I Led 3 Lives

The True Story of Herbert A. Philbrick's Television Program

by Martin Grams, Jr.

I Led Three Lives
The True Story of Herbert A. Philbrick's Television Program
© 2007 Martin Grams, Jr.

All rights reserved.

NBC is an acronym of the trade name National Broadcasting Company, Inc., and as their primary service trademark, is reprinted with permission.

ABC is an acronym of the trade name American Broadcasting Company, Inc., and as their primary service trademark, is reprinted with permission.

Disclaimer:
Information documented within the pages of this book is not meant to infringe on the privacy of anyone. All of the information contained within this book is (and has been) public knowledge for decades. Sources include special collections and archives available to the public at various libraries across the country including The Library of Congress, The Library of American Broadcasting of the University of Maryland, The Madison, Wisconsin Historical Society, and periodicals including *Time, The New York Times, Newsweek,* and many other unlimited sources that allow their information to be examined, reviewed and copied.

No part of this book may be reproduced in any form or by any means, electronic, mechanical, digital, photocopying or recording, except for brief inclusions in a review, without permission in writing from either the author or the publisher.

Published in the USA by:

BearManor Media
PO Box 71426
Albany, GA 31708

www.BearManorMedia.com

Library of Congress Cataloging-in-Publication Data:
Grams, Martin.

I led 3 lives : the true story of Herbert A. Philbrick's television program / by Martin Grams, Jr.

p. cm.
Includes bibliographical references and index.
ISBN 978-1-59393-092-9
1. I led 3 lives (Television program) 2. Philbrick, Herbert A. (Herbert Arthur), 1915-1993. I. Title.

PN1992.77.I24G73 2007
791.45'72--dc22

2007034658

Printed in the United States.

Design and Layout by Valerie Thompson.

Table of Contents

Dedication

*To all the fans of the television program,
and Herbert A. Philbrick, whose just cause and bravery
is an inspiration to all.*

INTRODUCTION

By 1952, the Red Scare was at a peak. Hollywood was attempting to cash in on the scare with such films as *Red Planet Mars* (1952), *Invasion U.S.A.* (1952), *I Was a Communist for the F.B.I.* (1951) and even the film short, *Red Nightmare* (1962), narrated by Jack Webb, has become regarded as essential viewing over the years. On radio, ZIV was syndicating a radio program entitled *I Was a Communist for the F.B.I.*, based on the book by Matt Cvetic. But since Warner Bros. owned the screen rights, ZIV could not take the successful radio program to television. His answer came in the form of Herbert A. Philbrick, who, in 1949, made headlines when he testified against eleven top Communists, and recounted his days as a counterspy for nine long years. His book, *I Led Three Lives*, was a big seller and the rest, as they say, is history.

Shortly before the completion of this book, I met a man at a convention who was apparently an admirer of my work, who asked me what my next book project was going to be. I kindly informed him that I was in the process of completing this book, about the history of the television series, *I Led Three Lives.* His remark to me took me by surprise. "Wasn't that the TV show that taught people all about Communism?" Only then did it occur to me that the series has never been broadcast since the early sixties, and sadly, is best remembered now as the popular answer to a crossword puzzle in *TV Guide*. I corrected the reader, informing him that *I Led Three Lives* was the story about a true American—who did indeed lead three lives, risking both his life and his family's, to help the Federal authorities crack down on a number of schemes perpetrated by members of the Communist Party. The show is

as American as it could get.

I met another man before the completion of this book, who told me his thoughts about the radio program, *I Led Three Lives.* His description of the radio program threw me for a loop until I realized that he was describing *I Was a Communist for the F.B.I.*, a different series based on the exploits of Matt Cvetic, but in the same vein as the Philbrick TV show. This led me to suspect that so little has been documented about the Herbert A. Philbrick series (including on-line encyclopedias that have very common errors in their entries) that many people were getting the two shows mixed up.

The television program was well conceived. Never once did the series suggest Communism was a good thing. The program always educated the viewers about the inner workings of Communism—how a character would explain the horrible ordeals they suffered from behind the Iron Curtain. How agents for the Communist Party found anyone, regardless of how valuable they were to the Party, as "expendable." Murder attempts, extortion attempts and far worse were exploited through the hands of the Communists.

Like the television series, this book was *not* written to promote Communism in any way, shape or form. Communism is a form of enslavement and this author personally despises the notion of the United States under a Communist rule. The purpose of this book was to reveal the facts behind the television series, and the true life of Herbert A. Philbrick. How his book came to be, and his involvement with the television series garnered the program a number of awards, and a detailed episode guide are included within these pages. With luck, encyclopedias and reference guides will make the necessary corrections.

Naturally, a book of this size could not be made without the help of a number of individuals who took time out of their busy lives to help me complete this task. In no specific order: Roy Bright, Rodney Bowcock, the staff at the Wisconsin Historical Society, the staff at the Billy Rose Theatre Collection in New York City, my wife Michelle for her patience, the numerous fans who sent me copies of the series on VHS and DVD, Alex Daoundakis, Terry Salomonson, Leo Gawroniak, and most importantly, John Ruklick, who spent a considerable amount of hours copying thousands of sheets of paper for me.

So, for all the fans of the series who wished a book of this nature was written and published, Here you go. The fascinating story of a true American, who for nine fantastic years, did indeed lead three lives. This is his story.

MARTIN GRAMS JR.
NOVEMBER 2006

Herbert A. Philbrick Biography

For nine years a quiet-spoken New Englander managed to pull off a greater feat. Thirty-six years old. Medium-build. Wore glasses. Active with the community church. Father of five children. His name was Herbert Arthur Philbrick.

Born May 11, 1915, he studied civil engineering at Northeastern University night school and graduated with a degree in engineering in 1938. His occupation was that of a Boston-area advertising executive who, acting as a citizen volunteer, successfully infiltrated the Communist Party USA between 1940 and 1949. Philbrick's nine-year adventure began innocently on a fine spring day in 1940. An ad salesman of 25 at the time, he was following his nose around Boston, sniffing for new business. At a door marked "Massachusetts Youth Council" he dropped in to run off his spiel. The comrade-in-charge, a pleasant-faced young woman, must have been amused at the spectacle of a man trying to sell direct-mail advertising to a front organization of the Communist Party.

Instead, she sold Philbrick on the need for a Youth Council in his neighborhood. She played up to his obvious interest in young people's organizations, to his starry-eyed belief that such groups could help keep the U.S. out of war, reduce unemployment and build "character, confidence and stability." With the help of some newfound friends and members of the Massachusetts Youth Council, Philbrick set up a Cambridge branch and was elected chairman—and then began to have the uneasy sensation of a man who is having the rug pulled slowly from under his feet. Gradually, it came to him that the friends, who were quietly taking over the organization, were Communists.

Herbert A. Philbrick

With his suspicions aroused by the strange power structure and positions taken by this group, Philbrick contacted the F.B.I. and, encouraged by them, began deepening his involvement in Communist activities, joining first the Young Communists League and later, as a secret member, the Communist Party itself

Philbrick was used by the Party for his advertising skills. Another asset was his public role as a Baptist youth leader. After time spent in local Party cells in Wakefield and Malden, Massachusetts, he received training in the fundamentals of Marxism-Leninism and worked for the Party in a variety of front groups. Later he was removed from local Party work and assigned to a cell of professionals where his main work consisted of working on the Progressive Party campaign of former Vice President Henry Wallace.

Important events which affected the Communist Party during Philbrick's tenure included the United Front, the Nazi invasion of the Soviet Union, Browderism and its end occasioned by the Ducios letter, and the 1948 campaign of Henry Wallace under the 3rd Party Progressive Party campaign.

While Philbrick was in the Party, Earl Browder, its General Secretary, enthusiastic about wartime cooperation between the United States and the Soviet Union and looking forward hopefully to postwar cooperation and the growing acceptance of the Communist Party by the American public, dissolved the Communist Party and reconstituted it as the Communist Political Association, apparently intending to set the Party on a reformist course. Philbrick himself made a brief show of opposing this new policy, a masterstroke, as policy was also opposed by William Z. Foster, longtime Chairman of the Communist Party. It was not much later when in July of 1945, as a result of the Ducios letter, a letter by a leading French Communist which actually was a policy directive which originated in Moscow, the Party turned away from Browderism and again took a Marxist-Leninist line while not completely abandoning the tactics of the United States.

For four years, Philbrick had given at least three nights a week to Communist work. In addition, he was carrying a full-time public-relations job with Paramount Pictures. On top of that, by his own inclination (and with Party approval), he was busy in neighborhood church work. And finally, late at night, after everything else was attended to, Philbrick had his reports to write for the FBI. There was not much time for home life with his wife and three children.

And there was the double risk of detection. If his employers found out he was a Communist, his career might be wrecked; if the Communists found out he was a counterspy, he felt pretty sure that his life would be in danger. The F.B.I. informed Philbrick in advance that if his secret was leaked, they would deny any affiliation with him, and could offer no protection. Already he suspected that he had been followed by Communist counterspies. Nevertheless, Philbrick felt that he had to go on.

He took out all the life insurance he could swing and, with the courageous support of his wife, who was eventually told of his counterspy role, stepped into the shadows as "Comrade Herb."

During the next five years, Herb wrote publicity and pamphlets for the cause, was named to the Party's "education" committee for New England (headed by Jack Stachel, of the Eleven), joined a super-secret professional group that collected U.S. financial and industrial data, arranged receptions for such personages as the very Reverend Hewlett Johnson, the "Red Dean" of Canterbury —and even, for a while, acted as a counter-counterspy, assigned to search for possible informers within the Party. Everything Comrade Herb saw and heard went into his reports to the F.B.I.

Herb Philbrick was a member of Pro-4—which was about as deep as one could get in the Communist underground. Composed of the Party's elite, intelligentsia, influential people—men and women posing as leading conservatives, as Right-Wing Democrats or

Republicans—the Pro-4 group carried out Soviet directives to the highest, least suspect quarters: in Universities, key industries, in medicine, law, in newspapers and banks, in state legislatures, and in national government.

The Pro-group also pulled the secret strings on the Communist front network. It set up organizations, or moved in on one already thriving, enlisted the support of innocent leaders and celebrities, and sometimes took over completely. Sometimes that organization was as large as the Progressive Party. Big or small, they worked according to a master plan—the overthrow the United States Government.

In a 1981 interview with *The Globe*, Philbrick commented, "I used to sit next to these people in these meetings and try to figure out why, why were they doing it? I don't know. All I can say is the communist mind is definitely a criminal mind. They seem to get a big thrill out of being part of this conspiracy, out of putting it over on people. 'We're the smart ones and they're the stupid ones.' Intellectual arrogance is definitely a part of it."

Philbrick said he read the Bible every night to avoid succumbing to communist propaganda. "I was sitting in cell meetings night after night, listening to stuff that was absolutely false but pretty powerful," he said. "But the contrast was the message of the Bible, which is absolutely at the opposite end. So I was able to see the difference between right and wrong and good and evil."

His task was not easy. Herb Philbrick spent a desperate nine years of battle, not only keeping his every move a guarded secret, but in keeping his own thinking straight and rational. He was shadowed and spied upon. His house was examined, but the young Communist agents failed to find the F.B.I. apparatus. Warned in advance by the F.B.I., Philbrick side-stepped a trap set for him in Party headquarters. He figured out a method for turning over the Party's files to the F.B.I. while Party members watched him from a hotel room across the street, waiting for that first misstep.

No exit. Another threat hung over Herb Philbrick's head. What if he should be arrested for his "subversive" activities? The answer was hard and simple: he would be on his own. He would get no recognition from the F.B.I. If any one of the many traps that surrounded him should click shut, there would be no exit.

The climax of Herbert Philbrick's multiple life in the Communist labyrinth came at Foley Square, New York, on April 16, 1949, and the story ran on all the front pages the next day. Reported the *Herald Tribune:*

"A Young Boston advertising executive, who joined the Communist Party as an undercover agent for the Federal Bureau of Investigation, took the witness stand yesterday against the eleven Party leaders on trial in U.S. District Court and began to reveal the secrets he had learned in nine years of investigation. The witness was a Party member in good standing until 2:01 p.m., when he disclosed his true identity to his sponsors. His appearance was a complete surprise to the defense.

"Defendants and their counsel stared at the soft-spoken agent, first incredulously and then evident distaste. They whispered among themselves and shook their heads. A member of the defense committee tip-toed from the courtroom and hurried to the telephone. 'During the entire nine years of my activities,' testified Philbrick, 'I have been continuously in touch with the F.B.I.' This remark drew an audible gasp from the left side of the spectators' benches—a section generally filled with relatives and friends of the defendants and fellow travelers. Throughout his testimony the defendants slumped in their chairs and watched him silently. Eugene Dennis, who was defending himself, peered at the witness intently.

"April 13th: During the three days of cross-examination, defense attorneys failed to shake Mr. Philbrick on any phase of his direct testimony.

"April 15th: The demeanor of the defendants and their attorneys as well as the reaction in *The Daily Worker* failed to conceal what amounted to shock at his five days of testimony."

The April 18, 1949 issue of *Time* reported the amazing story that broke in the courtroom titled "Unfair Surprise":

"In the marbled off pressroom one morning last week, newsmen surrounded blocky Frank Gordon, the Assistant U.S. Attorney. For nine and a half days in Manhattan's Federal Court, Witness Louis Budenz, the backslid Red, had made out the case against eleven top U.S. Communists charged with conspiring to advocate forcible overthrow of the U.S. Government. Now, the reporters asked, who would the prosecution's next witness be?

"Good-naturedly, Gordon fended off questions, held himself to one sententious answer: 'All I can tell you is that it's going to be a man.' The reason for this strategic evasion was soon understandable: the Government was ready with a real surprise.

"When young (age 33), studious looking Herbert A. Philbrick of Melrose, Massachusetts took the witness stand that afternoon, he was still a secret, dues-paying, in good standing member of the Massachusetts Communist Party. He was secure in its confidence and even a minor functionary in the underground apparatus.

"In a strong, confident voice, witness Philbrick matter-of-factly explained something that he and the Government had hidden well. 'During the entire nine years of my activities,' he said, 'I have been continuously in touch with the F.B.I.' The Government had reversed, with spectacular success, the old Red tactic of infiltration. As the wire-service reporters raced out of the courtroom for the telephones, the defendants and their lawyers sat stunned for a moment. Then the lawyers hopped to their feet in an attempt to head off the testimony of the unperturbed man in the witness chair. 'Unfair surprise,' muttered stooped, balding Abraham Isserman, and 'Outside the scope of the indictment.' Pint-sized Harry Sacher, barked similar objections. Judge Harold Medina, bitingly suave, then and later gave short shrift to their objections.

"What manner of man this curly-haired, spectacled witness who looked more like a peaceful, carefully dressed clerk than a secret Government agent? For nine years he had led a double life. To his wife, blonde, blue-eyed Eva, Herb Philbrick was a good husband and father (they have four little daughters). To his employers, a Boston motion-picture theatre chain, he was a go-getting assistant advertising manager, who knew how to turn out cute promotion pieces and ingratiate himself at newspaper drama desks. To his pastor, the Rev. Ralph Bertholf, he was a pillar of suburban Wakefield's first Baptist Church, a well-favored Sunday school teacher and editor of the church's paper, *Tall Spire.* To everyone else he was a friendly guy, who looked much younger than his years, liked a drink now then, foisted neither his religion nor his politics (whatever they were) on anybody.

"In 1940, witness Philbrick, who had been getting a flood of Communist-front literature in the course of his church work, helped to organize a group known as the Cambridge Youth Council. Almost at once, he spotted Reds in the fold. He took his suspicions to a member of the Young Communist League, from 1944 on, a member of the Communist Party. The F.B.I. paid his expenses; Party dues, and the cost of renting a recording machine on which he dictated some of his regular reports.

"The significance of Herbert A. Philbrick's testimony was that it demonstrated—on the neighborhood level—what ex-Communist Budenz had demonstrated to be the operating procedure of upper echelons in the Communist Party. Philbrick learned the need for increasing secrecy as U.S. policy toward U.S. Reds became tougher: the churning underground groups were narrowed down to five members apiece; last names were out; there was to be no communication (for security reasons) with any Communist Party member outside the unit.

"Early in the game, Philbrick had learned the Marxist-Leninist definition of revolution. Fanny Hartman, the divorced wife of the one-time boss of the Massachusetts Party, taught it: 'Violent revolution to be carried out by bands of armed workers against the existing state of government.' When would it come? Not 'next week,' or a war, 'in which case the conflict would be converted into civil war.' The working class must shatter, break up and blow up the whole state machinery . . .' Meanwhile, Party 'activists' were to get jobs in key industries: the General Electric plant in Lynn, Massachusetts, where jet engines are produced, textile plants, and the Boston & Maine Railroad. This, in the Party's circumlocutory 'Aesopian' language, was known as 'colonizing.'

"The witness made one more startling disclosure, before the Government turned him over to a defense that was scrabbling to get at him—one of the teachers at the secret schools for revolutionists was none other than Dirk Struik, Professor of Mathematics at the Massachusetts Institute of Technology, a long time sponsor of many organizations listed as subversive.

"In Cambridge, Struik denied that he was a Communist, though he defined himself as a 'Marxist scholar.' He furiously labeled Philbrick a 'stool pigeon.' In the courtroom, the defense shrilly trumpeted 'admitted F.B.I. spy,' and in the Communist press the whole clanking machinery of vituperation was cranked into motion; the *Daily Worker* could find something revolting even in the fact that Philbrick was wearing a red, white and blue tie.

"But such irrelevancies were just the point. The defense had nothing on Philbrick, and he gave no ground under the nagging cross-examination of bull-roaring, white-haired Louis McCabe. Said one Government official of Philbrick: 'They're going to have a tough time smearing him. He's clean as a whistle.' There was also another disturbing fact for the defendants to consider: Communists anywhere in the United States could no longer be sure who among them was a Communist."

© 1949 and 2006, Time, Inc. All rights reserved.
Reprinted with permission from Time *magazine, Time Reprints and Permissions, New York, NY.*

After the papers broke the story—with the F.B.I. validating Philbrick's co-operation—Herbert Philbrick was free to tell the whole, disturbing story of his work in the innermost councils of the U.S. Communist Party as an F.B.I. counterspy. The *New York Herald Tribune* persuaded Philbrick to write his memoirs documenting those nine incredible years. The McGraw-Hill Book Company caught on to Philbrick's story and persuaded him to write his tales in book form, entitled *I Led Three Lives.* McGraw-Hill thought so much of the story that they paid the author an extraordinary advance, and planned a first printing of over 40,000 copies of the book. *

The February 11, 1952 issue of *Time* magazine reviewed the book:

> "The Communists never really had a chance against Herb Philbrick. They tried to make a fool of a man who was not only a born salesman but an active and dedicated Baptist too, and they paid a high price for the blunder. Three years ago, at the trial of the eleven top U.S. Reds, Philbrick took the stand as a surprise Government witness. His testimony, compiled during nine years as an F.B.I. counterspy, helped to show the workings of the U.S. Communist Party.
>
> "Counterspy Philbrick tells the story of those nine years in *I Led Three Lives*. It is the story of a sane man who subjected himself to 'a manufactured schizophrenia,' who postponed indefinitely his own life, liberty, and pursuit of happiness, to get to the bottom of the great Communist conspiracy in the U.S."
>
> "At times, the strain of maintaining his three identities—citizen, Communist, counterspy—was almost more than Philbrick could stand. He would find himself involuntarily flushing during a

* Readers were able to read selected highlights in the *New York Herald Tribune* beginning January 1952. The book (should anyone today want to read this publication) tells the tale of daring courage and high adventure—a revealing, human, calmly-written document which has a deep urgency for every thinking American. Herbert Arthur Philbrick, *I Led Three Lives: Citizen, 'Communist,' Counterspy*, first published in 1952 by McGraw-Hill, reprinted by Grosset & Dunlap. Revised Edition, The Capitol Hill Press, 1973, Hardcover, ISBN 0882210033. The book retailed $3.50 and sold extremely well.

discussion of Party loyalty. And sometimes, in the darkness and exhaustion of the night, there came to his mind the bleak fear that 'the sheer power of the Party leaders with whom I worked' would break his will, and turn him into a real Communist.

"All at once, the ordeal was over. The FBI called him to the witness stand. As Comrade Herb began his testimony, he had some measure of reward for his pains in the looks of dazed astonishment that passed over the faces of the defendants.

"There have since been other rewards: public acclaim, a chance for some family life, the restoration of old friends who had been alienated as, one by one, they came to suspect something of his apparent political sympathies. But perhaps best of all for salesman Philbrick has been the chance to get back to selling only products which he can believe in. *The New York Herald Tribune*, which delegated a pair of staff writers to help Philbrick with his book and serialized *I Led Three Lives* on its front page, has also hired its author as an ad salesman."

About two months after the publication of *I Led Three Lives*, on April 13 and 20, 1952, ABC radio featured a two-part dramatization adapted from the Philbrick book, on the anthology program *The Great Adventure*, broadcast from 7:30 to 8:00 p.m., EST.

Although books had been written for the purpose of exposing the evils of Communism, *I Led Three Lives* was the first major book to lay bare the core of the Party's secrets—the full Communist conspiracy. From the small community projects of his first days in the Party to the startling international blueprints of the final days, Herbert Philbrick traced a compelling picture of intrigue. He revealed how the Communists intended to overthrow the United States Government . . . and when.

The victories of the Philbrick adventure, wrote J. Edgar Hoover to Mrs. Herbert Philbrick, "Were undoubtedly attributable in no small part to the additional responsibilities assumed by you and to your loyal and faithful devotion to [your husband] and your country. You must have endured endless suffering . . . I want to commend you for a task well done and to extend my sincerest appreciation."

After his well-publicized testimony, and best-selling book, Herbert A. Philbrick continued his personal crusade against communism as a columnist for the *New York Herald* and he was in tremendous demand on the lecture circuit during the later half of the 1950s, before turning toward other prospects such as being the operator of his own press agency that sent free editorials to small weekly newspapers during the 1960s and '70s. For a time, he even ran a country store in Rye, New Hampshire, which he sold sometime around 1965.

Although a staunch anti-communist, he turned down several invitations to testify before Sen. Joseph McCarthy's hearings in the mid-fifties. "I'm no McCarthyite," he told *The Globe*. "He [McCarthy] harmed the cause of anti-communism more than anybody I know."

Philbrick retired as a court reporter for the Rockinham County Newspapers. He lived at 15 Chapel Road, Little Boars Head, Northern Hampton, New Hampshire and for decades after his undercover work, Philbrick still seemed obsessed with the experience. Despite the fall of the Berlin Wall and the break up of the Soviet Union, he still feared retribution, keeping an unlisted phone number and post office box. "I always leave my back to the wall and one eye on the door," he said in a *Look Magazine* article in 1992.

On Monday, August 16, 1993, Herb Philbrick died in his home. He was 78. Arrangements were made by J. Verne Wood Funeral Home in Portsmouth, New Hampshire. Both the local newspapers and national periodicals covered the reports of his death, and the novel and television series he was associated with.

Philbrick's Involvement with the Series

When Herbert A. Philbrick was first approached by ZIV for the screen rights to his best-selling book, Philbrick immediately began working on plot outlines and summaries for suggested story ideas. He typed a complete chapter outline of the *I Led Three Lives* book, and the facts that he felt would become pertinent to the producers and writers when creating scripts for the series. He also typed up brief summaries and essays for the script writers, such as an outline for a Party meeting, the standard Communist Party cell procedure, and the theory and tactics of the Bolshevik Party on the question of war, peace and revolution. (Many of these outlines are found in the appendixes toward the back of the book.)

Before filming began, ZIV Productions gave Herbert A. Philbrick an all-expense trip to California for a tour of the ZIV Studios, and to chat at length with the producers, directors and writers regarding the formation of the television episodes. The production crew already had a breakdown of passages from the book which could be expanded into a flavorful television script (see appendices), research into the life of Herbert A. Philbrick through periodicals, and story ideas already in the works.

In one of Philbrick's earliest letters to John Sinn, Herb Gordon and Babe Unger:

> "First, many thanks for the very splendid visit to the studio last week. It was a great pleasure for me to meet all of you fellows, and I am looking forward to seeing you again in the near future. I was also greatly impressed by the excellent way in which you had started to work on the series. Even the rough drafts showed

that the writers had been briefed very well, and had pretty much caught on to the idea.

"I am sure that the thing we need to keep repeating is: this is a true story—stranger than fiction. We do not have the job of dreaming up impossible situations. We already have 'impossible' situations and facts, and the big job for us will be to make them believable to the television audience.

"Enclosed are two copies of suggested titles, which were considered during the work on the book period. Whether any of these will be any good for the TV series or not, I do not know, but at least they may serve as thought stimulation.

"You will note the first title, 'As It Happened.' I think this is most interesting due to the fact that John Sinn spotted this 'As It Happened' theme, and during our story conference indicated that the TV presentation should be on a 'As It Happened' basis, so that the TV viewer does not see what Philbrick recalls having happened ten years also, but is going along with Philbrick and seeing his actual thoughts and actions as it happened.

"Special memoranda. Using this dictation method, I will never in the world remember what I have put on the machine a few days later. Therefore, I request a copy of the dictated material be mailed back to me as soon as possible, because in many cases I shall have to depend on what preceded in order to know where to go from there.

"Also, I should like to see the proposed scripts so that corrections may be made so that the material will be as factual and accurate as possible. I think this is most necessary, because we do not want to leave ourselves open or vulnerable to attack from Communists and fellow travelers. As long as we keep the material factual, and documentary, they will not have a chance and we will have not only provided some excellent entertainment, but we will also have delivered a solid blow against the Communist Party—and I think that both are important.

> "Along with this transcript I am delivering another typewritten master of the book, which the stenographer may use in transcribing this material. Also, if any questions coming up about spelling of names and so forth, there is an index in the back of the book, 'I Led Three Lives' which will help out on any spelling.
>
> "Hope all goes well, and if anything further is needed, just give me a buzz."

Philbrick's request to review each outline was granted, for the purpose of adding valuable input regarding the realism of the stories and to avoid mistakes that might otherwise be made by the scriptwriters without a consultant. Most of the episodes from the first season were adapted from some passage or passages from the book. From New York he notified a rep for ZIV Productions, who wired or airmailed Philbrick's input to the firm on the West Coast which filmed the series, of his approval or disapproval. "When we first started the show, I wore slacks and a sport jacket, the way men dress out here in California," said actor Richard Carlson. "Philbrick said 'Remember, I'm an eastern advertising man in the story,' so I bought those suits with the vents in the back, the knit tie and button-down shirts. You know, real Boston. I used to wear a Windsor knot on my tie, a big knot, but I was told to make a smaller, eastern knot."

For the episode "Youth Movement," the severity of enemy agents required large sums of money, so a Communist campaign is used to infiltrate the local youth council program and its bank account. Since Philbrick first suspected Communist infiltration when he began working for the local youth council program, this was one episode that came close to home.

For scene 40 in "Youth Movement," Philbrick told the producers at ZIV: "Do we have time to squeeze in here the fact that we had not only the name of Vance, but the names of a number of other upstanding citizens . . . most of them non-communist . . . on the letterhead as sponsors. These people were dupes. The names were supplied to me by the Communist Party. You would be amazed to know how careless people are about lending their good names. The

CYC, a small organization to be sure, was able to victimize somewhere between 300 to 400 people, innocent people, by means of these tactics. We had on our list of sponsors, for example, the name of Kirtley Mather, well-known professor at Harvard University . . . a name, which the comrades were able to get somehow. Our headquarters were at the Cambridge YMCA. And at no cost to the Communist Party. Because the Party has been able to use the names of a terrific number of people, from Mrs. F. D. R. on down, the communist conspiracy in this country has been able to raise as much as $50,000,000 a year. Not bad for an organization which has never numbered more that 75,000 members at its peak. This is an opportunity for us to hammer home, in two or three sentences, the real meaning and danger behind this type of phony, fraudulent operation."

One interesting fact Philbrick pointed out in scene 73: "The F.B.I. is totally and completely unable to blow the whistle on anybody; it can only gather facts, it cannot reveal any. The Police Department may, or a local newspaper may do it. But the F.B.I., never."

One suggestion Philbrick revealed to the producers early in season one was reused in more than one episode throughout the series. "If you really want to make this the oomph, here's another little gimmick that the comrades have in order to help them track down and destroy a deviationist," Philbrick wrote. "In the wrapping of packages such as in this case, one way of tripping up a counterspy would be to wrap the envelope in such a way that any tampering would be detected. For example, they would seal the edges of the package with scotch tape; and they would also take a piece of hair from the head, and place this inside the package in such a position that it could easily be inadvertently unnoticed and misplaced in the unwrapping and rewrapping of the package. Or the piece of hair might be lightly tucked under one of the pieces of scotch tape. In this case, however, the wrapping would quite likely be done by someone other than Philbrick."

In one episode, there was a line for Carlson in the script that stated, "There is nothing in the educational propaganda that could possibly help the F.B.I." When Herb Philbrick read this, he commented, "This would not be a decision for Philbrick to make. There was actually no way that he could tell what information would be most valuable to the F.B.I.; his only job was to obtain any and all information, and then it was up to the Bureau itself to decide what was useful and what was not."

For the first pilot episode, Philbrick suggested that the words "social-patriots" be replaced with "social-democrats."

Another suggestion, Philbrick pointed out, was the church angle. "It worries me. Very touchy. It would have to be pointed out that Philbrick had been ordered to attend church as a cover for himself and the sisters had been ordered to attend in order to watch Philbrick. They were already attending the church with which Philbrick was instructed to affiliate. It was in connection with the development of the incident covered by this script that Philbrick realized it was not by accident he found himself in the same church with these two sisters and recognized it as a part of the Communist design to keep him under surveillance."

For an episode in which the Communists wanted to discredit and possibly murder a police officer, Philbrick clarified a few facts. "I note in the opening that the word 'elimination' is used. The communist term usually used is 'liquidation' and this is used by the comrades in the same impersonal, materialistic fashion as the word 'disintegrate.' The communists speak of a liquidation in about the same manner as one might speak of getting a haircut. Also, we might have the voiceover explain at this point, that the Review Board is the American equivalent of the Russian NKVD—the dreaded, secret police."

For another episode, Philbrick wrote: "'Sounds like a meeting's going on up front. How come I wasn't invited?' This, too, is the wrong philosophy. A Communist is never 'invited' to a meeting anymore than a PFC would be invited to fall in or about face. The Party orders you what to do."

On January 15, 1954, he wrote to the producers regarding episode 25, suggesting they delete a few lines of dialogue because he felt in real life, such an exchange was "much too risky to let you know your Comrade friend might be listening."

One of the major errors in the series was not caught until halfway through production of the first season. On the television program, Philbrick met up with a number of F.B.I. Agents. Special Agent Jerry Dressler (most popular with the fans and the chemistry between Dressler and Philbrick was magnificent), Special Agent Hal Henderson, Special Agent Steve Daniels, Special Agent Mike Andrews and others, including agents that helped on the sidelines in parks, secret offices, locked rooms and abandoned apartments. But as Philbrick himself pointed out *after* filming began for the series: "Philbrick's actual identity was known only to two F.B.I. agents inside the bureau. To all others, he was simply a code symbol. As a matter of fact, Philbrick (and any other confidential informant) would be highly nervous if the very fact that the name or identity was been bandied about, even inside the B itself. This was true right up to and including the preliminary stages of the government trial against the top eleven. When Philbrick made his trips to New York City to meet with special agents of the F.B.I. and with the Justice Department, he traveled under an alias."

ZIV TELEVISION PROGRAMS, INC.

Known throughout the industry as "the father of syndication," Frederick W. Ziv, with a University of Michigan law degree, landed a job at an advertising agency handling the publicity for radio programs. A year later, in 1929, he opened his own advertising agency and applied his trade to the booming radio market. It didn't take long for Ziv to recognize that local and regional advertisers could not compete with national-brand sponsors because they could not afford the budget of national coast-to-coast radio programs. So Ziv began producing prerecorded programs, "transcriptions" recorded onto acetate discs, bypassing the networks and selling his programs directly to local advertisers on a market-by-market basis. This was the foundation of "syndication." Programs were priced according to the size of each market; and this gave local sponsors a chance to break into radio with affordable quality programming that could be scheduled in any available slot on a station's schedule.

Ziv purchased the broadcast rights to many intellectual properties and began producing a large number of radio programs that were successful enough to warrant lengthy runs and the demand for additional episodes. *The Cisco Kid, Mister District Attorney, Boston Blackie, Favorite Story, Easy Aces,* and *Philo Vance* were a few. By 1948, statistically, he was the largest packager and syndicator of radio programs in the country. Throughout the forties other producers caught on and began their own production companies, often competing against ZIV in the first-run syndication market.

When television began retailing in stores during the mid-late forties, ZIV was the first to capitalize on the possibility of syndicating television programs. Television was then a medium laughed and shunned by other network producers, dismissed as a "fad." This paved a way for ZIV, who took some of his successful radio programs and adapted them into telemeters.

The Cisco Kid, starring Duncan Renaldo as the Cisco Kid and Leo Carillo as his sidekick, Pancho, became ZIV's first venture into television. His decision to shoot *The Cisco Kid* in color several years before color television sets were even available was a success. *The Cisco Kid* remained in production until mid-1956, and had a long life span in syndication thanks to the decision to shoot in color—all 156 episodes. From the first ten years alone of syndication, the series grossed about $11 million.

According to Christopher Anderson of the Museum of Broadcast Communications, "His fortunes in television were entirely tied to the market for first-run syndication, which grew enormously during the first half of the 1950s before going into a steep decline by the end of the decade. In the early years of U.S. television, local stations needed programming to fill the time slots outside of prime time that were not supplied by the networks. More importantly, local and regional sponsors needed opportunities to advertise their products on television. As in radio, ZIV supplied this market with inexpensive, pre-recorded programs that could be scheduled on a flexible basis. In 1948, the first ZIV series, *Yesterdays Newsreel* and *Sports Album*, featured 15-minute episodes of repackaged film footage."

Production budgets were usually $20,000 to $40,000 per 25-minute television episode, which were generally shot in two days. His fifth television series to go into production was *I Led Three Lives*, and it was this series that he made the biggest gamble of his career. To produce a series that exploited the methods of Communist activities, and chance that it would be accepted by television stations that preferred not to be associated with anything that bled the word "communism" in the program, was risky.

Frederick Ziv entered a disclaimer to any crusading intent. "We are not," a company rep told a reporter for *TV Guide*, "a corporate knight in shining armor. We're in the entertainment business. We're not trying to deliver a message. That's not our field. Our chief purpose is to find good story properties, turn them into good films and sell them. We think *I Led Three Lives* is good, exciting entertainment, and we know darned well we're selling it."

In order to save expenses in the event the show would be picked up by only a few stations, he gave Richard Carlson, the star of the series, an unusual three-year contract. Rather than be paid a large sum like most stars, ZIV offered Carlson the same pay scale as all other actors, and a percentage of the gross. The results were fantastic, and the demand for additional episodes was requested. The television series was filmed in color.

In January of 1955, the six-acre American National Studios, formerly the home of Eagle-Lion, surrendered to the television industry when ZIV Television Programs, Inc. bought the lot for the purpose of providing locations and studios for filming. This lot provided scenery for a handful of episodes toward the end of the second season, and new locations for much of the third season of *I Led Three Lives.* The financial rewards, for running a television studio, however, were only momentary.

In 1959, ZIV elected to sell 80% of his company to an alliance of Wall Street investment firms for $14 million. "I sold my business," he explained, "because I recognized the networks were taking command of everything and were permitting independent producers no room at all. The networks demanded a percentage of your profits, they demanded script approval and cast approval. You were just doing whatever the networks asked you to do. And that was not my type of operation. I didn't care to become an employee of the networks."

In 1960, United Artists purchased ZIV Television Programs, including the 20% share still held by chairman of the board, Frederick Ziv, and president, John L. Sinn, for $20 million. The newly merged production company was renamed ZIV-United Artists. United Artists had never been very successful in television, having placed only two series prime time, *The Troubleshooters* (1959–60) and *The Dennis O'Keefe Show* (1959–60). This pattern continued after the merger. ZIV-UA produced 12 pilots during the first year and failed to sell any of them. In 1962, the company phased out ZIV Television operations and changed its name to United Artists Television. Frederick Ziv left the board of directors at this time to return to Cincinnati, where he spent his retirement years donating his paperwork (scripts, shooting schedules, legal correspondence, etc.), for tax purposes, to various University libraries across the country.

RICHARD CARLSON: THE SCREEN PHILBRICK

Richard Carlson was born in Albert Lea, Minnesota, on April 29, 1914, the son of a Danish-born attorney. Richard and his family later moved to Minneapolis. It was at the University of Minnesota that he became interested in acting, through the campus drama club. On being graduated (Phi Beta Kappa) with a master's in English, Carlson was determined to become a playwright—eventually writing three plays, which he produced, directed and acted in, for a community theatre group in Minnesota. "Shortly after I graduated from Minnesota University," Carlson recalled, "my dad, who was a lawyer in Alberta Lea, Minnesota, wanted me to follow his profession. I wanted to continue my studies, attain a doctorate and then follow a career as a scholar."

Even from the beginning of his professional career, Carlson had been juggling four or five jobs at a time. "I thought then I'd like to teach—the academic life seemed appealing," he shrugged amiably, "so I took my M.A. degree, my Phi Beta Kappa key, and $2,500 in scholarship cash and opened my own repertory theatre in St. Paul!"

When that venture failed spectacularly, he fled to New York and made a fair name on Broadway. "I came to New York City and, while trying to make up my mind, looked up a classmate of mine who was connected with the theatre," Carlson continued. "When I dropped in on him backstage during a rehearsal, I was wearing my key dangling from a chain on my vest. Suddenly, I heard a call from one of the front rows. The caller identified himself as George Abbott (a name which meant nothing to me then) and asked me where I got the key. When I told him, he said they needed a college type for a small role in the play they were rehearsing. Did I want the job? It paid $50 a week! Remember, at the time there was a depression on, and $50 a week was a fabulous salary to a fellow just out of college."

"I knew I had to earn a living while writing," recalled Carlson, "and I figured actors had quite a bit of free time—so I decided to become an actor to pay the rent." Hollywood, then New York, followed, with various acting roles, primarily on tour and in stock. He completed a play, *Troubled Waters*, which was produced in New York with little success. Carlson's writing and acting got fairly good reviews, but the plays were not financial successes, and his company failed.

The play did attract film producer David O. Selznick, who, after he saw Carlson, gave him a writer-actor contract. So Carlson went out to Hollywood in 1936. He was not given the chance to do any writing, however. Instead, he was given his first film role in *The Young in Heart* (1938).

While in Hollywood he joined the Pasadena Community Playhouse, where he directed *Richard II* and played Prince Hal in both parts of *Henry IV*. Next, he went back to New York, where he got a part in *Three Men on a Horse* and spent 36 weeks on the road in the play, with Betty Field and Hume Cronyn. Later, he did the show for the Cape Playhouse at Dennis, Mass., and stayed with the company for two summers. While with the Playhouse, Carlson wrote his first play, *Western Waters*, which Warner Bros. financially optioned but did not bother to film.

After which he returned to New York. Subsequently, Carlson resigned himself to the fact that his career was in acting. "I decided early that acting was a good way to earn a living, while I concentrated on writing," Carlson noted. "The emphasis has since changed, but, it's still basically what I'm doing." There, Joshua Logan signed him for a song-and-dance role with Jimmy Durante and Ethel Merman in *Stars in Your Eyes*. With time out only for a hitch in the U. S. Navy, Carlson appeared in such films as *Back Street* (1941), *Valentino* (1951), *The Blue Veil* (1951), *Flat Top* (1952), *All I Desire* (1953), *Creature From the Black Lagoon* (1954), and many others. He also directed such films as *Riders to the Stars* (1954, written by *I Led Three Lives* scriptwriter Curt Siodmak) and *Four Guns to the Border* (1954), taking acting roles in them as well.

After a string of pictures in Hollywood, he took up writing columns for newspapers and periodicals. One of those movie jobs, *King Solomon's Mines* (1950), sent him to Africa, where he managed to kill his time between difficult scenes, mosquito-baiting, and big-game hunting to write lengthy reports of the movie company's activities for the *Saturday Evening Post.* Not only was he paid for his writing assignments, but the columns actually helped publicize the movie.

With such a wide variety of projects and acting jobs, it was no puzzle why ZIV Studios felt Carlson could play the role of Herbert A. Philbrick on the screen. Many Hollywood actors only made guest appearances on television series, with the belief that making the jump from big screen to a regular weekly television series was a step down in their acting career. For Carlson, the series only meant a step up.

Carlson disclaimed any intent to set himself up as a crusader. "The part," he said, "appealed to me for several reasons. I'd been offered a couple of routine private eye roles, but this thing had the ring of integrity. It tells the story of a guy who actually accomplished something. Further, it was a good financial deal. I stand to make more for this than I could ever make in pictures. Further still, it's paid over a period of time, which takes some of the sting out of the tax bite."

"But the big factor is that it gives me time to do a lot of other things," he continued, "I've always wanted to do—such as producing my own feature pictures. *I Led Three Lives* costs me maybe three months out of the year and makes a nice living for me. The rest of the time is mine to gamble with." The gamble, however, consisted of such feature films as *The Magnetic Monster* (1953), which was labeled by one critic, at the time of the film's release, as the most intelligent science-fiction picture made in Hollywood. Carlson played the role of Dr. Jerome Lockwood in *Riders to the Stars* (1954), a lone dreamer among a group of scientists who attempt to uncover the composition of meteors by capturing a meteor using three manned rockets. Both movies were produced by Ivan Tors, with the assistance of Frederic ZIV, and Carlson was even considered for a role in Tors' *Gog* (1954) but, because of *I Led Three Lives*, Carlson was not able to commit to the movie's shooting schedule.

Richard Carlson as Herbert A. Philbrick.

William Hudson as Special Agent Mike Andrews.

In between shooting schedules of *I Led Three Lives*, Carlson found time to portray William Travis in *The Last Command* (1955), a big-screen epic dramatizing the last days of the Alamo. Carlson also played Inspector Levering in *Bengazi* (1955) and supplied the narration for *An Annapolis Story* (1955). During the same years, Carlson found time to make guest appearances on other television programs, including *The Best of Broadway* and *General Electric Theater.*

"We shot 14 right off the bat [referring to episodes 2 through 15]," Carlson recalled of the first season, "doing the last five in just 10 days to free me for *Creature from the Black Lagoon* at Universal. They [*I Led Three Lives* episodes] may not be arty, but the exteriors are real, all shot on location, and the stories are 100 percent factual."

Those two factors apparently did the trick, for the series went into syndication in September of 1953 (before all of the episodes from the first season were completed!), and a month later had already been sold to 111 stations. "The only reaction I was afraid of," Carlson said, "was that we might be accused of Red-baiting, the temper of the times being what it is. But with Philbrick's book as our source, who can quarrel with us?"

Carlson did not look upon *I Led Three Lives* as any personal contribution to the fight against Communism. "I'm an actor," he recalled, "and the part is interesting and has stature. Philbrick is the guy who made the contribution, not me."

But *I Led Three Lives* was not Richard Carlson's first exposure to Communism tactics. The December 3, 1950 issue of the *New York Post* reported:

> "Being an active one of the Screen Actors' Guild's 44-member Board of Directors, he can and will talk knowingly of Communist tactics, anti-Communist measures, union problems, or any of the hundreds of subheadings of these subjects."

For reporter Archer Winsten of the same *New York Post,* Carlson explained his demands to do television shows. "My agent told me they wanted me to do a television show, and they said I asked an impossible price. I did, two thousand, and they accepted. So here I am and I've done two shows and can do six more if I want."*

"You see, television is a gold mine this year, right now, for featured players," Carlson continued. "The top stars can't go in,

* Carlson was referring to his appearances on *The Ford Theatre Hour* and *Pulitzer Prize Playhouse.*

either because their contracts won't let them or they're afraid of the primitive lighting conditions. So that leaves it up to the featured players to fill a demand nobody had foreseen. The television people themselves were caught off base. They simply didn't know that a dramatic show was going to sell merchandise. They had thought variety shows would be best. The result is that when they found out what dramatic shows could do in selling, everyone rushed to get them. The talent agencies are all swamped."

Carlson thought television could produce nerves in the most professional actor. In one of his earliest tries at TV, "The Canton Story" for the *Pulitzer Prize Playhouse,* he fluffed the first two lines. That made him so mad he settled down the rest of the way. "It's like doing summer stock or a little theatre in the pressure and the lack of time to prepare. But the difference is that instead of 600 people watching you, there are 16,000,000 and you don't see an audience, just two evil, little red eyes indicating whatever camera is on you."

Sponsors for the filmed series of *I Led Three Lives*, however, had many regional sponsors. They bought the show because of its documented anti-Communist format, figuring it was good public service material and thus a natural for their institutional kind of advertising. Oil and steel companies, banks, utility companies and other such concerns, many of whom never before used television as an advertising medium, picked up the series and were making noises that sounded like long-term renewal demands.

Carlson was enthusiastic about television, but primarily from an economic standpoint. He didn't watch it very often. "The actor who turns down a series," he said, "is out of his mind. It's hard work, to be sure, much harder than doing a feature picture, but you can make more money over a longer period of time and you have much more time to yourself. This is no longer a plaything. It makes good economic sense and I'm for it. I'm not only for it, I'm in it. Smartest move I ever made."

Carlson made his initial stab at TV about a year before *I Led Three Lives*, turning out two, 15-minute pilot films called *Richard's Poor Almanac.* The setting was the study of his Sherman Oaks home, with Carlson's wife and two youngsters running in and out of the proceedings, neighbors dropping by to chat and Carlson himself reading passages of poetry and prose. A little too erudite for the commercial market, the films, at the time of *I Led Three Lives*, were beginning to stir interest. "But," Carlson said, "they'll have to wait awhile. I'm already up to my ears with ZIV and my own features."

Carlson was a man apparently born to be versatile. He appeared in no less than 34 pictures and six Broadway plays, and he toured the nation as the lead in the road company of *Mister Roberts.* He was also a novelist, short story writer, director, producer, and versifier, contributor to national magazines, world traveler, husband and father. His two sons liked to kid him about being on television and had a weekly ritual whereby they announced in loud tones at 6:55 p.m. every Sunday night that they are going upstairs to watch *Private Secretary*, which played opposite *I Led Three Lives* in Los Angeles. "I was a little hurt first time they pulled it on me," Carlson chuckled, "but they came sneaking back downstairs at 7, giggling fit to bust. It's now a running gag—and I think I'd be hurt if they didn't pull it."

Playing the Role

"It's a tremendous responsibility to portray a real person every week," Carlson said. "Furthermore, we are dealing with material that is the most important thing in the world today and that's a responsibility. Also, the F.B.I. has to be satisfied with the scripts."

Financially, Carlson saw two distinct advantages by starring in syndicated programs. First, there's more money, particularly over the long pull, and second, for the versatile actor, there are fewer restrictions on what he can do. Under the contract with ZIV, Carlson was allowed to do live television appearances, direct pictures and act in features. He was free for virtually anything, provided it fit into the ZIV production schedule, and that was fast-moving and flexible enough to permit plenty of outside activity.

Despite much talk of the desirability and prestige of working on network shows from an actor's viewpoint, Carlson preferred to stay in the syndicated side of the business. "There are a number of advantages in doing films for syndication," he pointed out. "Most important of these is that there's more money in it, particularly over a long period of time. For example, look at what happened to me with *I Led Three Lives*, the first series I did for ZIV-TV. We stopped shooting two years ago and I'm making as much from the series as I did when we were in production. Many of the 117 episodes are still selling around the country. Since my contract called for me to get 10% of the gross, the checks are still coming in."

"I must have played every dramatic program on television," he explained to reporter Barbara Berch Jamison for the *New York Times*, "and pretty much all the guest shots there were to do, too.

I'd even had chances to do a series before this one—all private eyes—but I didn't see the point in tying myself down to a showoff that sort. When this came along it had all the elements I was looking for—truth, timeless, even a chance to be of public service. The only trouble was I didn't want to tie myself down to one job. I've got these other things I like to do, too."

Richard Carlson.

"The only solution was to have me 'marry' Philbrick—in other words, to take a piece of the show," Carlson continued. His contract paid him a low scale per day, the same cost every member of the supporting cast earned—an unheard of sum for someone who was the star of a series. (During the first season, the cost was $70 per day, with a usual 2-day filming schedule per episode. For the second season, the cost was $80 per day, again with a usual 2-day filming schedule per episode. For the third season, the cost was the same as the second; however the producers made a few attempts to shoot two episodes within a three-day filming schedule to keep costs down.)

According to a theatrical trade paper, Carlson's "take" had been a sizable one; ten percent of the gross. The *I Led Three Lives* series, comprising of 117 episodes or three years of production, according to *Variety* in September of 1958, "grossed a whopping $5,500,000 so far," and Carlson walked off with a hefty share of it. Which means Carlson grossed more than half a million.

Shortly after production of *I Led Three Lives* completed, Carlson made a similar arrangement with ZIV Television productions to star in a 39-episode run entitled *Mackenzie's Raiders*. Though the series was purchased by numerous stations across the country, the popular appeal was not as strong as *I Led Three Lives*, no doubt to the number of television Westerns invading the tube at the time. But Carlson sounded off publicly on what was commonly recognized as one of telefilms' major problems—how to come up with good, distinctive scripts in the beltline setup. Carlson felt that producers of action-adventure programs should follow a policy on writers adopted for comedy projects. One program should have a "stock company" of writers working on those particular series, rather than farming out the scripting to a large group of freelancers.

"The financial inducements are already more than satisfactory to attract good writers," Carlson told a reporter. "In recent years, a hard core of several hundred television writers has been developed. They get as many assignments as they can handle—from the standpoint of overall quality, almost too many. With residuals on top of initial payments, it's hard for a writer to turn down an offer no matter how busy he is. The answer lies in getting a small group of script writers to concentrate on one series."

Carlson claimed that such a system worked in favor of getting a distinctive consistent quality to the series, with the writers then well-acquainted with the characters and the motif of the project. He contended that *Raiders*, which operated on the "stock company of writers" principal, showed the fruits of such a system.

Back at home, he attempted to avoid tabloids reporting stories all Hollywood actors wish were suppressed. A casual visitor to the home of Richard Carlson would have discovered one of his hobbies—collecting Hollywood memorabilia. During the filming of Universal-International's *It Came from Outer Space*, the actor said that if he didn't curb his passion for collecting nostalgic cinematic souvenirs he might have been forced to rent a warehouse to take care of his ever-growing stock.

The actor began collecting objects d'art pertaining to the movie industry back in 1943. "It all began at a film charity bazaar," he explained, "when I held the winning ticket on the derby hat worn by Charlie Chaplin in *The Gold Rush* (1925). I hung it on a peg in my front hall. A week later a friend of mine typed up a label about the history. Then, as a gang for visitors of the hat, I framed it and tacked it up on the wall next to the hat rack. A friend of mine who had gotten a laugh out of my one-item brought me a set of false whiskers that John Barrymore had worn in some long-forgotten melodrama. With a hat and a beard, I was in business."

Through subsequent contributions and purchases Carlson managed to adorn his walls with such items as the leopard skin loincloth worn by Elmo Lincoln as the original Tarzan; a pair of Harold Lloyd's famed horned-rim spectacles; a Klansman's outfit from *The Birth of a Nation* (1915); an Arabian headdress worn by Rudolph Valentino in *The Sheik* (1921) and a solid gold cigarette holder, eight inches in length, sported in various silent melodramas by Lew Cody. Among his more treasured items was a 1909 model camera, a film splicer used by D.W. Griffith and a microphone used for the recording of *The Jazz Singer*. He had a difficult time saving any memorabilia from the television series, except for an occasional script, since the props had to be returned from where they came, and Philbrick's suits, jackets and automobiles changed from episode to episode. (Automobile buffs will notice how his vehicles changed from a Plymouth in one episode to a Packard in another.)

In July of 1959, reporter Murray Schumach, of the *New York Times*, quoted Carlson's publicity agent in New York saying that Mr. Carlson had become so successful, because of such television epics such as *I Led Three Lives* and *Mackenzie's Raiders*, that the movie companies could no longer afford him.

"Examine the men who have been successful in television," Carlson stated. "They're almost always people whose careers have gone down or, like myself, whose careers are not likely to get any bigger."

After Mackenzie's Raiders, Carlson directed episodes of other television series, such as *Men Into Space, Thriller* and *The Detectives.* He began writing scripts for Ivan Tors' *Daktari* series, and *O'Hara: U.S. Treasury.* He directed the 1966 motion picture, *Kid Rodelo* (1966).

On November 25, 1977, Richard Carlson died of a cerebral brain hemorrhage he suffered November 15, in Encino, California. He was 65. Almost all of his obituaries in newspapers and magazines made a reference to his portrayal as Herbert A. Philbrick on the *I Led Three Lives* television series. The November 27 issue of the *New York Times* actually headlined Carlson's death as "Star of *I Led Three Lives* on TV." The actor's body was cremated and a private funeral service was held.

THE MYTHS AND PRODUCTION OF *I LED THREE LIVES*

During this author's research, a number of reference guides made incorrect statements about the television series. After reviewing the numerous errors, I came to the conclusion that very little has been documented about the series to give those reference sources accurate cross-referencing. Oddly, had any of the people who did the write-ups actually viewed one or two episodes, they could have avoided those errors.

One encyclopedia listed that "Philbrick narrated each episode and served as a technical consultant and all scripts were approved by J. Edgar Hoover and the F.B.I." If that statement was referring to Philbrick as the character, and not the real Philbrick, this is accurate, but the statement about J. Edgar Hoover approving all of the scripts is inaccurate.

Neither J. Edgar Hoover nor the F.B.I. was involved with the series outside the use of the Federal Bureau's name. In the ZIV archives there was nothing referencing Hoover's endorsement for the series; there is, however, a wire sent from one producer to another, claiming that the censors, before approving the original pilot script for broadcast, suggested they "get clearance from F.B.I. to portray F.B.I. men in the story." This clearance was granted in the form of a letter, and this was the *only* communication between ZIV and the federal authorities during the entire production.

Another myth was that Herbert A. Philbrick starred as himself on the show. He never played the role of himself for any broadcast. The only documented work he did for network television was to pitch the television program for local TV commercials, and repeat guest appearances on *The Mike Douglas Show* (circa 1964) and *The*

Tonight Show (circa 1970).

The theme song for *I Led Three Lives* was composed by Ray Llewellyn, a pseudonym of Ray Bloch and David Rose, who wrote "under the table" for ZIV-TV and its World Broadcasting System music library.

By May of 1954, the program was seen on 157 stations and was among the top ten shows in the country, collecting several awards, including the George Washington honor medal of the Freedom Foundation at Columbia University. The September 30, 1953 issue of *Variety* reviewed the premiere episode:

> "There's no doubt that the ZIV beltline program operation has got the formula. They can grind 'em out quicker and faster than anybody in the business—and sell them twice as fast and on twice as many stations. (And if there's any doubt take a gander at those annual $25,000,000 radio-TV billings.)
>
> "For Exhibit 28 (or is it 82?) the ZIV packaging boys have come up with their latest TV entry—*I Led Three Lives*, which is as hot as Page 1 copy. Sold locally, as with all ZIV product, it bowed in the New York market on WNBT in the Sunday 10:30 p.m. slot, carrying the same thematic torch as the ZIV-made *I Was a Communist for the F.B.I.* series.
>
> "The technique is slick and surefire, with its continuing running commentary to supplement the visual escapades of Philbrick whose lot in life it was to dodge both the right guys and the wrongees, ducking in and out of cars, dark alleyways, trap doors, etc., as he ferrets out the Commie baddies and maneuvers secret huddles with the F.B.I. Pictorially, it's one of the best of the crop, with most of the footage filmed outdoors (and what a revelation to find that the streets, stores, restaurants, etc., are heavily peopled with a business-as-usual façade.)
>
> "The ZIV production boys haven't skimmed, for it's mounted with all the necessary trimmings. Eddie Davis' direction provides the correct tautness and suspense. It's a cinch that ZIV'll clean up on this one."

The October 2, 1953 issue of the *New York Times* also reviewed the premiere episode:

> "The initial installment was no assurance that the valuable volume will be used for maximum enlightenment on the devious operations of the organizers of front groups. The film's contents relied too much on trite preachment and corny melodrama to be either informative or valid theatre . . . Where the straightforward documentary technique might have been thoroughly absorbing, the film version sadly overdid the cloak-and-dagger routine. Virtually the whole half-hour consisted of scenes of Mr. Philbrick walking up and down streets, looking furtively over his shoulder every few seconds and momentarily expecting to be done in by the Reds. If in real life Mr. Philbrick has called attention to himself so childishly every time he went out on the street, both the F.B.I. and the Communists would have brought him in for questioning.
>
> "The scenes in the streets were a preliminary to the film's climax: a secret meeting of a Communist cell. The picture was on firm ground in underscoring that a Red could be most anyone and in appearance not distinguishable from the loyal citizen. But after the prolonged build-up of suspense, the cell meeting itself was anti-climactic.
>
> "First, a woman in the cell 'confessed' to deviating from the Party line—just how was not told—and thereupon she introduced the leader who would clarify matters. He made a brief statement that the goal of the Communist Party never changed and that ultimately workers would be armed for the overthrow of the government. With that the meeting adjourned. The film never did explain what was 'new' in the leader's words. To make a cell meeting seem a waste of time was hardly the most constructive introduction to an inside view of communism. Periodically throughout the film there was an offstage voice that in booming tones warned the viewer that the Communist menace was at his door, too.

"It must be hoped that the premiere will not prove typical of future installments of *I Led Three Lives*. The usefulness of Mr. Philbrick's book is that it avoided just what the initial film intended to do: oversimplification of the communism issue and substitution of emotion for information.

"In the book Mr. Philbrick quietly and earnestly tells of the computational nature of communism, of the devilishly clever methods used in the establishment of front groups, of the recruiting of dupes to serve the ends of card-carrying Communists, of the weird mental gyrations in which the Red indulges, of the essential drabness of life in the Party."

Actor Richard Carlson emphasized that the program was "not Red-baiting, not intended to teach anybody anything, but just to entertain. I hope since the TV show I will not lose my identity as Carlson and be known as Philbrick. But I am not sure. Around the studio here the telephone operator calls me 'Comrade Herb,' and others on the set say 'This is Philbrick.'"

If one considers continuity an important factor in the series, this program, like many television programs of the fifties, lacked any form of continuity that wasn't set in stone from the start. Philbrick's car varied from episode to episode, depending on the availability of the automobiles for the days of filming. In episode #108, for example, Philbrick drives a light Ford sedan and in the next episode (#109), he drives a green Plymouth.

In episode #55, Philbrick mentions he has a wife and five children. Yet only two children were ever seen on the television series and no mention is ever made during the rest of the series about him having five children!

The life of Eva Philbrick, however, was perhaps the biggest error on the series, but required for the sake of the television productions. The circumstances between the husband and wife relationship in the Communist Party was complicated by the nature of the conspiracy, as everything else. First, the Communist Party bosses were very nervous about any man or woman who was a member of the Party if the husband or wife was not also a member. This was especially true as the comrade continued to move up the ranks in the Party; and it was quite difficult for any person to move very deeply into the Party unless the comrades were certain that the husband or wife could be trusted.

However, despite this "trust," the Communist Party still did not trust anyone; therefore it was the duty of even married couples to distrust each other. In the Communist Party in the United States, the Party bosses expected both husband and wife to belong. However, they did not belong to the same cell. This was for security reasons; so that the husband did not necessarily know the specific Communist Party duties of the wife and the wife did not know of the specific Communist Party duties of the husband. In general, they both knew that they were Party members and that they adhered to Party discipline. Also, they were usually aware that one or the other was involved in Communist Party activities without knowledge of the details. But neither husband nor wife was supposed to tell the spouse the identities of the cell members, the number of cell members, their descriptions, the location of the meeting places, or anything of that nature.

Hence, in the instance of this television series, Eva would know that John Smith was upon a communist project; she would also assume that the courier was exactly what he was, and that was a conveyor of Communist Party messages; but she would not be entitled to know the nature of the message nor would she know the location of the meeting place John Smith was to go to.

Herb and Eva actually referred to this activity as their "hobby"; John Smith would quite often telephone his wife therefore to report that he was going to be doing some work on his hobby that evening; and that would alert her to the fact that he would be either attending a communist cell meeting, or be involved in some other Party activity. Any television episode in which Eva Philbrick actually gets involved with Party duties was rarely separated from Herb's duties. And when the duties were assigned, they were given their orders in the same room from the same cell leader.

In 1961, comedian Bob Newhart released an album featuring a selection of stand-up comedy routines entitled *Behind the Button Down Mind of Bob Newhart.* His routines are famous for being one-sided conversations, in which he has a conversation with someone, but only his side of the conversation is heard by the audience.

On this album, Newhart does a monologue entitled "Herb Phil Brick—Counterspy." In this routine, Newhart actually cracks a joke about Philbrick possibly being the leak week in and week out, questioning the logic of the Communists when they have yet to figure out . . . maybe it's Philbrick!

As funny as this fact may be, there were a number of episodes that centered on suspicion of Philbrick by the Party and/or the cell leaders. In episode #16, "Communist Cop," Philbrick passes a loyalty test and discovers that suspicion of a "leak" or "informant" is blame-shifted to another Comrade. In episode #24, "Infra-Red Film," Comrade Ormand is under suspicion as the F.B.I. informant when too many plans had been foiled in the recent months, and Ormand plays a game of cat and mouse to prove his innocence, and shed an eye toward Philbrick.

Episode #87, "Common Denominator," is perhaps the best of the episodes, since a number of Comrades use a computer to find the common denominator between all of the year's failed plots and Philbrick's name is brought up to play.

The truth was, many times Philbrick was under suspicion, but the F.B.I. often arranged for an arrest or an article in the newspaper that would give the Commies "evidence" that suggested otherwise. Always designed to throw them off the track—and more importantly, prevent them from suspecting Philbrick as an informant.

On September 14, 1960, ABC Television chose to broadcast an episode of *Hawaiian Eye*, entitled "I Wed Three Wives." The title was a pun on the name of the Philbrick/ZIV television series, and the plot had nothing to do with the counterspy series. This same pun on titles was done more than once. On November 1, 1987, an episode of the television series *Marblehead Manor* was entitled "I Led Three Wives."

Years before Lee Harvey Oswald, according to four United States government investigations, was responsible for the assassination of U.S. President John F. Kennedy, he became engrossed in the television series *I Led Three Lives*. According to his half-brother, Robert Oswald, "I think he just liked the atmosphere that you could do anything that you wanted to do, that you could imagine you could do." On November 24, 1963, Oswald, like Hebert Philbrick, made front page headlines when he was shot and killed by Jack Ruby on live television while in police custody.

In May of 1981, Arkham House published Stephen King's book *Danse Macabre*, which featured his recollections and memories of the days when E.C. Comics and late-night horror movies were the staple of his childhood. He wrote a brief recollection about his memories of watching the *I Led Three Lives* television series, and how it influenced him as a boy.

In the March 1995 issue of *Ladies Home Journal*, Lisa Stasi penned an article entitled "I Led Three Lives," an article about coping with change. Again, nothing related to the television series of the same name.

In 1998, Houghton-Mifflin published a book entitled *I Was a Communist* by Phillip Roth, written with an allusion to the popular television show *I Led Three Lives*, and readers were exposed to a lot of parody in the novel.

The Voice-Overs

Each episode of *I Led Three Lives* featured voice-overs from Philbrick (Richard Carlson) that were recorded separately from the days' filming.

This standard opener and closer were not the same for every episode.

For Pilot #1 . . .

Opening:

This is the story—the fantastic story—of Herbert A. Philbrick, who for nine frightening years *did* lead three lives . . . Average citizen, high-level member of the Communist Party, and Counterspy for the Federal Bureau of Investigation. For obvious reasons, the names, dates and places have been changed, but the story is based on fact.

It's the job of a counterspy to help find the enemies of the United States, to single out each one, to know his every move. This week's story concerns a secret Communist cell meeting and the search for one such hidden enemy.

Closing:

(Over film shot of insert of photo of Wilkerson being turned from back with question mark to front with photograph)

Because the files of the Federal Bureau of Investigation were completed on Leroy Wilkerson—his real name, his plans, his whereabouts known and reported—this man is no longer a hidden threat to the security of the United States.

(CARLSON AT TYPEWRITER IN SECRET ROOM)

Next week, another story from the files of a man who spent nine fantastic years as a counterspy for the Federal Bureau of Investigation.

FOR PILOT #2 . . .

OPENING:

This is the story—the fantastically true story—of Herbert A. Philbrick, who for nine frightening years *did* lead three lives . . . Average citizen, high-level number of the Communist Party, and Counterspy for the Federal Bureau of Investigation. For obvious reasons, the name, dates and places have been changed, but the story is based on fact.

In a moment, you are going to see an actual spy ring at work, an attempt by the Communist courier system to transit secret information through the Red underground.

CLOSING:

(OVER INSERT OF PRINTED PAPERS COMING OUT OF MACHINE IN F.B.I. OFFICE)

Government experts were able to de-code the secret plans of the Communist spy ring, eliminating another threat to our national security.

(CARLSON AT TYPEWRITER IN SECRET ROOM)

Next week, we'll bring you another story from the files of Herbert A. Philbrick—citizen . . . Communist . . . Counterspy.

FOR THE FIRST SEASON EPISODE (PRODUCTION #3B)

OPENING:

This is the story—the fantastically true story—of Herbert A. Philbrick, who for nine frightening years *did* lead three lives . . . Average citizen, high-level member of the Communist Party, and Counterspy for the Federal Bureau of Investigation. For obvious reasons, the names, dates and places have been changed, but the story is based on fact.

This week our story concerns a Communist narcotic ring and a plan to trade illegal drugs for American defense secrets.

Closing:
(Over insert of rag picker)
The photographic evidence supplied to the F.B.I. made it possible to destroy and later convict the Communist narcotic ring.
(Carlson at typewriter in secret room)
Next week, we'll bring you another story from the files of Herbert A Philbrick . . . The kind of a story that can only be told by a man who for nine fantastic years served as a counterspy for the Federal Bureau of Investigation.

For the first season episode (Production #4B)

Opening:
This is the story—the fantastically true story—of Herbert A. Philbrick, who for nine frightening years *did* lead three lives . . . Average citizen, high-level member of the Communist Party, and Counterspy for the Federal Bureau of Investigation. For obvious reasons, the name, dates and places have been changed, but the story is based on fact.
In this week's story, you'll see an attempt by a counterspy to secure vital information from the guarded and secret files—of Communist Headquarters itself.
Closing:
(Over insert of typewriter typing out names)
The list of Communists, once secret enemies of the United States, become pipelines of information to the F.B.I.—information no longer secret, no longer dangerous.
(Carlson at typewriter in secret room)
Next week, another story of Communist activities from the files of Herbert A Philbrick, counterspy—who for nine years posed as a member of the Communist Party.

By the third season of *I Led Three Lives*, the format material was set to a specific format. According to production material dated July 19, 1955:
Explanation: Our format Voice Over copy is divided into four sections which we'll call A-B-C-D. "A" is our Standard Opening over the Main Title and "B" is the variable portion of this that

changes each week with the script. "C" is the variable portion of the closing copy, and "D" is the Standard copy with Philbrick at the typewriter.

"A"

This is the story—the fantastically true story—from the files of Herbert A. Philbrick, who for nine frightening years *did* lead three lives . . . Citizen—Communist—Counterspy; and who has now revealed for the first time his secret files concerning not only his own activities, but those of other counter-espionage agents. For obvious reasons, the names, dates and places have been changed, but the story is based on fact. Herbert A. Philbrick is portrayed as the counterspy who . . .

(And then into the variable "B" copy that changes with the script)

"C"

(This is variable copy that changes with each script, and goes into...)

"D" (VERSION #1)

Next week, another story from the files of a man who spent nine fantastic years as a counterspy for the Federal Bureau of Investigation.

"D" (VERSION #2)

Next week, we'll bring you another story from the files of Herbert A. Philbrick—Citizen . . . Communist . . . Counterspy.

"D" (VERSION #3)

Next week, we'll bring you another story from the files of Herbert A. Philbrick . . . The kind of a story that can only be told by a man who for nine fantastic years served as a counterspy for the Federal Bureau of Investigation.

"D" (VERSION #4)

Next week, another story of Communist activities from the files of Herbert A. Philbrick, counterspy . . . who for nine years posed as a member of the Communist Party.

WHAT IS COMMUNISM?

Communism refers to a conjectured future classless, stateless social organization based upon common ownership of the means of production, and can be classified as a multi-variant branch of the broader socialist movement. Communism also refers to a variety of political movements which claim the establishment of such a social organization as their ultimate goal. Early forms of human social organization have been described as "primitive communism." However, communism as a political goal generally is a conjectured form of future social organization which has never been implemented. There are a considerable variety of views among self-identified communists. However, Marxism and Leninism, schools of communism associated with Karl Marx and of Vladimir Lenin respectively, have the distinction of having been a major force in world politics since the early 20th century. Class struggle plays a central role in the theory of Marxism. The establishment of communism is in this theory viewed as the culmination of the class struggle between the capitalist class, the owners of most of the capital, and the working class. Marx held that society could not be transformed from the capitalist mode of production to the communist mode of production all at once, but required a state transitional period which Marx described as the revolutionary dictatorship of the proletariat. The communist society Marx envisioned emerging from capitalism has never been implemented, and it remains theoretical. However, the term "Communism," especially when the word is capitalized, is often used to refer to the political and economic regimes under communist parties which claimed to be the dictatorship of the proletariat.

In the late 19th century, Marxist theories motivated socialist parties across Europe, although their policies later developed along the lines of "reforming" capitalism, rather than overthrowing it. The exception was the Russian Social Democratic Workers' Party. One branch of this Party, commonly known as the Bolsheviks and headed by Vladimir Lenin, succeeded in taking control of the country after the toppling of the Provisional Government in the Russian Revolution of 1917. In 1918, this Party changed its name to the Communist Party; thus establishing the contemporary distinction between communism and socialism.

After the success of the Red October Revolution in Russia, many socialist parties in other countries became communist parties, owing allegiance of varying degrees to the Communist Party of the Soviet Union. After World War II, regimes calling themselves communist took power in Eastern Europe. In 1949, the Communists in China, led by Mao Zedong, came to power and established the People's Republic of China. Among the other countries in the Third World that adopted a Communist form of government at some point were Cubs, North Korea, Vietnam, Laos, Angola, and Mozambique. By the early 1980s, almost one-third of the world's population lived under Communist states.

Communism carries a strong Social stigma in the United States, due to a history of anti-communism in America. Since the early 1970s, the term "Eurocommunism" was used to refer to the policies of communist parties in Western Europe, which sought to break with the tradition of uncritical and unconditional support of the Soviet Union. Such parties were politically active and electorally significant in France and Italy. With the collapse of the Communist governments in eastern Europe from the late 1980s and the breakup of the Soviet Union on December 8, 1991, Communism's influence has decreased dramatically in Europe, but around a quarter of the world's population still lives under Communist states.

In Russia, the 1917 October Revolution was the first time any Party with an avowedly Marxist orientation, in this case the Bolshevik Party, obtained state power. The assumption of state power by the Bolsheviks generated a great deal of practical and theoretical debate within the Marxist movement. Marx believed that socialism and communism would be built upon foundations laid by the most advanced capitalist development. Russia, however, was one of the poorest countries in Europe with an enormous, largely illiterate peasantry and a minority of industrial workers. Nevertheless, some socialists believed that a Russian revolution could be the precursor of workers' revolutions in the west.

The socialist Mensheviks opposed Lenin's communist Bolsheviks' plan for socialist revolution before capitalism was more fully developed. The Bolsheviks successful rise to power was based upon the slogans "peace, bread, and land" and "All power to the Soviets," slogans which tapped the massive public desire for an end to Russian involvement in the First World War, the peasants' demand for land reform, and popular support for the Soviets.

The usage of the terms "communism" and "socialism" shifted after 1917, when the Bolsheviks changed their name to the Communist Party and installed a single-Party regime devoted to the implementation of socialist policies under Leninism. The revolutionary Bolsheviks broke completely with the non-revolutionary social democratic movement, withdrew from the Second International, and formed the Third International, or Comintern, in 1919. Henceforth, the term "Communism" was applied to the objective of the parties founded under the umbrella of the Comintern. Their program called for the uniting of workers of the world for revolution, which would be followed by the establishment of a dictatorship of the proletariat as well as the development of a socialist economy. Ultimately, their program held, there would develop a harmonious classless society, with the withering away of the state. In the early 1920s, the Soviet Communists formed the Union of Soviet Socialist Republics, or Soviet Union, from the former Russian Empire.

Following Lenin's democratic centralism, the Communist parties were organized on a hierarchical basis, with active cells of members as the broad base; they were made up only of elite cadres approved by higher members of the Party as being reliable and completely subject to Party discipline.

In 1918–1920, in the middle of the Russian Civil War, the new regime nationalized all productive property. When mutiny and peasant unrest resulted, Lenin declared the New Economic Policy (NEP). However, Joseph Stalin's personal fight for leadership spelled the end of the NEP, and he used his control over personnel to abandon the program.

The Soviet Union and other countries ruled by Communist Parties are often described as "Communist states" with "state socialist" economic bases. This usage indicates that they proclaim that they have realized part of the socialist program by abolishing private control of the means of production and establishing state control over the economy; however, they do not declare themselves truly communist, as they have not established communal ownership.

As the Soviet Union won important allies by victory in the Second World War in Eastern Europe, communism as a movement spread to a number of new countries, and gave rise to a few different branches of its own, such as Maoism.

Communism had been vastly strengthened by the winning of many new nations into the sphere of Soviet influence and strength in Eastern Europe. Governments modeled on Soviet Communism took power with Soviet assistance in Bulgaria, Czechoslovakia, East Germany, Poland, Hungary and Romania. A Communist government was also created under Marshal Tito in Yugoslavia, but Tito's independent policies led to the expulsion of Yugoslavia from the Cominform, which had replaced the Comintern, and Titoism, a new branch in the world communist movement, was labeled "deviationist." Albania also became an independent Communist nation after World War II.

By 1950 the Chinese Communists held all of China, except Taiwan, thus controlling the most populous nation in the world. Other areas where rising Communist strength provoked dissension and in some cases actual fighting, include Laos, many nations of the Middle East and Africa, and, especially, Vietnam. With varying degrees of success, Communists attempted to unite with nationalist and socialist forces against what they saw as Western imperialism in these poor countries.

COMPARING "COMMUNISM" TO "COMMUNISM"

According to the 1996 third edition of *Fowler's Modern English Usage*, communism and derived words are written with the lowercase "c" except when they refer to a political Party of that name, a member of that Party, or a government led by such a Party, in which case the word "Communist" is written with the uppercase "C." Thus, one may be a communist (an advocate of communism) without being a Communist (a member of a Communist Party or another similar organization).

THE COMMUNIST PARTY

In modern usage, a Communist Party is a political Party which promotes communism, the sociopolitical philosophy based on Marxism. Communist parties today may or may not formally use the term "communist" in their name. Even if they do, not all follow a strict interpretation of any of the main "schools" of communism (chiefly Leninism, Maoism, Stalinism or Trotskyism).

The original Communist Parties first started to be widely established across the world in the early 20th century, after the creation of the Communist International by the Russian Bolsheviks. Communist parties have held power in 21 nations throughout history, first and most notably in the Soviet Union.

Members of communist parties were persecuted in many countries in the early Cold War period, when anti-communist sentiment was fueled by Western governments as part of their Cold War strategy. Nevertheless, in capitalist countries such as Italy and France, large Communist Parties gathered lots of popular support and played a prominent part in politics throughout the post-war decades. They developed a variant of Communist ideology known as Eurocommunism. This called for a socialist planned economy under the administration of a democratic government, and a multi-Party system of free elections. This was a clear break with the Soviet line, but many of these parties continued to maintain good, or at least diplomatic, relations with the Soviet Union.

All text above is available under the terms of the GNU Free Documentation License. Reprinted with permission from Wikipedia®.

Wikipedia® is a registered trademark of the Wikimedia Foundation, Inc.

I LED THREE LIVES: FACTS BEHIND THE BOOK

On the television series, Charlotte Lawrence played the recurring role of Philbrick's secretary, Carol. In the real world, Philbrick's secretary was named Gloria. One passage in the book described his secretary's suspicions, and how the F.B.I. will disavow any knowledge if any of his secret lives was discovered by any Party.

In the book, Philbrick described an incident when a Communist Party spy comes to work in Philbrick's office among the crew of new girls and gets into political discussions with Gloria, Philbrick's secretary. The comrade who tries to get Gloria to join the Party only succeeds in arousing Gloria's resentment—which turns to genuine concern when Philbrick fails to denounce communism in a discussion between the three of them. Gloria goes to Browning, the boss, and asks him to give Philbrick a raise. She argues that economic necessity is giving Philbrick to Communism. The F.B.I. warns Philbrick that if he is discovered by his business associates to be a Party member the Bureau would not stand behind him or acknowledge that he was a confidential informer: "If anything happens, we never heard of you . . ."

On the television series, there were two episodes in which Philbrick's boss almost caught wind of something foul when Philbrick was neglecting his job. In episode #36, "The Boss," Philbrick's boss starts showing concern for his employee, offering Eva and her husband a week-long vacation so he can settle his nerves. In episode #70, "Boss Number 2," Philbrick tells his boss that he has to leave town for 48 hours, and takes the first train north. To ensure the security of the mission, Comrades Reid and

Cooper are assigned to tail Philbrick all the way. On board the moving train, Herb's boss from the advertising agency bumps into Philbrick and together the two work alone on the project in a compartment.

In chapter six of the book, the Communist Party orders Philbrick to New York for a three-day weekend. The Young Communist League is to be dissolved officially; and a new organization is to be formed, as yet unnamed, but, he now learns to his shock, that this is already in Communist control, and he is to be state treasurer of this new group—the A.Y.D. Philbrick's problem is how to get away without attracting any suspicion. He calls a cousin in New York and arranges to stay with him. Then Eva calls the office the next day to explain that Philbrick is ill and unable to come to work. Meanwhile, he is on the way to New York.

The boss, Harry Browning, gets a generous inspiration and sends up a basket of fruit for Philbrick by two of the office help. Eva makes a red-faced explanation about sending him away from the city hubbub for a few days' rest. When Philbrick returns to his office Monday morning, he takes a vigorous ribbing from all, and a couple of suspicious looks, but manages to get his story accepted about visiting his family in Rye Beach while recovering from a sinus attack. On the surface—just a tall story to get a weekend off. To Philbrick, it means a great deal more.

Episode Guide

PILOT #1 "PILOT"
Production # 1001 / 1B
Typed script by Donn Mullally, n.d.
Typed script with producer's suggestions, n.d.
Mimeo (2 annotated versions), n.d.
Master mimeo (annotated), April 1, 1953
Revised master mimeo, May 9, 1953
Filmed April 3 and 4, 1953

Cast: Richard Carlson (Herbert A. Philbrick); Jeanne Cooper (Sally); Robert Anderson (Wilkerson); Walden Boyle (Adams); Emerson Treacy (Doc); John Frank (Comrade Lothar); Gregory Walcott (lawyer Bob); Mitchell Kowal (the man); William Grueneberg (the clerk); and Earl Keen (the prosecutor).

Production Credits

Production Chief:	Maurice Unger
Director:	Eddie Davis
First Assistant Director:	Eddie Stein
Second Assistant Director:	Bobby Ray
First Cameraman:	Curt Fetters
Second Cameraman:	Robert Hoffman
First Assistant Cameraman:	Hugh Crawford
Casting Director:	Ralph K. Winters
Sound Mixer:	Garry Harris
Recorder:	William Sosteleo
Boom Man:	Jay Ashworth

First Company Grip:	Carl Miksch
Second Company Grip:	Mel Bledsoe
Property Master:	Patterson
Set Decorator:	Lou Hafley
Script Supervisor:	Larry Lund
Film Editor:	Ace Clark
Gaffer:	Al Ronso
Set Labor:	Phil Casazza or Sal Inverso
Construction Chief:	Archie Hall
Electricians:	Charles Stockwell
Drivers:	Art Mynear
Third-grip:	Mel Bledsoe
Still Man:	Mr. Fullerton

Plot: Philbrick spends the day as John Q. Citizen, constantly strained by the fear of being watched and scrutinized, suspected by the Communist Party as a counterspy. Revealing to the television audience each of the members of the cell meeting as regular Joes about town, Philbrick points out which of them is a lawyer, a store owner, a scientist, and all with one common Red denominator. During the emergency cell meeting, Comrade Sally confesses to all in attendance that she is a deviationist, and hangs her head in shame. Comrade Wilkerson reinstates to the cell members that the policy is still the same—the violent overthrow of Capitalistic movement, and everything the United States stands for. The following day after the cell meeting, Philbrick meets up with Special Agent Adams of the F.B.I., who hands Philbrick a handful of photos captured outside the meeting place by an F.B.I. photographer. All of the men were identified except for one, who Philbrick recognizes with ease. Because the files of the F.B.I. were completed on Comrade Leroy Wilkerson, his plans and whereabouts were no longer a threat to the United States.

Memorable Quote: After Comrade Sally confesses, Philbrick remarked, "Confession is good for the soul. If the Comrades don't believe in the soul, they do believe in confessing. It's a big emotional thing with them, like a huge public bath where everyone scrubs everyone else's back. It's sickening . . ."

Trivia, Etc. Philbrick was to meet Special Agent James Adams, but when a Comrade enters the same diner, Philbrick gives the Agent a signal to let him know the coast is not clear. He lifts his thumb up when he takes a sip of his coffee, rather than tying his shoes, which was a signal used in all the other episodes. Agent Adams tells Philbrick that the special cell meetings are rare events—but not so rare as they appear in almost every episode. Philbrick registers his name in the ledger Richard Crown, an alias while working for the Party. This alias would not be used again in any other episode, nor the tactic and reasoning behind it.

The danger of discovery by the Party was revealed a number of times throughout the Philbrick book, and one such incident described when Philbrick had a rendezvous with an F.B.I. agent in a downtown restaurant. He arrived early, and while he was waiting for the agent to show, a comrade walked in. Philbrick could not risk being seen talking to the agent. When the agent entered, Philbrick gives him the prearranged signal with the glass of water . . . This same incident was dramatized in the pilot.

Production Notes: Comrade Wilkerson's car was needed for the second day of filming. A car for the F.B.I. was needed during both days of filming. Total cast cost for this episode was $980.00. No stock footage was used for this episode.

Total Crew Hours:	24
Make Ready and Film:	20 hours
Travel Time:	4 hours

◆ ❖ ◆

PILOT #2 "PILOT"

Production # 1002 / 2B
Audition script, May 4, 1953
Typed script (annotated) by Donn Mullally, May 15, 1953
Typed script (annotated), May 27, 1953
Mimeo script, May 27, 1953
Mimeo script, June 2, 1953
Mimeo script (annotated), post June 2, 1953

Mimeo script (annotated) ca. July 27, 1953
Filmed June 4 and 5, 1953

Cast: Richard Carlson (Herbert A. Philbrick); Elaine Sterling (Mrs. Philbrick); Lynn Davies (Arlene); Peter McCabe (Martin); Louis Nicoletti (Upstate Contact); Paul Keast (Kenyon); James Hyland (Evans); Wesley Hudman (the delivery boy); Harry Stanton (Ketchel); and Roy Engel (Cotton).

Production Credits

Director:	Eddie Davis
First Assistant Director:	Eddie Stein
Second Assistant Director:	Bobby Ray
First Cameraman:	Curt Fetters
Second Cameraman:	Robert Hoffman
First Assistant Cameraman:	Monk Askins
Casting Director:	Ralph H. Winters
Recorder:	Bob Post
Boom Man:	Jim Mobley
First Company Grip:	Carl Miksch
Second Company Grip:	Mel Bledsoe
Property Master:	Pat Patterson
Set Decorator:	Lou Hafley
Wardrobe Man:	Al Berke
Script Supervisor:	Larry Lund
Film Editor:	Ace Clark
Gaffers:	Joe Wharton and Lou Cortese
Set Labor:	Phil Casazza
Construction Chief:	Archie Hall

Plot: Philbrick receives a phone call from a member of the Communist Party who, speaking in code, requests his presence to attend an emergency cell meeting. While attempting to arrive at his destination, Philbrick meets up with an employee who works for the same advertising company Philbrick is employed with. While trying to eliminate suspicions against him, Philbrick is forced to turn down a car ride in an effort to be on time for the meeting.

Later, however, Philbrick discovers that his friend is actually a Comrade, an active member of the Communist Party. The reason for the meeting is soon revealed—their cell plans to make every effort to destroy Capitalistic Institutions—namely the United States Government. A code has been established to accomplish their mission. After the meeting, Philbrick attempts to contact the F.B.I. but with too many eyes about, he holds back until the time is right to pass on this information to the Feds. With the knowledge of how to crack the code, the authorities can keep monitoring all events and messages passed between one Comrade to another.

NOTES: This pilot introduces the audience to the basics involved with the premise, including Herb's hand signals warning Agent Adams to stay away because a Communist is following him (this code would later be changed in the series from raising a finger in the air to tying his shoes and drinking from a water fountain). Also revealed are verbal exchanges over the phone that are coded, and Herb's secret room that even Eva does not enter, and where Herb types his reports for both the F.B.I. *and* the Communist Party.

CODE CRACKER: The code property master was instructed to create a series of codes in the form of a pyramid.

7
212348
8168905472
89762435759621
786529856670124732

This pattern filled the page until a great pyramid of figures was completed. For the sake of the series, this was not an actual attempt at code, although the pyramid was a form of code that, when expertly handled, was nearly impossible to break and, as described by the prop master, "it is beautifully photographic and should stay with the audience until they see it reproduced again at the end of the picture."

EPISODE #3 "DOPE PHOTOGRAPHIC"

PRODUCTION # 1003 / 3B
OUTLINE, JULY 15, 1953
TYPESCRIPT (ANNOTATED) BY DONN MULLALLY, JULY 27, 1953
FINAL MASTER, JULY 27, 1953
REVISED PAGES, JULY 29, 1953
FILMED JULY 30 AND 31, 1953

CAST: Richard Carlson (Herbert A. Philbrick); Walden Boyle (Adams); John Tomecko (Dixon Liggett); Michael Audley (Sands); David McMahon (Henry); John Larch (Terry); Charlotte Lawrence (Miss Berdoni); Lynne Millan (Miss Barr); and Michael Riordan (Kirby).

PRODUCTION CREDITS

DIRECTOR:	EDDIE DAVIS
PRODUCTION CHIEF:	EDDIE DAVIS
FIRST ASSISTANT DIRECTOR:	EDDIE STEIN
SECOND ASSISTANT DIRECTOR:	BOBBY RAY
FIRST CAMERAMAN:	DAN CLARK
SECOND CAMERAMAN:	ROBERT HOFFMAN
FIRST ASSISTANT CAMERAMAN:	MONK ASKINS
CASTING DIRECTOR:	RALPH H. WINTERS
SOUND MIXER:	GARRY HARRIS
RECORDER:	BOB POST
BOOM MAN:	JAY ASHWORTH
FIRST COMPANY GRIP:	CARL MIKSCH
SECOND COMPANY GRIP:	MEL BLEDSOE (FIRST DAY ONLY)
PROPERTY MASTER:	YGNACIO SEPULVEDA
ASSISTANT PROPERTY MAN:	VICTOR PETROTTA
SET DRESSER:	LOU HAFLEY
SCRIPT SUPERVISOR:	LARRY LUND
GAFFER:	AL RONSO
SET LABOR:	PHIL CASAZZA
CONSTRUCTION CHIEF:	ARCHIE HALL

Plot: Special Agent Adams of the F.B.I. explains to Herb Philbrick that the Communist Party recently acquired a shipment of narcotics, which, if they can get key people in defense plants addicted, can lead to trades—vital defense plan information for free drugs. Since the pushers are already known to the police and F.B.I., moving in on the ring wouldn't shed suspicion on Philbrick. But to cinch the conviction, they need all the evidence they can get—including filming the exchanges on the street corner outside Philbrick's office. Herb buys a motion picture camera to capture a deal going down in the streets, and uses the excuse that he is trying a new advertising gimmick for a cover. But the Reds arrange for one of their own to be hired as a new secretary to keep tabs on Philbrick, suspecting foul play. After filming the streets for a number of days, avoiding the secretary and the nosy Comrades, the F.B.I. reviews the film, catches the peddlers in action, and crack down on the narcotics' ring.

Production Notes: A limo was needed on both days of filming. A sedan was needed on the second day of filming. Total cost breakdown: cast was paid $70 a day. Estimated Overtime: $100. With extras (total cost):$224.94. Total cost production for the film: $1,234.94. Total crew hours to film: 22 hours.

Location Shots:
7916 N. Beverly Blvd.
Roosevelt Hotel
Chandler Shoes, corner of 7th and Olive
Owl Drugs, 8th and Broadway
Westlake Park
Haas Bldg., corner of 7th and Broadway
One scene was filmed in a real Lab office.

Episode #4 "THE BAITED TRAP"
Production # 1004 / 4B
Story breakdown by Frank Burt.
Outline, July 22, 1953

TYPESCRIPT (ANNOTATED), N.D.
MASTER MIMEO, JULY 29, 1953
REVISED PAGES (ANNOTATED), AUGUST 3, 1953
FILMED AUGUST 4 AND 5, 1953

CAST: Richard Carlson (Herbert A. Philbrick); Alan Reynolds (Jack Blake); John Zaremba (Special Agent Jerry Dressler); Louise Kane (Comrade Agnes); Rankin Mansfield (the night attendant); Kevin Enright (Glenn Tucker); Aaron Spelling (the elevator operator); and Bob Lawson (extra in background).

PRODUCTION CREDITS

DIRECTOR:	LEW LANDERS
PRODUCTION CHIEF:	LEON BENSON
FIRST ASSISTANT DIRECTOR:	DON VERK
SECOND ASSISTANT DIRECTOR:	BOBBY RAY
FIRST CAMERAMAN:	WILLIAM WHITLEY
SECOND CAMERAMAN:	ROBERT HOFFMAN
FIRST ASSISTANT CAMERAMAN:	MONROE (MONK) ASKINS
SOUND MIXER:	GARRY HARRIS (FIRST ONLY)
RECORDER:	BOB POST (FIRST ONLY)
BOOM MAN:	JAY ASHWORTH (FIRST ONLY)
FIRST COMPANY GRIP:	CARL MIKSCH
PROPERTY MASTER:	YGNACIO SEPULVEDA
SCRIPT SUPERVISOR:	LARRY LUND
GAFER:	AL RONSO
DRIVERS:	ART MYNEAR AND CHARLIE BARR
CABLE MAN:	MR. DUFFY
ELECTRICIAN:	CHARLES STOCKWELL

PLOT: Philbrick is given a new assignment, one so valuable to the Party that they dare not give it to Comrade Agnes, a secretary from the inside. Comrade Jack wants Philbrick to put together a list of non-card carrying members, from a dummy list in code, from a restricted filing cabinet. When Special Agent Dressler explains to Philbrick that Comrade Jack rented a hotel room across the street on the same level as their stakeout, the opportunity to acquire a copy of the list is promising. But Philbrick suspects a baited trap to learn where his loyalties are. Rather than copy the list, he enters the room late that night at Commie Headquarters and performs his job, cracking the code as instructed, and types the list of names and addresses. Both Comrade Jack and the F.B.I. commend Philbrick for a job well done. For Comrade Jack, Philbrick passed all the tests with flying colors with no signs of deviation. For the F.B.I., having used a long-range telescope and a secretary dictating the names and address, once-secret enemies of the United States, have now become pipelines of information for the Feds.

TRIVIA, ETC. The role of the elevator operator was a young actor named Aaron Spelling, who would more than a decade later become a television producer, responsible for such programs as *Charlie's Angels, Fantasy Island, T. J. Hooker, Starsky and Hutch, S.W.A.T., Hart to Hart* and *Beverly Hills, 90210.*

This episode was based on an incident reported within the pages of Philbrick's book. In the book, Philbrick is scheduled to do some mimeographing and mailing one evening at Party headquarters. Chairman Otis Hood tells him that all the office personnel will be busy elsewhere, and gives Philbrick the key and tells him where to leave it and how to lock up. Philbrick goes out to supper. When he returns, the office is deserted. Now he has a perfect opportunity to go through all the files, get any info he wants for the F.B.I. The setup was too perfect. Across the street, in an upper story of the Hotel Touraine, Party members were watching Philbrick's every move through binoculars. The receptionist's desk where he is to leave the door key is directly in front of the window and can be seen clearly from their vantage point. Philbrick hesitates only a minute, and suspects a trap. He stays in the outer office all evening, right on the job, working at the mimeo, the card file, and the typewriter on that desk by the window. He leaves the key right where he was told, locks up, following instructions to the letter. The move was a smart and lucky decision.

PRODUCTION NOTES: A taxicab was rented for the second day of filming. Cast was paid $70 total for the two days filming. Estimated Overtime: $150. Extras (total cost) was $267.85.

Location Shots:
Equitable Building
The hotel where the character Jack resides was filmed in the Plaza Hotel.
All street scenes filmed within the vicinity of Hollywood & Vine.

Episode #5 "RAILROAD STRIKE ATTEMPT"

Production # 1005 / 5B
Outline dated July 20 and 21, 1953.
Typescript (annotated) by Gene Levitt, August 4, 1953
Master mimeo, August 4, 1953
Added pages, September 1, 1953
Filmed August 6 and 7, 1953

Cast: Richard Carlson (Herbert A. Philbrick); Norman Rainey (Dad); Duane Thorsen (Nichols); Jim Wade (Stanton); George Champe (the professor); and George Selk (Comrade Brockman).

Production Credits

Director:	Eddie Davis
Production Chief:	Eddie Davis
First Assistant Director:	Eddie Stein
Second Assistant Director:	Bobby Ray
First Cameraman:	Dan Clark
Second Cameraman:	Robert Hoffman
First Assistant Cameraman:	Monk Askins
Sound Mixer:	Garry Harris
Recorder:	Bob Post
Boom Man:	Jay Ashworth
First Company Grip:	Carl Miksch
Property Master:	Ygnacio Sepulveda
Wardrobe Man:	Al Berke
Script Supervisor:	Larry Lund

Plot: Philbrick learns that the Communist Party wants to start a railroad strike, in an effort to disrupt the transit system, thus slowing down our defense efforts; textiles, steel, auto manufacturing, etc. As an advertising man by occupation, Philbrick is assigned to create the usual leaflets using the right American words convincing employees of the railroad to strike—just skip the real issues, and maintain a stand for the strike. Such a strike can mushroom across the country within 24 hours. Days later, the pamphlets are printed and passed out throughout railroad yards, with a few verbal "suggestions" to strike or be subjected to Commie violence. Philbrick is watched with a close eye the entire time, preventing him from leaking the information to the F.B.I. until he gets one small break and a chance to tell the Feds what the ploy is. The next morning, a strike doesn't happen—men don't believe in the pamphlets, suspecting Communist infiltration. When the Commies send a few of their Goon Squad to set a violent example on some of the men at the railroad, the Government steps in and arrests the guilty parties.

Production Notes: Four car drivers were needed for the first day of filming. Five car drivers were needed for the second day of filming. Two sedans, a 33-passenger bus, and ZIV's station wagon were needed for both days' filming.

Total Crew Hours:	22
Estimated Overtime	$100.
Extras (total cost)	$483.76.

Production Trivia: The Party builds up its influence in key industries in order to be able to paralyze U.S. in case of war or revolution. This process is called "colonization." A good Party member must be prepared to shift his job or place of residence if called on to do a colonization job for the Party. This episode was adapted from a passage in chapter twelve of Philbrick's *I Led Three Lives* book, which revealed how Philbrick's father stormed into his office one afternoon. Old man Philbrick is a Railroad man, and has worked on the Boston and Maine line for years. The trainmen are negotiating for a raise in pay. The Party wants to use this opportunity. What Philbrick's father is mad about are some leaflets which he slams down on his son's desk. He obviously doesn't like what's in them. They are put out by the "Railway Employees Branch of the Communist Party of New England." "Who do these people think they are?" shouts the elder Philbrick. Philbrick, when writing about this in his book, looked back and thought it a humorous event that his father did not know that his own son had written and produced the leaflet.

LOCATION SHOTS:
U.P. FREIGHT YARDS, 4441 E. WASHINGTON
VACANT STORE, 1000 SOUTH OLIVE (AT OLYMPIC)
BROCKMAN'S HOME, CORNER OF INGRAHAM AND LITTLE STREETS
PRINTING OFFICE, 1121 NORTH LAS PALMAS
PHILBRICK'S HOME, 267 SOUTH LAFAYETTE PLACE
THE MARKET, CORNER OF 6TH AND VERMONT
GRIFFITH PARK AND ZOO

EPISODE #6 "CAMPUS STORY"
PRODUCTION # 1006 / 6B
TYPESCRIPT BY ROBERT YALE LIBOTT, AUGUST 5, 1953
MIMEO (ANNOTATED), AUGUST 5, 1953
MIMEO (ANNOTATED), AUGUST 12, 1953
MASTER MIMEO, AUGUST 12, 1953
REVISED PAGES (ANNOTATED), AUGUST 13, 1953
FILMED AUGUST 17 AND 18, 1953

CAST: Richard Carlson (Herbert A. Philbrick); Gene Reynolds (Dan Ellman); James Moloney (Jim Fielding III); Yvette Vickers (Sue Davis); Fred Beir (George Marvin); John Zaremba (Special Agent Jerry Dressler); John Lynch (Albert Maryatt); Peggy Wagner (Jeanne); Mark Bennett (Lawyer Gresham); and Harte E. Wayne (the campus cop).

PRODUCTION CREDITS

DIRECTOR:	LEW LANDERS
PRODUCTION CHIEF:	LEON BENSON
FIRST ASSISTANT DIRECTOR:	EDDIE STEIN

Second Assistant Director:	Bobby Ray
First Cameraman:	Dan Clark
Second Cameraman:	Robert Hoffman
First Assistant Cameraman:	Monroe (Monk) Askins
Sound Mixer:	Garry Harris
Recorder:	Robert (Bob) Post
Boom Man:	Jay Ashworth
First Company Grip:	Mel Bledsoe
Property Master:	Ygnacio Sepulveda
Script Supervisor:	Larry Lund
Gaffer:	Al Ronso
Drivers:	Art Mynear, Charlie Barr and Rot Hobbs

Plot: In Room 20, Fielding Hall, at a local College Campus, Comrade Dan Ellman is in charge of recruiting select students of prominent status who, many years in the future, might prove valuable to the Party—potential allies with Communist caliber. Among the chosen few are Jim Fielding III (whose family founded Fielding Hall), Howard Ainsworth, George Marvin and Sue Davis—all of whom have ties with community leaders. Philbrick is assigned to supervise and observe the program, which includes breaking in a fraternity dorm to investigate the background of one potential student. After clearing Jim Fielding of all wrong doings, Comrade Ellman believes he is successful in blackmailing the boy into becoming a member of the Party. Philbrick leaks a report to Special Agent Jerry Dressler, who explains that he cannot do anything to help convince Jim, who has already changed his mind about Democratic ways. The only thing the Federal Government can do is arrange for Jim to be quietly dropped at the end of the term, so no public scandal will come to the surface. Jim may have become a casualty, but they'll keep him on their "watch list" as he opens a door for the F.B.I. Who knows? Maybe the young lad will one day be giving the F.B.I. information. "We can't stop them from recruiting, Herb," Dressler comments, "but we can stop them from keeping secrets."

Memorable Quote: Philbrick comments, "You can't spot a traitor by his face."

PRODUCTION NOTES: One electrician, two policemen, three drivers, one bus, one camera truck, and one station wagon were needed for both days of filming. Seven extras were needed for the first day of filming. Five extras were needed on the second day of filming. One Ford convertible was needed on the second day of filming.

TRIVIA, ETC. One highly effective scene in this episode is when Sue Davis leads Jim into her dorm (keeping him occupied for a time so Philbrick and Comrade Dan Ellman can search Jim's room). Before Sue's invitation to come inside for a bite to eat, Jim has his tie straightened properly. When he leaves the dorm a short time later, his tie and shirt collar is ruffled—a visual gimmick that suggests he had a little more than a bite to eat. Changes were made to the script shortly before filming. Bradford College was changed to Branford College. Maria Davis was changed to Sue Davis. Special Agent Wells was changed to Special Agent Dressler.

LOCATION SHOTS:
CITY COLLEGE & CAMPUS, 955 N. VERMONT
MAREL'S SORORITY AND ROOM, 844 N. NORMANDIE
EXTERIOR AND INTERIOR OF THE MUSIC SHOP, 816 N. VERMONT AVE.
MALT SHOP, 850 N. VERMONT AVE.
EXTERIOR AND INTERIOR FIELDING'S ROOM AND HOUSE, 863 N. HELIOTROPE

EPISODE #7 "ARMY INFILTRATION"
PRODUCTION # 1007 / 7B
TYPESCRIPT (ANNOTATED) BY FRANK BURT, AUGUST 21, 1953
MASTER MIMEO (ANNOTATED), AUGUST 25, 1953
REVISED MASTER MIMEO, AUGUST 25, 1953
REVISED NARRATION, SEPTEMBER 24, 1953
FILMED AUGUST 27 AND 28, 1953

CAST: Richard Carlson (Herbert A. Philbrick); John Zaremba

(Special Agent Jerry Dressler); Jean G. Harvey (Jenny); Madge Cleveland (Amy Wharton); Lilyan Astaire (Margaret Wharton); James Nusser (Captain Norton); Maury Dexter (Corporal Wharton); Douglas Brooks (Sergeant); and John Frank (Lothar).

Production Credits

Director:	Les Goodwin
Production Chief:	Leon Benson
First Assistant Director:	Eddie Stein
Second Assistant Director:	Bobby Ray
First Cameraman:	Curt Fetters
Second Cameraman:	Robert Hoffman
First Assistant Cameraman:	Monk Askins
Sound Mixer:	Garry Harris (first day only)
Boom Man:	Jay Ashworth (first day only)
First Company Grip:	Carl Miksch
Second Company Grip:	Mel Bledsoe (first day only)
Property Master:	Max Pittman
Set Decorator:	Lou Hafley
Wardrobe Man:	Al Berke (first day only)
Script Supervisor:	Larry Lund
Film Editor:	Ace Clark
Gaffer:	Al Ronso
Construction Chief:	Archie Hall
Electricians:	Charles Stockwell (both days) and Knight (second day only)
Drivers:	Art Mynear and Charles Barr

Plot: The Communist Party has promoted Herb Philbrick to the position of Educational Director of the District. His new task will be the responsibility of distribution of printed materials, and this poses as a dual role as Party Security. During cell meetings, Philbrick plays the role of a motivational speaker, encouraging Party members to send materials to anyone abroad—this includes Amy and Margaret Wharton, two little old ladies who have been sending packages to their nephew George, a member of the Armed Forces. When Herb finds out, he leaks the information to Special Agent Jerry Dressler. Weeks later, when the Whartons' most recent package arrives at an American Military Base, George's superiors question him about the packages he has been receiving from his two aunts. George is shocked to discover that the sweet old ladies have been sending microfilm in disguise. Although arrests are made abroad, and the pipeline of information is broken, George's innocence is cleared of any wrong doing. Word reaches back to Philbrick who, playing the role of Educational Director, verbally reprimands Amy and Margaret that such errors are subject to disciplinary action. Thanks to Philbrick's leak to the F.B.I., a promising young man in the U.S. Military can continue doing what he does best.

MEMORABLE QUOTE: "A Communist will swear to anything—even on a stack of Bibles that they are not a Communist. After all, what's a Bible to them?"

PRODUCTION NOTES: A Chrysler car, a 50-passenger bus, and a camera truck were needed for the first day of filming. One stand-in was needed for both days of filming. A total of fifteen extras were needed to complete filming.

TOTAL CREW HOURS:	24
MAKE READY AND SHOOTING:	22 HOURS
TRAVEL:	2 HOURS

PROPS: The Property Master is responsible for arranging a large number of props be available for filming. An example, for the 22 1/2 minutes of film this episode required are keys on a ring, a note from Philbrick's wife, a notebook with lists of names, a wristwatch for Philbrick, "Commie" book and pamphlets, a crowbar, some books and boxes, pipe and tobacco, a key for a bookstore desk, a Party card, a billfold with a secret compartment, a clock set for 9:00, a newspaper, a large package with clothing and two pairs of shoes, a clipboard, a telephone, mail, and a strip of Microfilm.

LOCATION SHOTS:
INT. ANTIQUE SHOP, 5451 SANTA MONICA BLVD.

Ext. antique shop, on 3rd St. and Santa Monica Blvd.
Ext. St. Business District, 5530 Hollywood Blvd.
Ext. Bookstore, 203 N. Gramercy Pl.
U.S. Post Office, 1014 N. Vine St.

Episode #8 "THE SPY"
Production # 1008 / 8B
Typescript (annotated) by Donn Mullally, August 25, 1953
Mimeo (annotated), August 28, 1953
Master mimeo, August 28, 1953
Narration, September 25, and circa 29, 1953
Filmed August 29 and 30, 1953

Cast: Richard Carlson (Herbert A. Philbrick); Virginia Stefan (Eva Philbrick); Robert Clarke (Bernard J. Tippy); Peggy O'Connor (Mrs. Tipton); Richard Bryan (Special Agent Jenner); Mort Mills (Comrade Straight); Irvin Ashkenazy (Kloos); Roxanne Arlen (Zoe); and Kay Stewart (the nurse).

Production Credits

Director:	Eddie Davis
Production Chief:	Eddie Davis
First Assistant Director:	Don Verk
Second Assistant Director:	Bobby Ray
First Cameraman:	Curt Fetters
Second Cameraman:	Robert Hoffman
First Assistant Cameraman:	Monk Askins
Sound Mixer:	Garry Harris
Boom Man:	Jay Ashworth
First Company Grip:	Carl Miksch (second day only)
Second Company Grip:	Mel Bledsoe
Property Master:	Max Pittman
Set Decorator:	Lou Hafley
Wardrobe Man:	Al Berke
Script Supervisor:	Larry Lund

FILM EDITOR:	MARTIN COHN
GAFFER:	AL RONSO
SET LABOR:	PHIL CASAZZA
CONSTRUCTION CHIEF:	ARCHIE HALL
ELECTRICIAN:	CHARLES STOCKWELL
DRIVERS:	ART MYNEAR AND CHARLES BARR

PLOT: Comrade Bernard J. Tippy is suspected of being a deviant, and a possible traitor to the Communist Party. Herb Philbrick is assigned to question Tippy and, after getting to know him on a personal level, make out a report and forward it to Mr. Straight, a recent member of a Pro-4 Cell from Moscow. Philbrick actually sets up opportunities to test Tippy's loyalties, and soon suspects that if a war broke out between the U.S. and another country, Tippy would arm himself to defend the U.S. Even though this means the death of Tippy, Herb makes out an honest report and delivers it to Mr. Straight. After the whole shebang is completed, Agent Jenner plays a recording for Herb, a secret conversation between Tippy and Mr. Straight. Philbrick is shocked to learn that the entire assignment was a test to verify Herb's loyalties—not Tippy's. With Herb's loyalties established through an honest report, it is assumed by both Herb and Agent Jenner that he will soon be assigned to bigger and better jobs deeper in the Party. For the F.B.I., they now have confirmation of the top man of the Communist Secret Police in the area and will be able to watch his every move.

MEMORABLE QUOTE: "A lamb doesn't know anything about a slaughterhouse until he feels a knife at his throat."

PRODUCTION NOTES: Two prop makers, a laborer, two grips, two painters, two stand-ins and nine extras were needed to finish filming. Two policemen were needed for the second day of filming. A Ford car, a bus, a camera truck, and a station wagon were needed for the second day of filming.

TRIVIA, ETC. Herbert A. Philbrick himself was extremely pleased with this episode. "This is the first time I have ever seen the difference between liberalism and communism so emphatically and daringly put forth. It is my guess that this story, when it becomes known, will become the most talked about TV show on the air. There are a number of top-flight people who will be greatly interested, and who I think should be given advanced notice. Perhaps even an advanced screening. Such prominent liberals as Arthur Schlesinger, Jr., Max Lerner, Murray Kempton, Roger Baldwin, Morris Ernst, Mel Arnold, Dr. Daniel Poling and others connected with the *Freeman Magazine, The New Leader, Commentary*, etc., will I know, be very excited when they learn that such a dramatic presentation of communism vs. liberalism will appear on a TV screen."

Location Shots:
Filmed in the Interior of a Bowling Alley located at 7658 Beverly.
Filmed on location at a Miniature golf coarse located at 7716 Beverly.
Hotel, 1415 Ocean Ave.
City Street and Blood Bank, 1130 S. Vermont
Philbrick's home and bus stop, 267 S. Lafayette
Tippy's house was a real house located at 591 N. Bronson.

Episode #9 "THE JET ENGINE"
Production # 1009 / 9B
Typescript (annotated) by Stuart Jerome, n.d.
Typescript (annotated), August 6, 1953
Typescript, August 25, 1953
Master mimeo (annotated), September 2, 1953
Revised master mimeo, September 2, 1953
Revised pages (annotated), September 3, 1953
Filmed September 4 and 5, 1953.

Cast: Richard Carlson (Herbert A. Philbrick); John Zaremba (Special Agent Jerry Dressler); Alan Lee (Comrade Walker); Edith Craig (Comrade Mary); Herbert Lane (Comrade Al "Dan" Barrett);

Robert Berger (Comrade Becker); James Floyd Stone (the foreman); Joe Becker (the machinist); and Brick Sullivan (the factory guard).

Production Credits

Director:	Lew Landers
Production Chief:	Eddie Davis
First Assistant Director:	Eddie Stein
Second Assistant Director:	Bobby Ray
First Cameraman:	Curt Fetters
Second Cameraman:	Robert Hoffman
First Assistant Cameraman:	Monk Askins
Sound Mixer:	Garry Harris (second only)
Recorder:	Bob Post (second only)
Boom Man:	Jay Ashworth (second only)
First Company Grip:	Carl Miksch (second only)
Second Company Grip:	Mel Bledsoe
Property Master:	Ygnacio Sepulveda
Assistant Prop Man:	Max Pittman
Set Decorator:	Lou Hafley
Script Supervisor:	Larry Lund
Gaffer:	Al Ronso
Set Laborer:	Phil Casazza (second only)
Construction Chief:	Archie Hall
Electrician:	Charles Stockwell
Drivers:	Art Mynear and Charles Barr

Plot: Philbrick visits Comrade Mary's house to help stuff envelopes, and soon finds himself taking down shorthand. After printing fifty copies of a short survey, Philbrick learns that certain Party members are presently employed at important U.S. factories where top secret information about the production machinery is being reported to Comrade Walker, using these surveys. One such Comrade is Al Barrett (a.k.a. Dan) who, as shop steward, uses his position to jot down pertinent information about the milling machines. After Philbrick informs Special Agent Jerry Dressler, he discovers that Special Agent Moss has been employed at the same factory to keep close eyes on Barrett. With cooperation at top sources, the Feds arrange for Barrett to receive a transfer to a factory he thinks contains highly classified material—but it's not. The Reds, naturally, are pleased with the news, but with Barrett soon to begin delivering false information to the Reds, the espionage ring is foiled.

CASTING TRIVIA: Brick Sullivan, who played the role of a factory guard in this episode, was an unsung character actor. Sullivan played the role of a police officer, cop or prison guard in more than 130 films, including playing a military guard in *From Here to Eternity* (1953), a police officer in *Ma and Pa Kettle Go to Town* (1950), and a guard in *Miracle on 34th Street* (1947). One of his last few roles was playing a recurring role of a bartender in a few episodes of television's *Gunsmoke.*

PRODUCTION NOTES: Two prop masters, two painters, one laborer, two grips, two stand-ins, and eleven extras were needed for filming. Six extras were present the first day of filming, and five were present the second day of filming. A bus, a camera truck, Philbrick's car and Dressler's car were needed during the filming of this episode.

TOTAL CREW HOURS:	22 HOURS
MAKE READY AND SHOOTING:	19 HOURS
TRAVEL TIME:	3 HOURS

PRODUCTION TRIVIA: Philbrick wrote to the producers his personal feelings toward this episode: "I think that the script is a tremendous improvement over the first draft. However, somehow the impression I get from the overall script is a certain softness. It seems to be a little too Sunday Schoolish—not brittle enough. The male fist of the Communist conspiracy seems too well to be concealed with smooth velvet. This business of the F.B.I. lowering the shade before interviewing a visitor sounds much more like a tactic of the Communist Party than one of the F.B.I. Somehow, the symbolism of the lowered shade doesn't fit with the usual concept of the F.B.I. If this must be done, I would suggest that you use a Venetian blind. Or better still, build an interview room used for such purposes by the F.B.I. that is so located in the building as to face across a wing of a building with other F.B.I. offices on the other side or something of that nature."

Location Shots:
8715 Melrose Ave.
8901 Santa Monica
8715 Beverly
Streets and Highways in above vicinity
Consolidated lab
Building at Wilcox and Selma
Wilcox near Hollywood
Alley south of Hollywood Boulevard at Argyle
North American-Imperial at Aviation Blvd.

Episode #10 "HELPING HAND"
Production # 1010 / 10B
Outlines August 11, 1953, n.d.
Typescript by Gene Levitt, n.d.
Typescript (annotated), August 24, 1953
Mimeo (annotated), September 1, 1953
Master mimeo (annotated), September 8, 1953
Revised master mimeo, September 8, 1953
Filmed September 10 and 11, 1953

Cast: Richard Carlson (Herbert A. Philbrick); Virginia Stephan (Eva Philbrick); Lester Sharpe (Comrade Rudolph Draskin); William O'Neal (Comrade Baltim); Ed Hinton (Special Agent Hal Henderson); Roy Lennert (Comrade Phillips); Lucia Barclay (Comrade Ina); Jack Daly (the longshoreman); Heenan Elliott (the male guest); and Ruth Bennett (the wife).

Production Credits

Director:	Eddie Davis
Production Chief:	Eddie Davis
First Assistant Director:	Don Verk
Second Assistant Director:	Bobby Ray

First Cameraman:	Curt Fetters
Second Cameraman:	Robert Hoffman
First Assistant Cameraman:	Monk Askins
Sound Mixer:	Garry Harris
Recorder:	Bob Post
Boom Man:	Jay Ashworth
First Company Grip:	Carl Miksch
Second Company Grip:	Mel Bledsoe
Property Master:	Ygnacio Sepulveda
Assistant Property Man:	Robert Benton
Set Decorator:	Lou Hafley
Script Supervisor:	Helen Gailey (Sept. 10)
Script Supervisor:	Larry Lund (Sept. 11)
Film Editor:	Ace Clark
Gaffer:	Al Ronso
Set Labor:	Phil Casazza
Construction Chief:	Archie Hall
Electrician:	Charles Stockwell
Drivers:	Art Mynear and Charles Barr

Plot: At a recent cell meeting, Herb Philbrick is assigned to become a temporary floater for a special assignment. His mission is to pick up a man, Comrade Rudolph Draskin, who has been smuggled into the country. Philbrick's assignment is to take Draskin to a secret rendezvous where he is assigned a passport, credentials, photos, and other forms of fake identification. With Philbrick's connections with Hollywood commaderea and as an advertising man, the Party requests Philbrick introduce Draskin to the Hollywood elite so he can blend in, with the intentions of infiltrating the influential members of the film and screen industry. Philbrick does, earning Draskin's respect and trust. During Draskin's initial introductions to society members, Philbrick gathers fingerprints, statistics, and other vital information that could help assist the F.B.I. in their profiling. When Draskin finally lands a job in Hollywood, Philbrick sees his Comrade off at the airport—and observes Special Agent Henderson boarding the same plane . . .

COMMENT: The concluding remarks for this broadcast were specifically aimed toward the television viewers, with the intention of keeping Hollywood looking glamorous since the recent headlines trade papers printed about Hollywood actors testifying before the Un-American Activities Investigations made moviegoers and television viewers wonder who was leaning toward the wrong side.

"Many fine people have come to America from foreign lands and contributed substantially to the field of entertainment. When the Communists try to hide behind the clean records of this group, the authorities lost no time in clamping down on their operation. With this knowledge, the United States is continuously willing to welcome people from other countries, that they may add even more to their long list of achievements."

PRODUCTION TRIVIA: This episode features Eva Philbrick's concerns for her husband, and the men he has been frequently associated with. In chapter three of Philbrick's *I Led Three Lives* book, family tensions grew as Eva became disgusted with the people who came to the house and asked her husband to keep away from them. He tried to convince her he was doing the right thing, but instructions by the Bureau prevented him from telling her the truth. Since the intention of the television series was to progress along with the book's contents—especially the first season—this problem was resolved five episodes later in "The Wife."

PRODUCTION NOTES: A black 1948 Dodge, a bus, an inert car, and a station wagon were needed for the first day of filming. Two stand-ins each day were needed for filming and six extras were used on the first day of filming and two on the second day. Sets needed to be built were a Café, a boat cabin, a theatre lobby, and a speaker platform (i.e., no location shots for these four scenes).

TOTAL CREW HOURS:	24
TRAVEL TIME:	3
MAKE READY AND SHOOTING:	21

AN EXAMPLE OF THE PROPS REQUIRED FOR AN AVERAGE EPISODE: A portfolio, a taxi stand and phone, leaflets and books, a pier sign, a notebook, a banner reading "Life and Letter Club," a ticket envelope, a camera, a wristwatch, a suitcase, a wallet, a photo of Draskin, food for the restaurant, special matches, and an identification wallet were needed.

Location Shots:
Van Camp Sea Food Company, 772 Tuna Street
Partially filmed on a Ferry Boat and at Fish Harbor, located at Seaside & Tuna Streets
Western Airlines International

Episode #11 "PARCELS TO POLAND"
Production # 1011 / 11B
Outline by Donn Mullally.
Typescript (annotated) by Frank Burt, September 18, 1953
Mimeo (annotated), September 23, 1953
Master mimeo, September 23, 1953
Revised pages, September 24, 1953
Retakes, September 28, 1953
Filmed September 25 and 26, 1953

Cast: Richard Carlson (Herbert A. Philbrick); John Zaremba (Special Jerry Dressler); Diana Archer (Barbara); Elizabeth Cloud-Miller (the lady); Hugh Boswell (Platte); Charles Maxwell (Comrade George); and Jack Carol (Comrade Bill).

Production Credits

Director:	Les Goodwin
Production Chief:	Leon Benson
First Assistant Director:	Don Verk
Second Assistant Director:	Eddie Mull
First Cameraman:	Curt Fetters
Second Cameraman:	Robert Hoffman
First Assistant Cameraman:	Monk Askins
Sound Mixer:	Garry Harris (second day only)
Recorder:	Bob Post (second day only)

BOOM MAN:	JAY ASHWORTH (SECOND DAY ONLY)
FIRST COMPANY GRIP:	CARL MIKSCH
SECOND COMPANY GRIP:	TEX JACKSON (SECOND DAY ONLY)
PROPERTY MASTER:	LYLE REIFSNIDER
ASSISTANT PROPERTY MAN:	LLOYD MACLEAN
SET DECORATOR:	LOU HAFLEY
SCRIPT SUPERVISOR:	HELEN MCCAFFREY
GAFFER:	AL RONSO
SET LABOR:	SAL INVERSO (SECOND DAY ONLY)
CONSTRUCTION	CHIEF: ARCHIE HALL

PLOT: The Soviet Institute of Commerce is a front for a money-making scheme—a new trading company called "Christmas Parcels for Poland." The general idea is that they sell food parcels to American citizens, and guarantee delivery to needy families in Poland, unknowingly giving money for the Communist treasury, and a name and list of individuals in the U.S. who have contacts in Poland. Comrade Platte, who has been called to testify because of the recent newspapers reporting "Spy Queen Admits Communist Espionage," plans to expose the racket, but dies of a heart attack before reaching the stand. With their hands tied behind their backs, the F.B.I. and Philbrick are powerless to prevent the successful program from expanding into Easter. That is, until one of the victims gets her receipts for two packages she paid for . . . it turns out she was really working for a fascist Polish Refugee Organization. The names she gave them, the same on the receipts, were really kings and poets, who have been dead for hundreds of years. Having turned the receipts over to the newspapers, the Soviet Institute of Commerce is turned into a farce and the U.S. Government is able to begin an investigation for fraud.

PRODUCTION NOTES: A small bus, a camera car (truck), Philbrick's car, Dressler's car, and West's car were needed for the first day of filming. Sets needed to be built were the interior of the store, its backroom, upper hallway, artist studio, and library. There were four extras a day and one stand-in each day for the filming. No makeup man or wardrobe man was required for this episode.

Trivia, Etc. Actor Charles Maxwell, who plays Comrade George in this episode, later played the recurring role of Special Agent Joe Carey in future episodes. This was the only episode of the series where the cast and crew went back to retake additional or changed scenes, after the usual two-day filming.

Location Shots:
Roosevelt Building, 723 W. 7th Street
Alley between Hollywood and Ellentro
Parking lot at Wilcox and Selma
100 N. Hudson place
5518 Marathon
Store located at Melrose & Irving

Episode #12 "CAPTURED CONGRESSMAN"
Production # 1012 / 12B
Outline (annotated), July 16, 1953
Typescript (annotated), by Don Brinkley, n.d.
Master mimeo, (annotated), September 12, 1953
Typescript (annotated), September 14, 1953
Typescript (annotated), by Don Brinkley, rewrite by Stuart Jerome, September 18, 1953
Revised pages, September 22, 1953
Filmed September 23 and 24, 1953.

Cast: Richard Carlson (Herbert A. Philbrick); Ed Hinton (Special Agent Hal Henderson); Jo Gilbert (Mrs. Dayton); Paul Power (Kettner); Merle Weaver (Comrade Borden); and Gordon Barnes (Reynolds).

Production Credits

Director:	Eddie Davis
Production Chief:	Eddie Davis

First Assistant Director:	Eddie Stein
Second Assistant Director:	Eddie Mull
First Cameraman:	Dan Clark
Recorder:	Slim Haughton
Boom Man:	Jim Mobley
First Company Grip:	Mel Bledsoe
Property Master:	Lyle Reifsnider
Set Decorator:	Lou Hafley
Script Supervisor:	Helen McCaffrey
Set Labor:	Archie Hall
Drivers:	Art Mynear and Charles Barr

Plot: George Reynolds is running for Congress. With Philbrick's advertising campaign ideas, he is a cinch to win the upcoming election. Since Reynolds has sworn to conduct Anti-Communist investigations, and he proves to be an easy victim of a smear campaign, the Party prefers his certainty of office. For the coming months, Philbrick does his best to help win Reynolds the election and it appears he'll succeed—until the day before the election, when Reynolds is to give a radio speech. Philbrick learns that a woman named Mrs. Dayton made a contribution for his election campaign, and when he wins the election, he'll thank her publicly as usual—unaware that she'll announce publicly that he was funded by the Communist Party. Philbrick does his best to help, and during the radio address, George Reynolds skips the speech he was supposed to read and instead, exposes the true facts—including returning every penny of the funds to the Communist Party, and how he mortgaged his home to pay for the radio address himself. As a result of his investigation, Comrade Marie Dayton is exposed, as well as other top-ranking officials of the Communist Party.

Production Notes: A bus and Comrade Borden's car were needed for both days of filming. A station wagon (for sound), a camera truck, and a taxi cab were needed for the second day of filming. Two stand-ins each day were needed, and six extras on the first day and seven on the second day for filming. Sets needing to be built were a stage, a library and hall, backroom store (close shot), and

Radio B Studio. Oddly, no makeup man or wardrobe man were needed for this episode.

Total Crew Hours:	22
Make Ready and Shooting:	20 hours
Travel Time:	2 hours

Another example of the props required for an average episode:: Insert sign for Scene 4, push broom and pickup for janitor, briefcases, watches, glasses, cigarette lighter, money, signs for aquarium, "closed" sign, flags, posters, banners, map of the city, charts, insert map for Sc. 54, telephones, clocks, typewriters, phone bells, desk props, newspaper camera and flash bulbs, microphones for radio station, food card tables, mimeo machine, mail shoot, fish food, key for door, phone booth, and a taxi.

Production Trivia: The scene where Philbrick phones the F.B.I. from his office was changed between previous drafts and the final script. As Herbert A. Philbrick himself pointed out in a memo to the producers, "If he did they would answer 'F.B.I. office' in the normal manner, which would identify the call. If there was an emergency, he had a special number and they would call him back and disguise the call."

Location Shots:
7926 Beverly Blvd.
644 N. La Brea
624 N. Highland
Streets at Wilshire and La Brea

Episode #13 "PURLOINED PRINTING PRESS"
Production # 1013 / 13B
Outline August 24, 1953
Mimeo by Donn Mullally, September 16, 1953
Master mimeo, September 21, 1953
Revised master mimeo, September 25, 1953
Revised voice over, September 29, 1953

FILMED SEPTEMBER 28 AND 29, 1953.

CAST: Richard Carlson (Herbert A. Philbrick); David Vaile (Hedler); Joseph Kerr (Anderson); Sarah Spencer (Alice Dixon); Dean Cromer (Yaeger); Mary Adams (Mrs. Ives); Jack Nestle (the counterman); and Charlotte Lawrence (Miss Berdoni).

PRODUCTION CREDITS

DIRECTOR:	EDDIE DAVIS
PRODUCTION CHIEF:	EDDIE DAVIS
FIRST ASSISTANT DIRECTOR:	EDDIE STEIN
SECOND ASSISTANT DIRECTOR:	EDDIE MULL
FIRST CAMERAMAN:	CURT FETTERS
SECOND CAMERAMAN:	ROBERT HOFFMAN
FIRST ASSISTANT CAMERAMAN:	MONK ASKINS
SOUND MIXER:	GARRY HARRIS
RECORDER:	BOB POST
BOOM MAN:	JAY ASHWORTH
FIRST COMPANY GRIP:	CARL MIKSCH
PROPERTY MASTER:	LYLE REIFSNIDER
ASSISTANT PROPERTY MAN:	LLOYD MACLEAN
SET DECORATOR:	LOU HAFLEY
SCRIPT SUPERVISOR:	HELEN MCCAFFREY
GAFFER:	JOE WHARTON
SET LABOR:	PHIL CASAZZA
CONSTRUCTION CHIEF:	ARCHIE HALL

PLOT: A Communist Printing Press is aimed at destroying American liberties. In moving the Party underground, cell restructuring is established for reorganization, and Philbrick is assigned to purchase electric equipment and deliver it to an address where other equipment will eventually find their way to a destination, assembling such a printing press. In the event the big day comes, the Party will need all the printing presses they can handle. F.B.I. wants proof that Comrade Anderson is using a printing press, and making plates for an off-set press. Philbrick creates a set-up by using a client's advertising pamphlets as bait, forcing Comrade Anderson to exploit the off-set press to Herb, revealing how they accomplish their leaflets. Once the existence and location of the underground printing press was known to the F.B.I., its potential power as a line of communication was rendered completely useless.

PRODUCTION NOTES: A 33-passenger bus, a camera truck, a station wagon (for sound), Philbrick's car, Hedler's car, and a panel delivery were needed for the first day of filming. One stand-in and four extras each day were needed for filming. Sets needing to be built were interior press room, back of a fix-it shop & trap door, a club room (with a billiard table), Int. beanery, interior of a real estate office, interior of Ives home, and interior of Berdoni's office.

TOTAL CREW HOURS:	22
MAKE READY AND SHOOTING:	20 HOURS
TRAVEL TIME:	2 HOURS

PRODUCTION TRIVIA: According to correspondence, dated September 24, 1953, from Sanford Carter to Mr. Unger and Mr. Epstein of ZIV Studios, this script required a minor correction before being broadcast. "The only point I have to suggest is correction of an error that appears on page 34 in the narration," he explained. "Reference is made to Supreme Court Justice Brandeis stating that freedom of speech didn't license a man to cry 'fire' in a crowded theatre. This statement was made by Supreme Court Justice Holmes in Schenk v. U.S. 39, Supreme Court 249." The correction was made and the error was avoided before filming.

After filming completed on the second day, September 29, Richard Carlson remained at the ZIV Studio to help record the voice-over narration for numerous first-season episodes such as this one and episode 8.

One of the previous drafts of this episode called for Comrade Alice to say, "Thanks for coming out, Herb." Herbert A. Philbrick corrected the writer of the script, stating, "Nobody ever thanks him for anything in the Communist Party. They might say 'Thanks' in a sarcastic way or cutting manner, but they wouldn't say 'Thanks' under any circumstance. They might say 'Good' but never, 'Thanks.'" One of the previous drafts also stated that the Commies used photo-engraving equipment, and Philbrick corrected them stating that the Party "actually used a Multi- Lithograph Press machine.

This was a complete self-contained printing set-up—could do anything they wanted under one roof—didn't have to send out for any contacts or engravings—could do the entire job in nothing flat. The rotary press turned out 7,000 to 8,000 pieces in very short time."

THE BOOK VS. THE SHOW

This episode was based in part from a section in chapter eleven of the book, which Communist Party literature and propaganda were turned out on a vast network of printing presses—some open and legal, some secret and underground. As the government closed down more and more of the aboveground presses, the Party fell back on its reserve of secret underground printing establishments. Philbrick's connection with Boston printing and publishing trades made him useful to the Party as a member of the six-man education commission. Communist Party sandwiched front-group publication orders into his regular business orders.

Philbrick was ordered to inspect the Party's newest secret plant—an offset printing house. He did an extra-thorough job, obtaining an inventory of equipment and samples of the shop's work for the F.B.I. Following through in his triple function, he sent a business acquaintance to the shop with an order. For the Party, this would be a smoke screen for the shop's real function; for the customer, who couldn't get another printer to take on such a small job, it would be a favor; Philbrick would be accommodating the Party and the customer. Next time he sees the printer he learns that the job was turned down. Why? It was a U.S. Government job. Philbrick has a bad few minutes. Then he learns that the Party made a mistake too. Not caring to risk security investigations, which might be made before the job was assigned, they told the customer that they were not prepared to handle that many plates for a quick delivery.

LOCATION SHOTS:

252 N. HOOVER
2433 1/2TEMPLE
2601 BEVERLY
WESTMORELAND AND BEVERLY BLVD.
3474 WEST 1ST STREET

3145 Wilshire
Behind Bullock's Wilshire
1201 North Western
1203 N. Western
1560 N. Western

Episode #14 "CIVIL DEFENSE"
Production # 1014 / 14B
Step outline, September 2, 1953
Mimeo by Gene Levitt, September 18, 1953
Master mimeo, September 25, 1953
Revised pages (annotated), September 29, 1953
Filmed September 30 and October 1, 1953

Cast: Richard Carlson (Herbert A. Philbrick); Patrick Miller (Comrade Ted); Paul Richards (Comrade Don); Hal Alexander (Comrade Jack); Gayne Whitman (C.D. Man); Don Ross (the radio operator); and John Zaremba (Special Jerry Dressler).

Production Credits

Director:	Les Goodwin
Production Chief:	Leon Benson
First Assistant Director:	Don Verk
Second Assistant Director:	Eddie Mull
First Cameraman:	Curt Fetters
Second Cameraman:	Robert Hoffman
First Assistant Cameraman:	Monk Askins
Sound Mixer:	Garry Harris
Recorder:	Bob Post
Boom Man:	Jay Ashworth
First Company Grip:	Carl Miksch
Second Company Grip:	Tex Jackson
Property Master:	Lyle Reifsnider
Assistant Property Man:	Lloyd MacLean
Set Decorator:	Lou Hafley
Script Supervisor:	Helen McCaffrey

Gaffer:	Joe Wharton
Construction Chief:	Archie Hall
Electrician:	Charles Stockwell
Drivers:	Charles Barr and Art Mynear

Plot: A secret cell meeting is called to order, where Comrade Ted requires Party members to become active members of their local neighborhood Civil Defense Program, and later report on the number of ground patrol available, the location and strength of the U.S. Air Defense, and the position and strength of the aircraft. In the event of an impending attack, the Reds want to know what they could be up against. With a little help from Agent Dressler, Herb joins his local Civil Defense, and gives a report of all the names of known Comrades involved with the operation. After three Comrades are picked up by law enforcement because of this scheme, Comrade Ted suspects foul play and orders Philbrick to take a private drive into the country. There, Comrade Ted forces Philbrick to open every compartment, fold down the seats, and pop the hood and trunk for inspection. Satisfied there are no wire recordings or mobile radio transmitters, he clears Philbrick of any misdoings. Driving back home, Agent Dressler admits that it was a close call, but they did in fact have close tabs on Philbrick. The radio transmitter was hidden in the choke and the wire recorder was installed in the gas tank. Only a true mechanic would have found this.

Production Notes: A station wagon, a school bus, a camera car, and Philbrick's car were needed for the first day of filming. Sets were needed to be built for Commie Headquarters and Kitchen, office in the Armory and the interior of the Armory. One stand-in was needed each day of filming and three extras on the first day and six extras on the second day of filming. No stock shots were required for the film.

Total Crew Hours:	22 hours
Make Ready and Shooting:	19 1/2 hours
Travel Time:	2 1/2 hours

Location Shots:
Hollywood and Western
Griffith Park
Vermont Blvd to 3rd St.
771 N. Vermont
267 S. LaFayette Place

Episode #15 "THE WIFE"
Production # 1015 / 15B
Typescript (annotated) by Donn Mullally, Sept. 29, 1953
Master mimeo, September 30, 1953
Revised pages (annotated), October 1, 1953
Filmed October 2 and 3, 1953.

Cast: Richard Carlson (Herbert A. Philbrick); Virginia Stefan (Eva Philbrick); Ed Hinton (Special Agent Hal Henderson); Chris Alcaide (Norton); Gayne Sullivan (King); and Frank Pulaski (Chandler).

Production Credits

Director:	Eddie Davis
Production Chief:	Eddie Davis
First Assistant Director:	Eddie Stein
Second Assistant Director:	Bobby Ray
First Cameraman:	Curt Fetters
Second Cameraman:	Robert Hoffman
First Assistant Cameraman:	Monk Askins
Sound Mixer:	Garry Harris
Recorder:	Bob Post
Boom Man:	Jay Ashworth
First Company Grip:	Carl Miksch
Second Company Grip:	Mel Bledsoe
Property Master:	Ygnacio Sepulveda
Assistant Property Man:	Lyle Reifsnider
Set Dresser:	Lou Hafley
Script Supervisor:	Larry Lund

Gaffer:	Joe Wharton
Set Labor:	Phil Casazza
Construction Chief:	Archie Hall
Electrician:	Charles Stockwell
Drivers:	Art Mynear and Charles Barr

Plot: The Commies have intentions of getting Philbrick elected as an executive for the Youth Group of America. With his involvement in the community and a plot to rig the ballot counting, Herb is a cinch for the campaign. The Commies later plan to educate the youth with Communist propaganda, with Herb helping from the inside to prevent outside influence from distraction. The plan is a success, but at home, Eva Philbrick has become too suspicious of her husband's actions. The answers he gives her questions are running thin. With the Communist Party asking why Eva isn't a member, and Herb explaining his concern to Special Agent Henderson, the only logical solution is to have Eva become the newest member of the Party. This proves to be no easy task when she returns home one day to find one of Herb's "friends" switching religious books on the bookshelf for propaganda material. She even sneaks into Herb's secret closet when he is away, finds his papers and books, and burns them in the furnace. When Herb confronts his wife, she argues against his beliefs, which she has come to realize wholeheartedly. "You're a Communist. You don't believe in God," Eva cries. Returning from a trip to the mail box, Herb finds Eva talking in the living room with Agent Henderson. After their talk, Eva learns the truth about her husband, and tells Herb how proud she is of his bravery. She will continue to support him. Herb learns the good news through the newspapers that a sponsor for the Y.G.A. suspects Red influence, so the Party is backing down with their plan to have Herb elected.

Production Notes: This was one of the few episodes of the first season that was approved by Philbrick without any suggestive changes. A taxi, Philbrick's car, N.D. car, a small bus, a camera car, and a station wagon (for sound equipment) were needed on the first day of filming. Three extras total and a stand-in each day were needed for filming. Sets needed to be built were a Commie office, Philbrick's living room, children's room, and a music room.

Total Crew Hours:	22 hours
Make Ready and Shooting:	20 hours
Travel Time:	2 hours

Production Trivia: This episode was adapted from chapters two through six, but since the main focus of this episode was Eva's discovery and acceptance of Herb's position in the Party, the main aspects of the drama were adapted from two passages in Philbrick's *I Led Three Lives* book. In chapter five, his wife does some book-burning when she suspects the worst (including destroying evidence that was supposed to go to the Bureau). Due to this family tension, a decision was made by the Bureau to reveal Philbrick's secret to Eva. Eva does the same in this episode, which Philbrick realizes when he returns home to find the house baking like an oven because of the furnace. In chapter six, Eva begins to get upset about her husband's long hours, and the lack of a family life. Agent Healey comes to visit and explains to Eva in full what he is doing. Agent Healey was almost discovered in his house by two of the comrades and Eva's quick thinking got him out of sight just in time. For this episode, Special Agent Hal Henderson subs for the real Agent Healy, and Eva is more proud of her husband than ever.

Location Shots:

7200 Beverly Blvd.
351 S. La Brea or 619 N. La Brea
5711 Wilshire
267 S. Lafayette Street

Episode #16 "COMMUNIST COP"

Production # 1016 / 16B
Typescript (annotated) by Frank Burt, September 29, 1953
Mimeo (annotated), October 13, 1953
Master mimeo (annotated), November 3, 1953

Revised master mimeo, November 4, 1953
Filmed on November 5 and 6, 1953

Cast: Richard Carlson (Herbert A. Philbrick); John Zaremba (Special Jerry Dressler); John Tomecko (Comrade Dixon Liggett); Herb Ellis (Harper); Robert Curtis (Comrade Mike); Jeanette Keller (Phyllis); Bill Catching (Comrade Bud); and Troy Melton (Officer Jeffers).

Production Credits

Director:	Eugene Forde
Production Chief:	Leon Benson
First Assistant Director:	Eddie Stein
Second Assistant Director:	Bobby Ray
First Cameraman:	Curt Fetters
Second Cameraman:	Robert Hoffman
First Assistant Cameraman:	Monk Askins
Sound Mixer:	Garry Harris
Recorder:	Bob Post
Boom Man:	Jay Ashworth
First Company Grip:	Carl Miksch
Second Company Grip:	Mel Bledsoe
Property Master:	Ygnacio Sepulveda
Assistant Property Man:	Victor Petrotta
Set Decorator:	Lou Hafley
Script Supervisor:	Larry Lund
Gaffer:	Joe Wharton
Set Labor:	Phil Casazza
Drivers:	Charles Barr and Art Mynear

Plot: Picking up Red literature at a secret rendezvous in the country, and after discussing Comrade Mike's back aches, Philbrick volunteers to deliver the papers personally for him. At the bookstore where the men were sent to deliver the papers, Philbrick learns from Comrade Dixon Leggett that the Party suspects one of their members of being an informant. Since Herb passed the test (the literature was nothing more than plain newspapers), they have narrowed down the suspects to one remaining Party member, Comrade Rick Harper, of being the counterspy. After clever plans are established to eliminate Rick in the morning with an "auto accident," Philbrick is forced to remain at headquarters to memorize a file that has to be returned in the morning. Instead, Herb spends hours fighting the impulse to phone Agent Dressler and let him know about the impending murder, and finally meets up with him at the drugstore in town. With Dressler's cooperation with the local police, they arrange to have Comrade Mike picked up for "auto theft" before Comrade Rick is murdered. Obviously, when Comrade Mike learns that the Party attempted to have him eliminated, he agrees to tell the F.B.I. everything he knows, giving the Party the assumption that he was a counterspy and throwing off suspicion for Herb.

Production Notes: A white police car, a bus, and a station wagon for film and sound equipment were needed on the first day of filming. Five automobile drivers were needed for the second day of filming. Sets needed to be built were an alley-garage, a bookstore backroom, Rick's house, F.B.I. Radio Room, exterior of a Restaurant, and a green set. One stand-in and four extras were needed on the first day of filming, and one stand-in and one extra were needed the second day of filming.

Total Crew Hours:	22
Make Ready and Shooting:	19 hours
Travel Time:	3 hours

Episode #17 "DEFENSE PLANT SECURITY"

Production # 1017 / 17B
Typescript (annotated) by Frank Burt, October 30, 1953
Mimeo (annotated), October 30, 1953
Master mimeo, November 5, 1953
Filmed November 7 and 8, 1953

Cast: Richard Carlson (Herbert A. Philbrick); Ed Hinton (Special Agent Hal Henderson); Ed Parker (Comrade Clyde); Robert Pike

(Comrade Larry); Ewing Mitchell (Mr. Collins); George Denorman (Charles Tucker); and Pat Gallagher (Miss Bacon).

Production Credits

Director:	Eddie Davis
Production Chief:	Eddie Davis
First Assistant Director:	Don Verk
Second Assistant Director:	Bobby Ray
First Cameraman:	Curt Fetters
Second Cameraman:	Robert Hoffman
First Assistant Cameraman:	Monk Askins
Sound Mixer:	Garry Harris
Recorder:	Bob Post
Boom Man:	Jay Ashworth
First Company Grip:	Carl Miksch
Second Company Grip:	Mel Bledsoe
Property Master:	Ygnacio Sepulveda
Assistant Property Man:	Victor Petrotta
Set Decorator:	Lou Hafley
Script Supervisor:	Larry Lund
Gaffer:	Joe Wharton
Set Labor: P	Phil Casazza
Construction Chief:	Archie Hall
Electrician:	Charles Stockwell

Plot: The Evans Manufacturing Company recently employed a new factory worker named Clyde, who is best described as a ghost—leaving and entering buildings and meetings without being seen—avoiding F.B.I. photographers, and the Bureau desperately wants to know how he sneaks out of the Manufacturing Company unnoticed. Since the city is planning to undergo an air radio test tomorrow, Party members have agreed to use this opportunity to prove that they can gather at one central location in the near future, should an attack occur. Since their success as a whole relies on cooperation, everyone is required to attend—including Comrade Clyde. To make his boss at work pleased, Philbrick manages to create an advertising proposal for the Evans Manufacturing Company. At the plant during the air raid test, Philbrick observes

Clyde using a storm drain to exit the premises. Philbrick races to the cell meeting to observe Clyde's true intentions—uncover holes in security, and report his findings to the Party. Now that his task is completed, he will be transferred to a new plant. After Philbrick makes his report to Agent Henderson, he is shocked to learn that the F.B.I. has no plans to move in on Comrade Clyde. In fact, now that they know his true identity and motives, they plan to use him as a means of uncovering any holes in security as he continues to move from one factory plant to another.

Memorable Quote: Special Agent Tucker: "Sometimes I just don't understand what makes that guy tick. We're F.B.I. agents. This is our job. We get paid for it. His only pay is headaches and grief and a whole lot worse if he isn't careful. Yet it was his idea. He volunteered. Why?"

Agent Henderson: "You were in the Navy in the war, weren't you, Chuck? How did you happen to get in?"

Agent Tucker: "I volunteered."

Comment: This episode also reminds the viewers that no two Party members ever leave a meeting together, so they are never seen associating with each other, other than the privacy of the cell meetings.

Production Notes: A panel truck was needed on both days of filming. Philbrick's car, a panel truck, Henderson's car, a bus, and a camera and sound truck were needed for the second day of filming. Two stand-ins and three extras were needed for the first day of filming, and two stand-ins and seven extras were needed for the second day.

Production Trivia: Herbert A. Philbrick was personally pleased with the script for this episode. As he wrote to the producers, "Secure a copy of Communist Party directives dated October 1, 1950 and July 13, 1950 calling for the emergency mobilizations, which are referred to in this script. Frank Burke has again done a magnificent job in preparing this script. It is technically practically perfect."

Location Shots:
6715 Melrose
1714 N. Ivar
1720 N. Ivar
First and Cedar Burbank
1530 Hillburst
1726 N. Kenmore

Episode #18 "GUN RUNNING"
Production # 1018 / 18B
Typescript (annotated) by Gene Levitt, October 28, 1953
Mimeo (annotated), November 5, 1953
Revised pages (annotated), November 9, 1953
Revised final script, November 9, 1953
Revised pages, November 10, 1953
Revised master mimeo, November 11, 1953
Filmed November 11 and 12, 1953

Cast: Richard Carlson (Herbert A. Philbrick); John Zaremba (Special Agent Jerry Dressler); Vivi Janiss (Comrade Elaine); Ralph Van Nye (Collins); Bill Haade (the bus driver); Irmgard Dawson (the waitress); Charlotte Lawrence (Carol); and Alan Ray (unnamed Comrade).

Production Credits

Director:	Les Goodwin
Production Chief:	Henry S. Kesler
First Assistant Director:	Eddie Stein
Second Assistant Director:	Bobby Ray
First Cameraman:	Curt Fetters
Second Cameraman:	Robert Hoffman
First Assistant Cameraman:	Monk Askins
Sound Mixer:	Garry Harris

Recorder:	Bob Post
Boom Man:	Jay Ashworth
First Company Grip:	Carl Miksch
Second Company Grip:	Mel Bledsoe
Property Master:	Ygnacio Sepulveda
Assistant Property Man:	Victor Petrotta
Set Decorator:	Lou Hafley
Script Supervisor:	Larry Lund
Gaffer:	Joe Wharton
Set Labor:	Phil Casazza
Construction Chief:	Archie Hall
Electrician:	Charles Stockwell

Plot: The secret enemies of a nation have objectives that must be elaborately planned, and secretly carried out. Comrade Elaine rides along with Herb Philbrick as they pick up a small packet containing a coil spring, blue steel, three inches long and wrapped in an oily rag. Philbrick meets up with Special Agent Dressler and tells him what he saw, even handing Dressler a piece of the rag for analysis—which turn out to give them nothing. Later, after having conducted the same routine and pickup again with Comrade Elaine, Philbrick switches the piece of metal, and Dressler and his agents get a better opportunity to solve the mystery before returning the metal without Comrade Elaine noticing anything wrong. The metal was from a factory outside Meddowcrest and when the F.B.I. pieces together all of the parts, they discover that the Communists are smuggling parts of a handgun out of various metal factories, piece by piece. Once put together, the gun is untraceable without any serial numbers and at the rate of one gun a day at five days a week means 250 guns a year. With the knowledge of what the Communists are doing and how they accomplish this task, Agents for the Bureau make an attempt to prevent any future parts from being smuggled out of the metal factories.

Production Notes: A bus and a station wagon were needed for the first day of filming. Philbrick's car was needed for both days of filming. Stock footage was used for this film. Two stand-ins and six extras were needed for the first day of filming, and two stand-ins and four extras were needed for the second day of filming. Sets needed to be built were Elaine's office, the F.B.I. office, F.B.I. corridor, and cleanup.

TOTAL CREW HOURS: 24
MAKE READY AND SHOOTING: 21 HOURS
TRAVEL TIME: 3 HOURS

TRIVIA, ETC. Charlotte Lawrence played the role of Carol, Philbrick's secretary, in this episode. She played the recurring character of Carol in four other episodes throughout the series, but the character of Carol was never featured during any of the third season episodes, only the first two.

Herbert A. Philbrick commented to the producers: "I enjoyed reading the voice over, 'If the Communist Party would only work at overthrowing the United States for one week without Herbert A. Philbrick I might get caught up.' I certainly had *that* thought run through my head more than once!"

The comment Comrade Elaine makes in this episode, about the Communist Party taking over the territory of the world at the steady rate of 1,000 square miles a day, is indeed a fact. In November 1953, the same month this episode was filmed, in New York City, meetings were being sponsored by the Society for American-Soviet Friendship; undoubtedly, meetings are going to be taking place on the West Coast also—and the comrades were indeed bragging to each other that the Communist International had taken over the territory of the world at the steady rate of 1,000 square miles a day. As Philbrick explained in the same letter stated above, "I hope that in screening this, we really pound that fact home. The communist conspirators consider themselves to have been mighty successful during the past 36 years. It is extremely important that the average American citizen realize it. There is only one way that we are going to turn the tide in this cold war against the communist and that is that we must know the facts."

"It might also be well to point out that security regulations already existing in these plants had effectively prevented the smuggling of completely assembled weapons of any kind," Philbrick pointed out to the producers. "Every weapon was accounted for, and every employee is periodically checked upon leaving. This means of extracting the gun by means of one small part at a time, and which could be easily concealed, was a new and most important gimmick. The exposure of this technique enabled the manufacturing plants themselves to institute new and additional security regulations which effectively destroyed the carefully laid plans of the communists."

Location Shots:

Continental Trailway was filmed at Cahuenga & Hollywood Blvd.
The divided highway was really the Hollywood Freeway.
The drugstore was located at Magnolia & Lankershire Weddington & Lankershire
The gun factory was really filmed at Claybourn & Vineland.
The house was located on House Pdlss Ave. near Warner Bros.
The cigar store was located at Melrose and Bronson.
Sandwich shop was located at Vine & Santa Monica.
Filming was also completed on the lot of Troy's Café.

Episode #19 "PASSPORTS"

Production # 1019 / 19B
Typescript (annotated) by Gene Levitt, November 13, 1953
Mimeo (annotated), November 24, 1953
Revised pages (annotated), November 25, 1953
Revised master mimeo, November 25, 1953
Filmed November 30 and December 1, 1953

Cast: Richard Carlson (Herbert A. Philbrick); John Zaramba (Special Agent Jerry Dressler); Jan Arvan (Comrade Neil); Tim Graham (Ross of the F.B.I.); Marc Krah (Harry); Paul Maxey (Comrade George); and Don Brodie (the first forger).

Production Credits

Director:	Herbert L. Strock
Production Chief:	Henry S. Kesler
First Assistant Director:	Don Verk
Second Assistant Director:	Bobby Ray
First Cameraman:	Curt Fetters
Second Cameraman:	Robert Hoffman
First Assistant Cameraman:	Monk Askins
Sound Mixer:	Garry Harris
Recorder:	Bob Post
Boom Man:	Jay Ashworth
First Company Grip:	Carl Miksch
Second Company Grip:	Mel Bledsoe
Property Master:	Ygnacio Sepulveda
Assistant Property Man:	Victor Petrotta
Set Dresser:	Lou Hafley
Script Supervisor:	Larry Lund
Film Editor:	Duncan Mansfield, A.C.E
Gaffer:	Joe Wharton
Set Labor:	Phil Casazza
Construction Chief:	Archie Hall
Electrician:	Charles Stockwell

Plot: A walking file of Communist information—files, codes, charts, plans all memorized—has a problem getting out of the country without a passport, so Comrade Neil and Herb Philbrick have been assigned the job of getting a fake passport from a known underground passport forger. Philbrick makes contact with the shady operator and acquires the passport. To help assist the F.B.I. in identifying the forger (and picking up the forger might lead them to the Commie trying to leave the country), Philbrick bugs his briefcase with a wire recorder. But Comrade George, the new cell leader, is upset because of a new security leak, and no sooner does Philbrick hand over the passport, than he is picked up under escort and interrogated. After routine questioning, Philbrick's suitcase is opened for investigation but thankfully (and surprisingly) no wire recorder is found. Later, Philbrick learns, the Bureau felt this was too risky so they asked Philbrick to identify various voices of known forgers from a short film. Philbrick does identify the forger by the voice and the F.B.I. moves in to make the arrest.

Production Notes: A bus, a station wagon, and a Ford were needed for the first day of filming. Philbrick's car was needed for both days of filming. Two stand-ins were used each day of filming and three extras were used for the first day of filming.

Location Shots:
603 N. Irving
7658 Beverly Blvd.
627 N. June St.
5359 Clinton
Beverly and La Brea
Melrose and June
DeLongpre and Cherokee
Vine and Santa Monica
Selma and Cahuenga

Episode #20 "YOUTH MOVEMENT"
Production # 1020 / 20B
Typescript by Donn Mullally, October 19, 1953
Revised typescript, October 21, 1953
Mimeo (annotated), November 5, 1953
Master mimeo (annotated), November 20, 1953
Revised master mimeo, November 30, 1953
Revised master mimeo, December 2, 1953
Revised pages, December 1 and 2, 1953
Filmed December 2 and 3, 1953

Cast: Richard Carlson (Herbert A. Philbrick); Jack Carol (Comrade William [Bill] Hudson); Don Kennedy (Mays); John Zaremba (Special Agent Jerry Dressler); Ralph Montgomery (Mr. Nichols); and Michael Jeffrey (Mr. Vance).

PRODUCTION CREDITS

DIRECTOR:	LAMBERT HILLYER
PRODUCTION CHIEF:	LEON BENSON
FIRST ASSISTANT DIRECTOR:	EDDIE STEIN
SECOND ASSISTANT DIRECTOR:	BOBBY RAY
FIRST CAMERAMAN:	CURT FETTERS
SECOND CAMERAMAN:	ROBERT HOFFMAN
SOUND MIXER:	GARRY HARRIS
RECORDER:	BOB POST
BOOM MAN:	JAY ASHWORTH
FIRST COMPANY GRIP:	CARL MIKSCH
SECOND COMPANY GRIP:	MEL BLEDSOE (FIRST DAY ONLY)
PROPERTY MASTER:	YGNACIO SEPULVEDA
ASSISTANT PROPERTY MAN:	VICTOR PETROTTA (SECOND DAY ONLY)
SET DECORATOR:	LOU HAFLEY
SCRIPT SUPERVISOR:	LARRY LUND
FILM EDITOR:	DUNCAN MANSFIELD, A.C.E
GAFFER:	LOU CORTESE
SET LABOR:	PHIL CASAZZA (SECOND DAY ONLY)
CONSTRUCTION CHIEF:	ARCHIE HALL
ELECTRICIAN:	CHARLES STOCKWELL
DRIVER:	ART MYNEAR

PLOT: The severity of enemy agents require large sums of money, so a Communist campaign is used to infiltrate the local youth council program and its bank account. Comrade Hudson was voted in as treasurer and Mr. Vance, President of the Council, is unaware of Hudson's true intentions. To make matters worse, someone phoned the police anonymously and reported Philbrick as a Communist, which causes a local detective to begin inquiring on Philbrick's background. Comrade Hudson confesses to Herb that it was he who phoned the police. If someone's background is investigated and cleared of suspicion, it will mean a dead end to any possible future suspicion of Communist infiltration. Philbrick clears his name and weeks later, when Mr. Vance wants to look over the books to verify the council's financial stability, Hudson is put into a bind. It seems he's been using the funds for Communist purposes and needs Philbrick to help mail fund-raising letters to known Comrades in the area. When Herb tips off the police with an anonymous phone call of his own, payback doubles when authorities begin investigating a certain post office box linked with the letters and all of the names attached to the return addresses on the envelopes. Mr. Vance begins restructuring the council while an Anti-Red Squad starts making arrests, and the Party backs away from the Youth Center Fund Program.

PRODUCTION NOTES: A bus, May's car, a station wagon and Philbrick's car were needed for the first day of filming. One stand-in and five extras were needed for the first day, and one stand-in and one extra were needed for the second day of filming.

TOTAL CREW HOURS:	20
MAKE READY AND SHOOTING:	17 HOURS
TRAVEL TIME:	3 HOURS

CAST TRIVIA: Lambert Hillyer was also the director for numerous television episodes produced by ZIV Television Productions, including *Highway Patrol, The Man Called X* and *The Cisco Kid.* The ZIV productions were the last thing he ever directed. Before the television shows, he directed numerous B-westerns, the cliffhanger serial *The Batman* (1943, the first screen version of Batman), and Universal Studios' sequel to the 1931 Lugosi horror classic, *Dracula's Daughter* (1936).

PRODUCTION TRIVIA: Herbert Philbrick made a number of suggestions to an early draft for this episode. Regarding the loyalty oath, he remarked, "I was lucky. I never had to take one. The technique is correct, all right. A communist at that time would sign any loyalty oath quite readily. However, it was never necessary for Philbrick to do so. Have some other comrade take the thing."

For this episode, Philbrick commented in the form of a letter to the producers: "An excellent script, well done. Should make a bang-up good story. Over all, make sure that it is pointed out that this is a very typical communist front technique, used by the Party in hundreds of cases and in hundreds of organizations . . . . (The guide to subversive organizations by the House Un-American Activities Committee is a 156-page book, with six and seven organizations listed on every page. A terrifically big business, much bigger than most people realize.) This should serve as a warning to people *not* to lend their names to any group until they have thoroughly checked. Presented as a typical capsule case of a communist front maneuver, this program can render a tremendous public service."

LOCATION SHOTS:
1518 N. CAHUENGA
1511 N. CAHUENGA
HUDSON & SELMA
TAFT BUILDING
100 S. HUDSON & BEVERLY
ONE SCENE WAS FILMED ON THE EXTERIOR OF THE ZIV STUDIO PARKING LOT.
HAMBURGER HEAVEN

EPISODE #21 "MAP OF THE CITY"
PRODUCTION # 1021 / 21B
TYPESCRIPT BY JACK ROCK, NOVEMBER 24, 1953
FINAL TYPESCRIPT (ANNOTATED), DECEMBER 4, 1953
FILMED DECEMBER 7 AND 8, 1953

CAST: Richard Carlson (Herbert A. Philbrick); Ed Hinton (Special Agent Hal Henderson); Thayer Roberts (Manning); Jim Horan (Mawn); Joanne Jordan (Martha); Jack Lomas (Markam); Leo Curley (Gustave); and John Merrick (the policeman).

PRODUCTION CREDITS

DIRECTOR:	LAMBERT HILLYER
PRODUCTION CHIEF:	HENRY S. KESLER
FIRST ASSISTANT DIRECTOR:	EDDIE STEIN
SECOND ASSISTANT DIRECTOR:	BOBBY RAY

First Cameraman:	Curt Fetters
Second Cameraman:	Robert Hoffman
Sound Mixer:	Garry Harris
Recorder:	Bob Post
Boom Man:	Jay Ashworth
First Company Grip:	Carl Miksch
Property Master:	Ygnacio Sepulveda
Assistant Property Man:	Victor Petrotta
Set Decorator:	Lou Hafley
Script Supervisor:	Larry Lund
Film Editor:	Ace Clark
Construction Chief:	Archie Hall

Plot: At a recent cell meeting, Philbrick witnesses Party members making reports about possible sabotage. Meeting with Special Agent Henderson, Philbrick explains that the Comrades are making four maps of the city; one each for utilities, communications, industrial installations, and military targets, and noting down the details for possible structural collapse and weaknesses for all four of them. After the maps are completed, Philbrick is assigned to make a trip and deliver the maps to a courier. During the trip, Philbrick passes the maps on to Agent Henderson, who plans to photograph the maps in the back of his truck, with the condition that Philbrick needs the maps back in ten minutes because ten miles down the road he is to meet his courier. But after passing the maps to Henderson, Philbrick gets an unscheduled visit from his courier, Comrade Maun, and to make matters worse, the police get involved, suspecting both Philbrick and Maun as bank robbers—but only temporarily. When Philbrick and Maun reach their destination, Philbrick is surprised to find the maps back in the case—secretly replaced by the police at the side of the road. With copies of the maps, the F.B.I. is able to alert the potential weaknesses to the plants and installations, and safeguard measures are established, foiling months of work for the Communists.

Trivia, Etc. This episode features not one, but two times Philbrick is seen typing a report for the F.B.I., even reading a section of one of them out loud—rarely done on the television series.

PRODUCTION NOTES: Stock footage was used in this film. A bus, a car, a camera car, a truck, and Philbrick's car were needed for the first day of filming. Two stand-ins each day were needed and seven extras were needed for the entire filming. Sets needed to be built for an elevator, an F.B.I. office, and a secret room (on Stage 7), and Martha's living room and Martha's dining room (Stage 8).

TOTAL CREW HOURS:	20
MAKE READY AND SHOOTING:	20 HOURS

LOCATION SHOTS:
GRIFFITH PARK AREA

EPISODE #22 "CAVIAR"
PRODUCTION # 1022 / 22B
TYPESCRIPT (ANNOTATED) BY GENE LEVITT, DECEMBER 7, 1953
MASTER MIMEO (ANNOTATED), DECEMBER 15, 1953
REVISED MASTER MIMEO, DECEMBER 15, 1953
FILMED DECEMBER 18 AND 19, 1953

CAST: Richard Carlson (Herbert A. Philbrick); Ed Hinton (Special Hal Henderson); Lucia Barclay (Comrade Ina); George Pembroke (Comrade Rogers); Michael Hale (Petrie); David Eden (the golf pro); and John Breed (the delivery man).

PRODUCTION CREDITS

DIRECTOR:	LAMBERT HILLYER
PRODUCTION CHIEF:	HENRY S. KESLER
FIRST ASSISTANT DIRECTOR:	EDDIE STEIN
SECOND ASSISTANT DIRECTOR:	BOBBY RAY
FIRST CAMERAMAN:	ROBERT HOFFMAN
SECOND CAMERAMAN:	MONROE (MONK) ASKINS
FIRST ASSISTANT CAMERAMAN:	DICK RAWLINGS
SOUND MIXER:	GARRY HARRIS
RECORDER:	BOB POST
BOOM MAN:	JAY ASHWORTH
FIRST COMPANY GRIP:	CARL MIKSCH

Second Company Grip:	Mel Bledsoe (first day only)
Property Master:	Ygnacio Sepulveda
Assistant Property Man:	Victor Petrotta
Set Decorator:	Lou Hafley
Script Supervisor:	Larry Lund
Gaffer:	Joe Wharton
Construction Chief:	Archie Hall
Set Labor:	Phil Casazza (first day only)

Plot: Comrade Rogers explains to Philbrick that his next assignment is to be a "watchdog." After a courier receives his package, Philbrick is to keep an eye on the courier during and after the delivery to ensure that the package is safe and secure. Philbrick suspects Comrade Rogers of being a golfer, judging by a pamphlet on the table in Rogers' living room. But when Rogers voices his disgust of the sport, Philbrick gets puzzled. Agent Henderson suggests the pamphlet might be of importance, so the two men set up a trick to pick up the pamphlet. Only after Philbrick does, and returns to his office, does Comrade Ina show up. Philbrick sneaks the pamphlet out of the office and into Henderson's hands. At a chemist office, it is discovered that the instructional pamphlet is actually a highly technical manual on sabotage. Meanwhile, Philbrick continues his assignment which involves delivering small tins of imported caviar. Back at Henderson's, Philbrick is upset because he delivered the packages but is surprised to learn that the shipments were nothing more than caviar. It seems Henderson traced the ship at the harbor and after confiscating the "instructional pamphlets" inside caviar boxes, he switched the package with real caviar. The method of distributing subversive pamphlets was foiled, and the F.B.I. destroyed another dangerous threat to U.S. security.

Author's Comment: From a male standpoint, I can't help but notice Carlson staring at the woman's breasts continuously while in his office.

Trivia, Etc. Ygnacio Sepulveda and Victor Petrotta were responsible for the props in this episode. Among the props required were a golf manual, caviar tins and maps. Philbrick uses the alias "Arthur Trowbridge" in this episode, an alias he used more than once on the television series.

After reading the rough draft of this script, Herbert A. Philbrick pointed out to the producers that the F.B.I. would not order him to do a job as indicated in an exchange with Dressler. Instead, Philbrick suggested they change it to something like "You're a volunteer, Herb. We can't ask you to do it but I must let you know how important it is for us to get a copy of that map."

PRODUCTION NOTES: A bus, a station wagon, a comrade's car, and Philbrick's car were needed on the first day of filming. Two stand-ins were required each day, three extras on the first day and one on the second day of filming. Sets needed to be built were Philbrick's office, the F.B.I. lab, Rogers' living room, Del. Counter, and the back room in the art shop.

TOTAL CREW HOURS:	20 HOURS
MAKE READY AND SHOOTING:	18 HOURS
TRAVEL TIME:	2 HOURS

LOCATION SHOTS:
11030 WILSHIRE
10846 LINDBROOK

EPISODE #23 "THE KID"
PRODUCTION # 1023 / 23B
OUTLINE BY ARTHUR FITZ-RICHARD, DECEMBER 3, 1953
TYPESCRIPT, DECEMBER 14, 1953
MASTER MIMEO, DECEMBER 19, 1953
REVISED PAGES, DECEMBER 21, 1953
FILMED DECEMBER 22 AND 23, 1953

CAST: Richard Carlson (Herbert A. Philbrick); Pamela Duncan (Wanda); Stafford Repp (Allen); Charles Maxwell (Comrade George); John Zaremba (Special Agent Jerry Dressler); Richard Emory (Blaisdell); and Linda Bennett (Enid).

Production Credits

Director:	Herbert L. Strock
Production Chief:	Leon Benson
First Assistant Director:	Eddie Stein
Second Assistant Director:	Bobby Ray
First Cameraman:	Robert Hoffman
Second Cameraman:	Monroe (Monk) Askins
First Assistant Cameraman:	Dick Rawlings
Sound Mixer:	Garry Harris
Recorder:	Bob Post
Boom Man:	Jay Ashworth
First Company Grip:	Carl Miksch
Second Company Grip:	Mel Bledsoe (first day only)
Property Master:	Ygnacio Sepulveda
Assistant Property Man:	Victor Petrotta
Set Decorator:	Lou Hafley
Script Supervisor:	Larry Lund
Gaffer:	Joe Wharton
Set Labor:	Phil Casazza (first day only)
Construction Chief:	Archie Hall

Plot: Philbrick becomes a participant in a tragic situation when he is ordered by Red spy Allen to be ready for a mission to another city, carrying secret radar designs stolen by Comrade Wanda. Wanda is held in the Party by fear that something will happen to her small daughter Enid, and as a parent himself, Philbrick is much concerned over Enid's future. Obligated to reveal the spy plot to the F.B.I., Philbrick hopes the authorities can help trap her mother—even if it means giving a tip-off to the Comrades that he is an informant. The day after, with his Party mission completed successfully, Philbrick enables the F.B.I. to get a line on the spy ring's communications chain. Philbrick returns to find Wanda in custody and Enid spirited away by Party guardians who are holding her, to ensure Wanda's silence. Though forbidden to interfere, Philbrick can't help going to Enid's rescue when he chances on a lead to her whereabouts. After chancing his reputation and status with the Party, he rescues the child. Wanda gladly confesses—and the F.B.I. sees to it that Enid finds refuge with relatives while Wanda is in trouble. Philbrick, of course, remains the unsung, incognito hero.

PRODUCTION NOTES: A bus, a camera car, Philbrick's car and a Commie's car were needed on the first day of filming. One stand-in and one welfare worker were needed on both days of filming. Two extras were needed on the first day of filming.

TOTAL CREW HOURS:	22 HOURS
MAKE READY AND SHOOTING:	20 HOURS
TRAVEL TIME:	2 HOURS

LOCATION SHOTS:
EXPOSITION AND MENLO STREETS
913 W. 36TH STREET
663 W. 34TH STREET
890 JEFFERSON STREET
717 JEFFERSON STREET
1735 NO. CAHUENGA

EPISODE #24 "INFRA-RED FILM"
ORIGINAL COPYRIGHT FOR PRODUCTION #1024, MARCH 4, 1954.
ORIGINAL REGISTRATION #LP49041
PRODUCTION # 1024 / 24B
TYPESCRIPT (ANNOTATED) BY CURT SIODMAK AND STUART JEROME, DECEMBER 14, 1953
MASTER MIMEO (ANNOTATED), DECEMBER 22, 1953
REVISED MASTER MIMEO, DECEMBER 30, 1953
FILMED JANUARY 4 AND 5, 1954

CAST: Richard Carlson (Herbert A. Philbrick); Ed Hinton (Special Hal Henderson); Jack Reitzen (Comrade Ormand); Lewis Martin (Comrade Lester); Joseph Turkel (Comrade Leo); and Tor Johnson (Comrade Ziroc, the Turkish Bath owner).

Production Credits

Production Chief:	Eddie Davis
Director:	Eddie Davis
First Assistant Director:	Don Verk
Second Assistant Director:	Bobby Ray
First Cameraman:	Robert Hoffman
Second Cameraman:	Monroe (Monk) Askins
First Assistant Cameraman:	Dick Rawlings
Sound Mixer:	Garry Harris
Recorder:	Bob Post
Boom Man:	Jay Ashworth
First Company Grip:	Carl Miksch (first day only)
Second Company Grip:	Mel Bledsoe
Property Master:	Ygnacio Sepulveda
Assistant Property Man:	Victor Petrotta (first day only)
Set Decorator:	Lou Hafley
Script Supervisor:	Larry Lund
Film Editor:	Jack Woelz
Gaffer:	Joe Wharton
Set Labor:	Phil Casazza
Construction Chief:	Archie Hall
Drivers:	Charles Barr, Art Mynear and Ernie Reed

Plot: With the steady leak of information and recent arrests of cell members, Comrade Lester believes Comrade Ormond is the "leak." Ormond has been witnessed exiting the F.B.I. office in town at least a dozen times the past week. But when the cell members confront Ormond at the next cell meeting, he defends himself, claiming he is an N.K.U.D., an Agent for the Soviet Secret Police and he's been spending the past few weeks getting access to a list of all known counterspies in the Bureau. To prove his innocence, he invites Philbrick and Leo to join him as he retrieves negatives which—when developed—will shed light on the real guilty Party. Philbrick, fearing his name is on the list, joins the men but finds himself unable to contact Special Agent Henderson throughout the entire day. During the secret rendezvous, Comrade Ormond gets the film and takes it back to the meeting place to develop the negative. But Ormond is shocked when the film is blank. Comrade Lester, angry at Ormond for wasting their time, contacts Party Headquarters to receive orders on how to liquidate Ormond. Later that evening, Philbrick meets with Agent Henderson, who explains that they were aware of *their* leak, and used a special suitcase filled with radium to wipe the negative clean. They only played the game so they could learn who in the F.B.I. was secretly working for the Reds.

PRODUCTION NOTES: A policeman and a fireman were needed on the first day of filming, as well as a 33-passenger bus, station wagon, and Philbrick's car. Two stand-ins and three extras were needed on the second day of filming. Two stand-ins and two extras were needed for the first day of filming.

TOTAL CREW HOURS: 22
MAKE READY AND SHOOTING: 20 HOURS
TRAVEL TIME: 2 HOURS

TRIVIA, ETC. The character of Comrade Leo was originally called Comrade Gilbert in the rough drafts. The original ending conceived was to have Philbrick acquire blank 35mm film and switch it without the Comrades knowing, but this would obviously lack the suspense the episode gained from the final draft. Curt Siodmak, the author of this script, explained to the producers why this script has tremendous possibilities: "The use of micro film is standard practice in communist espionage circles today, as it has been for some time. Possibly the audience will not understand why 35mm. The idea is of course, that with the development of fine-grained film, pages of copy up to newspaper size can be photographed and reduced down to a 35mm negative size collar and still the film will hold all of the details of every tiny period and comma. The 35mm film is therefore mostly used for the photographing of important and secret government documents, maps, and other confidential material."

LOCATION SHOTS:
THE RAILROAD BRIDGE, 1300 N. BROADWAY
OUTSIDE FEDERAL BUILDING, 312 N. SPRING STREET

City Hall, 200 N. Spring
Real Turkish Bath, located at 903 Wilshire
Drugstore located at 3456 Wilshire
Uptown Theatre located at 1008 S. Western
Philbrick's house, 267 S. Lafette Park Place

Episode #25 "THE EDITOR"
Original copyright for production #1025, March 11, 1954.
Original Registration #LP49042
Production # 1025 / 25B
Mimeo by Stuart Jerome, December 28, 1953
Typescript (annotated), January 8, 1954
Master mimeo, January 8, 1954
Revised pages (annotated), January 11 and 13, 1954
Filmed January 15 and 16, 1954

Cast: Richard Carlson (Herbert A. Philbrick); Randolph Rees (Comrade Bryant); John Zaremba (Special Agent Jerry Dressler); Paul Bryar (Comrade Willis); Rose Plumer (Comrade Sarah); Carleton Young (Larry Edwards); Jeanne Woods (Mrs. Cooper); and Jack Henderson (the guard).

Production Credits

Director:	Lewis Allen
Production Chief:	Lewis Allen
First Assistant Director:	Eddie Stein
Second Assistant Director:	Joseph Wonder
First Cameraman:	Curt Fetters
Second Cameraman:	Monk Askins
First Assistant Cameraman:	Dick Rawlings
Sound Mixer:	Garry Harris
Recorder:	Bob Post
Boom Man:	Jay Ashworth
First Company Grip:	Carl Miksch
Second Company Grip:	Mel Bledsoe
Property Master:	Ygnacio Sepulveda

Assistant Property Man:	Victor Petrotta
Set Decorator:	Lou Hafley
Script Supervisor:	Helen McCaffrey
Gaffer:	Joe Wharton
Set Labor:	Phil Casazza
Construction Chief:	Archie Hall

Plot: Editor Larry Edwards prints proof in the local newspaper that the key foreman in the new Rock Falls Hydro-Electric Plant, George Cooper, is the leader of a local Communist cell. The report is true, Comrade Willis explains to Philbrick, and Cooper *was* assigned to find the best and simplified method of cutting off power to the plant in a single notice. Cooper vanished since the newspaper feature, and since Philbrick has gone north to Rock Falls to open advertising accounts in the past, it seems an appropriate cover for Philbrick and Comrade Bryant to visit the northern city in search of Cooper. There, Philbrick and Bryant meet Larry Edwards personally, who arranges for them a tour through the new plant. This proves valuable since Philbrick and Bryant learn from Cooper's wife that the plans were hidden in an envelope in a grate inside the building. During the tour, Philbrick fakes illness and sneaks off to finds the envelope—but is caught red-handed by a suspicious Edwards. The editor reveals that he works for the F.B.I. and together the men photograph the plans and return them to the envelope in time to be escorted out by the guard. While Philbrick is taken in high-esteem for his duty to the Party for recovering the plans, the F.B.I. uncovers the sabotage plan and makes the necessary precautions to prevent sabotage if and when it is attempted.

Production Notes: This was one of Philbrick's favorite episodes of the series. From the moment he read the rough draft, he was in favor of every little action and dialogue in the script. One electrician, three drivers, one stand-in, four extras, one policeman, and one fireman were needed for the first day of filming. Three electricians, one stand-in, and three extras were needed for the second day of filming. Philbrick's car, a bus, and a camera car were needed for the first day of filming.

Location Shots:

The scenes that take place in the antique shop were filmed on location at a real antique shop located at 5451 Santa Monica in Los Angeles. The scenes that take place at the power plant were filmed on location both outside and inside of a real electric hydro power plant located at Cahuenga & Whitnall (and Cahuenga & Camarillo) in North Hollywood, California. Opening scene for this episode was filmed on location at the California State Bank located on Santa Monica & Highland. The hotel was located at 1963 N. Cahuenga.

A parking lot at Western and Hollywood

Larchmont, between Beverly and 1st

Episode #26 "CONFUSED COMRADES"

Original copyright for production #1026, March 18, 1954.
Original Registration #LP49040
Production # 1026 / 26B
Typescript (annotated) by Jack Rock, December 22, 1953
Mimeo (annotated), January 5, 1954
Revised pages (annotated), January 15, 1954
Revised master mimeo, January 15, 1954
Filmed January 18 and 19, 1954

Cast: Richard Carlson (Herbert A. Philbrick); Ed Hinton (Special Agent Hal Henderson); Tom McKee (Comrade Brisson Laylock); John Frank (Comrade Lothar); and Jane Hampton (Comrade Mary).

Production Credits

Director:	Leigh Jason
Production Chief:	Henry S. Kesler
First Assistant Director:	Eddie Stein
Second Assistant Director:	Joseph Wonder
First Cameraman:	Robert Hoffman
Second Cameraman:	Monroe (Monk) Askins
First Assistant Cameraman:	Dick Rawlings

SOUND MIXER:	GARRY HARRIS
RECORDER:	BOB POST
BOOM MAN:	JAY ASHWORTH
FIRST COMPANY GRIP:	CARL MIKSCH
SECOND COMPANY GRIP:	MEL BLEDSOE
PROPERTY MASTER:	YGNACIO SEPULVEDA
ASSISTANT PROPERTY MAN:	VICTOR PETROTTA
SET DECORATOR:	LOU HAFLEY
SCRIPT SUPERVISOR:	LARRY LUND
GAFFER:	JOE WHARTON
SET LABOR:	PHIL CASAZZA
CONSTRUCTION CHIEF:	ARCHIE HALL

PLOT: In the Communist Party changes in policy often occurs so suddenly and completely that they sometimes leave the comrades themselves in semi-confusion. One such result is when Comrade Brisson Laylock, the new Red boss, gives the cell members orders for a new Party policy of tactical violence. As a testing ground for this program, Brisson explains that people are to assume acts of violence, vandalism, riots, broken windows, and so on to instill fear in the American people—thus establishing confusion, discontent, fear and unrest among the community. Laylock insists the new policy is a bad idea—the papers will eat it up and only drive the Party further underground. But the plan goes ahead without fail. A sudden wave of unexplained violence of bombs and broken windows has become inspiration for the Comrades. Philbrick leaks the information to Special Agent Henderson, who uses his men to apprehend and arrest some of the Comrades in the act of vandalism. No sooner does Comrade Laylock suspect a "leak," then Comrade Luther arrives at the meeting explaining that the Party studied the newspaper accounts and arrests and sees no benefit to the Party. The new policy as of now is to get to the American hearts. Comrade Laylock is pushed down in position for his failure to accept the new policy, and Philbrick, who stood up for his opinions in the first place, is asked to reprint his initial pamphlet of Communist infiltration through the heart, not the mind.

MEMORABLE QUOTE: When Philbrick protests the new Party policy at the cell meeting, Comrade Brisson Laylock uses Philbrick as an excuse to set an example to the rest of the cell members. "Comrade Herb. Your trouble is in clinging to this ridiculous thing you call 'individual thinking.' Now this can only lead to confusion. Because there are so many individuals who think so many different things. That's why there should be no reluctance in carrying out Party orders." Apparently, Laylock's comments boosted the morale of the cell members because after the members leave one-by-one, Comrade Brisson Laylock is beaten by a couple cell members. The beating was meant for Philbrick to learn a lesson about going against the Party rule.

PRODUCTION NOTES: One special effects artist and one police officer were needed for the first day of filming. One station wagon, a bus, and a Commie car were also needed for the first day of filming. Two stand-ins and nine extras were needed for the first day, and one stand-in and three extras were needed for the second day of filming.

TOTAL CREW HOURS:	20
MAKE READY AND SHOOTING:	19 HOURS
TRAVEL TIME:	1 HOUR

TRIVIA, ETC. Curt Fetters was supposed to be the first cameraman but Robert Hoffman took his place.

LOCATION SHOTS:
HOLLYWOOD PLAZA HOTEL
CAHUENGA AND HOLLYWOOD BLVD.
MRS. RING'S SHOP LOCATED AT MELROSE AND IRVING
IRVING AND VAN NESS
ONE SCENE WAS FILMED ON THE STUDIO LOT, ELECTRIC DEPARTMENT

EPISODE #27 "COMMUNICATIONS"
ORIGINAL COPYRIGHT FOR PRODUCTION #1027, MARCH 25, 1954.
ORIGINAL REGISTRATION #LP49039
PRODUCTION #1027 / 27B

Story Outline by Maurice Stoller.
Typescript (annotated) by Maurice Stoller, Jan. 8, 1954
Master mimeo (annotated), January 18, 1954
Revised master mimeo, January 19, 1954
Revised pages (annotated), January 21, 1954
Filmed January 25 and 26, 1954

Cast: Richard Carlson (Herbert A. Philbrick); Michael Fox (Comrade John); Howard Price (Comrade Pete); Michael Kowal (Comrade X); Pat Coleman (Comrade Al); Laura Mason (Comrade Jane); and John Zaremba (Special Agent Jerry Dressler).

Production Credits

Director:	Herbert L. Strock
Production Chief:	Herbert L. Strock
First Assistant Director:	Bobby Ray
Second Assistant Director:	George Loper
First Cameraman:	Robert Hoffman
Second Cameraman:	Monroe (Monk) Askins
First Assistant Cameraman:	Dick Rawlings
Sound Mixer:	Garry Harris
Recorder:	Bob Post
Boom Man:	Jay Ashworth
Film Coordinator:	John Tait
First Company Grip:	Mel Bledsoe
Second Company Grip:	Clarence Boyd
Property Master:	Ygnacio Sepulveda
Assistant Property Man:	J. Benton Sr.
Set Decorator:	Lou Hafley
Script Supervisor:	Helen McCaffrey
Film Editor:	Duncan Mansfield, A.C.E
Gaffer:	Lou Cortese
Construction Chief:	Archie Hall

Plot: The Communist Party wants to conduct research to smoothly paralyze the country's communications, should and when the country comes under attack. Helping deliver the layouts of all the radio stations in the area is one task. With Comrade Pete, Philbrick takes photographs both inside and outside of a local radio station, making notes about how much current is needed to run the offices, the equipment used in each office, and how much rope would be needed to scale the fences. All of this is done with ease since there is little or no security about. When the F.B.I. takes in one of the cell members for questioning, Plan B is put into effect—the destruction of the communication towers. Philbrick hands Special Agent Dressler an envelope containing copies of all the photographs taken, and details about the destruction of the towers. At the next cell meeting, Philbrick objects to Comrade Pete's idea of destroying the communications tower, stipulating they would be better guarded than the stations themselves, especially since the F.B.I. took one of their comrades in for questioning. To prove his point, Philbrick and Comrade John take a trip to a nearby tower and find that the tower is indeed safeguarded, thus spoiling any chance of destroying communications.

Production Notes: This was one of the few episodes to feature stock footage. The first day of filming required a lot of production, compared to the second day. A bus, a camera car, and three picture trucks were needed for the first day of filming, all rented or borrowed for the production. Five drivers, one policeman, three electricians, four extras, and one stand-in were also needed for the first day of filming. For the second day, all that were needed was one stand-in and two extras.

Total Crew Hours:	20
Make Ready and Shooting:	18 hours
Travel Time:	2 hours

Production Trivia: The initial draft of this episode was criticized by Herbert A. Philbrick himself, who, on January 11, 1954, suggested in writing a few changes to add realism to the story. He suggested that the script should be a "little more direct in explaining why the sabotage of radio and television communications was of such great importance to the Party." He wasn't happy that the script did not indicate as to how the transmitter was to be sabotaged, and felt that the script would be more interesting "if there were more specific details of the sabotage method."

Herbert A. Philbrick suggested solutions for this problem, recommending that they describe how "the fuse must be [blank] inches long, time to allow five minutes for escape and one pound charges of dynamite should be placed at four vital points." He even suggested making Comrade Pete "a demolition expert trained in the Spanish Civil War." The producers, however, had past experiences with the censorship department of NBC regarding showing in their scripts just how such things as bombs and explosive devices were rigged. Serious discussion and thought went into deciding whether the changes would be made or not, and after considerable thought, the decision to reveal details was disregarded for the sake of censorship.

LOCATION SHOTS:
533 7TH STREET
7TH & FLOWER
423 S. MAIN
338 WERDIN PL.
ONE SCENE WAS FILMED AT THE HOLLYWOOD POST OFFICE.
5939 SUNSET
VENICE NEAR LA BREA

EPISODE #28 "PHANTOM LABOR LEADER"
ORIGINAL COPYRIGHT FOR PRODUCTION #1028, APRIL 1, 1954.
ORIGINAL REGISTRATION #LP49038
PRODUCTION # 1028 / 28B
STORY BREAKDOWN BY ROBERT YALE LIBOTT.
TYPESCRIPT BY ROBERT YALE LIBOTT, SEPTEMBER 11, 1953
MIMEO (ANNOTATED), SEPTEMBER 17, 1953
REVISED MASTER MIMEO, JANUARY 20, 1954
REVISED PAGES (ANNOTATED), JANUARY 21, 1954
FILMED JANUARY 27 AND 28, 1954

CAST: Richard Carlson (Herbert A. Philbrick); Merritt Stone (Comrade Mitch); Mel Roberts (Roy Burns); Evelynne Eaton (Comrade Eve Baker); Dennis Moore (John Benton); and Ed

Hinton (Special Agent Hal Henderson).

Production Credits

Director:	Henry S. Kesler
Production Chief:	Henry S. Kesler
First Assistant Director:	Eddie Stein
Second Assistant Director:	Joseph Wonder
First Cameraman:	Curt Fetters
Second Cameraman:	Monroe (Monk) Askins
First Assistant Cameraman:	Dick Rawlings
Sound Mixer:	Garry Harris
Recorder:	Bob Post
Boom Man:	Jay Ashworth
Film Editor:	John B. Woelz
Sound Supervisor:	Herbert Norsch
Film Coordinator:	Donald Tait
Script Supervisor:	Larry Lund
First Company Grip:	Carl Miksch
Second Company Grip:	Mel Bledsoe
Property Master:	Lyle Reifsnider
Set Decorator:	Lou Hafley
Script Supervisor:	Larry Lund
Gaffer:	Joe Wharton (second day only)
Set Labor:	Phil Casazza (second day only)

Plot: The Communist Party has a new plan up their sleeve—the formation of a local union designed to sign up possible candidates and Party members. Before they can do this, however, they must first arouse trouble at various offices and plants, with the suggestions that current unions do not represent their clients to the fullest. Philbrick recognizes a well-organized, subversive organization when he sees it. Since the F.B.I. has no jurisdiction when it comes to labor disputes, Herb is on his own. While helping the Party create slogans and pamphlets designed to infiltrate the American worker with such notions of sweat shop conditions, the need for bigger pension plans and so on, Philbrick discovers that their plan is succeeding. Over a thousand new members sign up within the past week and if statistics are correct, Union 3133 only needs a few more days of recruits to apply for the formal permits making the Union official. With the help of the F.B.I. a Communist is picked up for questioning, and with evidence suggesting that Communist propaganda has invaded the so-called Union 3133—the Commies will have to find another way to gain recruits.

PRODUCTION NOTES: One policeman, one electrician, two stand-ins and five extras were needed for the first day of filming. Three electricians, two stand-ins, and five extras were needed for the second day of filming. A bus, a station wagon, a convertible, a panel truck, a police car, and a car were needed for the first day of filming.

TOTAL CREW HOURS:	20
MAKE READY AND SHOOTING:	18 HOURS
TRAVEL TIME:	2 HOURS

PRODUCTION TRIVIA: The subject matter for this episode was considered a little taboo. According to internal letters from production files, on September 16, 1953, Robert W. Friedheim wrote to Maurice Unger regarding this episode. "Dear Babe: Just for the record, in the event there should be any question on the subject matter of this script at any time, and in order to substantiate that this is only a very small segment of the complete picture of labor violence, Philbrick suggested we could strengthen our position by supplying a copy of substantial testimony before Government Investigating Committees on labor violence, with a letter along the lines of the following: 'ZIV regrets that it did not have time, in the half-hour period available for this film, to present all of the violent and vicious methods of the Communist conspiracy. We did the best we could with the time available, but in this Government report you will find still more factual material. We are glad to have stimulated your interest in this subject through our public service program, and we hope you will continue etc. etc. . . .' This is only an idea, Babe, in the event it should become important to us to support our position with Government record documentation at any time. Regards, Robert W. Friedheim."

Location Shots:
Exterior of an Appliance Store, Robinson's of Beverly Hills
Exterior and Interior of Kerr's, 9584 Wilshire
Loring and Wyton Drive, Westwood

Episode #29 "PROGRESSIVE"

Original copyright for production #1029, April 8, 1954.
Original Registration # LP49037
Production # 1029 / 29B
Typescript (annotated) by Gene Levitt, January 26, 1954
Final revised master script, January 26, 1954
Revised script, January 28, 1954
Final revised master script, January 28, 1954
Filmed February 1 and 2, 1954

Cast: Richard Carlson (Herbert A. Philbrick); Archie Twitchell (Ed Hughes); Clayton Post (Comrade Steve); Jo Gilbert (Comrade Eileen); Pat O'Hara (Comrade Gerald); Ed Hinton (Special Agent Hal Henderson); Bob Bruce (Comrade Walter); and Charles Postal (Comrade Fred).

Production Credits

Director:	Leigh Jason
Production Chief:	Leigh Jason
First Assistant Director:	Eddie Stein
Second Assistant Director:	Joseph Wonder
First Cameraman:	Robert Hoffman
Second Cameraman:	Lou Kunkle
First Assistant Cameraman:	Bud August
Sound Mixer:	Dean Thomas
Recorder:	John Bury
Boom Man:	Lyle Figlander
First Company Grip:	Mel Bledsoe
Property Master:	Lyle Reifsnider
Set Decorator:	Lou Hafley

SCRIPT SUPERVISOR: LARRY LUND
FILM EDITOR: DUNCAN MANSFIELD, A.C.E
GAFFER: LOU CORTESE
CONSTRUCTION CHIEF: ARCHIE HALL

PLOT: The Commies will go to any extreme to destroy an anti-Communist force. A new Citizen's Committee has been established by wealthy men with a conscience for anti-graft, anti-evil and especially anti-Communism. The local cell wants to put an end to this by infiltrating the committee with members of the Communist Party. Later, the Party will make an attempt to expose the committee as a dishonest organization created for the purpose of defrauding the public of funds, and defrauding the public's support for such committees. When Herb learns that the head of this committee is his next door neighbor, he hesitates—until Special Agent Hal Henderson convinces Herb to go through with it. If he doesn't, someone else will. Herb is voted in as Vice Chairman. The fall guy is Ed Hughes, who will be exposed as an embezzler once a rigged deposit is made into his bank account. An ink stain on the check, however, foils the Party's plan, and exposes the Commies for what they are, making their plan of integration collapse.

PRODUCTION NOTES: One electrician, two policemen, three drivers, one stand-in, and five extras were needed for the first day of filming. Three electricians, one stand-in, and eight extras were needed for the second day of filming. A bus, a camera car and Philbrick's car were needed only for the first day of filming.
TOTAL CREW HOURS: 22
MAKE READY AND SHOOTING: 19 1/2 HOURS
TRAVEL TIME: 2 1/2 HOURS

LOCATION SHOTS:
PIER AT SANTA MONICA
1301 OCEAN AVE
11TH & WILSHIRE BLVD.
PARK-DELONGPRE & MCCADDEN

Episode #30 "THE OLD MAN"
Original copyright for production #1030, April 15, 1954.
Original Registration #LP49036
Production # 1030 / 30B
Plot outline by Arthur Fitz-Richard, December 30, 1953
Typescript January 18, 1954
Mimeo (annotated), January 28, 1954
Revised master mimeo, February 1, 1954
Revised pages (annotated), February 1, 1954
Filmed February 3 and 4, 1954

Cast: Richard Carlson (Herbert A. Philbrick); Richard Collier (Comrade Kupke); John Zaremba (Special Agent Jerry Dressler); Lorraine Miller (Sarah Holman); Marshall Bradford (Frederick Holman); Larry Gelbman (Comrade Chuck); and Michael Harris (Carter).

Production Credits

Director:	Herbert L. Strock
Production Chief:	Herbert L. Strock
First Assistant Director:	Don Verk
Second Assistant Director:	Eddie Mull
First Cameraman:	Robert Hoffman
Second Cameraman:	Monroe (Monk) Askins
First Assistant Cameraman:	Dick Rawlings
Sound Mixer:	Garry Harris
Recorder:	Bob Post
Boom Man:	Jay Ashworth
First Company Grip:	Carl Miksch
Second Company Grip:	Mel Bledsoe (first day only)
Property Master:	Ygnacio Sepulveda
Assistant Property Man:	Victor Petrotta (first day only)
Set Decorator:	Lou Hafley
Script Supervisor:	Larry Lund
Film Editor:	Joe Ziegler

Gaffer:	Joe Wharton
Set Labor:	Phil Casazza (first day only)
Construction Chief:	Archie Hall

Plot: Fred Holman is responsible for a number of fund-raising fronts for the Party, but his daughter Sarah is worried. Although he is considered a financial wizard for the Party, his schemes and knowledge are regarded as extremely valuable. Her father was served a subpoena to testify and she fears he's a deviationist, but he retains his financial knowledge from his daughter "for her protection." When the Communists have Sarah report her father dead by arranging for her to identify a body, and then have it cremated, the papers report of his death (a heart attack), and she denies any knowledge of a subpoena. The F.B.I. isn't fooled by a fake funeral, but with the heat off Holman's back, it's a race to find him before the Commies do. A few days later, Philbrick witnesses Fred Holman leaving an office in a hurry—with papers that can incriminate names of Party members and the projects they are associated with. Sarah, having to choose between the safety of her father and the interests of the Party, chooses the former. When Philbrick and Sarah learn the whereabouts of Holman, the Party sends officials to tidy the mess but the goons are surprised when they arrive to find the F.B.I. waiting for them. A wire tap on Holman's home ensured his safety and his testimony in court naming names.

Production Notes: One electrician, one stand-in, and two extras were needed for the first day of filming. Three electricians and one stand-in were needed for the second day of filming. Sets were needed to be built for Holman's office, Kupke's office, Holman's den, a phone booth, an F.B.I. office, Holman's hotel hall and a newsstand. A bus, a camera car, Philbrick's car, Dressler's car, Sarah's car were needed for the first day of filming.

Total Crew Hours:	20
Make Ready and Shooting:	18 hours
Travel Time:	2 hours

Trivia, Etc. There was a demand for actor Larry Gelbman, who played the role of Comrade Chuck in this episode, to play the role of Germans in many television episodes. On *McHale's Navy*, he played the role of a German sub commander in the episode "McHale and his Schweinhunds." For *Combat!*, he played the role of a German sergeant, soldier, and sentry in four episodes: "Finest Hour," "Cry in the Ruins," "The Leader" and "The Flying Machine."

Location Shots:
Equitable Building, 6253 Hollywood Blvd.
Hollywood Roosevelt Hotel, 7000 Hwd. Blvd.
Vicinity of the Outpost, Franklin to La Prisa
Santa Monica and El Centro

Episode #31 "BIRTHDAY"
Original copyright for production #1031, April 22, 1954.
Original Registration #LP49104
Production # 1031 / 31B
Step outline ("The Anniversary"), by Jack Rock.
Typescript by Jack Rock, January 21, 1954
Mimeo (annotated), February 2, 1954
Revised master mimeo (annotated), February 4, 1954
Revised pages (annotated), February 4, 1954
Filmed February 5 and 6, 1954

Cast: Richard Carlson (Herbert A. Philbrick); Ed Hinton (Special Agent Hal Henderson); Virginia Stefan (Eva Philbrick); Norman Rainey (Dad); Pat Morrow (Constance Philbrick); Sandy Descher (Sandra); Charlotte Lawrence (Carol); Ralph Gamble (Comrade George); Richard Deems (Comrade Valentine); and Don Brodie (The Mouth).

Production Credits

Director:	Tim Whelan
Production Chief:	Henry S. Kesler
First Assistant Director:	Eddie Stein
Second Assistant Director:	Joseph Wonder

First Cameraman:	Robert Hoffman
Second Cameraman:	Monroe (Monk) Askins
First Assistant Cameraman:	Dick Rawlings
Sound Mixer:	Garry Harris
Recorder:	Bob Post
Boom Man:	Jay Ashworth
First Company Grip:	Carl Miksch
Second Company Grip:	Mel Bledsoe
Property Master:	Ygnacio Sepulveda
Assistant Property Man:	Victor Petrotta
Set Decorator:	Lou Hafley
Script Supervisor:	Larry Lund
Film Editor:	Jack Woelz
Gaffer:	Joe Wharton
Set Labor:	Phil Casazza (1 day only)
Construction Chief:	Archie Hall

Plot: The Philbrick family prepares a surprise birthday Party for Herb. When his secretary Carol informs him that he won "Employee of the Year" and an advertising trade journal banquet is planned for him the same evening, Philbrick is forced to choose which of the two events to attend. While the Party keeps him busy with an assignment as a telephone contact for an important big brass meeting that will take part most of the evening, Herb is put into a position where he cannot phone home. With a scheduled rendezvous in a nearby hotel, Special Agent Henderson is close by waiting for Herb, and a Red watchdog in the hotel lobby. Once a break opens, Herb takes a walk upstairs and alerts Henderson with the news of the secret meeting. Comrade Emerick snoops around and catches the boys talking. Agent Henderson plays the part of a potential advertising client and with the excuse accepted, Philbrick is asked to report to the cell leader to close his mission for the night. Back at the Philbrick residence, the children are sent to bed, upset because their father hasn't shown as he promised. Eva makes excuses with Herb's father. When Herb does return home, Eva breaks down and cries, confessing she was worried for him, but Herb reassures her that his family comes first, and their safety and well-being.

Production Notes: One electrician, one policeman and two stand-ins were needed for the first day of filming. Three electricians, two stand-ins, and two extras were needed for the second day of filming. Electrical Equipment rented was a Western Dolly. Sets needed to be built were a hotel, upper hall of the hotel, interior and exterior of Philbrick's office, Dad's house, Commie Headquarters, and various phone booths.

Total Crew Hours: 20
Make Ready and Shooting: 18 hours
Travel Time: 2 hours

Location Shots:

The interior scenes that take place in a hotel were filmed on location in the Hollywood Roosevelt Hotel, located at: 7000 Hollywood Blvd.
Ralph's Market, Sunset near Gardner
267 South LaFayette

Episode #32 "CELL LEADER"

Original copyright for production #1032, May 1, 1954.
Original Registration # LP49105
Production # 1032 / 32 B
Typescript by Stuart Jerome, January 29, 1954
Mimeo (annotated), February 10, 1954
Revised pages (annotated), February 11, 1954
Revised master mimeo, February 11, 1954
Filmed February 12 and 13, 1954

Cast: Richard Carlson (Herbert A. Philbrick); Grace Lenard (Comrade Baker); John Zaremba (Special Agent Jerry Dressler); Les Spears (Comrade Tyson); Jerry Hausner (Comrade Boyle); John McKee (the fire inspector); and Andy Andrews (F.B.I. Agent disguised as a fire inspector).

Production Credits

Director: Herbert L. Strock

Production Chief:	Herbert L. Strock
First Assistant Director:	Don Verk
Second Assistant Director:	Joseph Wonder
First Cameraman:	Curt Fetters
Second Cameraman:	Monroe (Monk) Askins
First Assistant Cameraman:	Dick Rawlings
Sound Mixer:	Garry Harris
Recorder:	Bob Post
Boom Man:	Jay Ashworth
First Company Grip:	Carl Miksch
Second Company Grip:	Cecil Haverty (second day only)
Property Master:	Ygnacio Sepulveda
Assistant Property Man:	Victor Petrotta
Set Decorator:	Lou Hafley
Script Supervisor:	Pearl Leiter
Film editor:	Duncan Mansfield, A.C.E
Gaffer:	Joe Wharton
Set Labor:	Phil Casazza
Construction Chief:	Archie Hall

Plot: A new cell leader is introduced, replacing the old one, and Philbrick is shocked when he is given an assignment of importance, involving $10,000 cash. Since his job as an advertising man will come in handy with the latest Red project, the Party gives him responsibility over the funds, and assigns Comrade Boyle and Comrade Tyson to keep an eye on Philbrick. After careful planning, Philbrick manages to get the money to the F.B.I. for investigation, before returning the bills so Philbrick can complete his mission. Thanks to Philbrick's co-operation, the F.B.I. begins their investigation, including arranging for a routine inspection from a fire inspector in order to shut down the latest Red tactic.

Production Notes: One electrician, one policeman, one fireman, one stand-in and one extra, and four drivers were needed for the first day of filming. Three electricians, one stand-in, and three extras were needed for the second day of filming. A bus, a camera car, Philbrick's car, and Dressler's car were needed for the first day of filming.

TOTAL CREW HOURS: 22
MAKE READY AND SHOOTING: 21 HOURS
TRAVEL TIME: 1 HOUR

PRODUCTION TRIVIA: This episode was originally intended to be episode 34 in the production schedule. Philbrick himself found several weaknesses in the script and made numerous suggestions for improvement. "In any operation such as this," he suggested, "the Comrades would be sure *not* to have any existing legal evidence. The information, therefore, would not be delivered by a special delivery letter, but by a Party courier to contact Philbrick on his way into the office, or else to come directly into the advertising office itself under the guise of some other matter of business."

Another suggestion Philbrick made was to keep his self from using the home telephone. "Philbrick would never use the home telephone. He would pay a visit to the corner cigar store, the one which is open until very late at night. As usual, this business of maintaining a pipe was always very handy: especially since it was necessary quite often to buy a new supply of tobacco. Of course, there were times when I had many more cans of tobacco hanging around than I could possibly use."

LOCATION SHOTS:
617 N. LA BREA
601 N. LA BREA
5769 WILSHIRE BLVD.
642 N. PLYMOUTH

EPISODE #33 "DRY RUN"
ORIGINAL COPYRIGHT FOR PRODUCTION #1033, MAY 8, 1954.
ORIGINAL REGISTRATION # LP49106
PRODUCTION # 1033 / 33B
MIMEO BY ARTHUR ORLOFF, FEBRUARY 1, 1954
TYPESCRIPT (ANNOTATED), FEBRUARY 10, 1954

Master mimeo (annotated), February 15, 1954
Revised master mimeo, February 15, 1954
Filmed February 17 and 18, 1954

Cast: Richard Carlson (Herbert A. Philbrick); Harlan Warde (Comrade Dave); John Zaremba (Special Agent Jerry Dressler); Virginia Stephan (Eva Philbrick); John Hedloe (Comrade Elroy); George Dunn (the police officer); and Jack Roberts (the bike shop man).

Production Credits

Director:	Henry S. Kesler
Production Chief:	Henry S. Kesler
First Assistant Director:	Don Verk
Second Assistant Director:	Eddie Mull
First Cameraman:	Robert Hoffman
Second Cameraman:	Monroe (Monk) Askins
First Assistant Cameraman:	Dick Rawlings
Sound Mixer:	Garry Harris
Recorder:	Bob Post
Boom Man:	Jay Ashworth
First Company Grip:	Carl Miksch (second day only)
Second Company Grip:	Mel Bledsoe
Property Master:	Lyle Reifsnider
Assistant Property Man:	J. Robert Benton, Sr.
Set Decorator:	Lou Hafley
Script Supervisor:	Larry Lund
Gaffer:	Joe Wharton
Set Labor:	Phil Casazza
Construction Chief:	Archie Hall
Electrician:	Charles Stockwell

Plot: Comrade Dave is suspicious of Herb Philbrick, and informs Comrade Elroy of his intentions of putting a lie detector on their suspect to gauge his faithfulness to the Party. In the meantime, Philbrick is handed an envelope and asked to deliver it to a Comrade at a bicycle shop. Later, when Philbrick was asked to accompany

Comrade Dave in a mission of valuable importance—to deliver tear bombs to a rendezvous—a stoke of fate hit the men when Comrade Dave's car stalls. When Philbrick searches for the tools, he discovers that there are no tear bombs in the car. Suspecting this was a dry run, and that Comrade Dave had tried to trap him, Philbrick toys with Dave, eliminating any suspicion or the use of a lie detector.

Trivia, Etc. When Philbrick is being tailed, he uses the water fountain as a way of sending a signal to Agent Dressler not to make contact.

Production Notes: One electrician, one policeman, five drivers and two stand-ins were needed for the first day of filming. Three electricians and two stand-ins were needed for the second day of filming. A bus, a station wagon, a police car, a camera car, and Philbrick's car were needed for the first day of filming. Sets needed to be built were Philbrick's living room, F.B.I. office, the picture frame shop, a telephone booth, and interior and exterior of the drugstore.

Total Crew Hours:	20
Make Ready and Shooting:	18 1/2 hours
Travel Time:	1 1/2 hours

Location Shots:
11214 Exposition Blvd.
Sepulveda and Exposition Streets
2127 Westwood Blvd.
300 Block Dalehurst in Westwood
Holmby Park in Westwood
Crawford Drugs, 10920 Kinross Avenue in Westwood

Episode #34 "COMRADE WANTS OUT"
Original copyright for production #1034, May 15, 1954.
Original Registration #LP49107
Production # 1034 / 34B
Typescript by Robert Mitchell, February 15, 1954

Mimeo (annotated), February 18, 1954
Master mimeo, February 18, 1954
Filmed February 22 and 23, 1954

Cast: Richard Carlson (Herbert A. Philbrick); Herbert Heyes (Comrade Ray); John Zaremba (Special Agent Jerry Dressler); Connie Weiler (Comrade Jane); Charles Victor (Comrade Burt); Michael Monroe (Bill Webber); and Fay Morley (the telephone clerk).

Production Credits

Director:	Herbert L. Strock
Production Chief:	Herbert L. Strock
First Assistant Director:	Don Verk
Second Assistant Director:	Eddie Mull
First Cameraman:	Robert Hoffman
Second Cameraman:	Fred Bentley
First Assistant Cameraman:	Paul Weddell
Sound Mixer:	Roy Meadows
Recorder:	William Sosteleo
Boom Man:	Wally Nogel
First Company Grip:	Mel Bledsoe
Second Company Grip:	Lou Hafley
Property Master:	Lyle Reifsnider
Assistant Property Man:	J. Robert Benton, Sr.
Set Decorator:	Lou Hafley
Script Supervisor:	Helen McCaffrey
Film Editor:	Bill Ziegler
Gaffer:	Lou Cotese
Set Labor:	Sol Inverso
Construction Chief:	Archie Hall

Plot: Freeworld Movement is a privately operated organization whose life blood is the flow of U.S. citizens. There are several methods to hand-string that campaign and Herb and three other Comrades are assigned various tasks to undermine people's confidence with the Movement. Herb observes Comrade Ray, a respected old-timer in the Party, acting peculiar, even dragging his feet with the project. Agent Dressler tells Philbrick that Comrade Ray may have seen the light and wants out—and he can be valuable to the Bureau. In order to discover Comrade Ray's true leanings, Philbrick spends time with Ray, attempting to make Ray dislike him with straight-hard Party lines. But Comrade Jane and Comrade Burt attempts to threaten Ray with blackmail and murder. When Ray's son comes home from college, Philbrick starts working on the boy with Communist lines that Ray would recognize—which naturally annoys the old-timer and causes Ray to make a decision that will save his son from exposure to the Communist Party and turns evidence to the F.B.I. exposing Party activities.

Memorable Quote: "Well, they never suspect cancer in the glow of health but it starts with one new, malignant cell."

Comment: Philbrick mails his report among a stack of bills so the usual mailbox snooper will find nothing but a stack of bills, not a report to the F.B.I.

Trivia, Etc. Paul Weddell was an assistant cameraman for only a few episodes of this television series. He remains an unsung name among assistant cameramen in Hollywood, whose credits include Cecil B. DeMille's *The Ten Commandments* (1956) and Alfred Hitchcock's *Vertigo* (1958) and *North by Northwest* (1959).

Production Notes: Three electricians, one stand-in, and two extras were needed for the first day of filming. One policeman, three drivers, one stand-in and two extras were needed for the second day of filming. Philbrick's car, a bus, and a station wagon were needed for the second day of filming. Stock footage was used.

Total Crew Hours:	22
Make Ready and Shooting:	21 hours
Travel Time:	1 hour

Location Shots:

Hollywood Mineral Baths, 625 Melrose

The public library featured in this episode was the John C. Fremont Freemont Library, located at 6121 Melrose.

Ray's Home, 603 June St.
Commie Headquarters, 6116 1/2 N. La Brea
Telephone Company, 1149 N. Gower Street

Episode #35 "DEPRESSION"

Original copyright for production #1035, May 22, 1954.
Original Registration # LP49108
Production # 1035 / 35B
Typescript (annotated), by Jack Rock, February 20, 1954
Revised pages (annotated), February 22, 1954
Revised master mimeo, February 22, 1954
Filmed February 23 and 24, 1954

Cast: Richard Carlson (Herbert A. Philbrick); Jane Hampton (Comrade Elsa); John Zaremba (Special Agent Jerry Dressler); Merritt Stone (Comrade Mitch); Charles Evans (McNeil); Rod O'Connor (Duncan Malone); John Goddard (Paul Donovan); Natalie Norwick (Heather); and Stanley Farrar (Victor Mason).

Production Credits

Director:	Lambert Hillyer
Production Chief:	Henry Kesler
First Assistant Director:	Eddie Stein
Second Assistant Director:	Eddie Mull
First Cameraman:	Robert Hoffman
Second Cameraman:	Fred Bentley
First Assistant Cameraman:	Paul Weddell
Sound Mixer:	Roy Meadows
Recorder:	William Sosteleo
Boom Man:	Wally Nogel
First Company Grip:	Mel Bledsoe
Property Master:	Lyle Reifsnider
Assistant Property Man:	J. Robert Benton, Sr.
Set Decorator:	Lou Hafley
Script Supervisor:	Helen McCaffrey
Film Editor:	Jack Woelz

Gaffer:	Lou Cotese
Set Labor:	Sol Inverso
Construction Chief:	Archie Hall

Plot: The closing of a local fire extinguishing company will only be temporary for a couple weeks, so that new tools and equipment can be assembled. The local Communist cell, headed by Comrade Mitch, wants to give the American public an impression that a depression has hit the town. Philbrick is assigned to write a radio commentary that is delivered to the public, suggesting we're in the midst of a depression, giving Americans a false sense of hope. Philbrick, incidentally, makes a mistake by switching the wrong radio commentary he was supposed to deliver to Comrade Mitchell Evans. When Warren McNeil, president of the extinguishing company, is called upon by Agent Dressler to put the public's mind to rest, the plan is foiled. As for the report, Comrade Mitchell asks Philbrick for an explanation. Philbrick explains how they should have been feeding a line or two, little by little, about the depression, instead of trying to cram it down their throats instead. Their efforts to bring about an economic crisis, even on a local scale, were a failure. The other Comrades agree, and Philbrick is allowed to continue his work.

Production Notes: Three electricians, two stand-ins, two extras, one policeman, and three drivers were needed for the first day of filming. One extra, three electricians, and two stand-ins were needed for the second day of filming. Philbrick's car, a bus, and a station wagon were needed for both days of filming.

Total Crew Hours:	20
Make Ready and Shooting:	19 hours
Travel Time:	1 hour

Location Shots:
5530 Melrose Ave.
1101 N. Vine
1161 N. Vine
Cahuenga & Romaine
329 N. Windsor

Episode #36 "THE BOSS"

Original copyright for production #1036, May 29, 1954.
Original Registration # LP49109
Production # 1036 / 36B
Typescript (annotated), by Stuart Jerome, Feb. 26, 1954
Typescript (annotated), February 27, 1954
Revised pages (annotated), March 1, 1954
Revised master mimeo, March 2, 1954
Filmed March 2 and 3, 1954

Cast: Richard Carlson (Herbert A. Philbrick); Ed Hinton (Special Hal Henderson); Virginia Stefan (Eva Philbrick); John Hamilton (Mr. Marshall); Charlotte Lawrence (Carol); Henry Corden (Comrade Howard); and Bob Carson (Special Agent Breen).

Production Credits

Director:	Eddie Davis
Production Chief:	Eddie Davis
First Assistant Director:	Bobby Ray
Second Assistant Director:	George Loper
First Cameraman:	Curt Fetters
Second Cameraman:	Fred Bentley
First Assistant Cameraman:	Paul Weddell
Sound Mixer:	Roy Meadows
Recorder:	William Sosteleo
Boom Man:	Wally Nogel
First Co. Grip:	Mel Beldsoe
Second Co. Grip:	Clarence Boyd
Property Master:	Ygnacio Sepulveda
Assistant Prop Man:	Victor Petrotta
Set Decorator:	Lou Hafley
Script Supervisor:	Helen McCaffrey
Film Editor:	Jack Woelz
Gaffer:	Lou Cortese
Set Labor:	Sol Inverso

Construction Chief: Archie Hall

Plot: Philbrick tells Special Agent Hal Henderson that the Party learned of a new atomic device at an American Defense Plant and, obviously, the Communist Party wants to get their hands on it, making plans to do so. They had an inside man who smuggled a model of the actual device outside the plant, and Philbrick is given the assignment of retrieving the device from the bottom of a boxcar, during a three-minute layover at the train station. Philbrick attempts to contact Agent Henderson when he learns the time and date of the pick-up, but fails to do so because Comrade Howard is keeping close tabs on him. Meanwhile, Philbrick's boss starts showing concern for his employee, offering Eva and her husband a week-long vacation so he can settle his nerves. Back at the station, while Philbrick is attempting to dislodge the package from the bottom of the boxcar, Comrade Howard keeps tabs on the security guard at the station. After succeeding with his mission, Philbrick reluctantly hands the package over to Howard, who leaves the station unaware that he's being followed by the F.B.I., who will make sure the package doesn't fall into the wrong hands.

Production Notes: The first day of shooting consisted of all the interior shots for this episode, filmed on a stage. The second day of shooting consisted of all the exterior shots for this episode. Three electricians and two stand-ins were needed for the first day of filming. One policeman, three drivers, two stand-ins and five extras were needed for the second day of filming. A Commie car, a bus, and a station wagon were needed for the second day of filming.

Total Crew Hours: 20
Make Ready and Shooting: 17 1/2 hours
Travel Time: 2 1/2 hours

Trivia, Etc. The scenes inside Philbrick's house were actually filmed in Richard Carlson's own residence, located at 257 Lafayette Park Place.

Location Shots:
U.P. R.R. Tracks, N. Broadway

THE FLOWER SHOP, BEVERLY AND RAMPART
DRUG STORE, 1921 WILSHIRE BLVD.
PHILBRICK'S HOME, 257 LAFAYETTE PK. PL.

EPISODE #37 "LOVE STORY"
ORIGINAL COPYRIGHT FOR PRODUCTION #1037, JUNE 5, 1954.
ORIGINAL REGISTRATION # LP49110
PRODUCTION # 1037 / 37B
TYPESCRIPT (ANNOTATED), BY ARTHUR FITZ-RICHARD, MARCH 9, 1954
MASTER MIMEO, MARCH 9, 1954
FILMED ON MARCH 11 AND 12, 1954

CAST: Richard Carlson (Herbert A. Philbrick); John Zaremba (Special Jerry Dressler); Judith Ames (Margaret); James Barrett (Paul); Ben Mazer (Mr. Blank); Bob Anderson (Harold Simmons); and Helen Brown (Mrs. Lillian Kinston).

PRODUCTION CREDITS

DIRECTOR:	LEON BENSON
PRODUCTION CHIEF:	LEON BENSON
FIRST ASSISTANT DIRECTOR:	DON VERK
SECOND ASSISTANT DIRECTOR:	GEORGE LOPER
FIRST CAMERAMAN:	CURT FETTERS
SECOND CAMERAMAN:	MONK ASKINS
FIRST ASSISTANT CAMERAMAN:	DICK RAWLINGS
SOUND MIXER:	GARY HARRIS
RECORDER:	BOB POST
BOOM MAN:	JAY ASHWORTH
FIRST CO. GRIP:	CARL MIKSCH
SECOND CO. GRIP:	CECIL HAVERTY
PROPERTY MASTER:	YGNACIO SEPULVEDA
ASSISTANT PROP MAN:	VICTOR PETROTTA
SET DECORATOR:	LOU HAFLEY
SCRIPT SUPERVISOR:	HELEN MCCAFFREY
FILM EDITOR:	DUNCAN MANSFIELD, A.C.E

GAFFER:	JOE WHARTON
SET LABOR:	PHIL CASAZZA
CONSTRUCTION CHIEF:	ARCHIE HALL

PLOT: Students are apparently studying more than art in school. Philbrick finds himself caught in the middle of numerous activities, and with various sides asking him to come up with the solutions. In the center of the story is Margaret, whose secret motives are unknown—but suspected—by Party members. Margaret rejects Paul's marriage proposal, so out of spite, Paul informs Philbrick that he suspects Margaret is a Communist. Mr. Blank and Mr. Simmons, both comrades for the cause, assign Philbrick the task of breaking up the romance between Paul and Margaret, and Simmons orders Philbrick to frame Paul for a crime he did not commit. Agent Dressler remains on the sidelines during this entire scenario. Margaret, in the meantime, manages to photograph vital plans and in desperation, locks Comrade Lillian in a room when caught red-handed. When Blank and Simmons catch wind of what Margaret has stolen, they corner her down a narrow street. Thankfully, Agent Dressler and an F.B.I. aide trap the two Commies and Margaret is free to send the microfilm to her rendezvous, on the side of freedom and democracy. Philbrick is not suspected of any involvement, since the Communist Party kept him too busy to deal with Margaret.

PRODUCTION NOTES: Three electricians and two stand-ins were needed on the second day of filming. One policeman, four drivers, two stand-ins, one electrician, and one fireman were needed on the second day of filming. Dressler's car, a bus, and a camera car, and a standby car were needed for the second day of filming.

TOTAL CREW HOURS:	22
MAKE READY AND SHOOTING:	21 HOURS
TRAVEL TIME:	1 HOUR

LOCATION SHOTS:
7304 MELROSE
7341 WILLOUGHBY
1000 FORMOSA

7400 MELROSE STREET
8129 MELROSE STREET
9010 MELROSE STREET

EPISODE #38 "UNEXPECTED TRIP"

ORIGINAL COPYRIGHT FOR PRODUCTION #1038, JUNE 12, 1954.
ORIGINAL REGISTRATION # LP49111
PRODUCTION #1038 / 38B
TYPESCRIPT BY TIM WHELAN, MARCH 19, 1954
MIMEO (ANNOTATED), MARCH 23, 1954
REVISED PAGES (ANNOTATED), MARCH 25, 1954
REVISED MASTER MIMEO, MARCH 25, 1954
FILMED ON MARCH 26 AND 27, 1954

CAST: Richard Carlson (Herbert A. Philbrick); John Zaremba (Special Jerry Dressler); Virginia Stefan (Eva Philbrick); Gayne Whitman (Reid); Howard Wright (Wyman); Vernon Rich (the farmer); and Jess Kirkpatrick (unnamed comrade).

PRODUCTION CREDITS

PRODUCTION CHIEF:	TIM WHELAN
DIRECTOR:	TIM WHELAN
FIRST ASSISTANT DIRECTOR:	DON VERK
SECOND ASSISTANT DIRECTOR:	BOBBY RAY
FIRST CAMERAMAN:	CURT FETTERS
SECOND CAMERAMAN:	MONK ASKINS
FIRST ASSISTANT CAMERAMAN:	DICK RAWLINGS
SOUND MIXER:	GARY HARRIS
RECORDER:	BOB POST
BOOM MAN:	JAY ASHWORTH
FIRST CO. GRIP:	CARL MIKSCH
SECOND CO. GRIP:	MEL BLEDSOE
PROPERTY MASTER:	YGNACIO SEPULVEDA
ASSISTANT PROP MASTER:	LYLE REIFSNIDER
SET DECORATOR:	LOU HAFLEY
SCRIPT SUPERVISOR:	HELEN MCCAFFREY

Film Editor:	Ace Clark
Gaffer:	Joe Wharton
Set Labor:	Phil Cassazza
Construction Chief:	Archie Hall

Plot: Philbrick receives a phone call from a Party member instructing him to report to the local airport immediately for a special assignment. There, Philbrick is handed plane tickets and ordered to deliver an important letter to a certain Party when he arrives at his destination. The task, however, is so vital to the Communist Party that Philbrick is assigned an escort—for dual control to ensure the letter does not fall into the hands of the opposition. Enter Comrade Reid, a cunning and determined Comrade, who foils Philbrick's every attempt at phoning his wife, the F.B.I., and on one occasion, trying to make a photocopy of the document for Agent Hal Henderson, who retains a close tail on the Comrades. Only after reaching his destination is Philbrick let in on the scheme of things. The letter was a McGuffin—a fake decoy—with no information of real value. Philbrick apparently passed the test. Before returning for home, he is given a real assignment—to deliver important papers that the Commies now trust will fall into the right hands. Now armed with two escorts, Philbrick must find a way to getting this information to the F.B.I. before it gets mailed. Thanks to a clever ploy involving an undercover agent and her fallen packages, Philbrick is able to slip the envelope among her boxes. The letter will reach its destination, but not before the F.B.I. gets a look at the contents first . . .

Notes: Throughout this episode, Eva Philbrick is greatly concerned over her husband's actions, whereabouts and people whom he associates himself with. When Philbrick receives the phone call in the beginning, he dismisses breakfast she prepared for him. After he arrived at his initial destination, Herb attempts to phone his wife but Comrade Reid cuts off the connection before a single word could be exchanged. This, naturally, starts to frighten Eva. Thankfully, this is what the author refers to as a keystone episode—an episode of the series that gives the program a dramatic change that will affect the storyline for the remainder of the broadcast:

Agent Dressler meets up with Eva in a church and discusses her husband's participation, and the reason why he kept secrets from her. As any supportive wife should be, Eva fully understands and accepts Herb's role in the scheme of things.

PRODUCTION NOTES: Three electricians, one policeman, and four extras, and two stand-ins were needed on the first day of filming. One policeman, two stand-ins, two extras, and three electricians were needed on the second day of filming. Two picture cars, a bus, and a station wagon were needed for both days of filming.

TOTAL CREW HOURS:	21
MAKE READY AND SHOOTING:	18 HOURS
TRAVEL TIME:	3 HOURS

TRIVIA, ETC. The airport scenes were filmed on location at the airport in Inglewood. The hotel scenes were filmed on location in the Hollywood Roosevelt Hotel located at 7000 Hollywood Blvd., Los Angeles, California. The Hollywood Roosevelt Hotel was the home of the very first Academy Awards (held in 1929) and was built as a glamorous gathering place for the screen colony, with investors including Douglas Fairbanks and Mary Pickford. Through the years, throngs of celebrities and people hoping to sight them have visited and resided at the hotel. The hotel still stands today.

EPISODE #39 "STRATEGIC MATERIAL"

ORIGINAL COPYRIGHT FOR PRODUCTION #1039, JUNE 19, 1954.
ORIGINAL REGISTRATION #LP49112
PRODUCTION #1039 / 39B
TYPESCRIPT (ANNOTATED), BY JACK ROCK, MARCH 26, 1954
MASTER MIMEO, MARCH 26, 1954
FILMED ON APRIL 2 AND 3, 1954

CAST: Richard Carlson (Herbert A. Philbrick); John Zaremba (Special Jerry Dressler); Marx Hartman (Ethan Dobe); Paul Keast (Captain Neilson); and Jonni Paris (the cashier).

Production Credits

Production Chief:	Herbert L. Strock
Director:	Herbert L. Strock
First Assistant Director:	Joseph Wonder
Second Assistant Director:	George Loper
First Cameraman:	Curt Fetters
Second Cameraman:	Fred Bently
First Assistant Cameraman:	Paul Weddell
Sound Mixer:	Roy Meadows
Recorder:	William Sosteleo
Boom Man:	Wally Nogel
First Co. Grip:	Carl Miksch
Property Master:	Lyle Reifsnider
Assistant Prop Master:	Bob Bowen
Set Decorator:	Lou Hafley
Script Supervisor:	Helen McCaffrey
Film Editor:	Duncan Mansfield, A.C.E
Gaffer:	Lou Cortese
Construction Chief:	Archie Hall

Plot: Philbrick's latest mission involves the secure transportation of hazardous chemicals to a rendezvous point where it will eventually be transported abroad. Philbrick finds no difficulty in giving information to Agent Dressler, including the name of the chemical plant where the chemicals apparently originate from. On the suspicious side is Comrade Ethan Dobe, who, after receiving one question too many from Philbrick, makes it a personal hobby to trail the counterspy. Even with someone following him, Philbrick exchanges information again with Agent Dressler, who explains to Herb that a mistake was apparently made, and that the chemicals are not the same as the Commies thought. They are highly dangerous. When Philbrick reveals this newfound information to Comrade Dobe, the two men start a search-and-destroy mission for the chemicals, following the actions of the carriers, and avoiding complications to ensure the stability of the Party. The trail closes in on a cargo ship, where Philbrick tests the chemicals, confirms the instability of the product, and saves all parties involved.

COMMENT: The script for this episode clearly suggests how accurate and stable the Communist Party wants to remain, even with the occasional foul-ups, and elimination of Party members who prove to be inefficient for the Party. One example includes Herb and Ethan's discussion in Philbrick's car, during the chase, regarding the efficient security methods of the Party. Another example is when Philbrick first meets Ethan, and the two men refer to the mission as what's "best for the Party."

PRODUCTION NOTES: Two electricians, one stand-in, one policeman, and four drivers were needed on the first day of filming. Four extras were needed for the first day and two extras were needed on the second day of filming. Philbrick's car, a 33-passenger bus, Dressler's car, a panel truck and a camera car were needed for this film.

TOTAL CREW HOURS:	22
MAKE READY AND SHOOTING:	17 1/2 HOURS
TRAVEL TIME:	4 1/2 HOURS

TRIVIA, ETC. This episode was originally scheduled to be filmed March 31 and April 1, but was instead pushed ahead a couple of days.

LOCATION SHOTS:
6225 SANTA MONICA BLVD.
1000 NORTH VINE STREET
PEDESTRIAN TUNNEL
6032 BARTON AVENUE
926 N. VINE STREET
PHONE COMPANY, NORTH VINE ST.
WILMINGTON BERTH 188
WILMINGTON STREETS

Season Two

Episode #40 "COUNTERFEIT"

Original copyright for production #1040, September 25, 1954. Original Registration #LP49113
Production # 1040 / 40B
Typescript (annotated), by Jack Rock, June 24, 1954
Revised pages (annotated), June 24, 1954
Revised master mimeo, June 26, 1954
Filmed June 30 and July 1, 1954

Cast: Richard Carlson (Herbert A. Philbrick); John Beradino (Special Agent Steve Daniels); Vivi Janiss (Comrade Endora); Richard Bartell (Comrade Irwin); Maureen Cassidy (Mary Castle); Ruth Bennett (Miss Shelby); George Barrows (Mako); and Mitchell Kowal (Joe).

Production Credits

Director:	Lew Landers
Production Chief:	Lew Landers
First Assistant Director:	Ralph Slosser
Second Assistant Director:	Harry Jones
First Cameraman:	Robert Hoffman
Second Cameraman:	Fred Bentley
First Assistant Cameraman:	Shirley Williams
Sound Mixer:	Phil Mitchell
Recorder:	Walt Teague
Boom Man:	Carl Miller
First Co. Grip:	Mel Bledsoe
Property Master:	Max Pittman
Second Company Grip:	Al Prince
Set Decorator:	Lou Hafley
Script Supervisor:	Emelie Ehrlick
Film Editor:	Ace Clark
Gaffer:	Don Scott
Set Labor:	Felix Chelecia
Construction Chief:	Archie Hall

PLOT: In an attempt to force its doctrine on other nations, the Communist Party respects no law other than its own. Case in point: Herb Philbrick informs Special Agent Steve Daniels that the Party is apparently getting desperate—they plan to bribe high officials in the community. Comrade Endora is assigned to make a chain store survey. Philbrick cannot explain what civic corruption and a survey have in common, and neither can Daniels, but after the courier is handed an envelope by Philbrick, the courier is hit by a car. Acting on instinct, Philbrick takes the letter back and returns to Comrade Irwin, whose reputation is taking orders, not making decisions. Irwin orders Philbrick to deliver the letter just as the courier would have. By switching a ten-dollar bill from one of the envelopes with one of his own, Philbrick turns the money over to the F.B.I. who quickly figures out the scheme. The Commies are printing counterfeit ten-dollar bills and has them put into circulation by means of the survey Comrade Endora conducts in the streets. In the event the fakes are noticed, only a high school or college student will take the fall—not knowing the true name of the man or woman who gave them the shopping survey and the counterfeit bill. Philbrick tells Comrade Irwin that a grocer recently picked up on a fake bill and this causes Irwin to drive to the house where the fake bills were being printed. The F.B.I. follows, makes arrests, prevents the destruction of evidence, confiscates the printing presses and half a million in fake currency, and round-up talkative Comrades ready to spill the beans. The campaign of political corruption came to an end, courtesy of the F.B.I. and a counterspy.

PRODUCTION NOTES: Three electricians, two stand-ins, and two extras were needed for the first day of filming. One policeman, one electrician, five drivers, one third-grip, two stand-ins, and six extras were needed for the second day of filming. A camera and sound car, a 33-passenger bus for crew, a station wagon, a Chevrolet, a Ford, a trailer for electrical equipment (crrd. by Nash), and a car for Nash were needed for the first day of filming. Stock footage was used.

TOTAL CREW HOURS:	21
MAKE READY AND SHOOTING:	19 1/2 HOURS
TRAVEL TIME:	1 1/2 HOURS

Location Shots:

The used car dealer scenes were shot on location at the Phil Hall Buick Dealer located at 6660 Sunset Blvd.
6812 Sunset (Burn & Strauss)
Bekins Van and Storage, 1025 N. Highland
Van Ness School
Castle Home, 404 No. Van Ness

Trivia: Episode #50 of the ZIV-produced radio program, *I Was a Communist for the F.B.I.*, entitled "The Wrong Green," featured a similar Communist scheme of passing counterfeit currency, and was probably the basis for the plot of this episode.

Episode #41 "RELATIVES"

Original copyright for production #1041, October 2, 1954.
Original Registration #LP49114
Production #1041 / 41 B
Typescript (annotated), by Ellis Marcus, June 28, 1954
Revised pages (annotated), July 6, 1954
Revised master mimeo, July 6, 1954
Filmed July 8 and 9, 1954

Cast: Richard Carlson (Herbert A. Philbrick); Ed Hinton (Special Hal Henderson); Michael McHale (Comrade Mike); Kem Dibbs (Comrade Ben); Fay Morley (Comrade Louise); Helen Mayon (Mrs. Baker); and Tony De Mario (Axel Bronstad).

Production Credits

Production Chief:	Eddie Davis
Director:	Eddie Davis
First Assistant Director:	Marty Moss
Second Assistant Director:	Bobby Ray
First Cameraman:	Robert Hoffman
Second Cameraman:	Monk Askins
First Assistant Cameraman:	Dick Rawlings
Sound Mixer:	Gary Harris

RECORDER:	JAY ASHWORTH
BOOM MAN:	ROBERT POST
FIRST CO. GRIP:	MEL BLEDSOE
PROPERTY MASTER:	YGNACIO SEPULVEDA
SET DECORATOR:	LOU HAFLEY
SCRIPT SUPERVISOR:	HELEN MCCAFFREY
FILM EDITOR:	DUNCAN MANSFIELD, A.C.E
GAFFER:	JOE WHARTON
CONSTRUCTION CHIEF:	ARCHIE HALL

PLOT: Philbrick flies out of town for an assignment, and takes lessons from Comrade Ben for conning people out of money, then donating the funds to the Communist Party. Using his bike shop as a front, Ben wants Philbrick to get in on the action, showing him just how the setup works. Philbrick doesn't want any part of the deceit schemes—at first—until he gives his report to Agent Hal Henderson, who agrees that Philbrick should play along. While almost getting caught tailing Comrade Ben and Comrade Mike, the F.B.I. moves in to arrest Mike. When Comrade Ben learns of the news, he informs Philbrick that the assignment has been cancelled—much to the relief of Philbrick.

PRODUCTION NOTES: Three electricians, two stand-ins, one motorcycle policeman, a fireman (at the airport), four drivers, and four extras were needed on the first day of filming. Three electricians and two stand-ins were needed on the second day of filming. A camera and sound car, a 33-passenger bus, a car for Philbrick, and a pick-up car were needed for the first day of filming.

TOTAL CREW HOURS:	20
MAKE READY AND SHOOTING:	17 HOURS
TRAVEL TIME:	3 HOURS

LOCATION SHOTS:

THE SCENES AT THE PLAYGROUND WERE FILMED ON LOCATION AT THE CULVER CITY PLAYGROUND AT CULVER AND OVERLAND IN CALIFORNIA.

INTERNATIONAL AIRPORT

ARMSTRONG'S BIKE SHOP, 9135 SOUTH SEPULEDA

Westchester Laundromat, 6227 West 87th Street
Gift Shop, 6203 West 87th Street
Bollona Creek (bridge), Overland and Ocean Aves.

Episode #42 "CLOSE FACTORY"
Production #1042 / 42B
Typescript (annotated), by Stuart Jerome, July 7, 1954
Revised master mimeo, July 9, 1954
Revised pages (annotated), July 9, 1954
Filmed July 14 and 15, 1954

Cast: Richard Carlson (Herbert A. Philbrick); John De Simone (Comrade Barker); Thayer Roberts (Comrade Harvey); Lorna Thayer (Mrs. Mallinson); Edward Coch (Mr. Mallinson); and Ed Hinton (Special Hal Henderson).

Production Credits

Production Chief:	Leigh Jason
Director:	Leigh Jason
First Assistant Director:	Ralph Slosser
Second Assistant Director:	Harry Jones
First Cameraman:	Curt Fetters
Second Cameraman:	Kenny Green
First Assistant Cameraman:	Bob McGowen
Sound Mixer:	T.T. Tuflett
Recorder:	Walt Teague
Boom Man:	Bill Hamilton
First Co. Grip:	Carl Miksch
Property Master:	Victor Petrotta
Set Decorator:	Lou Hafley and Bruce MacDonald
Wardrobe Man:	Irving Hill
Film Editor:	ack Woelz
Script Supervisor:	Larry Lund
Gaffer:	Lou Cortese
Construction Chief:	Archie Hall

PLOT: Information for Freedom Movement is a group of refugees from behind the Iron Curtain who help pass information to people who hate Communism. The Malisons, owners of a ceramics factory and former refugees, are the founders of this group. The ceramics factory functions as financial aid for the program, and doubles as a front at the same time. The products they export contain coded messages giving their friends hope that they are not alone in their fight for freedom. Since their program is a volunteer program, not a federally-funded program, the Malisons' true identity has been a secret until Comrade Harvey orders Philbrick, friends of the Malisons, to convince them to hire Comrade Barker as an employee. Days later, with Barker as an inside man, Philbrick is given the orders to plant a time bomb to eliminate both the plant and the Malisons. Since Comrade Harvey is forced to step out for a few minutes, Philbrick switches the boxes, leaving the bomb at Harvey's Photoshop. After planting the fake bomb, Philbrick is escorted by Barker to the photoshop to hear the news of the explosion on the radio, but Philbrick, realizing they are all about to die, fakes illness so the men leave briefly, just before the shop explodes. Comrade Harvey cries when he discovers that he gave Philbrick the wrong box, and the repercussions he will receive from the Party for his blunder.

COMMENT: Moral of the story was clear in this episode. As explained, "Communists don't always believe in passive resistance."

MEMORABLE QUOTE: Philbrick's closing comments: "What did the Bible say about people like you? They have sewn the wind, and they shall reap the whirlwind."

PRODUCTION NOTES: Three electricians, two stand-ins, one extra, one motorcycle policeman, a car for the "goon," and five drivers were needed on the second day of filming. One electrician, four drivers, two stand-ins, and eight extras were needed on the first day of filming. Philbrick's car, a 42-passenger bus, a camera and sound car, and a small panel truck (for electrical equipment) were needed for both days of filming.

TOTAL CREW HOURS: 21

Make Ready and Shooting: 10 hours
Travel Time: 1 hour

Trivia, Etc. Two casting notes: Carlyle Mitchell was originally slated to play the role of Comrade Harvey, and Veronica Pataky was originally slated to play the role of Mrs. Mallinson. The plot for this episode originated from a brief story idea dated May 26, 1954 by Stuart Jerome. Reprinted below, word-for-word:

Herb is ordered by his cell leader to head a concerted campaign against George and Teresa Ales, owners of a prosperous ceramic factory in the city. The idea is to put the Ales out of business. This puts Herb in a tough spot because his company handles their advertising. Also, he is at a loss to understand the reason for the Commies' activity against the Ales. True, they've been anti-Commie in local activities, but no more so than a lot of others.

Herb checks with the F.B.I., who can't understand the reason for the campaign either. The F.B.I. agrees with Herb that the only thing he can do is follow orders, since by sticking close to the project he'll have a chance to find out what it's all about.

Herb is forced to institute his campaign of terror against the Ales, trying to close down their factory. In the meantime, he tries desperately to find out what the upper-level Party has against them. Finally he learns that Mr. and Mrs. Ales have been devoting all their profits to a European refugee movement which has been smuggling people out of the iron curtain countries.

Then the F.B.I. moves in, arrests the Commie terrorists and saves the factory.

Location Shots:

The scenes filmed in the ceramics store were filmed on location at Sasha Brastoff, located at 11520 W. Olympia in Los Angeles, California. Jerry's Market at 5330 Melrose was used for location shots in the market.

The Patio at 500 No. Linden

Drive-in Theatre at Centinella & Sepulveda

Photo Gallery, 6209 Santa Monica

EPISODE #43 "MARTYR"

ORIGINAL COPYRIGHT FOR PRODUCTION #1043, OCTOBER 16, 1954.
ORIGINAL REGISTRATION #LP49116
PRODUCTION #1043 / 43B
TYPESCRIPT (ANNOTATED) BY DONN MULLALLY, JULY 12, 1954
MASTER MIMEO, JULY 13, 1954
REVISED PAGES, JULY 14, 1954
FILMED JULY 16 AND 17, 1954

CAST: Richard Carlson (Herbert A. Philbrick); Ed Hinton (Special Hal Henderson); Dorothy Adams (Mrs. Ballard); Guy Prescott (Carl Pressley); Paul Grant (Clark Ballard); J. Anthony Hughes (Thomas Kalfan); Marjorie Stapp (Elaine Walker); Willard Willingham (the Marine Guard); and Gregg Martell (Mr. Smith).

PRODUCTION CREDITS

PRODUCTION CHIEF:	EDDIE DAVIS
DIRECTOR:	EDDIE DAVIS
FIRST ASSISTANT DIRECTOR:	MARTY MOSS
SECOND ASSISTANT DIRECTOR:	BOBBY RAY
FIRST CAMERAMAN:	ROBERT HOFFMAN
SECOND CAMERAMAN:	MONK ASKINS
FIRST ASSISTANT CAMERAMAN:	DICK RAWLINGS
SOUND MIXER:	GARY HARRIS
RECORDER:	JAY ASHWORTH
BOOM MAN:	ROBERT POST
FIRST CO. GRIP:	MEL BLEDSOE
PROPERTY MASTER:	YGNACIO SEPULVEDA
SET DECORATOR:	LOU HAFLEY
SCRIPT SUPERVISOR:	HELEN MCCAFFREY
FILM EDITOR:	ACE CLARK
GAFFER:	JOE WHARTON
CONSTRUCTION CHIEF:	ARCHIE HALL

PLOT: When Comrade Ben learns that Philbrick is going south to

New York City on a business trip, he gives Philbrick a package to be delivered to an important Party functionary in New York. Philbrick reaches his destination, Comrade Louise, who opens the package to reveal he was a courier for $60,000. Comrade Louise asks Philbrick on a personal level whether he knows how Comrade Mike, a Communist floater who does rough jobs off the side to raise funds for the Party, gains the money he does. Philbrick does not know—but Special Agent Hal Henderson would also like know the answer to that question. When Philbrick learns that Comrade Mike is being promoted out West, he is assigned to take his place as a fundraiser. As the weeks pass, Philbrick learns how the game works—Comrade Mike is conning people who have victims (recently deceased) behind the Iron Curtain to pay for the passage of return for the relatives. Special Agent Henderson, in the meantime, learns that Comrade Louise is using the money to open new cells all over the country. When Philbrick uses a clever ploy, Special Agent Henderson has the evidence he needs to arrest Comrade Mike and Comrade Louise for extortion, using one of the victims as their source of information. With too much evidence against the Party, the project is dropped and Philbrick's neck is off the chopping block . . . for now.

MEMORABLE QUOTE: Philbrick questioning his assignment: "What could be so important that Comrade Ben felt it necessary to deliver it himself? Secret Party plans? Documents stolen from a defense plant? Or merely something to test your Party loyalty? Do they suspect you, Philbrick? Have they finally caught up with you . . . this business of leading three separate lives?"

COMMENTS: This is one of the better episodes of the series, revealing how the Communist Party attempted to extort money from innocent Americans, and how the victims took the loss. One woman, for example, optioned to sell her store—her only source of income—to gain the funds she needed to have her brother returned from abroad. What the Party did with the funds after they were gained was also explained. A discussion between Philbrick and Agent Henderson reminded listeners that the F.B.I. could not give Philbrick orders—Philbrick volunteered for his tasks. As much as the F.B.I. preferred Philbrick to continue doing what the Party wanted—making Philbrick sick to his stomach—they did not hesitate to remind Philbrick that he did not have to follow through all the way. How the F.B.I. got involved with gathering evidence against Comrade Mike and Comrade Louise was not revealed to the listeners, and the surprise was just that—a surprise. At the end of the drama, Philbrick realized that his trust in the project was disregarded to the Party, so to regain that trust from Comrade Ben, Philbrick optioned to pick up where he left off with the same project—this time with new victims selected.

PRODUCTION NOTES: Three electricians, two stand-ins, one motorcycle policeman, four drivers, and five extras were needed on the first day of filming. Three electricians, two stand-ins, and four extras were needed on the second day of filming. Philbrick's car, a 42-passenger bus, Dressler's car, a camera and sound car, and a trailer for electrical equipment were needed for the first day of filming. Stock footage was used.

TOTAL CREW HOURS: 23
MAKE READY AND SHOOTING: 20 HOURS
TRAVEL TIME: 3 HOURS

LOCATION SHOTS:
RAILROAD STATION, 5454 FERGUSON DR., NEAR ATLANTIC BLVD.

EPISODE #44 "HOMING STATION"
ORIGINAL COPYRIGHT FOR PRODUCTION #1044, OCTOBER 23, 1954. ORIGINAL REGISTRATION #LP49117
PRODUCTION #1044 / 44B
TYPESCRIPT (ANNOTATED), BY ARTHUR FITZ-RICHARD, JULY 12, 1954
REVISED PAGES (ANNOTATED), JULY 19, 1954
REVISED MASTER MIMEO, JULY 19, 1954
FILMED JULY 21 AND 22, 1954

CAST: Richard Carlson (Herbert A. Philbrick); Jack Jordan

(Comrade Fuller); Gil Warren (Jim Quentin); Lenore Kingston (Comrade Zirka); Alex Charpe (Ralph Sommers); and John Zaremba (Special Agent Jerry Dressler).

Production Credits

Production Chief:	Leon Benson
Director:	Leon Benson
First Assistant Director:	Marty Moss
Second Assistant Director:	Harry Jones
First Cameraman:	Curt Fetters
Second Cameraman:	Monk Askins
First Assistant Cameraman:	Dick Rawlings
Sound Mixer:	Gary Harris
Recorder:	Bob Post
Boom Man:	Jay Ashworth
First Co. Grip:	Carl Miksch
Property Master:	Max Pittman
Set Decorator:	Lou Hafley
Script Supervisor:	Larry Lund
Film Editor:	Duncan Mansfield, A.C.E
Gaffer:	Joe Wharton
Construction Chief:	Archie Hall

Plot: Herb Philbrick acts as carrier for the Communist Party, delivering electronic equipment to an old friend of his, Comrade Bob Quentin. He realizes that if the country comes under attack, the bombs and missiles will need to be radio guided—thus the reason for the equipment. Comrade Zirka, in the meantime, suspects Philbrick might be a thorn in the plans, having noticed how many comrades have been arrested in the past few months—all linked in some way with Philbrick. Suspecting Quentin's old cabin retreat as a prime location for the drop off, Philbrick takes a little fishing trip and begins snooping around. Cleverly blowing a short circuit, Philbrick is soon suspected of the sabotage but when an F.B.I. roadblock interferes with the Comrades' attempt at escape, the excuse the Federal Agents use for tailing and apprehending them eliminates any suspicions they had on Philbrick—pleasing Comrade Fuller since Philbrick's quick thinking saved his hide.

Production Notes: Three electricians, one stand-in, and one extra were needed on the first day of filming. One motorcycle policeman, six drivers, two stand-ins, one electrician, and one extra were needed on the second day of filming. Philbrick's car, a 33-passenger bus, a camera and sound car, a panel truck, Dressler's Car, and a police car were needed for the second day of filming. Stock footage was used.

Total Crew Hours:	23
Make Ready and Shooting:	20 hours
Travel Time:	3 hours

Episode #45 "INFILTRATION"

Original copyright for production #1045, October 30, 1954.
Production #1045 / 45B
Typescript by Jack Rock, July 15, 1954
Revised master mimeo, July 20, 1954
Filmed July 23 and 24, 1954

Cast: Richard Carlson (Herbert A. Philbrick); John Zaremba (Special Agent Jerry Dressler); John Dennis (Comrade Mitchell); Morgan Stock (Randolph); Jack Daly (Mr. Charles); Gloria Clark (Mrs. Charles); Bill Baldwin (Mr. Burkette); and David Parker (Comrade Murray).

Production Credits

Production Chief:	Lew Landers
Director:	Lew Landers
First Assistant Director:	Don Verk
Second Assistant Director:	Bobby Ray
First Cameraman:	Robert Hoffman
Second Cameraman:	Monk Askins
First Assistant Cameraman:	Dick Rawlings
Sound Mixer:	Gary Harris
Recorder:	Bob Post
Boom Man:	Jay Ashworth

First Co. Grip:	Mel Bledsoe
Property Master:	Victor Petrotta
Set Decorator:	Lou Hafley
Script Supervisors:	Larry Lund and Helen McCaffrey
Film Editor:	Jack Woelz
Gaffer:	Joe Wharton
Construction Chief:	Archie Hall

Plot: To achieve their purpose, ruthless Communist leaders will sacrifice anything—even a loyal comrade. The Party has an important project named Project F-10, but before the plan can be set, the Party wants to infiltrate and eliminate any traitors, spies and informants, including an amateur infiltration—a fanatic whose patriotism leads him to betrayal. Herb is assigned to find Randolph Bishop of the Emanon Chemical Company, and verify whether he is an honest Communist or not. When the Party suspects Randolph of deviating, they eliminate him, along with other Party members, by having them discredited of being Communists publicly. When Bishop loses his job because of the Party, he decides to get even by setting up a bomb at the Chemical plant. Project F-10, it is revealed, was to sabotage a fire at ten different chemical plants at the same time—only when the police start questioning, they'll learn all about the Communist project. Comrade Mitchum and Comrade Charles rush to the plant to put the fire out but find themselves too late—and arrested by the police. Philbrick secretly gives Dressler the list of Comrades who had a part in the Project, and the arson scheme is foiled to the fullest.

Comment: When Comrade Mitchell learns that Comrade Murray went to the authorities after learning certain information, he attempts to beat a confession out of Murray—but to no success. When questioned what disservice he did for the Party, Comrade Mitchell explains none—yet. "But the time to stop a traitor is to before he becomes a traitor. In Russia they deal with these things realistically. Here we have a Capitalist Government which spawns traitors—offers them sanctuary as a reward for their treason." The information was false, laid for Murray to see what he would do with that information and the beating was set as an example to the rest of the member of the Party in attendance.

PRODUCTION NOTES: Three electricians, one stand-in, one policeman, four drivers, and six extras were needed on the first day of filming. Three electricians, one stand-in and two extras were needed on the second day of filming. Mitchell's car, a 33-passenger bus, a black-and-white police car, a camera and sound car, and a standby car for Carlson were needed for the first day of filming.

TOTAL CREW HOURS:	20
MAKE READY AND SHOOTING:	18 1/2 HOURS
TRAVEL TIME:	1 1/2 HOURS

LOCATION SHOTS:
10717 VENICE BLVD.
10460 W. PICO
600 BLOCK NO. BRONSON
526 NORTH NORTON
522 NORTH NORTON

EPISODE #46 "ASSASSINATION"
ORIGINAL COPYRIGHT FOR PRODUCTION #1046, NOVEMBER 6, 1954.
PRODUCTION # 1046 / 46B
TYPESCRIPT BY STUART JEROME, JULY 22, 1954
REVISED PAGES (ANNOTATED), JULY 27, 1954
REVISED MASTER MIMEO, JULY 28, 1954
FILMED JULY 30 AND 31, 1954

CAST: Richard Carlson (Herbert A. Philbrick); Terry Frost (Comrade Taylor); Julie Bennett (Comrade Munson); Gordon Barnes (Tom Leary); Karolee Kelly (the salesgirl); Ted Maples (the ranger); and Ed Hinton (Special Agent Hal Henderson).

PRODUCTION CREDITS

PRODUCTION CHIEF:	EDDIE DAVIS

Director:	Eddie Davis
First Assistant Director:	Eddie Stein
Second Assistant Director:	Bobby Ray
First Cameraman:	Curt Fetters
Second Cameraman:	Monk Askins
First Assistant Cameraman:	Dick Rawlings
Sound Mixer:	Gary Harris
Recorder:	Bob Post
Boom Man:	Jay Ashworth
First Company Grip:	Carl Miksch
Second Company Grip:	Mel Bledsoe (second day only)
Property Master:	Ygnacio Sepulveda
Set Decorator:	Lou Hafley
Script Supervisor:	Larry Lund
Wardrobe Man:	Al Berke
Film Editor:	Art Bell
Gaffer:	Joe Wharton
Set Labor:	Sol Inverso (second day only)
Construction Chief:	Archie Hall

Plot: Congressman Tom Leahy and his committee have successfully been exposing youth camps run by the Communist Party. To prevent suspicion, Philbrick and Comrade Taylor go up to the mountains to liquidate all the pamphlets before the authorities snoop too close. In the cabin, the men are surprised to find all the pamphlets missing. Wandering through the woods, they find Congressman Leahy taking a walk. He explains that he's taking a brief vacation until tomorrow morning. Putting one and one together, Comrade Taylor decides to assassinate the congressman. Philbrick tries to talk him out of it, even attempting to steal the bullets from the rifle, but with no success. Thankfully, a Forest Ranger comes by and interrupts the assassination attempt. When the boys get back to Comrade Munson, she reprimands Comrade Taylor for taking matters into his own hands. A loyal Party member who lived near the forest had taken the pamphlets—not the congressman. Special Agent Hal Henderson informs Philbrick that due to the congressman's recent newspaper headlines, it was they who arranged for the Forest Ranger to keep tabs on the men just in case such an attempt was planned.

NOTES: An effective scene closes the first act of this episode, when Comrade Taylor reveals to Philbrick his intentions of killing Congressman Leahy, and no music score is featured as the screen fades to black, making the harsh revelation all the more terrifying. Episode #34 of the ZIV-produced radio program, *I Was a Communist for the F.B.I.* entitled "Kiss of Death," featured a similar Communist scheme and was probably the basis for the plot of this episode.

PRODUCTION NOTES: Three electricians, two stand-ins, and one extra were needed on the second day of filming. One ranger, five drivers, one electrician, and two stand-ins were needed on the first day of filming. A bus, a camera car, one Jeep, and two picture cars were needed for the first day of filming.

TOTAL CREW HOURS:	20
MAKE READY AND SHOOTING:	17 HOURS
TRAVEL TIME:	3 HOURS

EPISODE #47 "THE BOMB"

ORIGINAL COPYRIGHT FOR PRODUCTION #1047, NOVEMBER 13, 1954.
PRODUCTION #1047 / 47B
TYPESCRIPT BY FREDERICK STEPHANI, JULY 26, 1954
REVISED PAGES (ANNOTATED), AUGUST 4 AND 5, 1954
REVISED MASTER MIMEO, AUGUST 5, 1954
FILMED AUGUST 5 AND 6, 1954

CAST: Richard Carlson (Herbert A. Philbrick); Lillian Sayre (Comrade Ella); George Cooper (Special Miller); John Zaremba (Special Jerry Dressler); John Craven (Comrade Werner); Ken Duncan, Jr. (the comedian); Jack Reynolds (the service station attendant); Eleanor Tanin (the stewardess); Paul Peters (the radio operator); George Brand (Comrade X); and John Marshall (Mr. Average Man).

Production Credits

Director:	Eddie Davis
First Assistant Director:	Eddie Stein
Second Assistant Director:	Bobby Ray
First Cameraman:	Robert Hoffman
Second Cameraman:	Kenny Green
First Assistant Cameraman:	Dick Rawlings
Sound Mixer:	Gary Harris
Recorder:	Bob Post
Boom Man:	Jay Ashworth
First Company Grip:	Mel Bledsoe
Property Master:	Ygnacio Sepulveda
Assistant Property Man:	Victor Petrotta
Set Decorator:	Lou Hafley
Script Supervisor:	Larry Lund
Wardrobe:	Al Burke
Film Editor:	Jack Woelz
Gaffer:	Joe Wharton
Set Labor:	Sol Inverso
Construction Chief:	Archie Hall

Plot: Comrade Ella explains to Philbrick that Professor Marlowe is leaving for Washington to testify at a hearing. Having been purged from the Party because of his romantic beliefs, and disregard for the Manifesto, Comrade Ella gives Philbrick a two-fold assignment: to watch the Professor and report everything in full detail, and get the Professor's dossier and deliver it to Communist Party Headquarters in Washington. On board the plane, Philbrick discovers that the dossier he's carrying has a bomb inside. Special Agent Miller, on board the plane, helps Philbrick examine the contents to discover no bomb, just a small clock. Philbrick figures it to be a test, and he just failed since a special security seal was broken. The men repair the seal and return the dossier without any suspicion. At Headquarters, Philbrick is questioned numerous times and learns that he wasn't the only Commie with a ticking suitcase. Since

Marlowe's testimony is unimportant, there never was a bomb in any suitcase. An important job is coming up where members of the Party will be needed, who will follow orders faithful and loyal, without question, and having passed the test, will get the assignment.

TRIVIA: When Special Agent Jerry Dressler phones the airplane to contact Special Agent Miller, Dressler comments that Philbrick knows Morse code.

PRODUCTION NOTES: Three electricians, two stand-ins, four drivers, and six extras were needed for the first day of filming. All but the six extras were needed for the second day of filming. Two pix cars, a bus, and a camera and sound car were needed for both days of filming. Stock footage was used.

TOTAL CREW HOURS:	20
MAKE READY AND SHOOTING:	17 1/2 HOURS
TRAVEL TIME:	2 1/2 HOURS

LOCATION SHOTS:
INTERNATIONAL AIRPORT, INGLEWOOD, CA
AMERICAN AIRLINES
GRIFFITH PARK NEAR THE OBSERVATORY
2000 HILLHURST

EPISODE #48 "ATOMIC ANTIDOTE"
ORIGINAL COPYRIGHT FOR PRODUCTION #1048, NOVEMBER 20, 1954.
PRODUCTION # 1048 / 48B
OUTLINE, BY LEONARD HEIDERMAN
TYPESCRIPT (ANNOTATED), BY LEONARD HEIDERMAN, JULY 30, 1954
MASTER MIMEO (ANNOTATED), AUGUST 4, 1954
REVISED MASTER MIMEO, AUGUST 4, 1954
FILMED AUGUST 10 AND 11, 1954

CAST: Richard Carlson (Herbert A. Philbrick); John Zaremba

(Special Agent Jerry Dressler); William Justine (Jack Roscoe); Barbara Stuart (Martine Fenton); Robert E. Griffin (Roy Owens); and Adrienne Marden (Sally Owens).

PRODUCTION CREDITS

DIRECTOR:	HERBERT L. STROCK
PRODUCTION CHIEF:	HERBERT L. STROCK
FIRST ASSISTANT DIRECTOR:	JOSEPH WONDER
SECOND ASSISTANT DIRECTOR:	BOBBY RAY
FIRST CAMERAMAN:	ROBERT HOFFMAN
SECOND CAMERAMAN:	MONK ASKINS
FIRST ASSISTANT CAMERAMAN:	DICK RAWLINGS
SOUND MIXER:	GARY HARRIS
RECORDER:	BOB POST
BOOM MAN:	ELMER HAGLAND
FIRST COMPANY GRIP:	MEL BLEDSOE
PROPERTY MASTER:	VICTOR PETROTTA
ASSISTANT PROPERTY MAN:	BRUCE MCDONALD
SET DECORATOR:	LOU HAFLEY
SCRIPT SUPERVISOR:	LARRY LUND
FILM EDITOR:	ACE CLARK
GAFFER:	JOE WHARTON
SET LABOR:	PHIL CASAZZA
CONSTRUCTION CHIEF:	ARCHIE HALL

PLOT: Philbrick leaves town to Centerville to visit the farm of Roy and Sally Owens, who believe they have a way of keeping the U.S. from using Atomic weapons, thus making the country defenseless against an air attack. The Party is lacing the blame for bad weather and worse crops on the Atomic Energy Commission. Owens has been conducting a whispering campaign, succeeding in asking every farm family in the county to sign a petition to the Commission to stop all Atomic Bomb tests until a resolution can be made. Philbrick's job is to make a speech that will allow them to succeed in making their congressman sit up and take notice. The real reason for the failed crops is a drought that hits an all-time high, but that's no excuse to a "meeting of the minds." After their success, high-ranking Comrade Martine, who attended the voting, finds this method efficient and with a little sabotage across the country, she is certain that the same ploy would help cripple Atomic Weapon development throughout a national level. Back in town, Philbrick is handed the plans by Comrade Martine, and asked to review them and make a report that would reveal the success of her plan to higher authority. Back in town, Philbrick hands the plans to Dressler, who tells Herb that it just rained in Centerville—an act of God and Mother Nature foiling the Commies' plot.

Memorable Quote: Roy Owens explained to Herb: "People are afraid of what they don't understand. Atomic weapons are one thing they're plenty afraid of. Some of them think we're going to blow up the whole world. Others we're going to make the seas explode. But people around here . . . think that the big explosions change the weather."

Production Notes: One policeman, five drivers, one electrician, one stand-in and four extras were needed for the first day of filming. Three electricians, one stand-in, and three extras were needed for the second day of filming. Three picture cars, a bus, and a camera and sound car were needed for the first day of filming.

Total Crew Hours:	20
Make Ready and Shooting:	18 hours
Travel Time:	2 hours

Location Shots:
515 N. Larchmont
Larchmont and Beverly
10025 Farralone, Chatsworth
Devenshire and Farralone
Balboa and Devenshire

Episode #49 "DAY CAMP"

Original copyright for production #1049, November 27, 1954.

Production # 1049 / 49B
Typescript (annotated), by Robert Y. Libott, August 2, 1954
Master mimeo (annotated), August 8, 1954
Revised master mimeo, August 8, 1954
Revised pages (annotated), August 10, 1954
Filmed August 12 and 13, 1954

Cast: Richard Carlson (Herbert A. Philbrick); John Zaremba (Special Agent Jerry Dressler); Virginia Stefan (Eva Philbrick); Joan Lloyd (Betty Jane Masters); Ruth Robinson (Hilda Nettleton); Linda Stirling (Jeanette Lincoln); and Irving Mitchell (the stranger).

Production Credits

Director:	Leon Benson
Production Chief:	Leon Benson
First Assistant Director:	Don Verk
Second Assistant Director:	Bobby Ray
First Cameraman:	Robert Hoffman
Second Cameraman:	Monk Askins
First Assistant Cameraman:	Dick Rawlings
Sound Mixer:	Gary Harris
Recorder:	Bob Post
Boom Man:	Elmer Haglund and Jay Ashworth
First Company Grip:	Mel Bledsoe
Property Master:	Lyle Reifsnider
Set Decorator:	Lou Hafley
Script Supervisor:	Larry Lund
Wardrobe Man:	Al Berke
Film Editor:	Jack Woelz
Gaffer:	Joe Wharton
Construction Chief:	Archie Hall

Plot: When Philbrick takes Betty Jean Masters, the little girl who lives down the road, to the zoo, he meets up with Comrade Hilda, who suggests Philbrick take the girl to the Poconino Club, which offers everything a little girl needs—exercise, sports and instructions.

The Club is tied in with the Northwitch Foundation, which intrigues Herb and Eva, so the Philbricks visit the club personally, and with the approval of Betty Jean's father, induct Betty Jean into the day camp. As the days pass, Betty Jean starts acting different, even trying to raise money for the "oppressed, just like the Indians." Eva notices the change, and isn't very happy and threatens to blow the whole scam wide open if Herb doesn't get Betty Jean out of the club. The next day, before Eva states her position, Comrade Hilda explains to Herb that a member of the high-end review board is coming to the club to examine the project and give authorization for expansion on a national level. When Betty Jean is made to set an example, she uses "freedom" as the answer to why the Indians went West. The project is dismissed and Eva calms down, proud of Betty Jean. The next day, the Northwitch Foundation withdraws its support and the day camp folds.

COMMENTS: This episode fails on many levels. The set design for the camp doesn't look much like a camp except for a couple teepees and a picnic table (which was filmed, incidentally, at the Griffith Park baseball diamond). The premise is clever, but the way the Party set the system up isn't effective enough and even an eleven-year-old can figure by themselves that it wouldn't work. Comrade Hilda makes a lame excuse for her mistake, and anyone who comes up with a lame excuse like that shouldn't even be a member of the Party.

PRODUCTION NOTES: One fireman and truck, four drivers, one electrician, one stand-in, one welfare worker and six extras were needed for the first day of filming. Three electricians, one stand-in, and one welfare worker were needed for the second day of filming. Carlson's standby car, a 33-passenger bus, a camera and sound car, and a standby car and trailer were needed for the first day of filming.

TOTAL CREW HOURS:	22
MAKE READY AND SHOOTING:	20 1/2 HOURS
TRAVEL TIME:	1 1/2 HOURS

CASTING TRIVIA: Linda Stirling, who plays the role of Jeanette Lincoln in this episode, was previously under contract to Republic

Studios. She appeared in many cliffhanger serials, including the title role of The Black Whip in *Zorro's Black Whip* (1944).

Location Shots:

The scenes in the zoo were filmed on location at the Griffith Park Zoo. Other scenes in this episode were filmed on the Griffith Park baseball diamond.

Episode #50 "THE GUEST"

Original copyright for production #1050, December 4, 1954.
Production # 1050 / 50B
Typescript (annotated), by Arthur Fitz-Richard, August 13, 1954
Revised pages (annotated), August 17, 1954
Revised master mimeo, August 17, 1954
Filmed August 25 and 26, 1954

Cast: Richard Carlson (Herbert A. Philbrick); Virginia Stefan (Eva Philbrick); Pat Morrow (Constance Philbrick); John Beradino (Special Agent Steve Daniels); Les O'Pace (Joe MacKlin); and Tom McKee (Brissen Layloc).

Production Credits

Director:	Henry S. Kesler
Production Chief:	Henry S. Kesler
First Assistant Director:	Joseph Wonder
Second Assistant Director:	Bobby Ray
First Cameraman:	Curt Fetters
Second Cameraman:	Monk Askins
First Assistant Cameraman:	Dick Rawlings
Sound Mixer:	Gary Harris
Recorder:	Bob Post
Boom Man:	Elmer Haglund
First Company Grip:	Carl Miksch
Second Company Grip:	Colvy Kessinger (first day only)

PROPERTY MASTER: DON REDFORD
ASSISTANT PROPERTY MAN: VICTOR PETROTTA (FIRST DAY ONLY)
SET DECORATOR: LOU HAFLEY
WARDROBE MAN: AL BERKE
SCRIPT SUPERVISOR: LARRY LUND
FILM EDITOR: CHUCK CRAFT
GAFFER: JOE WHARTON
DIALOGUE DIRECTOR: EDDIE ANDERSON
CONSTRUCTION CHIEF: ARCHIE HALL

PLOT: Joe MacKlin was caught by the F.B.I. passing information to the Russians, but before he could testify, he skipped bail. Before Herb could take a weekend drive into the country, he finds himself assigned to tend a houseguest for the Party, Mr. MacKlin himself—who is dodging the F.B.I. long enough to escape the country. Comrade MacKlin makes himself at home, forcing Herb and Eva to feel like prisoners in their own home, preventing them from phoning the F.B.I. When Daniels phones the Philbrick residence, Herb answers the phone differently, and tells MacKlin that it was just a client on the other end. On the way to the airport, Philbrick tries everything he can to alert the authorities, including speeding, but fails every time. After helping MacKlin get to his plane, Herb meets up with Daniels, who explains the pilot works for the F.B.I.—the previous phone call was a successful tip-off. Thanks to the F.B.I.'s instant reaction to existing danger, this tale marked the beginning of the end of the unwelcome guest.

PRODUCTION NOTES: Three electricians, one motorcycle policeman, one driver, two stand-ins, and one welfare worker were needed for the first day of filming. One electrician, four drivers, two stand-ins, one welfare worker, and two extras were needed for the second day of filming. Philbrick's car was needed for both days of filming. A 33-passenger bus, Daniels' car, and a camera and sound car (and a trailer for props, no driver) were needed for the second day of filming.

TOTAL CREW HOURS: 20
MAKE READY AND SHOOTING: 17 1/2 HOURS
TRAVEL TIME: 2 1/2 HOURS

Location Shots:
Selma and Cahuenga
Hollywood Blvd. and Cahuenga
Santa Fe Bus Terminal, 1735 N. Cahuenga Blvd.
267 South Lafayette Park Place
Glendale School of Aeronautics (airport)
Griffith Park (near Roger Young Village)

Episode #51 "CHARITY"
Production # 1051 / 51B
Typescript (annotated), by Donn Mullally and Baruch J. Cohon, August 17, 1954
Master mimeo, August 24, 1954
Filmed August 31 and September 1, 1955

Cast: Richard Carlson (Herbert A. Philbrick); Virginia Stefan (Eva Philbrick); John Zaremba (Special Jerry Dressler); Joan Miller (Irene); Alan Reynolds (Jack Blake); and Stuart Nedd (Walker).

Production Credits

Director:	Leon Benson
Production Chief:	Leon Benson
First Assistant Director:	Eddie Stein
Second Assistant Director:	Harry Jones
First Cameraman:	Curt Fetters
Second Cameraman:	Monk Askins
First Assistant Cameraman:	Dick Rawlings
Sound Mixer:	Jay Ashworth
Recorder:	Larry Golding
Boom Man:	Bill Flannery
First Company Grip:	Carl Miksch
Property Master:	Victor Petrotta
Set Decorator:	Lou Hafley
Wardrobe Man:	Al Berke
Script Supervisor:	Phil Casazza
Film Editor:	Chuck Craft

Gaffer: Lou Cotese
Construction Chief: Archie Hall

Plot: The Communist Party does not believe in Church or God, and therefore Christmas also, except when they can turn it to their advantage. Comrade Irene explains to Philbrick that a whole slew of telephone salesmen will call around representing the "All Faith's United Christmas Fund," claiming to be endorsed by every church in the community. Philbrick is assigned to organize the leg men who go out to gather the donations. Philbrick shrewdly phones Agent Jerry Dressler instead of a customer on the list, and gives him the pitch. Before the next day's worth of phone calls, Agent Dressler arranges for a microphone to be hidden in the room and as Philbrick repeats the addresses, Dressler phones the victims in advance and tells them not to give the pledge, because of a holiday racket. When Comrade Jack, one of the leg men, returned to report the bad news, a very irate Comrade Irene insists on meeting some of the pledges. Choosing a page out of random (one supplied by the F.B.I., planted by Philbrick), she visits each of them to learn from the victims that they already gave the money, and Comrade Irene accuses Comrade Jack of stealing the money himself—especially with a dummy bank register planted by Philbrick. When the Party learns of the failure of the project, Comrade Irene will be drummed out of the Party, and Comrade Jack will take the blame—while the real money accidentally falls into the hands of the local Community Chest Fund.

Comments: When Comrade Jack discusses with Philbrick his preoccupation for trimming the Christmas tree, he comments how "germane to the whole concept of class revolt." Though not a perfect Christmas episode by any means (the lack of Christmas music substantiates this), the program's only holiday story is above average as Special Agent Jerry Dressler and Herbert Philbrick destroy the Party's racket by posing as a Christmas charity.

Production Notes: Three electricians, one policeman, one fireman, four drivers, two extras and two stand-ins were needed for the first day of filming. Three electricians, two stand-ins, and five extras were needed for the second day of filming. A 33-passenger bus, Philbrick's car, a car to pull trailer for electrical equipment, and a camera and a sound car were needed for the first day of filming.

Location Shots:
Building at 5757 Wilshire, Prudential Building
Ext. street corner, opposite the Prudential building
Interior of Bus Depot, 1735 North Cahuenga, Continental Trailways
Exterior apartment house, Lido apartments, Yucca and Wilcox

Episode #52 "NARCOTICS"
Production # 1052 / 52B
Typescript (annotated), by Stuart Jerome, August 23, 1954
Master mimeo (annotated), August 30, 1954
Revised master mimeo, August 30, 1954
Revised pages, August 31, 1954
Filmed September 3 and 4, 1954

Cast: Richard Carlson (Herbert A. Philbrick); Phil Pine (Jonathan Robinson); Nesdon Booth (Comrade Baker); Bobker Ben Ali (Steiger); John Zaremba (Special Agent Jerry Dressler); Fred Sherman (Mr. Hurley); and Charlotte Lawrence (Carol).

Production Credits

Director:	Henry S. Kesler
Production Chief:	Henry S. Kesler
First Assistant Director:	Joseph Wonder
Second Assistant Director:	Bobby Ray
First Cameraman:	Robert Hoffman
Second Cameraman:	Monk Askins
First Assistant Cameraman:	Dick Rawlings
Sound Mixer:	Gary Harris

Recorder:	Bob Post
Boom Man:	Elmer Haglund
First Company Grip:	Mel Bledsoe
Property Master:	Lyle Reifsnider
Set Decorator:	Lou Hafley
Wardrobe Man:	Al Berke
Script Supervisor:	Larry Lund
Film Editor:	Jack Woelz
Gaffer:	Joe Wharton
Construction Chief:	Archie Hall

Plot: Comrade Robinson explains how the Commies have recently acquired a huge shipment of opium narcotics, which control the decision-making of many juvenile delinquents. Philbrick's new assignment is to help strategically devise a mail order catalog that looks legit, yet hides within the pages a secret code so buyers can buy the opium. Philbrick is not told how the code works, but merely creates the layout for the catalog itself. After they succeed in devising the catalogs, the material is printed and distributed. But weeks later, when Comrade Robinson becomes addicted to the narcotics, he poses a risk and before being asked to leave the Party, is ordered to give the secret on how to decode the catalog, which reveals all of the locations and names of the pushers on the streets. Before the remaining catalogs can be destroyed, Philbrick overhears Robinson reveal the code, and quickly meets up with Agent Dressler to give him the information. Since the F.B.I. already has a catalog in their possession, they'll use the code to arrest each drug dealer off the streets one-by-one.

Production Notes: Three electricians, one motorcycle policeman, three drivers, two stand-ins, and four extras were needed for the first day of filming. Three electricians, one extra and two stand-ins were needed for the second day of filming. Philbrick's car, a 33-passenger bus, and a camera and sound car were needed for the first day of filming.

Total Crew Hours:	20
Make Ready and Shooting:	18 hours
Travel Time:	2 hours

Location Shots:
Ocean Park Pier
Street shots around Hollywood

Episode #53 "FIFTH AMENDMENT"

Production # 1053 / 53B
Typescript (annotated), by Donn Mullally, September 2, 1954
Master mimeo, September 2, 1954
Filmed September 10 and 11, 1954

Cast: Richard Carlson (Herbert A. Philbrick); Virginia Stefan (Eva Philbrick); John Zaremba (Special Agent Jerry Dressler); Carlyle Mitchell (Clay Jennings); John Fell (Comrade Rickard); and Ken Duncan (the unseen Comrade X).

Production Credits

Director:	Herbert L. Strock
Production Chief:	Herbert L. Strock
First Assistant Director:	Joseph Wonder
Second Assistant Director:	Lester Burke
First Cameraman:	Curt Fetters
Second Cameraman:	Monk Askins (first day only)
First Assistant Cameraman:	Dick Rawlings
Sound Mixer:	Gary Harris (first day only)
Sound Mixer:	Jay Ashworth (second day only)
Recorder:	Bob Post (first day only)
Recorder:	Larry Golding (second day only)
Boom Man:	Elmer Haglund (first day only)
Boom Man:	Bill Flannery (second day only)
First Company Grip:	Mel Bledsloe (first day only)

FIRST COMPANY GRIP:	CARL MIKSCH (SECOND DAY ONLY)
SECOND COMPANY GRIP:	WALTER CULP
PROPERTY MASTER:	MAX PITTMAN
SET DECORATOR:	LOU HAFLEY
WARDROBE MAN:	AL BERKE
SCRIPT SUPERVISOR:	PHIL CASAZZA
GAFFER:	JOE WHARTON
CONSTRUCTION CHIEF:	ARCHIE HALL

PLOT: The Committee on Subversive Action has subpoenaed Clay Jennings, a former member of the Communist Party, in hopes he'll testify regarding his twelve-month stint in the Party. If he testifies, he'll be forced to "name names"—including Herbert Philbrick. During a private meeting with Comrade X, a higher authority in the Party, Philbrick is ordered to convince Jennings to accept the Fifth Amendment. Special Agent Dressler of the F.B.I. makes arrangements for Jennings not to testify, to save their counterspy, but Herb insists otherwise. Snooping around, Herb discovers the identity of Comrade X. It turns out he is one of the most valuable assets to the Party, and Jennings can identify him by name—a Comrade reported to be dead some time ago. Realizing how important Comrade X is to the Party, Philbrick insists on personally delivering a message to the Comrade, giving Dressler and his men ample chance to follow and trace down the residence. Dressler succeeds and later tells Herb that Comrade X, alias James Eaton, will be tailed for a few weeks to get an idea of what his activities are, and more importantly, since they can later apprehend Comrade X, Jennings' testimony will not be needed—thus saving Philbrick from being named.

PRODUCTION NOTES: Three electricians, one motorcycle policeman, five drivers, one stand-in, and three extras were needed for the first day of filming. Three electricians, one stand-in, and three extras were needed for the second day of filming. Agent's car, a 33-passenger bus, two cars, and a camera and sound car were needed for the first day of filming.

TOTAL CREW HOURS: 20

Make Ready and Shooting: 19 hours
Travel Time: 1 hour

Trivia, Etc. Robert Hoffman was originally supposed to be the first cameraman during the second day of filming, but Curt Fetters took the position that day.

Location Shots:
267 South Lafayette Park Place
5511 Melrose Ave.
341 South Lafayette Park Place
6th and Occidental
6th and Lafayette Park Place
2628 West 6th Street

Episode #54 "REST HOME"
Production # 1054 / 54B
Typescript (annotated), by Jack Rock, September 2, 1954
Master mimeo, September 2, 1954
Filmed September 13 and 14, 1954

Cast: Richard Carlson (Herbert A. Philbrick); Herbert C. Lytton (Comrade Monroe); Ed Hinton (Special Agent Hal Henderson); William Hudson (Special Agent Mike Andrews); Laurie Mitchell (Mrs. Phyllis Britton); Harry Cody (Comrade Adams); Thom Carney (Martin); and Edward Earle (Randall).

Plot: Philbrick is taken to a rest home secretly operated by the Communist Party, and asked to pose as a patient recovering from headache attacks. The ploy is designed to be very convincing to millionaire Randall Milton, a former business acquaintance of Philbrick's, whose company is shipping various raw materials abroad. Since the Party wants to know when and where the materials are leaving, they hope by having Philbrick confide to Mr. Milton that the best cure for relieving headaches is to relieve information stored in the head. Philbrick thinks the idea won't work but as time passes, he begins to suspect it will. He tries to get word to the F.B.I. in hopes they might interfere. Meanwhile, worried the plan isn't working quickly enough, the Party accidentally drugs Mr. Milton too much, and the millionaire collapses. The F.B.I. arrives, posing as Health Inspectors, investigates the scene and arranges for Milton's transfer to the County Hospital. As for the guilty parties, they accidentally revealed their plot in the same room that concealed their own microphone, giving the F.B.I. evidence they need to convict.

Production Credits

Director:	Eddie Davis
Production Chief:	Eddie Davis
First Assistant Director:	George Loper
First Cameraman:	Robert Hoffman
Second Cameraman:	Charles Straumer
First Assistant Cameraman:	Jimmy Weston
Sound Mixer:	Jay Ashworth
Recorder:	Larry Golding
Boom Man:	Bill Flannery
First Company Grip:	Mel Bledsloe
Second Company Grip:	Walter Culp
Property Master:	Walter Culp
Set Decorator:	Lou Hafley
Wardrobe Man:	Al Berke
Script Supervisor:	Phil Casazza
Film Editor:	Jack Woelz
Gaffer:	S.H. Barton
Construction Chief:	Archie Hall

Production Notes: One bus and four stand-ins were required for this episode.

Total Crew Hours:	20
Make Ready and Shooting:	19 1/2 hours
Travel Time:	1/2 hour

Location Shots:

341 So. Layfayette Park Place

6th and Layfayette Park Place
6th and Occidental
2628 West 6th Street

Trivia: Episode #63 of the ZIV-produced radio program, *I Was a Communist for the F.B.I.*, entitled "Fifteen Minutes to Murder," featured a similar Communist scheme where Matt Cvetic, a counterspy, is ordered to visit a rest home and help assist in the murder of an F.B.I. agent. For this television episode, the plot was taken from this radio broadcast, only the means of why Philbrick was sent to the rest home was more realistic than murdering a Federal Agent.

Episode #55 "DEPORTATION"
Production # 1055 / 55B
Typescript (annotated), by Robert Yale Libott, September 8, 1954
Revised pages (annotated), September 14, 1954
Revised master mimeo, September 14, 1954
Filmed September 16 and 17, 1954

Cast: Richard Carlson (Herbert A. Philbrick); Cyril Delevanti (Comrade Valentine); Robert B. Williams (Comrade Joe Garth); Helen Mowery (Comrade Elena Moretz); Joy Lansing (the salesgirl); John Zaremba (Special Agent Jerry Dressler); and Ed Hinton (Special Agent Hal Henderson).

Production Credits

Director:	Leon Benson
Production Chief:	Leon Benson
First Assistant Director:	Joseph Wonder
First Cameraman:	Robert Hoffman
Second Cameraman:	Charles Straumer
First Assistant Cameraman:	Jim Weston
Sound Mixer:	Jay Ashworth
Recorder:	Larry Golding

Boom Man:	Bill Flannery
First Company Grip:	Mel Bledsloe
Second Company Grip:	Walter Culp
Property Master:	Leyle Reifsnider
Assistant Property Man:	Stan Walters
Set Decorator:	Lou Hafley
Script Supervisor:	Phil Casazza
Film Editor:	Duncan Mansfield, A.C.E
Gaffer:	S.H. Barton
Construction Chief:	Archie Hall

Plot: Comrade Joe Garth asks Philbrick to tail a woman named Elena who is spending her last day in America. Elena, however, proves to be a challenge as she is fully aware she is being followed and tricks Philbrick by giving him the slip. Reading a front-page newspaper, Philbrick discovers that Elena has been ordered to leave the U.S. for engaging with espionage activities. When Philbrick returns to Garth to report, he is informed that Comrade Elena is smuggling something out of the country and Philbrick is assigned to find her and retrieve her purse before she leaves. Special Agent Dressler keeps her in customs for a time while Philbrick explains the problem. During a "routine" in customs, Dressler and Philbrick find microfilm hidden in her lipstick and quickly photograph the negatives. Later, when the film is developed, Philbrick learns that the microfilm contains an efficiency report on known Communists, including a poor evaluation on Comrade Garth, and a good report on Philbrick.

Trivia, Etc. In this episode, Philbrick mentions he has a wife and five children. Yet only two children were ever seen on the television series!

Production Notes: Three electricians, one motorcycle policeman, four drivers, one fireman, one airport gendarme, six extras, and one stand-in were needed for the first day of filming. Three electricians, one driver, a camera car, and one stand-in were needed for the second day of filming. Carlson's car, a 33-passenger bus, a standby car, and a camera car were needed for the first day of filming.

Total Crew Hours:	22
Make Ready and Shooting:	20 hours
Travel Time:	2 hours

Location Shots:

International Airport, Pan American Section
Jewelry Store, 1009 1/2 North Western
Billy's Dress Shop, Western and Sunset
Alleyway at 1117 North Western
Corner of Bronson and Melrose

Episode #56 "THE SWITCH"

Production # 1056 / 56B
Typescript (annotated), by Rik Vollaerts, September 10, 1954
Master mimeo (annotated), September 14, 1954
Revised master mimeo, September 14, 1954
Filmed September 18 and 19, 1954

Cast: Richard Carlson (Herbert A. Philbrick); Charles Victor (Comrade Dan Burt); John Beradino (Special Agent Steve Daniels); Merritt Stone (Comrade Mitch); Gene Gilbert (Marion Lancing); Virginia Stefan (Eva Philbrick); and John Breed (Comrade Long).

Production Credits

Director:	Henry S. Kesler
Production Chief:	Henry S. Kesler
First Assistant Director:	Don Verk
First Cameraman:	Curt Fetters
Second Cameraman:	Harry Underwood (first day only)
Second Cameraman:	Charles Straumer (second day only)
First Assistant Cameraman:	Max Wook
Sound Mixer:	Jay Ashworth

RECORDER:	BILL FLANNERY
BOOM MAN:	WALTER TEAGUE (FIRST DAY ONLY)
FIRST COMPANY GRIP:	CARL MIKSCH
PROPERTY MASTER:	VICTOR PETROTTA
SET DECORATOR:	LOU HAFLEY
WARDROBE MAN:	AL BERKE
SCRIPT SUPERVISOR:	PHIL CASAZZA
FILM EDITOR:	JACK WOELZ
GAFFER:	S.H. BARTON
CONSTRUCTION CHIEF:	ARCHIE HALL

PLOT: During a special cell meeting, Comrade Dan Burt asks Philbrick to help choose an expendable Comrade in the Party as a plant for the F.B.I. The scheme is foolproof. One Comrade will visit the F.B.I., announce that they are a Communist, have seen the ways, and is willing to report to the Bureau all knowledge they have and to become a possible counterspy. This way the Party has an informant inside the Federal Agency and can have access to a list of real counterspies. For Philbrick, this could mean trouble. Herb explains the plan to Special Agent Daniels, who says he'll handle the situation in due course. After evaluating the deadwood among the Party cells, Philbrick is shocked to discover that Dan Burt will go himself—and with the papers Philbrick prepared selecting which cells are unimportant to the Party. Believing that his name will also appear in the newspapers, Philbrick prepares for the worst—and is shocked when he learns that Comrade Burt was laughed at when he entered the F.B.I., and Comrade Mitch assumed the plan would fail and moves up the ranks as Comrade Burt is escorted out by Party security.

PRODUCTION NOTES: Three electricians, one motorcycle policeman, four drivers, four extras and two stand-ins were needed for the first day of filming. Three electricians, and two stand-ins, were needed for the second day of filming. A Commie's car, a 33-passenger bus, Philbrick's car, and a camera & sound car were needed for the first day of filming.

TOTAL CREW HOURS: 20

Make Ready and Shooting: 18 1/2 hours
Travel Time: 1 1/2 hours

Location Shots:
267 Lafayette Park Place
2775 North Highland Ave.
6087 Sunset Blvd.
569 North Rossmore
Corner of Melrose & Windsor

Episode #57 "SERVICEMEN"
Production # 1057 / 57B
Typescript (annotated), by Leonard Heiderman, September 14, 1954
Revised pages (annotated), September 22, 1954
Revised master mimeo, September 22, 1954
Filmed September 23 and 24, 1954

Cast: Richard Carlson (Herbert A. Philbrick); Bill Boyett (Special Agent Bob Marshall); Dick Kaiser (Bud Hanson); Jarma Lewis (Cecil Davis); and Eleanor Moore (Comrade Myra Houk).

Production Credits
Director: Leon Benson
Production Chief: Leon Benson
First Assistant Director: Joseph Wonder
Second Assistant Director: Bobby Ray
First Cameraman: Robert Hoffman
Second Cameraman: Monk Askins
First Assistant Cameraman: Dick Rawlings
Sound Mixer: Gary Harris
Recorder: Bob Post
Boom Man: Elmer Haglund
First Company Grip: Mel Bledsoe
Property Master: Ygnacio Sepulveda
Set Decorator: Lou Hafley

Wardrobe Man:	Al Berke
Script Supervisor:	Larry Lund
Film Editor:	Ace Clark
Gaffer:	Joe Wharton
Construction Chief:	Archie Hall

Plot: "Sweethearts for Servicemen" is based on a simple idea: lonely servicemen returning from the front enjoy pretty eye candy. Comrade Myra explains to Philbrick that all of the women in the program are Communists and since men trust anything with a pretty face and a gentle voice—the Party assumes the plan will be a success by infiltrating servicemen. At the very least, the plan will give them military information about clothing issues, vaccines, and orientation courses. Philbrick is assigned to help educate and motivate the women, and at the same time, he attempts to gather all of the addresses of the women in this program to hand over to the F.B.I. Philbrick also attempts to protect serviceman Bud Hanson, a soon-to-be victim, who holds guided missile defense plans, and almost gets caught in the act by Comrade Myra. Instead, Philbrick does the best he can under the circumstances—by gathering fingerprints of all the women in the "Sweethearts" club. Special Agent Marshall informed Philbrick that they informed Hanson the other day, and planted the fake plans on purpose—with the cooperation of Hanson.

Production Notes: One electrician, one motorcycle policeman, four drivers, one extra and one stand-in were needed for the first day of filming. Three electricians, one stand-in, and four extras were needed for the second day of filming. Cecil Davis' car, a 33-passenger bus, Philbrick's car, and a camera and sound car were needed for the first day of filming. A motorcycle cop was featured during the first day of filming.

Total Crew Hours:	22 hours
Make Ready and Shooting:	20 1/2 hours
Travel Time:	1 1/2 hours

Trivia, Etc. This was the first of two episodes to feature Bill Boyett as Agent Bob Marshall. The other was the next episode,

"Asylum." Philbrick uses his alias, "Arthur Trowbridge," for this episode, an alias he uses on rare occasions during the series. The scenes outside of Myra Houk's house (including the garden) are actually Richard Carlson's own house, located 3827 Holly Lane in Sherman Oaks!

Location Shots:
Along Ventura Blvd.
Telephone Company, corner of Kester & Ventura
Hot Dog Stand, corner of Sepulveda & Ventura

Episode #58 "ASYLUM"
Production # 1058 / 58B
Typescript (annotated), by Richard G. Taylor, September 18, 1954
Revised pages (annotated), ca. September 24, 1954
Revised master mimeo, September 24, 1954
Filmed September 28 and 29, 1954

Cast: Richard Carlson (Herbert A. Philbrick); Bill Boyett (Special Agent Bob Marshall); Angie Dickinson (Comrade Margaret); William Hudson (Special Agent Mike Andrews); Anthony Jochim (Comrade Ashley); Dehl Berti (Comrade Alfred); and Harvey Dunn (the photography clerk).

Production Credits

Director:	Herbert L. Strock
Production Chief:	Herbert L. Strock
First Assistant Director:	Joseph Wonder
Second Assistant Director:	Bobby Ray
First Cameraman:	Curt Fetters
Second Cameraman:	Monk Askins
First Assistant Cameraman:	Dick Rawlings
Sound Mixer:	Gary Harris
Recorder:	Bob Post
Boom Man:	Elmer Haglund

First Company Grip:	Carl Miksch
Property Master:	Victor Petrotta
Set Decorator:	Lou Hafley
Wardrobe Man:	Al Berke
Script Supervisor:	Larry Lund
Film Editor:	Duncan Mansfield, A.C.E
Gaffer:	Joe Wharton
Set Director:	Sal Inverso
Construction Chief:	Archie Hall

Plot: Philbrick meets with Comrade Margaret, who assigns him the task of delivering a wristwatch camera to Comrade Alfred in Newton Springs. Alfred can deliver the camera to an inside man who manages to be in a position to photograph valuable documents at a defense plant. When Philbrick informs Special Agent Marshall, the F.B.I. suggests switching the wristwatch with one that had radioactive material inside. This way, when the Comrade wears the watch, janitors in the plant can seek out the guilty Party with a Geiger counter. When Comrade Margaret attempts to change plans for security reasons, Philbrick risks his loyalty to the Party, and the secret plans to route out the Commie Agent. Quick thinking on Philbrick's behalf helps the F.B.I. in succeeding, thus using the defense plant worker as Red Bait to route out other spies in defense plants.

Production Notes: One electrician, one policeman, five drivers, three extras and two stand-ins were needed on the first day of filming. Three electricians, and two stand-ins, and one extra were needed on the second day of filming. Marshall's car, a bus, Philbrick's car, a laundry truck, and a camera & sound car were needed for the first day of filming.

Total Crew Hours:	20
Make Ready and Shooting:	18 1/2 hours
Travel Time:	1 1/2 hours

Location Shots:

Street & running shots were filmed in the vicinity of 15800 Valley Vista.

Lot Coffee Shot, 5429 Melrose
The scenes outside the photo shop were filmed on location at a real photo shop located at Beverly and Fairfax.
12908 Magnolia
16117 Ventura

◆ ❖ ◆

Episode #59 "MOVING"
Production # 1059 / 59B
Typescript by Stuart Jerome, September 17, 1954
Revised pages (annotated), October 1, 1954
Revised master mimeo, October 1, 1954
Filmed October 2 and 3, 1954

Cast: Richard Carlson (Herbert A. Philbrick); Grace Lenard (Comrade Norma); Virginia Stephan (Eva Philbrick); Pat Morrow (Constance Philbrick); Jeri Weil (Dale Philbrick); Ed Hinton (Special Agent Hal Henderson); and Howard Hoffman (Mr. Kopp).

Production Credits

Director:	Herbert L. Strock
Production Chief:	Herbert L. Strock
First Assistant Director:	Eddie Stein
Second Assistant Director:	Bobby Ray
First Cameraman:	Curt Fetters
Second Cameraman:	Monk Askins
First Assistant Cameraman:	Dick Rawlings
Sound Mixer:	Gary Harris
Recorder:	Bob Post
Boom Man:	Elmer Haglund
First Company Grip:	Carl Miksch
Second Company Grip:	Mel Bledsoe
Property Master:	Ygnacio Sepulveda
Assistant Property Man:	Victor Petrotta
Set Decorator:	Lou Hafley
Script Supervisor:	Larry Lund

Film Editor:	Tom Scott
Gaffer:	Joe Wharton
Set Director:	Sal Inverso
Construction Chief:	Archie Hall

Plot: Philbrick's new assignment is going to affect his entire family. A new cell needs to be established in the middle-class neighborhood of Rexford, and Philbrick has been assigned to be the colonizer. This means moving into a new house, and out of the old one. When he confronts Eva, she is supportive, even encouraging the children, who already feel their father has been neglecting them. Herb appeals to Agent Henderson, who suggests he go along with the idea—this might just be another loyalty test. Eva's patience, however, is tested when Comrade Norma barges into the decision making—choosing the house they will live in. Herb doesn't mind the new house too much since there is space enough for a hidden room for which he can continue his work. After the Philbricks move into the new house, Comrade Norma walks in without invitation and almost catches Philbrick working on the secret room. When Comrade Norma orders Eva to choose a certain style of furniture, Eva decides enough is enough and stands her ground, putting Comrade Norma in her place—reminding her that a woman's house is a woman's choosing. As for Philbrick's children, they enjoy their new quarters and new friends.

Comments: Although this episode does meet up with the program's title, the suspense is very minimal and the F.B.I.'s involvement is almost not required except for padding the story and wasting film. The premise, however, allows for a transition since two future episodes, "Minority Control" and "Camera" make reference to Philbrick's new surroundings and the purchase of his new home.

The production, however, is above average. Emotions, especially Eva's, are demonstrated in a key scene. After Eva supports her husband's decision, he exits the room leaving her at the desk and typewriter. The camera only picks up a head shot but the sound of her hitting the keys on the typewriter twice and then ringing the bell before covering her head with her hands suggested her true opinion regarding the move to a new house.

Memorable Quote: Philbrick, when commenting to Eva why he wanted to resign from the F.B.I.: "There are a lot of reasons. I'm tired of being told what to do and what not to do. I'm tired of seeing disappointment on my kids' faces. I'm tired of seeing fear on your face."

Production Notes: Three electricians, one policeman, five drivers, two extras, one welfare worker, and one stand-in were needed for the first day of filming. Equipment needed: Henderson's car, a bus, Philbrick's car, a moving van, and a camera and sound car for the first day of filming. One stand-in was needed on the second day of filming.

Total Crew Hours: 20
Make Ready and Shooting: 19 hours
Travel Time: 1 hour

Location Shots:

The exteriors of Philbrick's new house were really a house located at 85 Westchester Place and owned by a woman named Mrs. Young. Scenes in the antique shop were filmed on location at Mr. Berardini's Antique Shop, located at 5451 Santa Monica. Exteriors of Philbrick's old house were filmed on location at 169 South Lafayette Place. The chase scenes were filmed in the vicinity of St. Andrews and San Marino Streets.

Episode #60 "MAILING LIST"

Production # 1060 / 60B
Typescript (annotated), by Arthur Fitz-Richard, October 2, 1954
Revised master mimeo, October 12, 1954
Filmed October 15 and 16, 1954

Cast: Richard Carlson (Herbert A. Philbrick); Austin Green (Comrade Mike Ferris / Joe); Alan Reynolds (Comrade Jack Blake); George Berkeley (Comrade Paul, the janitor); Tyler McVey (Miles

Brophy); Charles Seel (Saunders); and John Zaremba (Special Agent Jerry Dressler).

Production Credits

Director:	Leon Benson
Production Chief:	Leon Benson
First Assistant Director:	Eddie Stein
Second Assistant Director:	Bobby Ray
First Cameraman:	Curt Fetters
Second Cameraman:	Monk Askins
First Assistant Cameraman:	Dick Rawlings
Sound Mixer:	Gary Harris
Recorder:	Bob Post
Boom Man:	Elmer Haglund
First Company Grip:	Carl Miksch
Second Company Grip:	Mel Bledsoe
Property Master:	Max Pittman
Set Decorator:	Lou Hafley
Wardrobe Man:	Al Berke
Script Supervisor:	Larry Lund
Film Editor:	Jack Woelz
Gaffer:	Joe Wharton
Set Director:	Sal Inverso
Construction Chief:	Archie Hall

Plot: Comrade Jack Blake explains to Philbrick the importance of infiltrating the Brotherhood of Aviation Craftsman. An election will be held four weeks from today. Miles Brophy, a fascist dictator in the eyes of the Commies, needs to be undermined so the Reds can elect a shop steward in the Union. They already have one of their men nominated, but in order for the plan to succeed, Philbrick must first acquire the B.A.C. mailing list. A smear campaign using a simple mailing suggesting Brophy lose the election for the benefit of all, and applied just a day before the election, would mean Brophy has no chance of defending himself before the election. Philbrick accomplishes this task with ease and is then asked to fix the plate machine used to address the envelopes, putting him in good standing with the Comrades. Special Agent

Jerry Dressler, in a shrewd tactic, arranges for the arrest of Comrade Mike as a result of the mailing list purchase—which really won't prove beneficial since the Comrades were sold a bad list anyway.

Production Notes: Three electricians and two stand-ins were needed on the first day of filming. Three electricians, one policeman, one fireman, four drivers, two stand-ins, and three extras were needed on the second day of filming. Comrade Blake's car, a 33-passenger bus, Philbrick's car, and a camera & sound car were needed for the second day of filming.

Total Crew Hours:	22
Make Ready and Shooting:	20 1/2 hours
Travel Time:	1 1/2 hours

Location Shots:
DeLongpre Park, DeLongpre and Cherokee
Phlibrick's new house was a real house at 858 Westchester Place
Taft Building, Vine and Hollywood Blvd.

Episode #61 "CAMERA"
Production # 1061 / 61B
Typescript (annotated), by Ellis Marcus, October 1, 1954
Revised pages (annotated), October 5, 1954
Revised master mimeo, October 5, 1954
Filmed October 7 and 8, 1954

Cast: Richard Carlson (Herbert A. Philbrick); Harlan Warde (Comrade Dave); Butler Hixon (Comrade Chester Lang); Gail Bonney (Comrade Bess); Virginia Stephan (Eva Philbrick); Leo Needham (Comrade Alec); and John Beradino (Special Agent Steve Daniels).

Production Credits

Director:	Leon Benson
Production Chief:	Leon Benson

FIRST ASSISTANT DIRECTOR:	DON VERK
SECOND ASSISTANT DIRECTOR:	BOBBY RAY
FIRST CAMERAMAN:	ROBERT HOFFMAN
SECOND CAMERAMAN:	MONK ASKINS
FIRST ASSISTANT CAMERAMAN:	DICK RAWLINGS
SOUND MIXER:	GARY HARRIS
RECORDER:	BOB POST
BOOM MAN:	ELMER HAGLUND
FIRST COMPANY GRIP:	MEL BLEDSOE
PROPERTY MASTER:	YGNACIO SEPULVEDA
ASSISTANT PROPERTY MAN:	VICTOR PETROTTA
SET DECORATOR:	LOU HAFLEY
SCRIPT SUPERVISOR:	LARRY LUND
GAFFER:	JOE WHARTON
SET DIRECTOR:	SAL INVERSO
CONSTRUCTION CHIEF:	ARCHIE HALL

PLOT: Comrade Dave and Herb compile a report on the past year's activities and deliver it to Comrade Chester Lang's house. At the house, Philbrick notices a large number of important Party figures and takes advantage of the opportunity by filming them together with his new movie camera—using the colonial architecture of the house as his excuse. After handing the film to Special Agent Steve Daniels, Comrade Bess orders Philbrick to bring her the roll of film. Realizing he must have captured someone of great importance, he contacts Agent Daniels—avoiding Comrade Alex following him—and assigns names to the photos for Agent Daniels (except for one man in particular). Obviously the unknown man is the key to the mystery, but Philbrick is completely baffled as to his identity. Taking the film back to Comrade Bess, Philbrick cleverly tells her that he was followed while retrieving the film from the developer, but as any good Party member, was able to shake them off her tail. Back in her good graces, Philbrick leaves playing the victim to Comrade Dave, who apparently knew what was going on the entire time, and Dave, attempting to gain Philbrick's confidence, gives him the details of the mysterious man who is really a chemical engineer and disloyal defense plant manager.

PRODUCTION NOTES: Three electricians, one policeman, three drivers, four extras and two stand-ins were needed on the first day of filming. Three electricians, and two stand-ins, and one extra were needed on the second day of filming. A bus, Philbrick's car, and a camera and sound car were needed for the first day of filming.

TOTAL CREW HOURS: 22
MAKE READY AND SHOOTING: 21 HOURS
TRAVEL TIME: 1 HOUR

PRODUCTION TRIVIA: The real Herb Philbrick was a camera fan and often filmed events and people during his outings, whenever he had the opportunity. This episode was based on this fact. Those motion pictures were processed and turned over to the F.B.I. for identification of members—all the members who didn't persistently turn their backs to the lens.

LOCATION SHOTS:
FILM SERVICE LAB, 6327 SANTA MONICA BLVD.
STREET SHOTS WITHIN THE VICINITY OF VINE STREET, BETWEEN SANTA MONICA AND SUNSET BLVD.
CHESTER HOUSE, 3959 LONGRIDGE AVE.

EPISODE #62 "MINORITY CONTROL"
PRODUCTION # 1062 / 62B
TYPESCRIPT (ANNOTATED), BY JACK ROCK, N.D.
MASTER MIMEO, OCTOBER 11, 1954
MASTER MIMEO (ANNOTATED), N.D.
REVISED PAGES (ANNOTATED), N.D.
FILMED OCTOBER 13 AND 14, 1954

CAST: Richard Carlson (Herbert A. Philbrick); William Hudson (Special Agent Mike Andrews); Frank Fowler (Comrade Farrell Ames); Darlene Fields (Comrade Lucille); Junius Mathews (Comrade Felix); William Neff (Joe); and Harry Hickox (the president).

Production Credits

Production Chief:	Herbert L. Strock
Director:	Herbert L. Strock
First Assistant Director:	Joseph Wonder
Second Assistant Director:	Bobby Ray
First Cameraman:	Curt Fetters
Second Cameraman:	Monk Askins
First Assistant Cameraman:	Dick Rawlings
Sound Mixer:	Gary Harris
Recorder:	Bob Post
Boom Man:	Elmer Haglund
First Company Grip:	Carl Miksch
Second Company Grip:	Mel Bledsoe
Property Master:	Ygnacio Sepulveda
Assistant Property Man:	Victor Petrotta
Set Decorator:	Lou Hafley
Script Supervisor:	Larry Lund
Film Editor:	Jack Woelz
Gaffer:	Joe Wharton
Set Director:	Sal Inverso
Construction Chief:	Archie Hall

Plot: Comrade Farrell Ames tells Philbrick that they are closing Party Headquarters. With growing suspicions among the police here in the States and empty stomachs back at the homeland, the Party is going underground. Their latest plan is to take control of all institutions—civil, political and industrial. Their first target is the Tax Payer's Alliance, which Philbrick is assigned to apply for membership and get familiar with their bylaws. Comrade Farrell also joins the Alliance, and almost immediately requests one of the bylaws to be changed. Instead of the 40% membership requirement for a quorum, he wants any members regardless of the percentage, to allow a change to policy. This bylaw is revised (but not without protest from a couple members). An election is soon held for president, and with a rigged ballot box, Comrade Farrell is successful. Philbrick, being an inside man, continues to second all of Farrell's motions. One Saturday evening, Comrade Farrell calls for a meeting—with barely any members present—calling for the

Alliance's immediate support for Fred Braxton for candidacy. Braxton is obviously a communist, and two different letters are issued to selected members that would guarantee the election results. As a last minute solution, Philbrick switches the letters so the opposite members would receive the wrong ones. When members of the Tax Payer's Alliance receive them, the men turn Comrade Farrell over to the police to begin an investigation, on suspicion of Communist infiltration. Special Agent Mike Andrews later explains to Herb that the Commies called an emergency council of war without Philbrick's knowledge—Philbrick is too important to the Party to be blamed for the mishap so he is free from suspicion. Comrade Farrell, however, is reprimanded and his secretary Lucille, also a member of the Party, will become the sacrificial goat.

Memorable Quote: Philbrick, listening to Comrade Lucille's speech, thinks to himself: "This is what you are fighting, Philbrick. The creature that screams patriotism to your face and holds the dagger of Communism to strike it into your back."

Production Notes: Three electricians, one policeman, three drivers, one extra and one stand-in were needed on the first day of filming. Three electricians, one stand-in, and seven extras were needed on the second day of filming. A bus, Philbrick's car, and a camera & sound car were needed for the first day of filming.

Total Crew Hours:	20
Make Ready and Shooting:	19 1/2 hours
Travel Time:	1/2 hour

Location Shots:

Hoover Real Estate Office, 4701 Los Feliz Blvd.
Telephone Company, 1107 North Gower

Episode #63 "COMIC STRIP"

Production #1063 / 63B

Typescript (annotated), by Stuart Jerome, October 15, 1954
Revised pages (annotated), October 18, 1954
Revised master mimeo, October 18, 1954
Filmed October 25 and 26, 1954

Cast: Richard Carlson (Herbert A. Philbrick); John Cliff (Comrade Shaw); John Zaremba (Special Agent Jerry Dressler); Alan Harris (Comrade Nyby); Micheal Dengate (Comrade Whalen); and John Lehmann (Comrade Hale).

Production Credits

Production Chief:	Herbert L. Strock
Director:	Herbert L. Strock
First Assistant Director:	Joseph Wonder
Second Assistant Director:	Bobby Ray
First Cameraman:	Robert Hoffman
Second Cameraman:	Monk Askins
First Assistant Cameraman:	Dick Rawlings
Sound Mixer:	Gary Harris
Recorder:	Bob Post
Boom Man:	Elmer Haglund
First Company Grip:	Mel Bledsoe
Property Master:	Max Pittman
Assistant Property Man:	Victor Petrotta
Set Decorator:	Lou Hafley
Wardrobe Man:	Al Berke
Script Supervisor and Production Manager:	Larry Lund
Film Editor:	Jack Woelz
Gaffer:	Joe Wharton
Set Director:	Sal Inverso
Construction Chief:	Archie Hall

Plot: Comrade Nyby, a former Communist Party member of two years, is the cartoonist of a popular comic strip hero named Captain Champion. Even though he's been in hiding for seven years, the Comrades have caught up to him and blackmail him into paying the Party $200 a week for back dues. Philbrick is assigned as the courier. Feeling sorry for the old man, Philbrick gives the details to Special Agent Dressler, who confesses they cannot do anything until Nyby comes to them first—and Philbrick cannot convince Nyby to turn himself in, because of the fear of losing his stature with the Party. As the weeks pass, the blackmail is raised to $300 a week and the submission of a plot for Nyby's next strip. Apparently, the Party wants to use his weekly comic strip as a means of spreading propaganda, and the money he makes from his strip. Even with the threat of his wife's safety, Nyby goes to the F.B.I., just days before the Party decided Nyby has outlived his usefulness. Agent Dressler warns Philbrick not to make the last pickup, as agents will be on hand to arrest the courier, and as a counterspy, Philbrick has no protection. Comrade Shaw wants to ensure Nyby's final payment goes without a flaw, and tags along with Philbrick to make the pickup. But Philbrick is surprised when the F.B.I. does not appear. Later that evening, Agent Dressler explains to Philbrick that a tape recorder was hidden instead, and Comrade Shaw and his men have been picked up. It's stroke of luck on Philbrick's part, as he can continue his service for both parties.

Production Notes: One electrician, one motorcycle policeman, five drivers, two extras and one stand-in were needed on the first day of filming. Three electricians and one stand-in were needed on the second day of filming. Dressler's car, a bus, Philbrick's car, Shaw's car, and a camera & sound car were needed for the first day of filming.

Total Crew Hours:	19
Make Ready and Shooting:	18 hours
Travel Time:	1 hour

Location Shots:

Parking Lot (Melrose), across from Nickodell's
Exterior of Jewelry Store, 5324 Melrose
Griffith Park, Picnic Grounds and Park
House at 5411 Red Oak Road

EPISODE #64 "GOON SQUAD"

PRODUCTION # 1064 / 64B
TYPESCRIPT (ANNOTATED) BY DONN MULLALLY, OCTOBER 28, 1954
REVISED PAGES (ANNOTATED), OCTOBER 25, 1954
REVISED MASTER MIMEO, OCTOBER 25, 1954
FILMED OCTOBER 30 AND 31, 1954

CAST: Richard Carlson (Herbert A. Philbrick); Bill Traylor (Comrade Andrew); Peter Adams (Dixon); Tom McKee (Comrade Brisson Laylock / Kramer); Allan Douglas (Comrade Logan); Ken Duncan Jr. (the masked man); Jack Gardner (Comrade Anderson); and John Zaremba (Special Agent Jerry Dressler).

PRODUCTION CREDITS

PRODUCTION CHIEF:	HENRY S. KESLER
DIRECTOR:	HENRY S. KESLER
FIRST ASSISTANT DIRECTOR:	JOSEPH WONDER
SECOND ASSISTANT DIRECTOR:	BOBBY RAY
FIRST CAMERAMAN:	CURT FETTERS
SECOND CAMERAMAN:	MONK ASKINS
FIRST ASSISTANT CAMERAMAN:	DICK RAWLINGS
SOUND MIXER:	GARY HARRIS
RECORDER:	BOB POST
BOOM MAN:	ELMER HAGLUND
FIRST COMPANY GRIP:	CARL MIKSCH
SECOND COMPANY GRIP:	MEL BLEDSOE
PROPERTY MASTER:	MAX PITTMAN
ASSISTANT PROPERTY MAN:	VICTOR PETROTTA
SET DECORATOR:	LOU HAFLEY
FILM EDITOR:	ACE CLARK
GAFFER:	JOE WHARTON
SET DIRECTOR:	SAL INVERSO
CONSTRUCTION CHIEF:	ARCHIE HALL
DIALOGUE DIRECTOR:	BILL ANDERSON

PLOT: Fear of everything and everyone outside the Communist world is a lesson in Communism. How that fear is kept alive is revealed during a routine Pro-4 cell meeting, when three masked men storm into Comrade Brisson's house. While everyone escapes out the back door, Philbrick overhears Brisson taking a beating. This "goon squad" is the act of overzealous patriots and their mission sets the Commie High Command on their toes. One by one, the men of the cell are questioned, but no one fesses up. A few days later, Comrade Anderson takes a beating from a personal visit from the "goon squad." Philbrick, fearing he might be next on the list, visits Party Headquarters and suggests that they might become a target themselves. Special Agent Dressler suggests that the "goon squad" is merely a rouse. After all, Hitler burned down his own Reichstad to convince his own men to get tough with their enemies. With this notion put in effect, Herb spends the afternoon with Dressler, as they witness Comrade Logan cleaning out files from his office—just in case such an event occurs. When the "goon squad" does arrive, Dressler gives the signal and the men are arrested. The publicity makes headlines and, afterwards, Dressler phones Comrade Logan to come to the office to sign a charge of vandalism (against his own men).

TRIVIA, ETC. In this episode, Philbrick has to attend a meeting and, in doing so, parks two blocks from the meeting place, walks three, and arrives exactly on time. This is something all Party members do when they attend a cell meeting. Not one minute early and not one minute late, and nothing to attract suspicion. Later in the episode, when the question of who initiated the "goon squad" comes up, Philbrick explains, "The question of Communist affiliation is a relative one at best. Somebody, somewhere along the line, has to know who is a Communist and who isn't. Somewhere along the line there has to be a link."

PRODUCTION NOTES: Three electricians, one motorcycle policeman, four drivers, three extras and one stand-in were needed on the first day of filming. Three electricians and one stand-in were needed on the second day of filming. Goon's car, a 33-passenger bus, Philbrick's car, and a camera and sound car were needed for the first day of filming. Stock footage was used.

TOTAL CREW HOURS:	20
MAKE READY AND SHOOTING:	19 1/2 HOURS
TRAVEL TIME:	1/2 HOUR

LOCATION SHOTS:

TETAM AUTO PARK, HOLLYWOOD BLVD. [BY WARNER BROS. THEATRE]
FLORIST SHOP, 5501 MELROSE
CRAMER'S HOUSE, 1803 NORTH CANYON, HOLLYWOOD
BUNGALOW, 407 NORTH CLINTON, HOLLYWOOD
STREET AND SCHOOL, 400 BLOCK OF NORTH CLINTON

EPISODE #65 "CONVICTS"

PRODUCTION # 1065 / 65B
TYPESCRIPT (ANNOTATED), BY RIK VOLLAERTS, OCTOBER 28, 1954
MASTER MIMEO (ANNOTATED), NOVEMBER 1, 1954
REVISED MASTER MIMEO, NOVEMBER 1, 1954
FILMED NOVEMBER 4 AND 5, 1954

CAST: Richard Carlson (Herbert A. Philbrick); John Beradino (Special Agent Steve Daniels); Richard Benedict (Comrade Jordan); Paul Weber (Comrade Lee Terrence); Clarence Badger, Jr. (Emory Long); and Nick Blair (Pat Lawson).

PRODUCTION CREDITS

PRODUCTION CHIEF:	LEW LANDERS
DIRECTOR:	LEW LANDERS
FIRST ASSISTANT DIRECTOR:	EDDIE STEIN
SECOND ASSISTANT DIRECTOR:	BOBBY RAY
FIRST CAMERAMAN:	CURT FETTERS (FIRST DAY ONLY)
FIRST CAMERAMAN:	BOB HOFFMAN (SECOND DAY ONLY)
SECOND CAMERAMAN:	MONK ASKINS
FIRST ASSISTANT CAMERAMAN:	DICK RAWLINGS

Sound Mixer:	Gary Harris
Boom Man:	Elmer Haglund
First Company Grip:	Carl Miksch (first day only)
First Company Grip:	Mel Bledsoe (second day only)
Property Master:	Ygnacio Sepulveda and Max Pittman
Assistant Property Man:	Victor Petrotta
Set Decorator:	Lou Hafley
Film Editor:	Ace Clark
Gaffer:	Jud Leroy
Set Director:	Sal Inverso
Construction Chief:	Archie Hall
Dialogue Director:	Bill Anderson
Policemen Supplied by:	Morgan Windbill.

Plot: The Communist Party thrives on injustice. Case in point: Comrade Terrance explains to Herb his new membership drive. At the State Penitentiary, Comrade Jordan has a key man or two inside, choosing selected inmates who really hate the capitalistic society, men who have had personal experience with injustice, and after their release arranges for transportation, good clothes and food, and a place to live. Befriending the ex-cons and making them into members of the Party is true Marx policy and Philbrick, smelling trouble, gives this information to Special Agent Steve Daniels. Philbrick's part in the scheme is to help select the members and oversee the operation. While Philbrick does his best to play Party member, Daniels encourages Mr. Long, a local factory plant owner, to join the Chamber of Commerce and hire ex-cons so they have a true purpose when they get out of the pen. When Jordan learns of the Chamber of Commerce's plan, he threatens to use the cons to overpower Terrance. Philbrick leaks this information to Daniels, who plans to pick up Jordan using the inside man in the Penitentiary as the "leak."

Production Notes: One policeman, five drivers, six extras and two stand-ins were needed on the first day of filming. Three electricians, and two stand-ins, and four extras were needed on the second day of filming. Daniels' car, a bus, Philbrick's car, a Commie car, and a camera and sound car were needed for the first day of filming. Stock footage was used.

Total Crew Hours:	20
Make Ready and Shooting:	19 hours
Travel Time:	1 hour

Location Shots:
Construction Site at Grand and Court Street
Office Building, Grand and Temple
Penitentiary, 1630 North Main Street
Gas Station at 766 Castelar
Café and Alleys, 416 Alpine Street

Episode #66 "INVESTMENTS"
Production #1066 / 66B
Typescript (annotated), by Leonard Heiderman, November 1, 1954
Master mimeo, (annotated), November 3, 1954
Revised master mimeo, November 3, 1954
Filmed November 6 and 7, 1954

Cast: Richard Carlson (Herbert A. Philbrick); William Hudson (Special Agent Mike Andrews); Carolyn Scott (Comrade Patty, the nurse); John Zaremba (Special Agent Jerry Dressler); John Stephenson (Robert Faulk); Charlotte Lawrence (Carol); and Helen Van Tuyl (Mrs. Shelby).

Production Credits

Production Chief:	Henry S. Kesler
Director:	Henry S. Kesler
First Assistant Director:	Don Verk
Second Assistant Director:	Bobby Ray
First Cameraman:	Robert Hoffman
Second Cameraman:	Monk Askins

FIRST ASSISTANT CAMERAMAN:	DICK RAWLINGS
SOUND MIXER:	GARY HARRIS
RECORDER:	DALE KNIGHT
BOOM MAN:	ELMER HAGLUND
FIRST COMPANY GRIP:	MEL BLEDSOE
PROPERTY MASTER:	MAX PITTMAN
ASSISTANT PROPERTY MAN:	VICTOR PETROTTA
SET DECORATOR:	LOU HAFLEY
MAKE-UP MAN:	GEORGE GRAY
WARDROBE MAN:	AL BERKE
FILM EDITOR:	DUNCAN MANSFIELD, A.C.E
GAFFER:	JOE WHARTON AND JUD LEROY
CONSTRUCTION CHIEF:	ARCHIE HALL
DIALOGUE DIRECTOR:	BILL ANDERSON

PLOT: Robert Falk is a suspected Commie financial businessman who handles some of the Party's most important funds and investments and asks Philbrick, an experienced advertising man, to foster the notions of Mrs. Shelby. Six years ago Mrs. Shelby's husband passed away, eventually closing a plant that was the largest employer in town. Falk would like to see her illusions become a reality, so he can use the Bull and Bear market to grow the Party's assets ten-fold. When the market opens with her newly available stock, the value will raise and later, when his intention is to fold on a loan to Mrs. Shelby, the stock will fall—giving the Party $50,000 for every point the stock drops. Falk predicts that one day the American business will fall the same way. Philbrick plays along with the scheme, with Dressler admitting that he cannot interfere—the old-fashioned stock market scheme is legal. Later, Agent Andrews visits Mrs. Shelby in private and informs her of the Communist infiltration scheme. With this information, she makes sure that the price of the stock keeps going up instead of down. Falk is forced to sell and take a loss. Since the Party doesn't like failure, Falk knows his time is at hand and to save face, hands Philbrick a complete list of stocks and names owned by the Communists, and gives him an address to deliver it to—but not before Special Agent Dressler gets a copy . . .

Production Notes: Three electricians, one motorcycle policeman, one cableman, three drivers, one extra and two stand-ins were needed on the first day of filming. Three electricians and two stand-ins were needed on the second day of filming. A 33-passenger bus, Philbrick's car, and a camera and sound car were needed for the first day of filming.

Total Crew Hours:	20
Make Ready and Shooting:	19 hours
Travel Time:	1 hour

Location Shots:
McArthur Park Boat House, Corner of Wilshire & Alvarado
2010 Wilshire Blvd.
Los Angeles Public Library at 5th and Grand
310 South Lafayette Park Place
Phone Booth at 6th and Occidental
Store at 5423 Melrose

◆ ❖ ◆

Episode #67 "THE SON"
Production # 1067 / 67B
Typescript (annotated), by Arthur Fitz-Richard, November 29, 1954
Master mimeo (annotated), December 7, 1954
Revised master mimeo, December 7, 1954
Filmed December 15 and 16, 1954

Cast: Richard Carlson (Herbert A. Philbrick); Allan Gruener (Comrade Peters); William Hudson (Special Agent Mike Andrews); Fred Nurney (Comrade Otto); Cliff Gould (Bill Hoffman); Patricia Walter (Lona Nedick, Hoffman's secretary); and Hans Herbert (Dr. Heinz Hoffman).

Production Credits

Production Chief:	Herbert L. Strock
Director:	Herbert L. Strock

First Assistant Director:	Eddie Stein
Second Assistant Director:	Bobby Ray
First Cameraman:	Curt Fetters
Second Cameraman:	Monk Askins
First Assistant Cameraman:	Dick Rawlings
Sound Mixer:	Gary Harris
Recorder:	Bob Post
Boom Man:	Elmer Haglund
First Company Grip:	Carl Miksch
Second Company Grip:	Mel Bledsoe (second day only)
Property Master:	Victor Petrotta
Assistant Property Man:	Tom Shaw
Set Decorator:	Lou Hafley
Wardrobe Man:	Al Berke
Script Supervisor:	Larry Lund
Film Editor:	Chuck Craft
Gaffer:	Joe Wharton
Set Director:	Sal Inverso (second day only)
Construction Chief:	Archie Hall

Plot: Dr. Heinz Hoffman has been working on increasing the operating range of jet engines. The Communist Party wants this information but since the only copies of the work known to exist are at high-level security plants, the Party sees one option—Hoffman's son Bill, who has been working alongside his father. Using a clever scheme, Lona Nedick, Hoffman's secretary, uses her wiles to encourage the boy to see the truth about his mother—that she is alive and well in East Germany. Since the father and son have not met eye to eye in recent years, Bill believes her lies and makes plans to fly to the East. If the plan succeeds, the Communists hope to brainwash him into working for them—and thus revealing the plans. Special Agent Blake Edwards, using information given to him by Philbrick, approaches the good doctor and explains what is happening. The doctor, not wanting to see his son branded as a traitor, breaks security protocol and hands the plans to Lona to put into the safe. With the F.B.I. keeping tabs on the secretary, Lona and her associates are arrested with the plans in her possession, and Dr. Hoffman visits the airport to save his son from a mistake before it is too late.

PRODUCTION NOTES: One electrician, one motorcycle policeman, one fireman, four drivers, and one stand-in were needed on the first day of filming. Three electricians, one stand-in, and two extras were needed on the second day of filming. A 33-passenger bus, Philbrick's car (a light grey Ford), F.B.I. car (a black Nash), and a camera and sound car (station wagon) were needed for the first day of filming.

TOTAL CREW HOURS: 20
MAKE READY AND SHOOTING: 18 HOURS
TRAVEL TIME: 2 HOURS

LOCATION SHOTS:
PARK AT OLYMPIC AND RIMPAU
INTERNATIONAL AIRPORT, AMERICAN AIRLINES
APARTMENT HOUSE AND MEETING PLACE, 820 SOUTH MANSFIELD
PARKING LOT, CORNER OF MANSFIELD AND WILSHIRE
INSTITUTE BUILDING, 1138 NORTH LAS PALMOS
STREET NEAR INSTITUTE BUILDING
BUS STOP IN THE VICINITY OF THE INSTITUTE BUILDING

EPISODE #68 "VANDALISM"

PRODUCTION #1068 / 68B
MASTER MIMEO BY JACK ROCK, NOVEMBER 30, 1954
MASTER MIMEO (ANNOTATED), DECEMBER 16, 1954
REVISED MASTER MIMEO, DECEMBER 16, 1954
FILMED JANUARY 3 AND 4, 1955

CAST: Richard Carlson (Herbert A. Philbrick); Allan Douglas (Comrade Logan); John Beradino (Special Agent Steve Daniels); Bernie Rich (Roger Meredith); John Tuggle (Mickey); Ann Seaton (Mrs. Doreen Bennett); and Dennis McCarthy (Doctor Lawrence Hiller).

Production Credits

Production Chief:	Henry S. Kesler
Director:	Henry S. Kesler
First Assistant Director:	Eddie Stein
Second Assistant Director:	Bobby Ray
First Cameraman:	Robert Hoffman
Second Cameraman:	Monk Askins
First Assistant Cameraman:	Dick Rawlings
Sound Mixer:	Gary Harris
Recorder:	Elmer Haglund
Boom Man:	Bob Post
First Company Grip:	Mel Bledsoe
Property Master:	Ygnacio Spulveda
Set Decorator:	Lou Hafley
Script Supervisor:	Larry Lund
Film Editor:	Chuck Craft
Gaffer:	Joe Wharton
Construction Chief:	Archie Hall
Dialogue Director:	Bill Anderson

Plot: Philbrick is asked by Doreen Bennett and Lawrence Hiller, members of the "Juvenile Vandalism Committee," for help. Acts of vandalism are being committed in schools. No thefts; just wanton destruction. Herb is asked by the couple to help write pieces for the local newspaper to help establish a coat hanger for tomorrow's growth. When Comrade Logan learns of Philbrick's assignment, he hands Herb some material to be incorporated into the pieces. Herb protests that such an act would reveal the Communist Party's infiltration too quickly—much to the dislike of Logan. At the schools, Comrade Logan uses capitalism as an excuse in motivational chats with students, encouraging them to "fight" for a just cause—"protection and freedom" of mankind. This new youth movement, however, is caught in the act by local police and Special Agent Steve Daniels explains to the kids that they were working for the Communist Party all along. He explains how they were disillusioned, and as a means of setting things straight, the boys are encouraged to speak on a radio broadcast as misguided witnesses for all to know. Comrade Logan, hearing the broadcast from the mouths of the same youths he tried to poison, is run out of town and the Party thanks Herb for not exposing them in the newspaper articles.

COMMENT: Mickey, one of the young boys, is misguided by Comrade Logan's pep talk, commenting, "Whoever thought you could smear up a school room and be doing something for your country at the same time?" But when Agent Daniels gives the boys his own talk, the lesson meant for the children is also meant for any youth watching the program. "Vandalism is like an epidemic," he explains. "To hear or read about it creates a wave of mass hysteria among youngsters. Wakens a desire to go out and smash things. What's the result? Sooner or later they get caught and it's a session in reform school. When they come out they're bitter and disillusioned because Mr. Logan and his friends didn't stand by them. So when they're released from reform school, they are easy prey for the Communists, who then assure them that something like this will never happen if the Comrades are in charge."

PRODUCTION NOTES: Three electricians, one foot policeman, three drivers, two extras and two stand-ins were needed on the first day of filming. Three electricians and two stand-ins were needed on the second day of filming. A bus, standby car, and a camera & sound car were needed for the first day of filming.

TOTAL CREW HOURS: 20
MAKE READY AND SHOOTING: 19 1/2 HOURS
TRAVEL TIME: 1/2 HOUR

LOCATION SHOTS:

SHOESHINE STAND, 5631 MELROSE AVENUE
PHONE BOOTH, 5925 MELROSE AVENUE
STREET NEAR SCHOOL (NEAR POLAR PALACE), VAN NESS AND CLINTON
SCHOOL AND HALIWAY, VAN NESS SCHOOL, 501 NORTH VAN NESS
BARBERSHOP, MARATHON NEAR IRVING (OPPOSITE PARAMOUNT STUDIO)

EPISODE #69 "BRAINWASH"
PRODUCTION # 1069 / 69B
TYPESCRIPT (ANNOTATED), BY DONN MULLALLY, DECEMBER 29, 1954
REVISED PAGES (ANNOTATED), DECEMBER 31, 1954
REVISED MASTER MIMEO, DECEMBER 31, 1954
FILMED, JANUARY 5 AND 6, 1955.

CAST: Richard Carlson (Herbert A. Philbrick); George Brand (James Hillary); John Zaremba (Special Agent Jerry Dressler); Beatrice Maude (Mrs. Hillary); Robert Jordan (Comrade Kapotek); Harry Fleer (Jack Graves); Ken Duncan, Jr. (Kirk); Maurice Hart (Barb); and Harry Martin (the voice of Brooks Clark).

PRODUCTION CREDITS

DIRECTOR:	HERBERT L. STROCK
PRODUCTION CHIEF:	HERBERT L. STROCK
FIRST ASSISTANT DIRECTOR:	JOSEPH WONDER
SECOND ASSISTANT DIRECTOR:	BOBBY RAY
FIRST CAMERAMAN:	ROBERT HOFFMAN
SECOND CAMERAMAN:	MONK ASKINS
FIRST ASSISTANT CAMERAMAN:	DICK RAWLINGS
SOUND MIXER:	GARY HARRIS
RECORDER:	BOB POST
BOOM MAN:	ELMER HAGLUND
FIRST COMPANY GRIP:	MEL BLEDSOE
PROPERTY MASTER:	MAX PITTMAN
SET DECORATOR:	LOU HAFLEY
WARDROBE MAN:	AL BERKE
SCRIPT SUPERVISOR:	LARRY LUND
FILM EDITOR:	JACK WOELZ
GAFFER:	JOE WHARTON
SET DIRECTOR:	SAL INVERSO (ONE DAY ONLY)
CONSTRUCTION CHIEF:	ARCHIE HALL

PLOT: Mr. And Mrs. James Hillary disappeared behind the Iron Curtain and were never seen again for many years. Back among the living, Mr. Hillary speaks very little of what he witnessed, but has a scheduled radio broadcast a week from today. Comrade Kapotek assigns Philbrick to learn all that he can from Mr. Hillary, become close friends, and discover where his true loyalty lies. Day after day Philbrick turns in his report to both Kapotek and Special Agent Jerry Dressler, but Philbrick is still unsure where Hillary's loyalties lie. Finally, the morning of the broadcast, Hillary cracks and locks himself in his bedroom. Philbrick manages to get inside and in private, Hillary explains he has been brainwashed—a British correspondent named Clark committed suicide when he was trying to escape the Red country because Hillary named Clark as a member of a spy ring that in reality, doesn't exist. He did so because under all the torture, he wanted a moment's silence and a good meal. Now that Hillary is a tool of propaganda, he can't cancel the radio broadcast. Philbrick tells Dressler, who arranges for a transatlantic call thirty minutes before the broadcast from Brooks Clark, who admits he had to keep his head down. When the radio broadcast fails to assist the Communist Party, Kapotek attempts to leave, knowing his mission is a failure, but a welcoming committee at home will soon eliminate Comrade Kapotek.

PRODUCTION NOTES: Three electricians, one policeman, one fireman, one cableman, four drivers, two extras and one stand-in were needed for the first day of filming. Three electricians, one stand-in, and five extras were needed for the second day of filming. Dressler's car, a bus, a Commie car, and a camera and sound car were needed for the first day of filming. Stock footage was used.

TOTAL CREW HOURS: 20
MAKE READY AND SHOOTING: 20 HOURS

LOCATION SHOTS:
849 SOUTH GRAMERCY PLACE
PIER 179, SAN PEDRO
IL&W-U HIRING HALL, SAN PEDRO
FISHING DECK, FISHERMAN'S ASSOCIATION, SAN PEDRO

◆ ❖ ◆

Episode #70 "BOSS # 2"
Production #1070 / 70B
Typescript (annotated), by Stuart Jerome, January 6, 1955
Revised pages (annotated), January 11, 1955
Revised master mimeo, January 11, 1955
Filmed January 15 and 16, 1955

Cast: Richard Carlson (Herbert A. Philbrick); John Zaremba (Special Agent Jerry Dressler); Merrit Stone (Comrade Mitch); John Mallory (Comrade Cooper); Bob Swan (Comrade Reid); John Ayres (Mr. Stevens); Walter Beaver (Doctor Haven); Syl Lamont (first unnamed Comrade); Joseph Hamilton (the conductor); and Rosemary Day (the girl clerk).

Production Credits

Production Chief:	Henry S. Kesler
Director:	Henry S. Kesler
First Assistant Director:	Eddie Bernoudy
Second Assistant Director:	Harry Jones
First Cameraman:	Curt Fetters
Second Cameraman:	Bud Mautino
First Assistant Cameraman:	Dick Johnson
Sound Mixer:	Jay Ashworth
Recorder:	Bill Denby
Boom Man:	Bill Flannery
First Company Grip:	Carl Miksch
Second Company Grip:	Colly Kessinger
Property Master:	Lyle Reifsnider
Assistant Property Man:	Stanley Walters
Set Decorator:	Lou Hafley
Script Supervisor:	Helen Gailey
Gaffer:	Jimmy Viana
Set Director:	John Burrill
Construction Chief:	Archie Hall

Plot: Comrade Mitch assigns Philbrick to go to Woodland City with a special envelope and deliver it to a designated Comrade. Herb tells his boss that he has to leave town for 48 hours, and takes the first train north. To ensure the security of the mission, Comrade Reid and Cooper are assigned to tail Philbrick all the way. This doesn't give Special Agent Jerry Dressler much of an opportunity to assist Herb, but the envelope is passed to the F.B.I. agent with the assurance that the envelope will be returned before Herb reaches his destination. While Dressler and a another agent set about retrieving the information in a closed compartment, Herb bumps into his boss from the advertising agency and together the two work on a project in a separate compartment. Comrade Reid and Cooper, suspicious, insist Herb hand over the envelope, but, using security as an excuse, he fails to do so. Dressler eventually copies the contents of the envelope—blueprints of a Government facility for use of sabotage—and returns the envelope to Philbrick just as Cooper and Reid lose their patience. The conductor, suspicious of the events on board, phones the police and has Cooper and Reid picked up—making it appear they failed the mission, but not Philbrick, who will succeed with his boss and deliver the envelope to the scheduled rendezvous.

Production Notes: Three electricians, one patrolman, three drivers, four extras and one stand-in were needed on the first day of filming. Three electricians, one stand-in, and one special effects man, were needed on the second day of filming. Carlson's car, a bus, and a camera & sound car were needed for the first day of filming. Stock footage was used.

Total Crew Hours:	16
Make Ready and Shooting:	15 1/2 hours
Travel Time:	1/2 hour

Location Shots:
Southern Pacific Station, Glendale
TV Motors Used Car Lot, corner Brand & Las Felix
Cosmo Street, 1/2 block off Hollywood Blvd.

Episode #71 "REVOLT"
Production #1071 / 71B
Typescript (annotated), by Ellis Marcus, December 29, 1954
Revised pages (annotated), January 3, 1955
Revised master mimeo, January 3, 1955
Filmed January 22 and 23, 1955

Cast: Richard Carlson (Herbert A. Philbrick); Virginia Stefan (Eva Philbrick); John Beradino (Special Agent Steve Daniels); Michael Fox (Comrade John); Stagg Salem (Comrade Don); Maria Gregory (Comrade Louisa Palmer); Mitch Kowal (Comrade Joe Burton); and Arlene Solof (Miss Burke).

Production Credits

Production Chief:	Henry S. Kesler
Director:	Henry S. Kesler
First Assistant Director:	Don Verk
Second Assistant Director:	Harry Jones
First Cameraman:	Curt Fetters
Second Cameraman:	Bud Mautino
First Assistant Cameraman:	Dick Johnson
Sound Mixer:	Jay Ashworth
Recorder:	Bob Post
Boom Man:	Bill Flannery
First Company Grip:	Carl Miksch
Property Master:	Lyle Reifsnider
Assistant Property Man:	Victor Petrotta
Set Decorator:	Lou Hafley
Script Supervisor:	Helen Gailey
Film Editor:	Duncan Mansfield, A.C.E
Gaffer:	Jimmy Viana
Construction Chief:	Archie Hall

Plot: When Philbrick learns that Comrade Kurt and Comrade Louisa are withholding Party funds and keeping secrets behind a closet door, he asks Special Agent Steve Daniels whether he should be loyal to Comrade John, the cell leader, or keep his silence. Daniels suggests he stay faithful to the cell leader. Philbrick tells Comrade John what he saw and John, suspecting Philbrick is playing a game, orders him to find positive proof he can use against Kurt and Louisa. With the help of Eva, Herb finds weapons and after snooping a little more, finds an armory in the locked closet. Herb leaks this knowledge to Daniels and then tries to inform Comrade John, but is shocked to learn that the National Committee demoted John, and promoted Kurt. Back at the antique store that Kurt uses as a front, Comrade John learns from a detective (who is actually Agent Steve Daniels) that the firearms were discovered during a routine fire department inspection and Party members were arrested. Comrade John, happy that his reinstatement will be soon at hand, apologizes to Herb for not listening to him initially, and has more faith and trust in Philbrick than he ever had.

PRODUCTION NOTES: Three electricians, one policeman, one fireman, four drivers, three extras and one stand-in were needed on the first day of filming. Three electricians, one stand-in, and one extra were needed on the second day of filming. A black Nash, an electrical trailer, a 33-passenger bus, Philbrick's car, and a camera and sound car were needed for the first day of filming.

TOTAL CREW HOURS:	20
MAKE READY AND SHOOTING:	18 3/4 HOURS
TRAVEL TIME:	1 1/4 HOURS

LOCATION SHOTS:
GITTLESON BROTHERS AMUSEMENT PARK, 5257 HOLLYWOOD BLVD.
STEVE'S SHOE REPAIR SHOP, 5257 MELROSE AVE.
5043 ROSEWOOD AVE.

◆ ❖ ◆

EPISODE #72 "MR. AND MRS."

PRODUCTION # 1072 / 72B
TYPESCRIPT (ANNOTATED), BY RICHARD G. TAYLOR, JANUARY 12, 1955

Revised pages (annotated), January 20, 1955
Revised master mimeo, January 20, 1955
Filmed January 25 and 26, 1955

Cast: Richard Carlson (Herbert A. Philbrick); Jack Edwards (Comrade Phil); George Jerome Becwar (Comrade Dan / Remler); Virginia Stefan (Eva Philbrick); John Zaremba (Special Agent Jerry Dressler); and Rod O'Conner (Duncan Malone).

Production Credits

Production Chief:	Jon Epstein
Director:	Lambert Hillyer
First Assistant Director:	Eddie Bernoudy
Second Assistant Director:	Bobby Ray
First Cameraman:	Curt Fetters
Second Cameraman:	Bud Mautino
First Assistant Cameraman:	Dick Rawlings (first day only)
First Assistant Cameraman:	Dick Johnson (second day only)
Sound Mixer:	Jay Ashworth
Recorder:	Bill Denby
Boom Man:	Bill Flannery
First Company Grip:	Mel Bledsoe
Second Company Grip:	Colly Kessinger
Property Master:	Lyle Reifsnider
Assistant Property Man:	Ygnacio Sepulveda
Set Decorator:	Lou Hafley
Script Supervisor:	Helene Gailey
Film Editor:	Jack Woelz
Gaffer:	Joe Wharton
Construction Chief:	Archie Hall

Plot: Eva and Herb Philbrick are active members of the Mr. and Mrs. Club, designed to head a refugee committee, to bring a displaced couple over from Europe for a vacation. Comrade Phil tells Herb that his involvement will prove useful to the Party. Harry and Anna Remler have been living in a displaced camp in West

Germany after the war. The Remlers are really Soviet-trained agents in disguise, to help sabotage an electric plant that supplies power to the nation's local defenses—a test in U.S. vulnerability. Though it will look like an operational failure, Herb's job is to keep the members of the club from meeting the fake Remlers until the job is done. Herb reports the foul play to Special Agent Dressler, who suggests he can have the local authorities "innocently" get involved as long as the details of the location are given in advance. Philbrick does so, but shortly after, the plans and location are changed for security reasons. Using a piece of paper and a phone call delivered to Eva in code, Herb is able to get the new location to Dressler in time for the plan to fail—and the fake Remlers are picked up for illegal entry into Canada the day after.

PRODUCTION NOTES: Three electricians, one motorcycle policeman, a fireman, five drivers, four extras and one stand-in were needed on the first day of filming. Three electricians, one stand-in, and six extras were needed on the second day of filming. Comrade Phil's car, a 33-passenger bus, Philbrick's car, Comrade Dan's car, and a camera and sound car were needed for the first day of filming.

TOTAL CREW HOURS:	19
MAKE READY AND SHOOTING:	17 3/4 HOURS
TRAVEL TIME:	1 1/4 HOURS

PRODUCTION TRIVIA: This episode was based on a brief section in Philbrick's book. In the book, Philbrick described how a phase of his life as a Citizen was his participation in a "Mr. and Mrs." Club at his church. Both he and Eva were charter members, and the club's first presidents. As a member of a Pro-group in the Party, Philbrick was ordered to push the current communist peace crusade into his church club. He arranged a meeting at which a guest speaker, a prominent Bostonian not known as a communist, was to address the club on the subject of "peace." The man spoke well, followed the Party line to the letter, but very few of the club members are na˝ve enough to fall for his point of view. Philbrick was not looked at favorably in the church for a time, but he kept his membership in the Party secured.

Location Shots:
The car chases took place in a street nearby the Exposition Park in Los Angeles.
Exterior of Music store, Figueroa and 40th Place

Episode #73 "OILFIELD"
Production # 1073/ 73B
Typescript (annotated), January 19, 1955
Revised pages (annotated), January 26, 1955
Revised master mimeo, January 26, 1955
Filmed January 27 and 28, 1955

Cast: Richard Carlson (Herbert A. Philbrick); Virginia Stefan (Eva Philbrick); John Zaremba (Special Agent Jerry Dressler); Voltaire Perkins (Comrade Gregory Collins); Glenn Denning (Comrade Dan Steller); Steve Ritch (Comrade John Deering); and Ted Stanhope (Comrade Dr. Pauling).

Production Credits

Director:	Herbert L. Strock
Production Chief:	Herbert L. Strock
First Assistant Director:	Eddie Stein
Second Assistant Director:	Harry Jones
First Cameraman:	Bobby Hoffman
Second Cameraman:	Bud Mautino
First Assistant Cameraman:	Dick Johnson
Sound Mixer:	Jay Ashworth
Recorder:	Bill Denby
Boom Man:	Billy Flannery
First Company Grip:	Mel Bledsoe
Second Company Grip:	Clarence Boyd
Property Master:	Victor Petrotta
Assistant Property Man:	Cecil Smith
Set Decorator:	Lou Hafley
Script Supervisor:	Helen Gailey
Film Editor:	Jack Woelz

GAFFER: JOE WHARTON
CONSTRUCTION CHIEF: ARCHIE HALL

PLOT: Gregory Collins, a man of both wealth and power among society, gives Herb a promotion in the Party. Herb is assigned the advertising account of the Green Diamond Oil Company, and Comrade John Deering of the Oil Company explains to Herb that the company is presently an American company that expects to branch out in the Middle East. Since this will mean recruiting men for overseas, this project will need Philbrick to screen each and every applicant and decide who to hire for the job—a sheer brilliance of smuggling (legally) Commies overseas; as Philbrick describes it, "exporting Communism." After being briefed, Special Agent Jerry Dressler gives Philbrick a small camera to capture photos and documents—an easier way to pass on information since Philbrick's promotion will mean tighter security. Philbrick accomplishes this task with ease and passes the film to F.B.I. contacts as the project gets underway . . . until the Reds get suspicious of foul play. It seems the men Philbrick selected were not issued passports and Gregory Collins is picked up by the police as a "security leak," thus foiling the export business.

COMMENTS: Philbrick puts on a good show as a loyal Party member when he barks his orders to Dan Steller, a man assigned to work with Philbrick not only as security, but as the leg man. "Every man walks alone in the Party," Philbrick explains. "Each man must be complete. Sufficient unto himself, until the day the world belongs to the Party."

PRODUCTION NOTES: One electrician, one motorcycle policeman, six drivers, three extras and one stand-in were needed on the first day of filming. Four electricians and one stand-in were needed on the second day of filming. A police car, a bus, Philbrick's car, one limousine, a panel truck, and a camera & sound car were needed for the first day of filming.

TOTAL CREW HOURS: 20
MAKE READY AND SHOOTING: 18 1/2 HOURS
TRAVEL TIME: 1 1/2 HOURS

LOCATION SHOTS:
SHELL OIL CO. REFINERY, 20945 SOUTH WILMINGTON BLVD.
CHASES AND SHOTS IN VICINITY OF PLANT AND SEPULVEDA AND DOLORES STREETS.
COLLIN'S HOME & GARDENS, 310 SOUTH LAFAYETTE PARK PLACE
CAMERA SHOP, 7901 SANTA MONICA BLVD.

EPISODE #74 "CHURCH"
Production # 1074 / 74B
Typescript (annotated) by Jack Rock, January 26, 1955
Revised pages (annotated), February 1, 1955
Revised master mimeo, February 1, 1955
Filmed February 5 and 6, 1955

CAST: Richard Carlson (Herbert A. Philbrick); Tom McKee (Comrade Laylock); Charles Victor (Comrade Burt); Virginia Stefan (Eva Philbrick); John Zaremba (Special Agent Jerry Dressler); Mike Ragan (Comrade Garry); and Thom Conroy (Dr. Ewing).

PRODUCTION CREDITS

DIRECTOR:	HENRY S. KESLER
PRODUCTION CHIEF:	HENRY S. KESLER
FIRST ASSISTANT DIRECTOR:	EDDIE STEIN
SECOND ASSISTANT DIRECTOR:	HARRY JONES
FIRST CAMERAMAN:	BOBBY HOFFMAN
SECOND CAMERAMAN:	BUD MAUTINO
FIRST ASSISTANT CAMERAMAN:	DICK JOHNSON
SOUND MIXER:	JAY ASHWORTH
RECORDER:	BILL DENBY
BOOM MAN:	BILL FLANNERY
FIRST COMPANY GRIP:	MEL BLEDSOE
PROPERTY MASTER:	TOM SHAW
SET DECORATOR:	LOU HAFLEY
WARDROBE MAN:	AL BERKE
SCRIPT SUPERVISOR:	HELEN GAILEY

Film Editor: Duncan Mansfield, A.C.E
Gaffer: S.H. Barton
Construction Chief: Archie Hall

Plot: Knowing full well that you can take a physical church away from the people, but you cannot take the spiritual church out of the people, a determined Communist cell leader establishes a church infiltration program—using a psychological means, thus destroying their faith in God. Every undercover Comrade is instructed to join a church, nationwide, and start a series of gossip and lies, and later make a report on their findings. Philbrick is hired to gather all the reports and draw a conclusion from a final report to the head office. Since Eva has been asked to become a member of the House and Grounds Committee, this proves an opportune moment for the Philbricks to become personally involved. Shortly after the Party discovers that racial overtones against various other religions is a key factor to destroying churches. But the cell leader is angry when he learns about a series of news articles that exposes the plot, proving a serious setback to their plans. Suspecting a leak in the cell, rather than poor workmanship of the infiltrating Comrades, the cell leader insists on background checks, which partially include barging into the Philbricks' house uninvited. They find nothing, of course, and Herb and Eva Philbrick remain cleared of any wrongdoing.

Memorable Quotes: When Philbrick is called to a meeting on Sunday afternoon, Eva shows disgust toward the invitation. But as Herb tells his wife, "To the Communists, Sunday is just another day of the week."

The closing comments by the cell leader is as much shocking as it is horrifying, when he predicts the fall of religion, and the doctrine of Communism will be preached in its place. "When that time comes," he predicts, "a man's salvation will be measured by his loyalty to the Party, and not by some devotion to a whimsical and elusive deity."

Production Notes: One electrician, one cableman, one policeman, five drivers, and two stand-ins were needed on the first day of filming. Four electricians, and two stand-ins, and two extras were needed on the second day of filming. Dressler's car, a bus, Philbrick's car, a Commie car, and a camera & sound car were needed for the first day of filming.

Total Crew Hours:	20
Make Ready and Shooting:	18 hours
Travel Time:	2 hours

Location Shots:

The church featured in this episode was St. Gregory's Catholic Church, located on 9th and Norton Street.

Philbrick home and streets, 858 South Westchester

Car Wash Rack, 5920 Sunset Blvd.

Commie headquarters (apt. building & street), 6231 Afton Place "Amerstern Apts."

Telephone booth and Andy's Service, Melrose & Cole Ave.

Episode #75 "LOST REPORT"

Production # 1075 / 75B

Typescript (annotated), by Arthur Fitz-Richard, January 25, 1955

Revised pages (annotated), February 1, 1955

Revised master mimeo, February 1, 1955

Filmed February 9 and 10, 1955

Cast: Richard Carlson (Herbert A. Philbrick); Jefferson Searles (Comrade Goss); Ferris Taylor (Comrade Allard); Virginia Stefan (Eva Philbrick); Larry White (Bobby Masters); William Hudson (Special Agent Mike Andrews); Jeane Wood (Comrade Rhoda Cooper); Tom Chapman (Bill Shipstad); and George Spaulding (Mr. Burns).

Production Credits

Director:	Herbert L. Strock
Production Chief:	Herbert L. Strock
First Assistant Director:	Eddie Bernoudy

SECOND ASSISTANT DIRECTOR:	BOBBY RAY
FIRST CAMERAMAN:	CURT FETTERS
SECOND CAMERAMAN:	MONK ASKINS
FIRST ASSISTANT CAMERAMAN:	DICK RAWLINGS
SOUND MIXER:	GARY HARRIS
RECORDER:	BILL DENBY
BOOM MAN:	ELMER HAGLUND
FIRST COMPANY GRIP:	CARL MIKSCH
PROPERTY MASTER:	TOM SHAW
SET DECORATOR:	LOU HAFLEY
WARDROBE MAN:	AL BERKE
SCRIPT SUPERVISOR:	LARRY LUND
FILM EDITOR:	DUNCAN MANSFIELD, A.C.E
GAFFER:	JOE WHARTON
CONSTRUCTION CHIEF:	ARCHIE HALL

PLOT: While the Philbricks are settling down in their new house, a moment's peace is all but impossible. Between the interruptions of Bobby Masters, the little neighbor boy, and Party assignments, Herb is certain his luck will run out sooner or later. While Eva stuffs envelopes with codes for Party members alerting them of the day and time they are to have their next cell meeting, Philbrick finishes his report for Special Agent Steve Daniels of the F.B.I. Soon after the letters are mailed, Herb realizes the F.B.I. report is missing. Realizing it was accidentally stuffed into an envelope, Herb and Special Agent Daniels spend the next 24 hours filling out "stop delivery" forms, tracing the envelope routes with mail couriers, and with each letter found, the men come to a dead end. Herb is eventually caught snooping in Comrade Rhoda's mailbox, and after she beats him to the envelope, she tells Comrade Goss that Philbrick is a spy. Her accusations are put to the test—but she says nothing of the envelope she received in the mail. Philbrick is cleared of any wrongdoing when it is revealed that she had already told members of the Party how much she hated Philbrick and would take any advantage to discredit him. Back at the Philbrick house, Comrade Goss finds a paper airplane young Bobby made (the F.B.I. report) and without opening it, unsuspecting and unknowingly hands it back to Herb.

PRODUCTION NOTES: One electrician, one motorcycle policeman, five drivers, three extras and one stand-in were needed for the first day of filming. Four electricians, one third-grip, one cableman, one stand-in, and one welfare worker were needed for the second day of filming. Andrews' car, a 33-passenger bus, Philbrick's car, a station wagon, and a camera and sound car were needed for the first day of filming. A crab dolly was rented for the second day of filming.

TOTAL CREW HOURS:	20
MAKE READY AND SHOOTING:	18 1/2 HOURS
TRAVEL TIME:	1 1/2 HOURS

LOCATION SHOTS:
BACK OF HOLLYWOOD POST OFFICE, HOLLYWOOD ON WILCOX
RESIDENTIAL STREET, 9TH & WESTCHESTER
POST OFFICE STATION, OAKWOOD STATION, 316 NORTH WESTERN AVE.
REAL ESTATE OFFICE, 1230 NORTH LA BREA
PHILBRICK'S HOUSE, 858 WESTCHESTER PLACE
RHODA'S HOUSE
DELONGPRE PARK, DELONGPRE & CHEROKEE
RESIDENTIAL STREET ON WESTCHESTER NEAR 9TH

EPISODE #76 "CHILD COMMIE"
PRODUCTION # 1076 / 76B
TYPESCRIPT (ANNOTATED), BY LEONARD HEIDERMAN, FEBRUARY 7, 1955
REVISED PAGES (ANNOTATED), FEBRUARY 8, 1955
REVISED MASTER MIMEO, FEBRUARY 8, 1955
FILMED FEBRUARY 12 AND 13, 1955

CAST: Richard Carlson (Herbert A. Philbrick); Virginia Stefan (Eva Philbrick); Pat Morrow (Constance Philbrick); Peter Adams (Martin (Vorch) Dixon); Isa Ashdown (Beth (Vorch) Dixon); Jack Shea (Alvin Bolt); and John Beradino (Special Agent Steve Daniels).

Production Credits

Director:	Henry S. Kesler
Production Chief:	Henry S. Kesler
First Assistant Director:	Joseph Wonder
Second Assistant Director:	Harry Jones
First Cameraman:	Bobby Hoffman
Second Cameraman:	Bud Mautino
First Assistant Cameraman:	Dick Johnson
Sound Mixer:	Jay Ashworth
Recorder:	Bill Denby
Boom Man:	Bill Flannery
First Company Grip:	Mel Bledsoe
Property Master:	Victor Petrotta
Set Decorator:	Lou Hafley
Wardrobe Man:	Al Berke
Script Supervisor:	Helen Gailey
Film Editor:	Jack Woelz
Gaffer:	Joe Wharton
Construction Chief:	Archie Hall

Plot: Alan Dixon, in charge of the Communist Youth Program, arrives in the local area to see what methods are needed to make American children more receptive to Communism. Since he has to leave town for a couple days, he asks the Philbricks to baby-sit his daughter, Beth. Herb is completely unaware that Beth is really a spy, assigned to report any misconduct of Herb's loyalty to the Party. Shortly after her arrival, Beth attempts to poison young Connie Philbrick with Communist propaganda, but Herb intervenes in time—suggesting Beth is more poison than hindrance. Later, after Herb returns Beth to her home, he sets out to deliver his report to Dixon, unaware that Beth stole a copy. Before Herb can begin a search for the missing report, Herb is escorted to Dixon's office. It seems Dixon's daughter accuses Herb of being a spy. Herb quickly covers his tracks by insisting that the copy was made should the initial report get destroyed. In fact, Herb insisted, stealing such reports—even if they are copies—is a breach of security and he threatens to report Dixon and his daughter to the review board. Dixon, fearing his position (and loyalties) questioned, dismisses the matter altogether, and destroys the copy of the report. Realizing how Philbrick looked after the best interests of the Party, Dixon hands Philbrick plans of a secret publishing company designed to print children's books designed for future Communist infiltration, and asks him to finalize the grammar. Philbrick leaves, satisfied that the close shave was nothing but, and hands the publishing plans to the F.B.I.

Production Notes: Three electricians, one foot patrolman, five drivers, three extras, one welfare worker, and two stand-ins were needed for the first day of filming. Three electricians, two stand-ins, and one welfare worker were needed for the second day of filming. Daniels' car, a 33-passenger bus, Philbrick's car, Bolt's car, and a camera and sound car were needed for the first day of filming.

Total Crew Hours:	20
Make Ready and Shooting:	19 hours
Travel Time:	1 hour

Location Shots:
Gaylord Apartments, Wilshire & Ambassador
9th & Westchester, 851 Westchester Street
Corner of 4th and Western

Episode #77 "COMMIE DIES"
Production # 1077 / 77B
Typescript (annotated), by Ellis Marcus, February 7, 1955
Revised pages (annotated), February 9, 1955
Revised pages (annotated), February 17, 1955
Revised master mimeo, February 17, 1955
Filmed February 19 and 20, 1955

Cast: Richard Carlson (Herbert A. Philbrick); Jeanne Bates (Comrade Joan); Victor Rodman (Comrade Arthur); John Zaremba (Special Agent Jerry Dressler); Eva McVeagh (Miss Cutler); James Craven (Dr. Freeman); and Peter Hanson (Reverend Murkland).

PRODUCTION CREDITS

DIRECTOR:	HENRY S. KESLER
PRODUCTION CHIEF:	HENRY S. KESLER
FIRST ASSISTANT DIRECTOR:	EDDIE STEIN
SECOND ASSISTANT DIRECTOR:	HARRY JONES
FIRST CAMERAMAN:	BOBBY HOFFMAN
SECOND CAMERAMAN:	JIM BELL
FIRST ASSISTANT CAMERAMAN:	BUD MARTINO
SOUND MIXER:	JIM MOBLEY
RECORDER:	D. KNIGHT
BOOM MAN:	CARL W. DANIELS
FIRST COMPANY GRIP:	MEL BLEDSOE
SECOND COMPANY GRIP:	WALTER CULP
PROPERTY MASTER:	TOM SHAW
SET DECORATOR:	LOU HAFLEY
WARDROBE MAN:	AL BERKE
SCRIPT SUPERVISOR:	GLORIA MORGAN
FILM EDITOR:	TOM SCOTT
GAFFER:	J. VIANO
SET DIRECTOR:	SAL INVERSO
CONSTRUCTION CHIEF:	ARCHIE HALL

PLOT: An example of the Party's merciless gratitude when a member can no longer perform his duties is clearly revealed when Comrade Arthur becomes bedridden. Arthur has been considered one of the most valuable members of the Party, and his fundraising programs have been flawless. But Comrade Joan failed to keep abreast of Arthur's methods. Comrade Arthur only has a few days left, and should he die before administering his affairs to Comrade Joan, the financial donations to the Party will slow to a halt and she will have to answer to a disciplinary committee. Philbrick is assigned to learn all of Comrade Arthur's schemes and methods, but Arthur is not cooperative, withholding all the names, details and funds. With pressure on both sides, Philbrick finds himself in between a grudge match. In private, as the hours and days pass, Philbrick gains Arthur's respect and the bedridden old man starts to suspect Philbrick of thoughtfulness—a chink in the Red armor, so Arthur confesses privately that before he dies . . . he'd like to make peace with God. Herb visits a neighboring church and arranges for a pastor to visit the old man—and does so successfully just minutes before Arthur passes on. With Comrade Joan forced to explain her mistakes to the committee, Philbrick goes home happy knowing that a man, toward the end of his life, who served for the Communist Manifesto, one of the best in the Party, disregarded the system for the Bible.

PRODUCTION NOTES: Three electricians, one foot patrolman, four drivers, six extras and two stand-ins were needed for the first day of filming. Three electricians, two stand-ins, one third-grip, one cableman, and one driver were needed for the second day of filming. Dressler's car, a 33-passenger bus, Philbrick's car, and an interior truck were needed for the first day of filming.

TOTAL CREW HOURS:	19
MAKE READY AND SHOOTING:	17 1/2 HOURS
TRAVEL TIME:	1 1/2 HOURS

LOCATION SHOTS:
6233 HOLLYWOOD BLVD.
HOLLYWOOD AND VINE
TIPS RESTAURANT, VINE NEAR HOLLYWOOD BLVD.
1724 VINE STREET, DHK PARK
ARTS SERVICE STATION, MELROSE AND COLE STREETS
ROSSMORE AND CLINTON, 165 MURFIELD
547 NORTH CHEROKEE

EPISODE #78 "COMRADE EVA"
PRODUCTION # 1078 / 78B
TYPESCRIPT (ANNOTATED), BY STUART JEROME, FEBRUARY 16, 1955
REVISED PAGES (ANNOTATED), FEBRUARY 22, 1955
REVISED MASTER MIMEO, FEBRUARY 22, 1955
FILMED FEBRUARY 25 AND 26, 1955

CAST: Richard Carlson (Herbert A. Philbrick); Pat Morrow

(Constance Philbrick); Ruth Perrott (Comrade Claire); Paul Birch (Comrade Jack); Virginia Stefan (Eva Philbrick); John Zaremba (Special Agent Jerry Dressler); and Jack Harris (the policeman).

PRODUCTION CREDITS

DIRECTOR:	HENRY S. KESLER
PRODUCTION CHIEF:	HENRY S. KESLER
FIRST ASSISTANT DIRECTOR:	DON VERK
SECOND ASSISTANT DIRECTOR:	EDDIE MULL
FIRST CAMERAMAN:	DAN CLARK
SECOND CAMERAMAN:	KENNY GREEN
FIRST ASSISTANT CAMERAMAN:	C. MARQUARD
SOUND MIXER:	JIM MOBLEY
RECORDER:	BILL DENBY
BOOM MAN:	(?) ERLINGER
FIRST COMPANY GRIP:	CLARENCE BOYD
SECOND COMPANY GRIP:	DELMAR HOLLOWAY
PROPERTY MASTER:	GENE STONE
ASSISTANT PROPERTY MAN:	STAN WALTERS
SET DECORATOR:	LOU HAFLEY
WARDROBE MAN:	AL BERKE
SCRIPT SUPERVISOR:	GLORIA MORGAN
FILM EDITOR:	DUNCAN MANSFIELD, A.C.E
GAFFER:	JIM VIANA
SET DIRECTOR:	SAL INVERSO
CONSTRUCTION CHIEF:	ARCHIE HALL

PLOT: As a Party member, Eva Philbrick's duties have been kept minimal and Comrade Claire wants Eva to participate more. Herb, learning that his wife was picked up for a job, panics. Meeting with Special Agent Dressler, Herb asks for the F.B.I.'s intervention. But Dressler will not do anything to help, insisting that any intervention would discredit the Philbricks, and cause endangerment to Herb. Herb decides to take matters into his own hands, and very slowly causes suspicion on himself, asking too many questions—all related to the what, where and when of his wife's mission. Later in the afternoon, Herb receives a phone call from Comrade Claire. It seems Eva was assigned to distribute Communist propaganda to people outside a defense plant. But when Eva learned what she was distributing, she turned against her orders and thus caused suspicion. Comrade Claire insists Eva is not a true Communist and wants to hold both the Philbricks responsible. Eva uses the excuse of "Party Security," and when Comrade Claire receives a phone call, she dismisses both Herb and Eva. Down the road from the cleaners, Special Agent Dressler reveals what happened. It seems the police "happened" to pass by and picked up two people for distributing without a license. Comrade Claire apparently made a mistake by forgetting about the license, and as such, will be held accountable for her actions.

Production Notes: Four electricians, one cableman, one welfare worker, and two stand-ins were needed for the first day of filming. One electrician, one policeman, four drivers, two stand-ins, and four extras were needed for the second day of filming. Dressler's car, a 33-passenger bus, Philbrick's car, and an International station wagon were needed for the second day of filming. A crab dolly was rented for the electrical department for the first day of filming.

Total Crew Hours:	20
Make Ready and Shooting:	19 hours
Travel Time:	1 hour

Location Shots:
6641 Santa Monica Blvd.
700 North Vine Street
Corner Melrose and Cole
858 Westchester

SEASON THREE

Episode #79 "RENDEZVOUS"
Production # 1079 / 79B
Typescript (annotated) by Ellis Marcus, July 12, 1955
Master mimeo, July 12, 1955
Filmed July 19 and 20, 1955

Cast: Richard Carlson (Herbert A. Philbrick); Robert Christopher

(Comrade Harvey); Mel Welles (Comrade Willy); Virginia Stefan (Eva Philbrick); John Zaremba (Special Agent Jerry Dressler); Henry Hunter (Comrade Ben); and Helene Hawley (Comrade Felice).

Production Credits

Director:	Eddie Davis
Production Chief:	Eddie Davis
First Assistant Director:	Dick McWhorter
Second Assistant Director:	Bobby Ray
First Cameraman:	Monk Askins
Second Cameraman:	Dick Rawlings
First Assistant Cameraman:	Jim Bell
Sound Mixer:	Gary Harris
Recorder:	Bob Post
Boom Man:	Elmer Haglund
First Company Grip:	Carl Miksch
Second Company Grip:	Tex Jackson (second day only)
Property Master:	Ygnacio Sepulveda
Assistant Property Man:	Don Smith
Set Decorator:	Bruce "Bud" MacDonald
Wardrobe Man:	Al Berke
Script Supervisor:	Larry Lund
Film Editor:	Jack Woelz
Gaffer:	S.H. Barton
Set Director:	Ted McCaskey
Construction Chief:	Archie Hall
Electricians:	Charles Stockwell, Mr. Hanger, and Cortesse

Plot: Philbrick finds himself caught in the machinery of Communist justice in action, when, after tipping off a hunch to Special Agent Dressler that Comrade Felice was to be liquidated, her life is saved in the nick of time. Almost overnight, Commie headquarters is moved to a new location and none of the cell members will talk to Philbrick. Herb soon learns that Comrade Willy, a member of the NKDV and wannabe leader of a dangerous group of revolutionists, is making Philbrick look like an informant, suspecting the tip-off. Special Agent Dressler discovers Comrade Willy is a former Nazi, who enjoys cracking a few skulls to gain power and move up the ranks, and gives Herb the details. During a private inquiry, Philbrick is tried and found guilty of contacting the F.B.I., until Philbrick reveals a newspaper article with a picture of Comrade Willy as a Nazi during the war, working with the same Hitler that invaded Russia. Once Willy's credibility is put to the test, the Communist leader is found guilty of blame-shifting for power. Philbrick, in the meantime, is cleared of any wrongdoing and briefed on the new location of Communist Headquarters.

PRODUCTION NOTES: Five drivers, seven extras and two stand-ins were needed on the first day of filming. Three electricians, two stand-ins, and three extras were needed for the second day of filming. Dressler's car (a brown Plymouth), a 33-passenger bus, Philbrick's car (a green Ford), a truck, Harvey's car (a green Plymouth station wagon), and a camera car (station wagon) were needed for the first day of filming.

COLORFUL TRIVIA: All of the episodes from the first season were shot in black and white. The entire second season was filmed in color, though color prints from the second season are not easy to come by among collectors and fans of the series. The color was primitive and cheap, and sadly, many color prints have turned pinkish over time. For the third season, beginning with this episode, the production crew went back to black and white, shot with 35mm black and white both plus—& tri—x film.

LOCATION SHOTS:
1919 SOUTH MAIN STREET
EXPOSITION PARK, NORTH FIGUERA DRIVE
918 WESTCHESTER PLACE
858 SOUTH WESTCHESTER PLACE
7000 ROMAINE
7201 SANTA MONICA
7200 BLOCK SANTA MONICA
FULLER AND ROMAINE

Episode #80 "HOUSE BREAKING"

Production # 1080 / 80B
Typescript (annotated) by Stuart Jerome, July 11, 1955
Master mimeo, July 12, 1955
Revised pages (annotated), July 18, 1955
Filmed July 21 and 22, 1955

Cast: Richard Carlson (Herbert A. Philbrick); Robert Griffin (Comrade Mullen); William Vaughn (Comrade Roach); Virginia Stefan (Eva Philbrick); John Zaremba (Special Agent Jerry Dressler); Bob Harris (Comrade Hagan); and Don Hix (Comrade Kirk).

Production Credits

Director:	Henry S. Kesler
Production Chief:	Henry S. Kesler
First Assistant Director:	Jack Gertsman
First Cameraman:	Curt Fetters (first day only)
First Cameraman:	Bobby Hoffman (second day only)
Second Cameraman:	Ken Williams (first day only)
Second Cameraman:	Bud Mautino (second day only)
First Assistant Cameraman:	Spec Jones (second day only)
Sound Mixer:	Roy Meadows (first day only)
Sound Mixer:	Jay Ashworth (second day only)
Recorder:	Bill Hanks (first day only)
Recorder:	Larry Golding (second day only)
Boom Man:	William Morris (first day only)

Boom Man:	Jim Flannery (second day only)
First Company Grip:	Carl Miksch (first day only)
First Company Grip:	Mel Bledsoe (second day only)
Second Company Grip:	Vernon Marshall (first day only)
Property Master:	Robert Benton, Sr.
Assistant Property Man:	Don Smith
Set Decorator:	Robert Bradfield
Wardrobe Man:	Al Berke
Script Supervisor:	Wesley Jones (first day only)
Film Editor:	Duncan Mansfield, A.C.E
Gaffers:	S.H. Barton
Set Director:	Ted McCaskey
Construction Chief:	Archie Hall
Electricians:	Charles Stockwell

Plot: The Philbricks return from a week-long vacation (a second honeymoon) to find their house ransacked, and before Herb can discover whether or not his hidden room was uncovered, Comrade Roach appears and orders Philbrick to attend a cell meeting. It seems they plan to expose a traitor. Roach also blackmails Herb for $200 for his silence, since he claims he was the man who had broken into the Philbrick house, and that Herb will be exposed as the traitor. Still unable to find out if his secret room was discovered, Herb reluctantly pays the blackmail and hopes Comrade Roach was bluffing. During the meeting, Comrade Mullen explains to Philbrick that he and Roach went through the house and found a stack of papers listing F.B.I. Agents, and threatened to pour boiling water on him. When Philbrick discovers that the papers were forged and planted by Roach, the committee discovers the truth by Roach's impulse for self-preservation—and blackmail money to prove it. Thus, a counterspy under suspicion for treachery is spared liquidation.

Comment: There is really great suspense in this episode; even suggesting that the Party found Herb's hidden room and the copies of his reports addressed to the F.B.I. By the unwritten laws of television programs of the fifties, the hero wouldn't be exposed anyway to the villains, but with a show that prides itself on changing aspects of the series during the progression of the episodes, and being early in the third season, there was cause to suspect that the Communists had discovered his secret.

PRODUCTION NOTES: Two electricians, one policeman, one extra, and one stand-in were needed for the first day of filming. Two electricians and two stand-ins were needed for the second day of filming. Dressler's car (a 1955 Nash Ambassador) and Comrade Roach's car (a 1955 Nash Lemans) were needed for the first day of filming. Philbrick's car (a 1955 Chevrolet) was used in both days of filming.
TOTAL CREW HOURS: 20

LOCATION SHOTS:
CARTHAY CENTER
SECURITY 1ST NATIONAL BANK, 6320 SAN VINCENTE BLVD.
CIVIC PLAYHOUSE, 755 NORTH LA CIENGA
STAGE 5 AT ZIV STUDIOS

EPISODE #81 "ATTACK AREA"
PRODUCTION # 1080 / 81B
TYPESCRIPT BY JACK ROCK, CIRCA JULY 19, 1955
MASTER MIMEO (ANNOTATED), JULY 26, 1955
REVISED MASTER MIMEO, JULY 26, 1955
FILMED JULY 29 AND 30, 1955

CAST: Richard Carlson (Herbert A. Philbrick); Gordon Wynn (Comrade Sedare); Don C. Harvey (Comrade Nycheck); Joan Danton (Comrade Luvana); John Beradino (Special Agent Steve Daniels); and Bill Layne (Carl).

PRODUCTION CREDITS
DIRECTOR: HENRY S. KESLER

Production Chief:	Henry S. Kesler
First Assistant Director:	Eddie Stein
Second Assistant Director:	Willard Kirkham
First Cameraman:	Monk Askins
Second Cameraman:	Bud Mautino
First Assistant Cameraman:	Spec Jones
Sound Mixer:	Jay Ashworth
Recorder:	Larry Golding
Boom Man:	Jim Flannery
First Company Grip:	Mel Bledsoe (first day only)
First Company Grip:	Tex Jackson (second day only)
Second Company Grip:	Walter Culp (second day only)
Property Master:	Ygnacio Sepulveda
Assistant Property Man:	Stanley Walters
Set Decorator:	Robert Bradfield
Wardrobe Man:	Al Berke
Script Supervisor:	Jane Ficker
Film Editor:	Tommy Scott
Gaffer:	Wade Huff
Construction Chief:	Archie Hall
Electrician:	Mike Hudson and Hap Manley
Policeman supplied by:	Jess Haggerty

Plot: Comrade Nycheck, a member of the Communist Goon Squad, delivers a package to Philbrick's garage and orders him to keep it secure, against the temptation of Herb Philbrick. When Special Agent Steve Daniels and Special Agent Carl visit the garage and open the crate, they discover enough T.N.T. to blow the city apart, and are surprised by an unscheduled visit from two Comrades, and close the container quickly. Later, Comrade Nycheck is ordered to load the box's contents into the back of a car, a little at a time. When the phone rings, Philbrick is given coordinates for the location to plant the explosives. While the Comrades plant the explosives at the assigned locations, Philbrick takes a picture of the map with his cufflink camera and drops the roll of film where the F.B.I. can pick it up. When they return to Philbrick's house to relax and listen to the radio for the news reports, Comrade Sedare is shocked to discover that the explosives never went off. Later that evening, Steve Daniels explains to Herb that the Comrades were picked up at every delivery point, courtesy of the map. Comrade Sedare will take the rap for the failure of the project, and the F.B.I. will pick him up later when he is alone, so no suspicion will fall on Philbrick.

PRODUCTION NOTES: Three electricians, one policeman, five drivers, and three stand-ins were needed for the first day of filming. Three electricians, one third-grip, a cableman, and three stand-ins were needed for the second day of filming. A standby car, a heavy's car, and a panel truck were needed for the first day of filming. A cab dolly was rented for use on the second day of filming.

TOTAL CREW HOURS:	19
MAKE READY AND SHOOTING:	17 1/2 HOURS
TRAVEL TIME:	1 1/2 HOURS

LOCATION SHOTS:
MCCADDEN AND ROMAINE STREET, 5311 MELROSE AVE.
LEMON GOVE ST. TUNNEL
WESTCHESTER ST. & 9TH
858 SOUTH WESTCHESTER ST.
700 NORTH COLE

EPISODE #82 "SACRIFICED"
ORIGINAL COPYRIGHT FOR PRODUCTION #1082, OCTOBER 15, 1955. ORIGINAL REGISTRATION #LP49218
PRODUCTION # 1082 / 82B
TYPESCRIPT (ANNOTATED), BY DONN MULLALLY, N.D.
MASTER MIMEO, JULY 19, 1955
REVISED PAGES (ANNOTATED), JULY 25, 1955
FILMED JULY 27 AND 28, 1955

Cast: Richard Carlson (Herbert A. Philbrick); Virginia Stefan (Eva Philbrick); John Zaremba (Special Agent Jerry Dressler); Edith Leslie (Comrade Grant); Bob Malcolm (Colonel Paxton); Paul Baxley (Cummins); Morgan Windbiel (Hillman); Matty Fain (Marsen); and Harry Guardino (Duncan).

Production Credits

Director:	Leon Benson
Production Chief:	Leon Benson
First Assistant Director:	Jack Gertsman
Second Assistant Director:	Bobby Ray
First Cameraman:	Monk Askins (first day only)
First Cameraman:	Curt Fetters (second day only)
Second Cameraman:	Dick Rawlings
First Assistant Cameraman:	Jim Bell
Sound Mixer:	Gary Harris
Recorder:	George Anderson
Boom Man:	Elmer Haglund
First and Second Company Grip:	Mel Bledsoe
Property Master:	Robert Benton, Sr.
Assistant Property Man:	Harry Ott
Set Decorator:	R. Bradfield
Wardrobe Man:	Al Berke
Script Supervisor:	Larry Lund
Film Editor:	Duncan Mansfield, a.c.e
Gaffer:	S.H. Barton
Set Director:	Art Sweet
Construction Chief:	Archie Hall
Electrician:	Charles Stockwell
Policeman supplied by:	Jess Haggerty

Plot: Philbrick is surprised when he visits headquarters to learn that his next mission for the Reds will also be his last. Colonel Paxton and his fundraising campaign are too valuable to be jeopardized, including his membership with the Anti-Communist

Committee. To eliminate suspicion from himself, Paxton will go on local TV and name names of people who are active members of the Party. During this broadcast, Philbrick is going to be named the "leader" of the Communist group . . . and become a sacrificial lamb for the cause. Herb has no choice but to break the news to Agent Dressler, who suggests that he convince Comrade Grant that Colonel Paxton is a traitor—even an F.B.I. informer. With assistance from Agents of the Federal Bureau, a letter and other suspicious objects are planted in Paxton's house, so Comrade Grant can see for himself that Paxton has been "secretly" disloyal to the Party. Even when Paxton is being tailed, he is witnessed talking to an F.B.I. Agent—courtesy of Agent Dressler—all the more convincing. The plan to "name names" to eliminate suspicion is foiled quickly and the F.B.I. gains a bonus—the Party lost one of their most important members—turning to the other side to save his own skin.

MEMORABLE QUOTE: Philbrick remarked to himself: "I haven't done anything for the F.B.I. It's been a selfish one-way street the whole time. I just want a free country for my kids."

PRODUCTION NOTES: One electrician, one policeman, one fireman, four drivers, five extras and two stand-ins were needed for the first day of filming. Three electricians and two stand-ins were needed for the second day of filming. Grant's car (a blue four-door Lincoln), a 33-passenger bus, Philbrick's car (a light grey Plymouth Sedan), a mail car (tan Ford station wagon), and a camera and sound car (an Interior station wagon) were needed for the first day of filming. Stock footage was used. A fireman was available for one particular scene, in case of an emergency.

LOCATION SHOTS:

L.A. INTERNATIONAL AIRPORT, PAN AMERICAN WORLD AIRWAYS
9136 SEPULVEDA
U.S. POST OFFICE, WESTCHESTER
858 SOUTH WESTCHESTER PLACE
510 SOUTH ARDEN BLVD.

EPISODE #83 "EVA SICK"

ORIGINAL COPYRIGHT FOR PRODUCTION #1083, OCTOBER 22, 1955. ORIGINAL REGISTRATION #LP49217
PRODUCTION # 1083 / 83B
TYPESCRIPT (ANNOTATED), BY STUART JEROME, AUGUST 12, 1955
MASTER MIMEO, AUGUST 12, 1955
FILMED AUGUST 19 AND 20, 1955

CAST: Richard Carlson (Herbert A. Philbrick); Mauritz Hugo (Comrade Esteban); Patricia Morrow (Connie Philbrick); Virginia Stefan (Eva Philbrick); John Zaremba (Special Agent Jerry Dressler); Donna Drew (girl in phone booth); Lainey Elliot (telephone operator); Laura Sexton (girl receptionist); Charles Conrad (Dr. Blankfort); James Macklin (garage man); and Robert A. Vanselow (policeman).

PRODUCTION CREDITS

DIRECTOR:	EDDIE DAVIS
PRODUCTION CHIEF:	EDDIE DAVIS
FIRST ASSISTANT DIRECTOR:	ERICH VON STROHEIM, JR.
SECOND ASSISTANT DIRECTOR:	BOBBY RAY
FIRST CAMERAMAN:	BOBBY HOFFMAN
SECOND CAMERAMAN:	TOMMY MORRIS
FIRST ASSISTANT CAMERAMAN:	GEORGE LEPICARD
SOUND MIXER:	BOB POST
RECORDER:	KEN CORSON
BOOM MAN:	CARL DANIELS
FIRST COMPANY GRIP:	TEX JACKSON
PROPERTY MASTER:	YGNACIO SEPULVEDA
ASSISTANT PROPERTY MAN:	CHARLES CHICETTI
SET DECORATOR:	VIN TAYLOR
SCRIPT SUPERVISOR:	DORIS AUGUST
FILM EDITOR:	CHUCK CRAFT
SET DIRECTOR:	DON GRAY
CONSTRUCTION CHIEF:	ARCHIE HALL

ELECTRICIANS:	BERT JONES
POLICEMEN SUPPLIED BY:	MORGAN WINDBIEL.
DRIVERS:	ARNOLD BALLARD AND ED FITZGERALD

PLOT: Herb Philbrick is assigned to pick up an envelope at a newsstand and deliver it to a hotel. At a corner phone booth, Herb phones to check in on the status of Eva, who was feeling sick earlier in the morning. Upon learning that the doctor rushed Eva to the hospital, Herb makes a mad rush to the clinic. After learning that Eva's condition is not life-threatening (she merely has the chicken pox), he realizes he absentmindedly forgot the envelope in the phone booth. Realizing his error, he returns to discover the envelope missing. Back at Comrade Esteban's, Herb learns that the envelope contained America's Radar Defense Plans, but before he can make excuses for his mistake, he is shocked to learn that the plans were safely delivered to their destination outside the U.S. Puzzled, Herb visits Agent Dressler, who explains that Herb was being followed and an F.B.I. Agent picked up the envelope, switched the real blueprints for fake ones, and arranged to have them delivered at the rendezvous point where Herb was supposed to deliver them. The Communists will never know.

PRODUCTION NOTES: One electrician, one policeman, four drivers, a third-grip, one extra, and one stand-in were needed for the first day of filming. Four electricians, one third-grip, one cableman, one stand-in, and one welfare worker were needed for the second day of filming. A bus, an insert car, and a camera and sound car were needed for the first day of filming.

LOCATION SHOTS:
OAKWOOD & LA JOLIA, 8166 BEVERLY BLVD.
8165 BEVERLY BLVD.
CORNER OF YUCCA AND LAS PALMAS
CORNER OF WESTERN AVE. AND HOLLYWOOD BLVD.
1707 HOLLYWOOD BLVD.
PRESBYTERIAN HOSPITAL

1322 North Vermont Ave.
1776 Hilhurst

Episode #84 "ATHLETE"

Original copyright for production #1084, October 29, 1955. Original Registration #LP49216
Production #1084 / 84B
Typescript (annotated) by Leonard Heideman, August 11, 1955
Master mimeo, August 11, 1955
Revised pages (annotated), August 17, 18, 1955
Filmed August 24 and 25, 1955

Cast: Richard Carlson (Herbert A. Philbrick); John Zaremba (Special Agent Jerry Dressler); Robert Wehling (Ralph Brooks); Jeanne Tatum (Rita Brooks); Mark Damon (Fred Semper); Jim Hyland (Coach Miller); and Judson Taylor (Comrade Steve).

Production Credits

Production Chief:	Henry S. Kesler
Director:	Henry S. Kesler
First Assistant Director:	Jack Gertsman
Second Assistant Director:	Jud Cox
First Cameraman:	Monk Askins
Second Cameraman:	Al Green
First Assistant Cameraman:	Spec Jones
Sound Mixer:	Bob Post
Recorder:	Ken Corson
Boom Man:	Carl Daniels
First Company Grip:	Tex Jackson
Property Master:	George Stewart
Assistant Property Man:	Stanley Waiters
Set Decorator:	Clarence Stenson
Script Supervisor:	Jack Ficker
Film Editor:	Duncan Mansfield, a.c.e

GAFFER: JOHN MILLMAN
CONSTRUCTION CHIEF: ARCHIE HALL

PLOT: Comrade Ralph Brooks, a sports writer, wants to hire Herb Philbrick to write a bad article about a rising young track star named Fred Sanford, to discredit the boy. This Communist ploy, entitled "Project Athlete," is not a new gimmick. The method of discrediting good athletes to show American citizens how corrupt fame and fortune inflicts problems to an average athlete can be a powerful tool in psychology. Philbrick informs Agent Dressler, who explains to Herb that Russian Athletes always look good in the Russian papers, and jealousy has always been their downfall. In the passing weeks, Herb gets to know young Fred very well, including how he overcame a physical handicap. When Comrade Ralph wants Fred to go to South America for a race, and offers to fund the boy's trip, Fred will not sign—knowing full well who they are and their motives. Philbrick writes an editorial for the local paper, exposing Fred as a young man who won't take bribes, and his credibility improves. The Party dissociates itself with Brooks and all aspects of "Project Athlete." In fact, a new project is handed to Herb as a form of promotion.

PRODUCTION NOTES: One policeman, three drivers, five extras and two stand-ins were needed for the first day of filming. Three electricians, two stand-ins, and one extra were needed for the second day of filming. A 1954 Lincoln Convertible and a 1955 Plymouth Sedan were needed for the first day of filming.

LOCATION SHOTS:
459 LORING AVE., WEST L.A.
CORDINGLY HOTEL (CORNER OF WILSHIRE AND BEV GLENN), WEST L.A.
WESTWOOD-GAYLEY, BETWEEN WAYBURN AND WILSHIRE
ALL OF THE TRACK-AND-FIELD SCENES WERE FILMED ON LOCATION AT THE UCLA CAMPUS TRACK FIELD.
UCLA ALSO LENT USE OF THEIR ART BUILDING FOR FILMING.
STAGE 5 AT ZIV STUDIOS

Episode #85 "LAWYER"

Original copyright for production #1085, November 5, 1955. Original Registration #LP49210
Production # 1085 / 85B
Typescript (annotated) by Ellis Marcus, August 18, 1955
Master mimeo, August 18, 1955
Revised pages (annotated), August 25, 1955
Filmed August 31 and September 1, 1955

Cast: Richard Carlson (Herbert A. Philbrick); John Zaremba (Special Agent Jerry Dressler); Stuart Nedd (Comrade Bob); Robin Short (Jeff Donahue); Paul Hahn (Comrade Zach Draper); and Vicki Bakken (Gloria Penrose).

Production Credits

Production Chief:	Jack Herzberg
Director:	Jack Herzberg
First Assistant Director:	Bert Glazer
Second Assistant Director:	William Kirkham
First Cameraman:	Monk Askins (first day only)
First Cameraman:	Bill Sickner (second day only)
Second Cameraman:	Al Green (first day only)
Second Cameraman:	John Hickerson (second day only)
First Assistant Cameraman:	Spec Jones (first day only)
Sound Mixer:	Bob Post (first day only)
Sound Mixer:	Harry Mills (second day only)
Recorder:	Ken Corson (first day only)
Recorder:	Walter Peague (second day only)
Boom Man:	William Hamilton (first day only)

Boom Man:	Ace Beall (second day only)
First Company Grip:	Tex Jackson
Second Company Grip:	Larry Yutronich
Property Master:	E. Smith
Assistant Property Man:	Stanley Walters
Set Decorator:	Bruce "Bud" MacDonald
Wardrobe Man:	Frank Tauss
Script Supervisor:	Doris August
Film Editor:	Duncan Mansfield, A.C.E
Gaffer:	John Millman
Construction Chief:	Archie Hall
Electricians:	John Millman, Mr. Hounshell, Mr. Gediman and Roy Slocum
Policeman supplied by:	Morgan Windbeil

Plot: Comrade Bob asks Philbrick to get acquainted with Jeff Donahue, a lawyer, so Jeff can defend Comrade Zack Draper in court. It seems Comrade Draper was arrested on an aggravated assault charge by a piano player. Comrade Draper needs a good defense so he can be free to continue his work for the Party. Philbrick consults Jeff and hires him to take to Draper's defense. After questioning a witness, Herb and Jeff discover that Draper is innocent of the crime he is charged with. Meanwhile, Comrade Bob gives Phil the bail money and Jeff discovers by accident that the witness did not have a piano recital as she stated. Now an innocent lawyer will be put in a fix if he loses and in the hands of the Communist Party if he wins. Philbrick cleverly tricks Comrade Draper into revealing where the piano was during the evening of the assault, and forces Draper to uncover an error in his story. This satisfies Jeff, who sternly decides not to represent Comrade Draper in court . . . and walks away with his hands clean. Since Philbrick was not let in on the scheme, he is not found guilty of "accidentally" revealing Draper's mistake. Comrade Bob, however, will have to explain to the Party why the scheme failed. To close matters, a Commie strong-arm makes for Draper's residence in the hopes of preventing any testimony in court, but the F.B.I. arrives on the scene and take Draper in for questioning.

Production Notes: One electrician, one extra and one stand-in were needed for the first day of filming. Four electricians, one policeman, one stand-in, and one extra were needed for the second day of filming. Zach's car (white-and-blue hardtop Mercedes-Benz), a bus, Philbrick's car (a light green Chevy), a police car, and a camera insert car (requires high set-up for running shots) were needed for the first day of filming.

Location Shots:
401 McCadden
United Cerebral Palsy, 5201 Beverly Blvd.
1438 North Wilcox
Dick & Leo's, Highland and Waring
Hollywood Police Station, Wilcox and DeLongpree
Mr. Brown's House, 623 North Citrus Street
DeLongpree Park, June and DeLongpree

Episode #86 "NEWSREEL"
Original copyright for production #1086, November 12, 1955. Original Registration #LP49211
Production # 1086 / 86B
Typescript (annotated) by Rik Vollaerts, August 11, 1955
Master mimeo (annotated), August 23, 1955
Revised master mimeo, August 23, 1955
Revised pages (annotated), August 26, 1955
Filmed September 6 and 7, 1955

Cast: Richard Carlson (Herbert A. Philbrick); John Zaremba (Special Agent Jerry Dressler); Ralph Clanton (Comrade Marvin Tanner); Robert Fatten (Comrade Gary Schooner); Doug Henderson (Ralph Desmond); and Richard Beach (Special Agent Will Congdon).

Production Credits
Production Chief: Henry S. Kesler
Director: Henry S. Kesler

FIRST ASSISTANT DIRECTOR:	BERT GLAZER
SECOND ASSISTANT DIRECTOR:	WILLARD KIRKHAM
FIRST CAMERAMAN:	MONK ASKINS
SECOND CAMERAMAN:	AL GREEN
FIRST ASSISTANT CAMERAMAN:	SPEC JONES
SOUND MIXER:	JAY ASHWORTH
RECORDER:	ROY CROPPER
BOOM MAN:	BILL FLANNERY
FIRST COMPANY GRIP:	CARL MIKSCH
SECOND COMPANY GRIP:	TEX JACKSON
PROPERTY MASTER:	ERNIE SMITH
ASSISTANT PROPERTY MAN:	BOB MURDOCH
SET DECORATOR:	CLARENCE STENSON
WARDROBE MAN:	FRANK TAUSS
SCRIPT SUPERVISOR:	JANE FICKER
FILM EDITOR:	JACK WOELZ
GAFFER:	BERT JONES
SET DIRECTOR:	ART SWEET
CONSTRUCTION CHIEF:	ARCHIE HALL
ELECTRICIANS:	BERT JONES AND MIKE HUDSON
DRIVERS:	MR. THETFORD, MR. HELMICK, MR. DAIBER, MR. MORPHIS AND JACK OSBORN

PLOT: Comrade Marvin Tanner explains to Philbrick that the Party just acquired the Aurora Newsreel Corporation and knowledge of the new ownership will be kept a secret. Their goal is to create newsreels for shipment abroad, and they are to be edited to show police brutality, slums, starving people, and mistreatment of minorities so that viewers abroad will believe what they see about the United States—not just what they hear. Tanner also tells Philbrick that he suspects one of his cell members of being a counter-spy for the F.B.I. and the Party has plans to eliminate him quickly. Philbrick tells Special Agent Dressler, who admits they do have another counterspy, but like Philbrick, are unable to protect him. Since there is no law against making newsreels, the F.B.I. is powerless to stop the Party. Philbrick, however, suggests to the Party that they use the filmmaking facilities to create indoctrinate and educational training films, which puts Philbrick in the Party's good graces and doubles for the F.B.I. since this new task is a violation of the Smith Act. After learning from a Comrade that the counterspy has been eliminated, Philbrick purposely switches the film labels, and an educational short is shown in a local theater. The federal authorities have what they need to begin arrests of everyone involved—except for Philbrick who wasn't listed as an employee of Aurora Studios.

Production Notes: Two electricians, five drivers, and one stand-in were needed on the first day of filming. Four electricians and one stand-in were needed on the second day of filming. Dressler's car (green hard-top Mercury), Philbrick's car, and Desmond's car were needed for both days of filming. A bus and a station wagon were needed on the second day only.

Location Shots:
Gilmore Drive-In, 6201 West 3rd Street

Episode #87 "COMMON DENOMINATOR"
Production #1088 / 87B
Typescript (annotated), by Donn Mullally, August 18, 1955
Master mimeo, August 18, 1955
Revised pages (annotated), September 1, 1955
Filmed September 8 and 9, 1955

Cast: Richard Carlson (Herbert A. Philbrick); Virginia Stefan (Eva Philbrick); John Beradino (Special Agent Steve Daniels); Hy Anzel (Comrade Fulton); George Meader (Hiltener); Brad Trumbull (Comrade Garro); and Fredd Villani (Comrade Walsh).

Production Credits

Production Chief:	Jon Epstein
Director:	Lambert Hillyer

FIRST ASSISTANT DIRECTOR:	JACK GERTSMAN
SECOND ASSISTANT DIRECTOR:	WILLARD KIRKHAM
FIRST CAMERAMAN:	BOBBY HOFFMAN
SECOND CAMERAMAN:	DICK RAWLINGS
FIRST ASSISTANT CAMERAMAN:	JIM BELL
SOUND MIXER:	GARY HARRIS
RECORDER:	WILLIAM HANKS
BOOM MAN:	ELMER HAGLUND
FIRST COMPANY GRIP:	MEL BLEDSOE
SECOND COMPANY GRIP:	TOM MATHIS
PROPERTY MASTER:	ROBERT BENTON SR.
ASSISTANT PROPERTY MAN:	CECIL SMITH
SET DECORATOR:	CLARENCE STENSON
WARDROBE MAN:	AL BERKE
SCRIPT SUPERVISOR:	LARRY LUND
FILM EDITOR:	DUNCAN MANSFIELD, A.C.E
GAFFER:	JOHN MILLMAN
SET DIRECTOR:	ART SWEET
CONSTRUCTION CHIEF:	ARCHIE HALL
ELECTRICIANS:	MIKE HUDSON, WALTER GIDEMAN AND ROY SLOCUM

PLOT: Since the Party has been growing increasingly annoyed with the failure of numerous plans in the area, two Comrades are secretly assigned to use a special machine that will find a common denominator—and the answer turns up Herbert A. Philbrick. Comrade Fulton decides to test Philbrick, by giving him a "special assignment." The Philbricks are ordered to put two men up for a spell, Comrade Garrow and Comrade Walsh. With no knowledge of why they are there, the Philbricks play along until Special Agent Steve Daniels explains that Antonio Prado, a South American bigwig, is arriving in the U.S. and a special convoy, en route from the airport, will pass through Herb's neighborhood. But if they deviate from that route, the Reds will figure Herb at fault and "eliminate" him. As each day and hour passes, the Philbricks are forced to play along with the assassination attempt, even being tied down to their beds to eliminate any chances of interference. After the cars pass and no gunplay is exchanged, Herb and Eva are released. Comrade Fulton confesses Herb's loyalty and assumes a human element with the machine caused a factor of failure. As for Prado's route, Daniels explains to Philbrick that Prado went by bus through the city. An F.B.I. Agent took Prado's place during the escort through the suburbs.

Production Notes: Three electricians, one third-grip, and two cablemen were needed on the first day of filming. One electrician, one cableman, one policeman, and five drivers were needed on the second day of filming. Fulton's car (a blue Mercury convertible), a bus, Philbrick's car (a green Ford Sedan), an Escort car (black Lincoln Sedan) were all needed. A motorcycle and a camera and sound car were needed for the second day of filming. A crab dolly was rented for use on the second day of filming.

Location Shots:
South Kratz Building Corp., 260 South Beverly Dr.
Westwood Nursery, 9786 West Pico
Motor Ave. south of Pico Blvd.
Chevrolet Hills Playground
858 South Westchester Place

Episode #88 "STOLEN PASSPORT"
Production # 1088 / 88B
Typescript (annotated), by Leonard Heiderman, September 2, 1955
Master mimeo, September 2, 1955
Master mimeo (annotated), September 10, 1955
Revised pages (annotated), September 10, 1955
Revised pages, September 10, 1955
Filmed September 13 and 14, 1955

Cast: Richard Carlson (Herbert A. Philbrick); John Zaremba (Special Agent Jerry Dressler); Lyn Guild (Charlene Ordway); William S. Meigs (Comrade Albert Anders); Monty Ash (Paul

Edward Kulaki); Jeanne Baird (Ellen Kulaki); Robert Sheldon (the attendant); and Albert Carrier (the waiter).

Production Credits

Production Chief:	Eddie Davis
Director:	Eddie Davis
First Assistant Director:	Eddie Stein
Second Assistant Director:	Bobby Ray
First Cameraman:	Curt Fetters
Second Cameraman:	Dick Rawlings
First Assistant Cameraman:	Jim Bell
Sound Mixer:	Gary Harris
Recorder:	William Hanks
Boom Man:	Elmer Haglund
First Company Grip:	Carl Miksch
Second Company Grip:	Tex Jackson (second day only)
Property Master:	Ygnacio Sepulveda
Assistant Property Man:	Stanley Walters
Set Decorator:	Bruce "Bud" MacDonald
Wardrobe Man:	Al Berke
Script Supervisor:	Jane Ficker
Film Editor:	Tom Scott
Gaffer:	Bert Jones
Set Director:	Art Sweet
Construction Chief:	Archie Hall
Electricians:	Mike Hudson, Mr. Kraus and Roy Slocum
Drivers:	Arnold Ballard, Harry Dalstrom, Mr. Spencer, Mr. Goodman and Ernie Reed

Plot: Herb is assigned by Comrade Anders to go to Los Angeles and move in with Paul Edward Kulaki and his wife, to supervise his work for the Party. Kulaki came from Canada under a British passport, and now teaches English in a high school while serving an intellectual purpose for the Party—not physical. But one evening on the way home, Kulaki is trailed by Herb, who observes Kulaki making contacts, and picking up envelopes—information about the local guided missile plant. After finding a secret photography room downstairs, Philbrick is caught red-handed by Mrs. Kulaki, who accuses him of being a spy. After Herb passes his information to Agent Dressler, he is forced to meet Comrade Anders face-to-face and does not deny any of his actions. Herb claims Kulaki was careless in his job and as a result, Philbrick was able to learn what he knows and this jeopardizes Party security. Comrade Anders agrees, and eliminates Kulaki, assigning Philbrick a new task—of handing the microfilm containing all of Kulaki's work to a destination in Ottawa. Philbrick passes the film to Dressler, who, after viewing the pictures, agrees that it cannot fall into the wrong hands. Philbrick stalls for time from his Canadian contact long enough for Dressler to return the film—now containing fake documents. With knowledge of the Canadian contact, the F.B.I. will follow the trail and smash the espionage ring up north.

Trivia, Etc. Since the series takes place in Massachusetts, the film crew had always been cautious of filming palm trees, but since this episode takes place in Los Angeles, palm trees actually make an appearance in this episode.

Production Notes: Two stand-ins and two extras were needed on the first day of filming. Three electricians, two stand-ins, one extra, and five drivers were needed on the second day of filming. A Nash Rambler (for the aircraft workers), a 33-passenger bus, Philbrick's car (a red Ford Convertible), a camera car (station wagon), and Kulaki's car were needed for the first day of filming.

Location Shots:

Filmed on location at Grauman's Chinese Theatre, when Philbrick moves into the courtyard and speaks to the F.B.I. Agent who tells Philbrick the story about Kulaki and the Canadian government tie-up. Hollywood High School, located at 1521 North Highland, is used when Kulaki, with books under his arm, comes out of the building, and moves past Philbrick hiding behind a street map.

1600 North Orange
Tanner Garage
Westchester District
International Airport

Episode #89 "EXCHANGE STUDENT"
Production # 1089 / 89B
Typescript (annotated), September 3, 1955
Master mimeo, September 3, 1955
Revised pages (annotated), September 15, 16, 1955
Filmed September 17 and 19, 1955

Cast: Richard Carlson (Herbert A. Philbrick); John Beradino (Special Agent Steve Daniels); Charles Maxwell (Special Agent Joe Carey); David Post (Leevack Charaine); Doralyn Gordan (Comrade Nita); Russell Whiteman (Dean Harris); and Maxwell Wagner (Morgan).

Production Credits

Director:	Les Goodwin
Production Chief:	Jack Herzberg
First Assistant Director:	Eddie Mull
Second Assistant Director:	Jud Cox
First Cameraman:	Monk Askins
Second Cameraman:	Al Green (first day only)
First Assistant Cameraman:	Spec Jones
Sound Mixer:	Jay Ashworth
Recorder:	Roy Cropper
Boom Man:	Bill Flannery
First Company Grip:	Tex Jackson
Second Company Grip:	Bing Hall (second day only)
Property Master:	Robert Benton Sr.
Assistant Property Man:	Stanley Waltere
Set Decorator:	Clarence Stenson

Wardrobe Man:	Al Berke
Script Supervisor:	Ruth Brownson
Film Editor:	Duncan Mansfield, A.C.E
Gaffer:	S.H. Barton
Set Director:	Herb Pritchard
Construction Chief:	Dee Bolhius
Electricians:	S.H. Barton
Policeman supplied by:	Jess Haggerty
Drivers:	Arnold Ballard, Steddard, Snyder and Jack Osborn

Plot: In an effort to salvage communication difficulties with Party members abroad, a Student Exchange program is established. With an increase in couriers being picked up, codes being cracked, and a postal system that cannot be trusted, the Commies are getting desperate. Philbrick is assigned to escort and follow a foreign exchange student named Leevack, and if need be, fill his every request. This task comes in the form of picking up a brush and comb, taking a broken watch to a repair man, and so on. Agent Steve Daniels of the F.B.I. helps Philbrick discover the method by which Leevack is using to send messages in and out of the country. It seems the watch repair man "fixes" the watch so a message in the form of a magnetic recording is coded on a metal spring. During a pool party, Philbrick dodges bullets for the F.B.I. by creating a distraction, while Agent Daniels and his associate find the recording in the wristwatch. Later, when the repair man gets suspicious, he attempts to smash the next watch—but the F.B.I. prevents him from succeeding. Philbrick, in the meantime, personally sees Leevack to the airport, knowing full well that future messages will not be as reliable as they cross the border.

Production Notes: Two electricians, one policeman, four drivers, one stand-in, and five extras were needed for the first day of filming. Four electricians and one stand-in were needed for the second day of filming. A props car, a 40-passenger bus, Philbrick's car, a station wagon, and a camera car were needed for this film. Also, Doralyn Gordan requested to use the last name of Cartwright on the end credits.

Location Shots:
Burbank Blvd. and Woodman
4421 Murietta
14010 Chandler
One scene was filmed at Richard Carlson's residence, located at Hollywood Drive and Valley Vista.

Episode #90 "EX G.I."
Production # 1090 / 90B
Typescript (annotated) by Stuart Jerome, September 3, 1955
Master mimeo, September 3, 1955
Revised pages (annotated), September 21, 1955
Filmed September 23 and 24, 1955.

Cast: Richard Carlson (Herbert A. Philbrick); John Zaremba (Special Agent Jerry Dressler); Eddie Garr (Alex Bulgov); Mack Williams (Comrade Boden); and Ted Jacques (Comrade Halliday).

Production Credits

Director:	Jack Herzberg
Production Chief:	Jack Herzberg
First Assistant Director:	Eddie Stein
Second Assistant Director:	Willard Kirkham
First Cameraman:	Curt Fetters
Second Cameraman:	Dick Rawlings
First Assistant Cameraman:	Jim Bell
Sound Mixer:	Gary Harris
Recorder:	William Hanks
Boom Man:	Elmer Haglund
First Company Grip:	Carl Miksch
Second Company Grip:	Bud Busick
Property Master:	Ygnacio Sepulveda
Assistant Property Man:	Bob Murdock
Set Decorator:	Bruce "Bud" MacDonald
Wardrobe Man:	Al Berke
Script Supervisor:	Larry Lund

Film Editor:	Sam Starr
Set Director:	Art Sweet
Construction Chief:	Dee Bolius
Electricians:	Mike Hudson, Bert Jones and someone named Graham
Drivers:	Arnold Ballard, Harry Dalstrom, Mr. Spencer, Mr. Goodman and Ernie Reed

Plot: Alex Bulgov, an old Army buddy of Philbrick's, fears the Soviet Police has been following him, and asks Herb to visit a cottage out of town to pick up a consignment for the U.S. Herb reluctantly agrees but before he can do so, Comrade Boden explains that Alex has in his possession some coded papers of electro-turbine installations, and before the Party can eliminate the traitor, they want to know where the papers are and more importantly—why he chooses Philbrick as his contact. When Alex returns to pay Herb a visit, he forces him to drive out of town at the point of a gun. On the way, Alex explains to his old friend that while he was overseas, the secret police took his wife away and he never saw her again. His consignment is a small boy, his seven-year-old son Paul, who he smuggled off a ship with the promise of America. Alex hands Philbrick an envelope with the coded papers the Commies want—and Alex assures Philbrick that the plans are useless. But the boy is his main concern. When Comrade Boden's goons show up at the cabin, having tailed the men, Alex attempts to make a break for it and is gunned down. Philbrick hands Comrade Halliday the documents, and is told that he did a good job. After the goons leave, Philbrick takes the sleeping lad to Special Agent Dressler, who promises the boy will be relocated in the U.S. with a loving home. Perhaps one day Philbrick will be allowed to visit the boy and explain that his father did not die in vain.

Production Notes: Three electricians, one cableman, one motorcycle policeman, one fireman, four drivers, two stand-ins, one welfare worker, and one extra were needed for the first day of filming. Four electricians, one cableman, two stand-ins, five extras, and one welfare worker were needed for the second day of filming. A 33-passenger bus, Philbrick's car, a camera and sound car, a Commie's car, and a trailer were needed for the first day of filming. A crab dolly was rented on the second day and a western dolly was rented on the first day.

LOCATION SHOTS:
LOUIE DUBEWY, 7314 SUNSET BLVD.
ST. THOMAS CHURCH, 7501 HIGHWAY
L. STRAUSS, GRIFFITH PARK AT VERMONT (CABIN)
ICE CAPADES BUILDING, 6121 SANTA MONICA
FATHE BUILDING, 6823 SANTA MONICA
STAGE #5 AT ZIV STUDIOS

EPISODE #91 "PRISONER"
PRODUCTION # 1091 / 91B
TYPESCRIPT (ANNOTATED), BY RIK VOLLAERTS, SEPTEMBER 20, 1955
MASTER MIMEO, SEPTEMBER 20, 1955
REVISED PAGES (ANNOTATED), SEPTEMBER 22, 1955
REVISED PAGES (ANNOTATED), SEPTEMBER 26, 1955
FILMED SEPTEMBER 28 AND 29, 1955

CAST: Richard Carlson (Herbert A. Philbrick); John Zaremba (Special Agent Jerry Dressler); Pierce Lydon (Bill Carter); Guy Rennie (Frank Norris); Dean Cromer (Fred Zimmer); James Bronte (Bill Johnson); and Edward Colebrook (James Swasey).

PRODUCTION CREDITS

DIRECTOR:	LAMBERT HILLYER
PRODUCTION CHIEF:	JACK HERZBERG
FIRST ASSISTANT DIRECTOR:	ERICH VON STROHEIM, JR.
SECOND ASSISTANT DIRECTOR:	WILLARD KIRKHAM
FIRST CAMERAMAN:	MONK ASKINS
SECOND CAMERAMAN:	DICK RAWLINGS
FIRST ASSISTANT CAMERAMAN:	JIM BELL

Sound Mixer:	Gary Harris
Recorder:	William Hanks
Boom Man:	Elmer Haglund
First Company Grip:	Carl Miksch
Property Master:	Ygnacio Sepulveda
Assistant Property Man:	Cecil Smith
Set Decorator:	Bruce "Bud" MacDonald
Wardrobe Man:	Al Berke
Script Supervisor:	Larry Lund
Film Editor:	Duncan Mansfield, A.C.E
Gaffer:	S. H. Barton
Set Director:	Sol Inverso
Construction Chief:	Dee Bolius
Electricians:	S.H. Barton
Drivers:	Arnold Ballard, Harry Dalstrom and Brown

Plot: James Swasey, a former member of the Communist Party, is turning evidence. Swasey is old and tired and a conviction under the Smith Act will finish him. It is this reason that the Party feels Swasey is dangerous, so they decide to silence him for good. Philbrick is chosen to deliver $1,000 to a paid assassin, Jack Norris, a gangster whose reputation for committing such acts even behind bars in front of armed guards is just what the Party needs. But when Norris finds out who the live target is, he demands more money for the job. Philbrick, with permission from his superior, pays Norris a return visit with a few muscles, and demands the job be completed at the original price—or else. Norris agrees and reveals the method of operation—an inmate behind bars will do the job from the inside. With this knowledge, Philbrick is able to leak the info to the F.B.I., who places an undercover agent behind the steel bars to help protect Swasey. After the assassination job is foiled, Swasey, upset and shocked at having seen with his own eyes what the Communists attempted, tells the F.B.I. everything he knows without waiting for a trial. To eliminate suspicion of Philbrick's involvement, the F.B.I. fakes a credible reason for the assassination attempt to reporters for the local newspapers.

Production Notes: One electrician, one cableman, two policemen, four drivers, two stand-ins, and three silent parts were needed for the first day of filming. Four electricians, one cableman, two stand-ins, five extras, and one silent bit part were needed for the second day of filming. A 33-passenger bus, Philbrick's car, Norris's car, and a camera car were needed for the first day of filming.

Location Shots:
Top of cutting room building
Corner of Poinsettia and Romine
Poinsetta Park at Fuller and Romaine
Waring and Martell
Pan Pacific Auditorium is where the final scene with Philbrick and Dressler discussing what happened to Swasey and Zimmer at the prison takes place.
6399 Wilshire Blvd.
All of the scenes that take place inside a building (the cell block, Philbrick's office, Warden's office, etc.) were all filmed during the second day of filming on Stage #7 at ZIV Studios.

◆ ❖ ◆

Episode #92 "INSTRUCTIONAL CAMP"
Production # 1092 / 92B
Typescript (annotated), by Evelyn Lawson and Herbert L. Strock, September 21, 1955
Master mimeo, September 22, 1955
Revised pages (annotated), October 4, 1955
Filmed October 10 and 11, 1955

Cast: Richard Carlson (Herbert A. Philbrick); Paul Harber (Comrade Gertz); Jean Harvey (Mother Strumm); Ed Hinton (Special Agent Hal Henderson); George Fairchild (Mr. Rose); Harry Rand (Mr. Laurel); Charles Macauley (Mr. Aster); James Rawley (Communist Information Chief); and William Taylor (the gatekeeper).

Production Credits

Director:	Herbert L. Strock
Production Chief:	Herbert L. Strock
First Assistant Director:	Don Verk
Second Assistant Director:	Bobby Ray
First Cameraman:	Monk Askins
Second Cameraman:	Dick Rawlings
First Assistant Cameraman:	Jim Bell
Sound Mixer:	Gary Harris (first day only)
Sound Mixer:	Bob Post (second day only)
Recorder:	William Hanks (first day only)
Boom Man:	Elmer Haglund (first day only)
Boom Man:	Steve Marshall (second day only)
First Company Grip:	Carl Miksch (first day only)
Second Company Grip:	Walter Culp
Property Master:	Ygnacio Sepulveda
Assistant Property Man:	Cecil Smith
Set Decorator:	Bruce "Bud" MacDonald
Wardrobe Man:	Al Berke
Script Supervisor:	Jane Ficker
Film Editor:	Chuck Craft
Set Director:	Herb Pritchard
Construction Chief:	Dee Bolius
Electricians:	Charles Stockwell
Drivers:	Ray Stoddard, J. A. Brown, Jack Osborn and George Cox

Plot: Philbrick is compelled to accept an invitation to Camp Pleasure Pines. This camp, available to only high-ranking comrades, is presided over by the fabulous and notorious Mother Strumm, one of the five top Communists in the country. Mother Strumm is also adept in brainwashing and detecting traitors within the Party ranks. On his arrival in camp, Philbrick is put in charge of three agents—specialists trained at the camp—now ready to be released to set up propaganda schools throughout the country. Although aware of the camp's activities, the F.B.I. has never been able to penetrate the camp or "get anything" on Mother Strumm. Therefore, the agents, their operations and conspirators are completely unknown to the F.B.I. How Philbrick, under constant surveillance, conveys the descriptions and destinations of these malignant men to the F.B.I., nipping the project in the bud, is the basis of this episode.

PRODUCTION NOTES: One electrician, one second assistant cameraman, one policeman, four or five drivers, two stand-ins, and five extras were needed for the first day of filming. One electrician, one second assistant cameraman, three drivers, one stand-in, and two extras were needed for the second day of filming. A bus for cast and crew, Philbrick's car, Carlson's car, a camera car, a Ford station wagon, a Commie car, a Mercedes-Benz, and Kulaki's car (a Chrysler Sedan) were needed for the first day of filming.

LOCATION SHOTS:

ALL SCENES THAT TAKE PLACE IN THE CAMP WERE FILMED ON LOCATION AT BRONSON CANYON ON THE FIRST DAY OF FILMING. ALL OTHER SCENES WERE FILMED DURING THE SECOND DAY OF FILMING.

159 SOUTH CENTRAL, GLENDALE

GLENDALE TRAIN STATION

1521 GARDENA AVE., GLENDALE

HARVEY HOTEL, SANTA MONICA BLVD. HOLLYWOOD

900 NORTH MISSION AT RICHMAN (TRAIN YARDS)

EPISODE #93 "SECOND COURIER"

PRODUCTION # 1093 / 93B

TYPESCRIPT (ANNOTATED), BY STUART JEROME, OCTOBER 7, 1955

MASTER MIMEO, OCTOBER 7, 1955

REVISED PAGES (ANNOTATED), OCTOBER 13 AND 14, 1955

FILMED OCTOBER 15 AND 17, 1955

Cast: Richard Carlson (Herbert A. Philbrick); John Zaremba (Special Agent Jerry Dressler); Judith Ames (Comrade Jeannete); George Slocum (Comrade Marin); Robert Patten (Comrade Gary Schooner); George Taylor (the second courier); and William Hughes (the driver).

Production Credits

Director:	Herbert L. Strock
Production Chief:	Herbert L. Strock
First Assistant Director:	Willard Kirkham
Second Assistant Director:	Bobby Ray
First Cameraman:	Bob Hoffman
Second Cameraman:	Dick Rawlings
First Assistant Cameraman:	Jim Bell
Sound Mixer:	Gary Harris
Recorder:	William Hanks
Boom Man:	Elmer Haglund
First Company Grip:	Mel Bledsoe
Second Company Grip:	Jack Chambers
Property Master:	Max Pittman
Assistant Property Man:	Stanley Walters
Set Decorator:	Clarence Steenson
Wardrobe Man:	Al Berke
Script Supervisor:	Jane Ficker
Film Editor:	Duncan Mansfield
Gaffer:	S.H. Barton
Set Director:	Ted McCaskey
Construction Chief:	Dee Bolius
Electricians:	Charles Stockwell
Drivers:	Ray Stoddard, J. A. Brown, Jack Osborn and George Cox

Plot: At the Hotel Harvey, now a central Commie State Headquarters, Philbrick is given a typewriter case and told to deliver it to a special rendezvous point. On board a train, he delivers the case personally to another Party member. When the Party members discover the contents contain an incendiary bomb, a problem comes up. The timer is jammed and the device could go off any time. No one knows how the device operates, but Comrade Jeannete insists on staying to the very end in hopes of switching the bomb off. Her assistant, in the meantime, Comrade Marin, attempts to make a break for his life. Philbrick wants to phone the F.B.I., but is stuck in a situation where he cannot place a phone call, leaving the bomb ticking away. Finally, the F.B.I. arrives at the train station and the Commies—including Philbrick—make haste. While the F.B.I. easily turns the bomb off and confiscates the explosive, the female Comrade accuses Philbrick of phoning the police. But she is in for a surprise. It seems the head man of the Commie State Headquarters was responsible for the anonymous call to the authorities. After all, the bomb had to be turned off. But since Philbrick was the only level-headed man in the scheme of things, he is free to go—unlike Comrade Jeannete and Comrade Marin, who will face death-defying consequences.

Production Notes: One electrician, one second assistant cameraman, one policeman, four or five drivers, two stand-ins, and five extras were needed for the first day of filming. One electrician, one second assistant cameraman, three drivers, one stand-in, and two extras were needed for the second day of filming. A bus for cast and crew, Philbrick's car, Carlson's car, a camera car, a Ford station wagon, a Commie car, a Mercedes-Benz, and Kulaki's car (a Chrysler Sedan) were needed for the first day of filming.

Location Shots:
159 South Central, Glendale
Glendale Train Station
1521 Gardena Ave., Glendale
Harvey Hotel, Santa Monica Blvd. Hollywood
900 North Mission at Richman (train yards)

Episode #94 "PHONY BROTHER"
Production # 1094 / 94B
Typescript (annotated) by Lee Berg, October 5, 1955

Master mimeo (annotated), October 14, 1955
Revised master mimeo, October 14, 1955
Revised pages (annotated), October 17, 1955
Filmed October 18 and 19, 1955

Cast: Richard Carlson (Herbert A. Philbrick); John Zaremba (Special Agent Jerry Dressler); Meg Randall (Lottie Carp); Norman Bartold (Peter Carp); Donald Kirke (Roger Standish); Watson Downs (George Thompson); and Frederic Melchior (Col. Mikhael).

Production Credits

Director:	Henry S. Kesler
Production Chief:	Henry S. Kesler
First Assistant Director:	Don Verk
Second Assistant Director:	Bobby Ray
First Cameraman:	Monk Askins
Second Cameraman:	Dick Rawlings
First Assistant Cameraman:	Jim Bell
Sound Mixer:	Gary Harris
Recorder:	William Hanks
Boom Man:	Elmer Haglund
First Company Grip:	Carl Miksch
Second Company Grip:	Coley Kessinger
Property Master:	Victor Petrotta
Assistant Property Man:	Stanley Walters
Set Decorator:	Bruce "Bud" MacDonald
Wardrobe Man:	Al Berke
Script Supervisor:	Larry Lund
Film Editor:	Chuck Craft
Gaffer:	S.H. Barton
Set Director:	Sol Inverso
Construction Chief:	Dee Bolius
Electricians:	Mike Hudson, Charles Stockwell and Mr. Hanger
Drivers:	J.A. Brown and Ray Stoddard

Plot: Lottie Carp and her brother Peter return from behind the Iron Curtain, and Philbrick is hired as press agent for an

Anti-Commie Tour where Peter is to give a number of lectures. But during the tour, as Philbrick continues to type speech after speech, he suspects something wrong. Playing on Lottie's nerves, Philbrick discovers that Peter is a fake. Her real brother is still behind the Iron Curtain. The Commies used the best surgeons and dialecticians to create a duplicate Peter. During the entire tour, the fake Peter has been meeting up with important Comrades in various cities to establish a massive spy ring, threatening Americans with the lives of their relatives who are still behind the Iron Curtain. This scheme forces the victims to reveal information about the power plants and engineering factories they work. Philbrick cleverly gets a hold of Peter's list of names and copies it for the F.B.I. With this information, the fake Peter will return to his homeland with the good news that the spy ring is established, unaware that the F.B.I. will be arranging for fake information to leak to the Commies, thanks to the list of names. Lottie, however, learns from the Feds the sad news that her real brother has been dead for some time, and that they were using her—much like they tried with other Americans during the tour.

PRODUCTION NOTES: Four electricians, one cableman, one third-grip, two drivers, and two stand-ins were needed for the first day of filming. Two electricians, one cableman, one third-grip, two drivers, and two stand-ins were needed for the second day of filming. Philbrick's car and a camera car (an International station wagon) were needed for the first day of filming. A crab dolly was rented for both days of filming.

LOCATION SHOTS:
STUDIO, INTERNATIONAL BUILDING 22
POINSETTA PLAYGROUND AT FULLER AND ROMAINE
STAGE #5 AT ZIV STUDIOS

EPISODE #95 "TRAPPED"
PRODUCTION # 1095 / 95B
TYPESCRIPT (ANNOTATED), BY ELLIS MARCUS, OCTOBER 7, 1955
MASTER MIMEO, OCTOBER 7, 1955

Revised pages, October 14, 1955
Filmed October 20 and 21, 1955

Cast: Richard Carlson (Herbert A. Philbrick); Virginia Stefan (Eva Philbrick); Charles Maxwell (Special Agent Joe Carey); Emmaline Henry (Comrade Martha); Sidney Gordan (Comrade Dave); George Mather (Comrade Rudi); and Gary Roark (Comrade Johann).

Production Credits

Production Chief:	Jack Herzberg
Director:	Jack Herzberg
First Assistant Director:	Eddie Stein
Second Assistant Director:	Bobby Ray
First Cameraman:	Monk Askins
Second Cameraman:	Dick Rawlings
First Assistant Cameraman:	Jim Bell
Sound Mixer:	Gary Harris
Recorder:	William Hanks
Boom Man:	Elmer Haglund
First Company Grip:	Carl Miksch
Second Company Grip:	Coley Kessinger
Property Master:	Max Pittman
Assistant Property Man:	Stanley Walters
Set Decorator:	Bruce "Bud" MacDonald
Wardrobe Man:	Al Berke
Script Supervisor:	Larry Lund
Film Editor:	Chuck Craft
Gaffer:	S.H. Barton
Set Director:	Sol Inverso
Construction Chief:	Dee Bolius
Electricians:	Mike Hudson, Mr. Lipney and Charles Stockwell
Drivers:	Arnold Ballard, Jack Osborn and Ray Stoddard

Plot: In Berlin, Germany, Philbrick overhears Comrade Martha shoot a member of their Party because of his incompetence and capitalist sentiment, and threatens her motives toward Philbrick: "The difference between us here and you American Communists is that we do not compromise." She suspects Philbrick of being subjected to the soft American way of life, and hands him the shell from the bullet as a reminder. Back in the U.S., Philbrick is assigned to escort a visiting Comrade through town—Comrade Martha, who is on assignment. As the days pass, a suspicious Martha jots notes about Philbrick's motives and actions, unaware that he is trying to find out what her mission is. During a confrontation with Comrade Dave, Philbrick is forced to defend himself in front of the accusing Comrade Martha—who finds herself in a position when she is ordered to return to Berlin since her job was foiled (courtesy of Philbrick and the F.B.I.) and scared that she will not survive the interrogations abroad, fails to pleads for her safety.

Production Notes: One electrician, one motorcycle policeman, three drivers, two stand-ins, and two extras were needed on the first day of filming. Three electricians, one cableman, third-grip, two stand-ins, and two extras were needed on the second day of filming. A 33-passenger bus, Philbrick's car, Daniels' car, a camera & sound car were needed for the first day of filming. A crab dolly was rented on the second day.

Location Shots:
8251 Beverly
Travel Agency, 8432 Beverly
Commie Headquarters, 8445 Melrose
Garden and back yard, 1400 North Genessee
Driveway only, Philbrick's house, 1400 North Genessee
Telephone booth, Hayworth and Sunset
House and country roads, 2625 Nichols Canyon

Episode #96 "MOTHER-IN-LAW"
Production # 1096 / 96B
Typescript (annotated), by Leonard Heiderman, October 12, 1955

Master mimeo, October 12, 1955
Revised pages (annotated), October 26, 1955
Revised Script (annotated), November 3, 1955
Filmed November 1 and 2, 1955

Cast: Richard Carlson (Herbert A. Philbrick); Virginia Stefan (Eva Philbrick); Ruth Clifford (Eva's Mother); Marjorie Stapp (Comrade Wanda Harris); John Zaremba (Special Agent Jerry Dressler); Robert Nash (Burl Kirk); and Patricia Morrow (Constance Philbrick).

Production Credits

Production Chief:	Henry S. Kesler
Director:	Henry S. Kesler
First Assistant Director:	Robert Hoffman
First Cameraman:	Dick Rawlings
Assistant Director:	Ed Stein
Production Coordinator:	Joe Wonder
Sound Mixer:	Garry Harris
Video Supervisor:	Donald Tait
Film Editor:	Thomas Scott
Audio Supervisor:	Quinn Martin
Sound Editor:	Gus Galvin
Property Master:	Max Pittman
Set Decorator:	Bruce "Bud" MacDonald
Set Designer:	Jack Collis
Script Supervisor:	Larry Lund

Plot: Comrade Wanda assigns Herb and Eva some important tasks to perform, on the same weekend Eva's mother comes to visit. The jobs Comrade Wanda wants the Philbricks to perform is not as important as keeping their Party membership a secret from Eva's mother. Young Connie recounts a few events of the past to her grandmother, giving the elderly woman something to ponder. Finding a book in the house entitled "History of the Communist Party of the Soviet Union," Eva's mother confirms her suspicions and confronts her daughter and son-in-law. Eva's mother tells her daughter that they will have to explain to her satisfaction, or she will find someone who will. After Herb returns home from his mission, and assisting the F.B.I. at the same time, he confronts his mother-in-law who remains unsure about what action she will take, even when Herb assures that he and Eva are *not* Communists. Before retiring for the evening, Eva's mother overhears Connie praying by the bedside and when she asks who taught the prayer to her, Connie replies, "Dad did." Eva's mother decides not to go to the police, and like her grandchild, will rely on a little love and a lot of "faith."

TRIVIA, ETC. The florist shop in this episode was filmed on location at a real Florist shop, Idella Florist, located at 5501 Melrose Avenue.

EPISODE #97 "CENTRAL AMERICAN"
PRODUCTION # 1097 / 97B
TYPESCRIPT (ANNOTATED), BY ELLIS MARCUS, OCTOBER 27, 1955
MASTER MIMEO, OCTOBER 27, 1955
FILMED NOVEMBER 8 AND 9, 1955

CAST: Richard Carlson (Herbert A. Philbrick); John Zaremba (Special Agent Jerry Dressler); Anna Navarro (Senorita Constanza); Mercedes Shirley (Comrade Rose); Charles Davis (Bill Pringle); Albert Carrier (Tomaso); and Burton Kaiser (Finito).

PRODUCTION CREDITS

PRODUCTION CHIEF:	HENRY S. KESLER
DIRECTOR:	HENRY S. KESLER
FIRST ASSISTANT DIRECTOR:	WILLARD KIRKHAM
SECOND ASSISTANT DIRECTOR:	BOBBY RAY
FIRST CAMERAMAN:	MONK ASKINS
SECOND CAMERAMAN:	DICK RAWLINGS
FIRST ASSISTANT CAMERAMAN:	JIM BELL
SOUND MIXER:	GARY HARRIS
RECORDER:	WILLIAM HANKS
BOOM MAN:	ELMER HAGLUND
FIRST COMPANY GRIP:	CARL MIKSCH

SECOND COMPANY GRIP:	COLEY KESSINGER
PROPERTY MASTER:	YGNACIO SEPULVEDA
ASSISTANT PROPERTY MAN:	VICTOR PETROTTA
SET DECORATOR:	BRUCE "BUD" MACDONALD
WARDROBE MAN:	AL BERKE
SCRIPT SUPERVISOR:	LARRY LUND
FILM EDITOR:	TOMMY SCOTT
GAFFER:	S.H. BARTON
SET DIRECTOR:	SOL INVERSO
CONSTRUCTION CHIEF:	DEE BOLIUS
ELECTRICIANS:	MR. LIPNEY (4 DAYS ONLY)
DRIVERS:	JACK OSBORN, HARRY DALSTROM, RAY STODDARD AND ERNIE REED

PLOT: In what is probably the only episode of the series in which he carries a loaded gun, Herb Philbrick is asked to fly to Panagua to help assist the Communist Party in their attempt to take over the country. His cell member insists he memorizes all of Communist action he can and report back to her when he is done. It seems down south, their plan of overthrowing the government failed and having been run out of town, Communist guerillas require a little American influence to help accomplish their mission. But when Herb arrives, he discovers he was just a pawn in a gun-smuggling game. After learning how the Communist guerillas plan to commit a murder to prevent a planned election, he is surprised to learn that he has been chosen to be the triggerman. Taking calculated risks, Herb leaks information to Constanza, his contact in town, and the villain exchanges gunfire with another Party, foiling the murder plot. Philbrick is free to return to the States with information that will make both Comrade Rose and Special Agent Joe Carey very happy.

PRODUCTION NOTES: One electrician, four drivers, four extras, and two stand-ins were needed on the first day of filming. Three electricians, two stand-ins, were needed on the second day of filming. A bus, a honey wagon, and two picture cars were needed for the first day of filming.

Total Crew Hours:	19
Make Ready and Shooting:	17 1/2 hours
Travel Time:	1 1/2 hours

Location Shots:
American National Studio, ZIV, Studio Lot and Street
Much of this episode was filmed at Franklin Canyon.
Stage # 3 of ZIV Studios, for interior scenes on day two.

Episode #98 "KIDNAP"
Production # 1098 / 98B
Typescript (annotated) by Risk Vollaerts, November 4, 1955
Master mimeo, November 4, 1955
Revised pages (annotated), November 10 and 17, 1955
Filmed November 18 and 19, 1955

Cast: Richard Carlson (Herbert A. Philbrick); Charles Maxwell (Special Agent Joe Carey); Fred Grimes (Konrad Bergenauer); Dennis King Jr. (George Curran); Robert Whitney (the police officer); and Leslie Kimmell (the ship's captain).

Production Credits

Production Chief:	Jack Herzberg
Director:	Jack Herzberg
First Assistant Director:	Eddie Stein
Second Assistant Director:	Bobby Ray
First Cameraman:	Curt Fetters
Second Cameraman:	Dick Rawlings
First Assistant Cameraman:	Jim Bell
Sound Mixer:	Gary Harris
Recorder:	William Hanks
Boom Man:	Elmer Haglund
First Company Grip:	Carl Miksch
Second Company Grip:	Mel Bledsoe
Property Master:	Max Pittman
Assistant Property Man:	Stan Walters

Set Decorator:	Bruce "Bud" MacDonald
Wardrobe Man:	Al Berke
Script Supervisor:	Larry Lund
Film Editor:	Duncan Mansfield, a.c.e
Gaffer:	S.H. Barton
Set Director:	Sol Inverso
Construction Chief:	Dee Bolhius
electricians:	Charles Stockwell, Mr. Kreiger and Mr. Gediman
Drivers:	Arnold Ballard, Harry Dalstrom, Jack Osborn, J.A. Brown, Ray Stoddard and Ernie Reed

Plot: Konrad Bergenauer, son of the famed Hans Bergenauer, smuggles himself into the U.S. and claims asylum. Since Hans Bergenauer is a legendary figure to the Communist Party, the impact this news brings to the public is motivational and naturally the Communists want the boy returned—at any cost. While in the States, if the boy speaks about the evils of Communism, the propaganda can work against the Communist Party. With the help of Comrade Curran, Philbrick lures the boy outside of police custody and drives him through town to the pier, where a specially-selected ship will escort the lad back to his home country. Philbrick leaks this knowledge to Special Agent Joe Carey, who arranges for two armed police officers to "happen" pass the sailor and captain of the vessel, at the time they gain possession of the goods. Unable to answer any questions legitimately, the men are hauled in for questioning—including the kidnapped boy. Comrade Curran and Herb Philbrick watch from a distance, not suspecting any foul play, and return to their cell leader to give the bad news.

Production Notes: Two Electricians, one motorcycle policeman, one fireman, one harbor cop, six drivers, two stand-ins, and three extras were needed on the first day of filming. Two electricians, one motorcycle policeman, three drivers, and two stand-ins were needed on the second day of filming. A 33-passenger bus, Philbrick's car, a camera and sound car, Curran's car, police sedan, a 1 1/2-ton truck were needed for the first day of filming. Philbrick's car, camera and sound car, 3-passenger bus, and a 1 1/2-ton truck were used on the second day of filming. One harbor cop and one fireman were on hand for some of the filming. One dog and one trainer were also used for filming.

Total Crew Hours:	20
Make Ready and Shooting:	17 hours
Travel Time:	3 hours

Location Shots:
Indies Terminal, Pier 170
Streets adjacent to pier
Other locations vicinity Wilmington
A real art store at 6412 Selma Ave
Streets in vicinity
Stage # 5 of ZIV Studios

Episode #99 "HISTORICAL SOCIETY"
Production # 1099 / 99B
Typescript (annotated), by Jack Rock, November 4, 1955
Master mimeo (annotated), November 17, 1955
Revised master mimeo, November 17, 1955
Filmed November 28 and 29, 1955

Cast: Richard Carlson (Herbert A. Philbrick); John Zaremba (Special Agent Jerry Dressler); Nyra Monsour (Comrade Janecha); Charles Tannen (Comrade Lanzing); Tiger Fafara (Joe Lawrence); and Eileen Robbins (Mrs. Lawrence).

Production Credits

Production Chief:	Herbert L. Strock
Director:	Herbert L. Strock
First Assistant Director:	Willard Kirkham
Second Assistant Director:	Jud Cox
First Cameraman:	Monk Askins
Second Cameraman:	Bob Johannes

First Assistant Cameraman:	Dick Batcheller
Sound Mixer:	Jay Ashworth
Recorder:	Roy Cropper
Boom Man:	Bill Flannery
First Company Grip:	Carl Miksch
Second Company Grip:	Coley Kessinger
Property Master:	Max Pittman
Assistant Property Man:	Stanley Walters
Set Decorator:	Lou Hafley
Wardrobe Man:	Al Berke
Script Supervisor:	Jeanne Lippman
Film Editor:	Duncan Mansfield, A.C.E
Gaffer:	Al Ronso
Set Director:	Herb Pitchard
Construction Chief:	Dee Bolius
Drivers:	Harry Dalstrom and Ray Stoddard

Plot: Philbrick is ordered by the Party to dig through the history of a number of American Heroes and find a period of time in their experience in which no record of their movements is available. The Party will then represent it as unearthed hitherto, unknown information about these people and this information will be designed to discredit the person or persons involved; these lies to be sandwiched in between true facts—not derogatory—about the person, and then published in a book which is to be called *Handbook of American Heroes.* In a contact with Special Agent Jerry Dressler, Philbrick finds that there is little that can be done about stopping the book from being published, but at great risk to himself he finds a way to discredit the book.

Production Notes: Three electricians, one policeman, two drivers, one stand-in, one welfare worker, and two extras were needed on the first day of filming. Two electricians, one cableman, two stand-ins, and two extras were needed on the second day of filming. A camera car (International station wagon), and Carlson's car (Plymouth Sedan) were needed for the first day of filming. A crab dolly was rented for the second day of filming.

Location Shots:

Sidewalk of Poinsetta Park at Fuller and Romaine
Exterior World Building, ZIV Studios represented the Historical Publishing Society.
7329 Santa Monica Blvd.
Zippy Cleaners
Stage # 5 of ZIV Studios

Episode #100 "HIT AND RUN"

Production # 1100 / 100B
Typescript (annotated), by Lee Berg, November 4, 1955
Revised Script (annotated), November 23, 1955
Revised master mimeo, November 23, 1955
Revised pages (annotated), November 28, 1955
Revised pages, November 28, 1955
Filmed November 30 and December 1, 1955

Cast: Richard Carlson (Herbert A. Philbrick); Valeri Gratton (Comrade Sonia); Coulter Irwin (Comrade Jager); Paul Sorenson (Comrade Brown); John Beradino (Special Agent Steve Daniels); James Waters (the gas station attendant); Elmore Vincent (Mr. Willard); Dennis Cross (Sgt. Ritter); and Cliff Gould (the lab technician).

Production Credits

Production Chief:	Jack Herzberg
Director:	Lew Landers
First Assistant Director:	Eddie Stein
Second Assistant Director:	Jud Cox
First Cameraman:	Robert Hoffman
Second Cameraman:	Bob Johannes
First Assistant Cameraman:	Ed O'Toole (first day only)
First Assistant Cameraman:	Dick Batcheller (second day only)
Sound Mixer:	Jay Ashworth
Recorder:	Roy Cropper

Boom Man:	Bill Flannery
First Company Grip:	Mel Bledsoe
Second Company Grip:	Robert West (second day only)
Property Master:	Everett Richardson
Assistant Property Man:	Stanley Walters
Set Decorator:	Bruce "Bud" MacDonald
Wardrobe Man:	Al Berke
Script Supervisor:	Jeannette (Jeanne) Lippman
Film Editor:	Charles Craft, a.c.e.
Gaffer:	Al Ronso
Production Coordinator:	Joe Wonder
Video Supervisor:	Donald Tait
Audio Supervisor:	Quinn Martin
Sound Editor:	Sidney Sutherland
Set Designer:	Jack Collis
Set Director:	Herb Pritchard
Construction Chief:	Dee Bolius
Electricians:	Al Ronso and Charles Stockwell
Drivers:	Arnold Ballard, Harry Dalstrom, J.A. Brown and Ray Stoddard

Plot: Comrade Sonia asks Herb Philbrick for his car keys and orders him to remain in the room while Comrade Jager uses Herb's vehicle to transport something vital to the Party. But during the trip across town, the overseas courier accidentally hits a woman and, panicking, he drives off. After wiping his fingerprints from the automobile, he returns to give Sonia the bad news. Realizing she would have to account for the error, she explains to Philbrick the problem. She orders him to be the fall guy if questioned by the police. Herb threatens to go above her head if forced to do what is asked, on the basis that he won't be the fall guy for *her* mistakes. This dilemma is brought directly to the attention of Comrade Brown, who supports Comrade Sonia's position—until an eyewitness identifies Comrade Jager—who was picked up by Special Agent Steve Daniels, thus clearing Philbrick of any wrongdoing . . . and Comrade Sonia now has to face a disciplinary meeting.

Trivia, Etc. Actor Paul Sorenson was misspelled "Sorensen" in the closing credits. Comrade Sonia reminds Philbrick that no matter how important he was to the Party, a good Comrade is always expendable. "The man who drove your car is on a top secret mission," she explains to him. "He must be protected at all costs. You, Comrade Herb, are expendable. You know something, Comrade Herb? I enjoy this. You—the perfect Party member, one who has always been held up to my eyes as an example. *You* are expendable."

Production Notes: Two electricians, one motorcycle policeman, five drivers, two stand-ins, and two extras were needed on the first day of filming. Three electricians, one policeman, three drivers, and two stand-ins were needed on the second day of filming. A 33-passenger bus, Philbrick's car, and an inert car were needed for both days of filming. A police sedan and Daniels' car were needed for the first day of filming.

Location Shots:
Les Williams Garage, 7150 Melrose
Hollywood Police Station on Wilcox Avenue was used in the scene where Agent Daniels talks to Sgt. Ritter.
Rand's Parking Lt., Beverly and Fairfax
Mrs. Geltzeiler, 133 North Edinsburgh
Streets near first and Edinburg
P.E. Alley and spur, Willoughby and Detroit
Studio Lot, Stage # 5 of ZIV Studios

Episode #101 "NEW MEMBER"
Production # 1101 / 101B
Typescript (annotated), by Leonard Heiderman, November 30, 1955
Master mimeo, November 30, 1955
Filmed December 5 and 6, 1955

Cast: Richard Carlson (Herbert A. Philbrick); John Zaremba (Special Agent Jerry Dressler); Jim Salem (Howard Cole); Faith Geer (Edna); Wade Cagle (Steven Burke); Ruta Lee (Louise Burke); and Wayne Scott (Jack Shea of the F.B.I.).

Production Credits

Production Chief:	Henry S. Kesler
Director:	Henry S. Kesler
First Assistant Director:	Erich Von Stroheim, Jr.
Second Assistant Director:	Jud Cox
First Cameraman:	Curt Fetters (first day only)
First Cameraman:	Robert Hoffman (second day only)
Second Cameraman:	Bob Chewing (first day only)
Second Cameraman:	Bob Johannes (second day only)
First Assistant Cameraman:	Jim Bell (first day only)
First Assistant Cameraman:	Dick Batcheller (second day only)
Sound Mixer:	Gary Harris (first day only)
Sound Mixer:	Phil Mitchell (second day only)
Recorder:	Lloyd Hansk
Boom Man:	Dick Williams (first day only)
Boom Man:	Elmer Haglund (second day only)
First Company Grip:	Glyn Harris (first day only)
First Company Grip:	Mel Bledsoe (second day only)
Second Company Grip:	Robert West
Property Master:	Victor Petrotta
Assistant Property Man:	Harry Ott
Set Decorator:	Clarence Stenson
Wardrobe Man:	Al Berke
Script Supervisor:	Betty Fancher (first day only)

Script Supervisor:	Larry Lund (second day only)
Film Editor:	Jack Woelz
Gaffer:	Al Ronso
Set Director:	Herb Pritchard
Construction Chief:	Dee Bolius
Electricians:	Mike Hudson, S.H. Barton, Jud Leroy and Mr. Zaslove
Drivers:	Mr. Balzeretti, Mr. Busselle, Harry Dalstrom and Ray Stoddard
Motorcycle Policeman supplied by:	Morgan Windbiel

Plot: Comrade Herb and Comrade Cole are assigned to investigate the background of Steven Burke, a man who has spent the past few years serving the Party, but has yet become initiated as a full-fledged member. Herb and Cole investigate Burke's religious affiliations, his standing with his wife, how he handles stress under psychological conditions, and so on. Comrade Edna gives Herb a key so he can gain access to Burke's house, and he is forced to hide when Burke and his wife arrive prematurely. While stuck in his position, Herb overhears an argument between the couple. It seems his wife has her suspicions and wants an explanation for Burke's actions and motives—or she's leaving. Burke cannot explain right now, but asks that she return in the evening so he can explain in detail. Later, Special Agent Jerry Dressler explains to Herb that Steven Burke is really a counterspy and his admission to the Party is vital to the F.B.I. With this knowledge, Herb agrees to give a favorable report. Later that evening, after Steven explains the truth to his wife (now satisfied), Herb learns that Comrade Cole hid a tape recorder in the living room to capture anything incriminating. With a little quick thinking, Herb erases the tape.

Production Notes: One motorcycle policeman, four drivers, one stand-in, one silent bit, and one extra were needed on the first day of filming. Four electricians and one stand-in were needed on the second day of filming. A 33-passenger bus, Philbrick's car, a camera car, Burke's car (Chrysler Sedan) were needed for the first day of filming.

Location Shots:
623 Afton Pl. Holly (Amesbury Apts.)
Corner of Hudson Place and West 2nd
Corner of Melrose and Alta Vista
Corner of Melrose and Fuller

Episode #102 "DEAD MAN"
Production # 1102 / 102B
Original copyright for production #1102, March 10, 1956.
Original Registration #LP49152
Typescript (annotated), by Stuart Jerome, December 1, 1955
Master mimeo (annotated), December 5, 1955
Revised master mimeo, December 5, 1955
Filmed December 9 and 10, 1955

Cast: Richard Carlson (Herbert A. Philbrick); Charles Maxwell (Special Agent Joe Carey); Jeanne Bates (Nancy Perkins); Thomas McKee (Brisson Laylock); Sherwood Price (Comrade Adams); and Bert Rumsey (the tailor).

Production Credits

Production Chief:	Henry S. Kesler
Director:	Henry S. Kesler
First Assistant Director:	Eddie Stein
Second Assistant Director:	Bobby Ray
First Cameraman:	Robert Hoffman
Second Cameraman:	Harry Marble
First Assistant Cameraman:	Lou Anderson
Sound Mixer:	Jay Ashworth
Recorder:	Roy Cropper
Boom Man:	Bill Flannery
First Company Grip:	Mel Bledsoe

Second Company Grip:	Robert West (second day only)
Property Master:	Everett Richardson
Assistant Property Man:	Stanley Walters
Set Decorator:	Bruce "Bud" MacDonald
Wardrobe Man:	Al Berke
Script Supervisor:	Jeanne Lippman
Film Editor:	Chuck Craft
Gaffer:	Al Ronso
Set Director:	Herb Pritchard
Construction Chief:	Dee Bolhius
Electrician:	Mike Hudson
Drivers:	J. A. Brown and Jack Osborn

Plot: Herb Philbrick is ordered by the Party to break into a house to find some hidden papers. Instead, he discovers a dead man on the floor, and then he is discovered by the man's wife. Herb learns that the dead man was one of America's top Commies, and that he died of a heart attack. The papers concerned one of the Party's most vital secrets, but his widow refuses to surrender them. Then the Party calls on Herb to perform the most fantastic feat of his career—he is to impersonate an F.B.I. Counterspy—so that he can win the widow's confidence and obtain the papers for the Party. This proves easier said than done.

Production Notes: One electrician, one motorcycle policeman, five drivers, two stand-ins, and two extras were needed on the first day of filming. Three electricians, two stand-ins and one extra were needed on the second day of filming. A 33-passenger bus, Philbrick's car, a camera and sound car and Laylook's car was needed for the first day of filming.

Location Shots:

Poinsetta Park at Fuller and Romaine
460 North Las Palmas
Cross Roads of the World, Selma and Cherokee
Subterranean Garage, 569 North Rossmore

Tailor Shop, 5460 Melrose Ave.
Phone booth 2 blocks east of La Brea on Melrose
Stage # 5 of ZIV Studios

Episode #103 "MISSING"
Original copyright for production #1103, March 17, 1956.
Original Registration #LP49160
Production # 1103 / 103B
Typescript (annotated), by Ellis Marcus, November 30, 1955
Master mimeo (annotated), December 8, 1955
Revised master mimeo, December 8, 1955
Filmed December 12 and 13, 1955

Cast: Richard Carlson (Herbert A. Philbrick); John Zaremba (Special Agent Jerry Dressler); Richard Norris (Joe Evarts); Dawn Richard (Mae Evarts); Larry Harmon (Comrade Crane); Opal Euard (Mrs. Dow); and James McHale (Bud Leffingwell).

Production Credits

Production Chief:	Herbert L. Strock
Director:	Herbert L. Strock
First Assistant Director:	Willard Kirkham
Second Assistant Director:	Jud Cox
First Cameraman:	Robert Hoffman
Second Cameraman:	Harry Marble
First Assistant Cameraman:	Lou Anderson
Sound Mixer:	Jay Ashworth
Recorder:	Roy Cropper
Boom Man:	Bill Flannery
First Company Grip:	Mel Bledsoe
Second Company Grip:	Robert West (second day only)
Property Master:	Max Pittman
Assistant Property Man:	Harry Ott

SET DECORATOR:	BRUCE "BUD" MACDONALD
WARDROBE MAN:	AL BERKE
SCRIPT SUPERVISOR:	JEANNE LIPPMAN
FILM EDITOR:	CHUCK CRAFT
GAFFER:	AL RONSO
SET DIRECTOR:	HERB PRITCHARD
CONSTRUCTION CHIEF:	DEE BOLIUS
DRIVERS:	L. BROWNIE, HARRY DALSTROM, JACK OSBORN AND RAY STODDARD

PLOT: Herb Philbrick is ordered by the Communists to locate Comrade Joe and his wife, Mae, who are suspected of deserting the Party. Knowing that if Joe has deserted, he and Mae may become victims of an accidental death perpetrated by the Party, Philbrick contrives to utilize the F.B.I. in the search. He soon locates Joe in another town but is tricked and Joe and Mae escape. At this point, Jerry Dressler of the F.B.I. steps in with a strange gem that enables Joe and Mae to remain among the "disappeared" (murdered) and helps Philbrick convince the Communists that Joe and Mae are dead.

PRODUCTION NOTES: Four drivers, one stand-in, and two extras were needed on the first day of filming. One stand-in and one extra were needed on the second day of filming. A 33-passenger bus (driven by Jack Osborn), a camera car, Joe's car (driven by Ray Stoddard), and a rented car (driven by L. Brownie) were needed for the first day of filming.

LOCATION SHOTS:
RANCHO GOLF COURSE
10501 BUTTERFIELD RD.
10575 TROON AVE.
2759 DUMFRIES
GEO. HOFBERG'S STATION
9921 WEST PICO BLVD.
STAGE # 5 OF ZIV STUDIOS

Episode #104 "COMMIE PHOTO"

Original copyright for production #1104, March 24, 1956.
Original Registration #LP49161
Production # 1104 / 104B
Typescript (annotated), by Lee Berg, December 10, 1955
Master mimeo (annotated), December 12, 1955
Revised master mimeo, December 12, 1955
Filmed December 16 and 17, 1955

Cast: Richard Carlson (Herbert A. Philbrick); John Zaremba (Special Jerry Dressler); Ralph Clanton (Comrade Marvin Tanner); Kay Cousins Johnson (Comrade Anna); Robert J. Stevenson (Comrade Gregor); Gerald Marshall (Comrade Alfred Embers); Pandora Bronson (Comrade Louise); and Jeff Alexander (Arthur Collins).

Production Credits

Production Chief:	Henry S. Kesler
Director:	Henry S. Kesler
First Assistant Director:	Eddie Stein
Second Assistant Director:	Jud Cox
First Cameraman:	Monk Askins
Second Cameraman:	Harry Marble (first day only)
Second Cameraman:	Dick Rawlings (second day only)
First Assistant Cameraman:	Lou Anderson (first day only)
First Assistant Cameraman:	Jim Bell (second day only)
Sound Mixer:	Jay Ashworth (first day only)
Sound Mixer:	Gary Harris (second day only)
Recorder:	Roy Cropper (first day only)

Recorder:	Lloyd Hanks (second day only)
Boom Man:	Bill Flannery (first day only)
Boom Man:	Elmer Haglund (second day only)
First Company Grip:	Mel Bledsoe
Second Company Grip:	Robert West (second day only)
Property Master:	Everett Richardson
Assistant Property Man:	Stanley Walters
Set Decorator:	Bruce "Bud" MacDonald
Production Coordinator:	Joe Wonder
Video Supervisor:	Donald Tait
Set Designer:	Jack Collins
Wardrobe Man:	Al Berke
Script Supervisor:	Jeanne Lippman
Film Editor:	Chuck Craft
Gaffer:	Al Ronso
Set Director:	Herb Pritchard
Construction Chief:	Dee Bolius

Plot: A new policy directive arrived, giving orders for all cell leaders to eliminate any and all members who have been showing signs of deviation. The Party apparently wants to prune from the ranks all undesirables. Comrade Tanner, a man considered to be very dangerous to anyone concerned, orders all cell leaders to make a list of at least five suspects and report their findings to him personally. Comrade Herb, however, is assigned to help assist Comrade Anna and Comrade Gregor of the Soviet Security to eliminate Alfred Embers—a man who has been suspected of treason. Herb protests his cooperation and is threatened by Comrade Anna both verbally and physically. When a reporter from a local paper catches the attention of the angry Anna, he takes her picture on the street and she protests. Wondering why the protest, Herb digs a little to uncover her secret. Comrade Anna was at one time Hilda Meister, a former Nazi with a bad reputation. When Comrade Anna learns Philbrick knows too much, she prepares to eliminate him for "being a deviationist." Philbrick beats her to the punch by telling Comrade Tanner the truth and Tanner takes the matter into his own hands. Philbrick's cooperation with Embers will not be needed—the Party has bigger issues at hand such as dealing with Anna and Gregor.

Trivia, Etc. Actor Robert J. Stevenson is billed as Bob Forrest in the closing credits.

Production Notes: One electrician, one motorcycle policeman, three drivers, two stand-ins, and one extra were needed on the first day of filming. Three electricians, two stand-ins, and one extra were needed on the second day of filming. A 33-passenger bus, Philbrick's car, and a camera car were needed for the first day of filming.

Location Shots:
Lumber yard, 6641 Santa Monica blvd.
Exterior of city streets, ABC Building, 1551 North Vine St. and vicinity
Building Construction, PE Property, Santa Monica and Highland
Phone booth at Santa Monica and La Brea

Episode #105 "AIRMAN"
Original copyright for production #1105, March 31, 1956.
Original Registration #LP49162
Production # 1105 / 105B
Typescript (annotated), by Leonard Heiderman, December 29, 1955
Master mimeo (annotated), January 4, 1956
Revised master mimeo, January 4, 1956
Filmed January 9 and 10, 1956

Cast: Richard Carlson (Herbert A. Philbrick); Scott Douglas (Karl Mueller); Marilyn O'Conner (Wanda); Charles Maxwell (Special Agent Joe Carey); Brad Jackson (Dick Andrews); Ted Lehmann

(Hans Coleman); William Vaughan (Comrade Roach); and Dick Wilson (the commandant).

Production Credits

Production Chief:	Henry S. Kesler
Director:	Henry S. Kesler
First Assistant Director:	Eddie Stein
Second Assistant Director:	Bobby Ray
First Cameraman:	Bobby Hoffman
Second Cameraman:	Dick Rawlings
First Assistant Cameraman:	Jim Bell
Sound Mixer:	Gary Harris
Recorder:	Lloyd Hanks
Boom Man:	Elmer Haglund
First Company Grip:	Mel Bledsoe
Second Company Grip:	Carl Miksch
Property Master:	Victor Petrotta
Assistant Property Man:	Stanley Walters
Set Designer:	Jack Collis
Audio Supervisor:	Quinn Martin
Production Coordinator:	Joe Wonder
Set Decorator:	Bruce "Bud" MacDonald
Wardrobe Man:	Al Berke
Script Supervisor:	Larry Lund
Film Editor:	Chuck Craft
Gaffer:	Al Ronso
Set Director:	Bill Bentham
Construction Chief:	Dee Bolius
Electricians:	Mike Hudson, Charles Stockwell and Jud Leroy
Drivers:	Arnold Ballard, Harry Dalstrom, Ray Stoddard, J.A. Brown and Jack Osborn

Plot: American newspapers report of a murder on a U.S. Airbase in West Germany, the act apparently committed by a post-war American soldier. The Party sends Philbrick on an unscheduled trip to West Germany to help write pamphlets and newspaper articles that would aid in the Communist cause. Exploiting such an incident might start a concentrated effort (and possibly support) to have all U.S. Airbases removed from West Germany. But as Philbrick begins questioning Dick Andrews, the accused, he discovers the murder to be nothing more than a frame-up. The kid is innocent. To make matters worse, the Chief of Police in town, Karl Mueller, is actually a Party member, who uses his position to ensure the success of this mission. The only way that Andrews can be cleared of any wrongdoing is the discovery of the murder weapon—which Mueller is suppressing from the public. Philbrick soon takes advantage of a witness by cleverly staging a solution that comes in the form of Hans Coleman, the true murderer. With this exposed, the German police start investigating Karl Mueller's background and Andrews is set free.

Production Notes: One electrician, one policeman, five drivers, two stand-ins, and two extras were needed on the first day of filming. Three electricians, two stand-ins, and two extras were needed on the second day of filming. A 33-passenger bus, a taxi cab, Mueller's car, and an insert car were needed for the first day of filming.

Location Shots:
1500 Cross Roads of the World
Street shots of Hollywood
Stage #5 of ZIV Studios

Episode #106 "RADIOACTIVE"
Production # 1106 / 106B
Original copyright for production #1106, April 7, 1956.
Original Registration # LP49163
Master mimeo, by Robert Wesley (a.k.a. Gene Roddenberry), January 3, 1956
Master mimeo (annotated), January 9, 1955
Revised master mimeo, January 9, 1955
Filmed January 13 and 14, 1956

CAST: Richard Carlson (Herbert A. Philbrick); John Zaremba (Special Agent Jerry Dressler); Cynthia Leighton (Comrade Rita); Joe Hamilton (Comrade Prentice); and Gilbert Frye (Leon).

PRODUCTION CREDITS

PRODUCTION CHIEF:	HERBERT L. STROCK
DIRECTOR:	HERBERT L. STROCK
FIRST ASSISTANT DIRECTOR:	EDDIE STEIN
SECOND ASSISTANT DIRECTOR:	BOBBY RAY
FIRST CAMERAMAN:	MONK ASKINS
SECOND CAMERAMAN:	DICK RAWLINGS
FIRST ASSISTANT CAMERAMAN:	JIM BELL
SOUND MIXER:	GARY HARRIS
RECORDER:	LLOYD HANKS
BOOM MAN:	ELMER HAGLUND
FIRST COMPANY GRIP:	CARL MIKSCH
SECOND COMPANY GRIP:	MEL BLEDSOE
PROPERTY MASTER:	VICTOR PETROTTA
ASSISTANT PROPERTY MAN:	STANLEY WALTERS
SET DECORATOR:	BRUCE "BUD" MACDONALD
WARDROBE MAN:	AL BERKE
SCRIPT SUPERVISOR:	LARRY LUND
FILM EDITOR:	JACK WOELZ
GAFFER:	AL RONSO
SET DIRECTOR:	HERB PRITCHARD
CONSTRUCTION CHIEF:	DEE BOLIUS
DRIVERS:	HARRY DALSTROM, RAY STODDARD, TED GARBER AND JACK OSBORN

PLOT: Philbrick learns that Comrade Rita was in town for a brief stay before disappearing. Since she was in possession of a valuable item, the Party wants all members to be on the lookout for this woman. During a meeting with Special Agent Dressler, Philbrick learns that Comrade Rita has a radioactive element—a plutonium isotope. Dressler knows where she is, having allowed her to steal the isotope, because they wanted to learn who her contacts were. Dressler arms Philbrick with a Geiger counter and when Comrade

Rita isn't home, Philbrick sneaks in to locate the isotope. Hiding in a closet from the Commies, Philbrick overhears Comrade Rita as a deviationist, with plans to sell the isotope for $100,000. Later, he assists the F.B.I. in switching the isotope for one that is worthless. After being caught in the house, Philbrick claims he was ordered to find Comrade Rita and with suspicion on his head, is given a test to verify whether or not he knows anything about the isotope. Philbrick passes the test, and is asked to leave before the transaction between Comrade Rita and the Party escalade.

Production Notes: One electrician, one policeman, four drivers, one stand-in, and one extra were needed on the first day of filming. Three electricians, one cableman, a third-grip, and one stand-in were needed on the second day of filming. A 33-passenger bus, Philbrick's car, a camera and sound car, and Dressler's car were needed for the first day of filming.

Location Shots:
Lumber yard, 6641 Santa Monica
Parking lot, Santa Monica & MacCadden
Alley near of stakeout, Vista near Santa Monica
Rita's House, 860 North Vista
Stakeout house and opposite Rita's house, 849 North Vista
Stage # 5 of ZIV Studios

Episode #107 "DETECTOSCOPE"
Production # 1107 / 107B
Original copyright for production #1107, April 14, 1956.
Original Registration #LP49164
Typescript (annotated), by Jack Rock, n.d.
Master mimeo (annotated), January 20, 1956
Revised master mimeo, January 20, 1956
Revised pages (annotated), January 26, 1956
Filmed February 1 and 2, 1956

Cast: Richard Carlson (Herbert A. Philbrick); John Zaremba

(Special Agent Jerry Dressler); Virginia Stefan (Eva Philbrick); Patricia Morrow (Connie Philbrick); Mike Garth (Comrade Norbert); Jack Haddock (Sergeant Johns); and Michael Legend (Sergeant Johns).

PRODUCTION CREDITS

PRODUCTION CHIEF:	HEBERT L. STROCK
PRODUCER-DIRECTOR:	HERBERT L. STROCK
FIRST ASSISTANT DIRECTOR:	EDDIE STEIN
SECOND ASSISTANT DIRECTOR:	BOBBY RAY
FIRST CAMERAMAN:	ROBERT HOFFMAN
SECOND CAMERAMAN:	DICK RAWLINGS
FIRST ASSISTANT CAMERAMAN:	JIM BELL
SOUND MIXER:	GARRY HARRIS
RECORDER:	LLOYD HANKS
BOOM MAN:	ELMER HAGLUND
FIRST COMPANY GRIP:	MEL BLEDSOE
SECOND COMPANY GRIP:	CARL MIKSCH
PROPERTY MASTER:	MAX PITTMAN
ASSISTANT PROPERTY MAN:	VICTOR PETROTTA
SET DECORATOR:	BRUCE "BUD" MACDONALD
SCRIPT SUPERVISOR:	LARRY LUND
FILM EDITOR:	JACK WOELZ
GAFFER:	AL RONSO
CONSTRUCTION CHIEF:	DEE BELHIUS

PLOT: Herb Philbrick is assigned as security to help assist the Party in a new plan labeled "top secret." The plan calls for converting vacuum cleaners into miniature missile launchers and to ensure nothing leaves the factory unauthorized, future meetings will require a metal detector. Philbrick designs the detector and by accident, smuggles his cufflink camera into the safe zone. Taking advantage of the opportunity, he takes photos for the F.B.I. Unable to leave without setting off the metal detector, Philbrick attempts to stall for time, so he can sneak the camera into the only bag allowed to exit through the metal detector. After doing so, he arranges with Special Agent Dressler to have a police officer pull a Comrade over for "suspicion of robbery," and take the camera out of the bag without the Comrade suspecting. With the photographic evidence, the F.B.I. comes one step closer to preventing an attack on civilian life.

Episode #108 "THE FIANCÉ"

Production # 1108 / 108B
Original copyright for production #1108, April 21, 1956.
Original Registration #LP49165
Typescript (annotated), by Ellis Marcus, January 12, 1956
Master mimeo, January 12, 1956
Revised pages (annotated), February 1 and 2, 1956
Filmed in three days between February 13 and 17, 1956
(Episodes 108 and 109 were filmed on the same days)

Cast: Richard Carlson (Herbert A. Philbrick); John Zaremba (Special Agent Jerry Dressler); Jacqueline Park (Comrade Susan); Paul Hahn (Comrade Zach); and Dennis McCarthy (Wallace Dunmar).

Production Credits

Producer:	Jon Epstein
Director:	Jack Herzberg
First Assistant Director:	Bert Glazer
Second Assistant Director:	Bob Templeton
First Cameraman:	Curt Fetters
Second Cameraman:	Bob Johannes
First Assistant Cameraman:	Jim Bell
Sound Mixer:	Jay Ashworth
Recorder:	Roy Cropper
Boom Man:	Bill Flannery
First Company Grip:	Carl Miksch
Second Company Grip:	Robert Dabke
Third Company Grip:	Ed Berger
Property Master:	Victor Petrotta
Assistant Property Man:	Stan Walters
Set Decorator:	Bruce "Bud" MacDonald
Wardrobe Man:	Al Berke

Script Supervisor:	Jeanne Lippman
Film Editor:	Jack Woelz
Gaffer:	Al Ronso
Set Labor:	Herb Pritchard
Construction Chief:	Dee Bolius
Electricians:	Mr. Fields, Mike Hudson, Jud Leroy, and Charles Stone
Policeman supplied by:	R.C. Laird.
Drivers:	J.A. Brown, Arnold Ballard, Harry Dalstrom and Jack Osborn

Plot: After a school lesson for young Communist wannabes, Philbrick realizes one of his students, Comrade Susan, accidentally left her gloves in the room. Visiting her house that night to return them, Philbrick accidentally started a chain of events that causes a breakup between Susan and her fiancé, Wallace Dunmar. When ordered to fix the error, Philbrick learns that Susan's romance is a Party assignment—Dunmar works for a missile defense plant and his knowledge is valuable. Philbrick tells Special Agent Dressler, who advises that he continues with fixing the relationship, which he succeeds. With the F.B.I. watching Dunmar's every move, Philbrick keeps a close observation on Susan to learn how she passes on her information. After learning about Dunmar's loyalties to the U.S., the F.B.I. moves in on Susan, who confesses her involvement with the Party. Dunmar, in the meantime, is cleared of all suspicion, having realized how easily he was duped.

Production Notes: Stock footage was used in this film. Welfare workers were given $26.51 each per day. Three electricians, one policeman, four drivers, one stand-in, two Welfare workers, and three silent bits were needed for the first day of filming. Three electricians, one third-grip, one cableman, one stand-in, two extras, and one silent bit were needed for the second day of filming. Two electricians, one policeman, one extra, and one stand-in were needed for the third day of filming. A crab dolly was rented on the second day for filming. Philbrick's car and Wally's car were needed for the first day of filming. Philbrick's car, Collins' car, and a Dodge Highway Patrol car were needed on the second day of filming.

TRIVIA, ETC. Unsure why the continuity was not enforced on this series, Philbrick's car varied from episode to episode. For this episode, Philbrick drives a light Ford Sedan and in the next episode he drives a green Plymouth. And to think that both episodes were filmed on the same days! Automobile buffs have been able to realize this error with ease, after watching multiple episodes back-to-back. For the casual television viewer, who watched an episode once a week, this was not as easy to spot.

EPISODE #109 "PUBLIC IDOL"

PRODUCTION # 1109 / 109B
ORIGINAL COPYRIGHT FOR PRODUCTION #1109, APRIL 28, 1956.
ORIGINAL REGISTRATION #LP49166
TYPESCRIPT (ANNOTATED), BY STUART JEROME, JANUARY 12, 1956
MASTER MIMEO, JANUARY 12, 1956
REVISED PAGES (ANNOTATED), FEBRUARY 2, 1956
FILMED IN THREE DAYS BETWEEN FEBRUARY 13 AND 17, 1956
(EPISODES 108 AND 109 WERE FILMED ON THE SAME DAYS)

CAST: Richard Carlson (Herbert A. Philbrick); Charles Maxwell (Special Agent Joe Carey); Mickey Simpson (Barry Collins); Jeanne Cooper (Janet Collins); Gene Roth (Mr. Drake); Ann Morriss (Comrade Lili); Brad Trumbull (Comrade Garro); and Robert Whitney (the policeman).

PRODUCTION CREDITS

PRODUCER:	JON EPSTEIN
DIRECTOR:	JACK HERZBERG
FIRST ASSISTANT DIRECTOR:	BERT GLAZER
SECOND ASSISTANT DIRECTOR:	BOB TEMPLETON
FIRST CAMERAMAN:	CURT FETTERS
SECOND CAMERAMAN:	BOB JOHANNES
FIRST ASSISTANT CAMERAMAN:	JIM BELL

SOUND MIXER:	JAY ASHWORTH
RECORDER:	ROY CROPPER
BOOM MAN:	BILL FLANNERY
FIRST COMPANY GRIP:	CARL MIKSCH
SECOND COMPANY GRIP:	ROBERT DABKE
THIRD COMPANY GRIP:	ED BERGER
PROPERTY MASTER:	VICTOR PETROTTA
ASSISTANT PROPERTY MAN:	STAN WALTERS
SET DECORATOR:	BRUCE "BUD" MACDONALD
WARDROBE MAN:	AL BERKE
SCRIPT SUPERVISOR:	JEANNE LIPPMAN
FILM EDITOR:	JACK WOELZ
GAFFER:	AL RONSO
SET LABOR:	HERB PRITCHARD
CONSTRUCTION CHIEF:	DEE BOLIUS
ELECTRICIANS:	MR. FIELDS, MIKE HUDSON, JUD LEROY, AND CHARLES STONE
POLICEMAN SUPPLIED BY:	R.C. LAIRD
DRIVERS:	J.A. BROWN, ARNOLD BALLARD, HARRY DALSTROM AND JACK OSBORN

PLOT: Mr. Drake, a high-profile client of Philbrick's Associated Advertising Company, wants to hire Barry Collins, an athlete and former Communist, as an employee for his Sporting Goods Company. Mr. Drake knows the Communist Party will apply any tactic to prevent a former Party member a decent job and a promising future, but goes ahead with the plan anyway. Philbrick makes the arrangements, which pleases Collins, who has had problems getting a job since he went public—courtesy of Party persecution. When Comrade Lili learns of the news, she helps organize a murder attempt against Drake's wife. Philbrick learns the details and in an attempt to foil the scheme, sneaks into the Collins house to save her, without being seen by any member of the Party. Special Agent Joe Carey arranges for the newspapers to report the details of how Janet Collins fell, knocking the phone off the hook and breaking up a Party line. Naturally, the police were called in to investigate and with Barry Collins' testimony regarding the Communists' smear campaign, the guilty parties will answer for their murder attempt.

Production Notes: Three electricians, one policeman, and four drivers were needed for the first day of filming. Three electricians, one third-grip, one cableman, and stand-ins were needed for the second day of filming. Two electricians, one policeman, were needed for the third day of filming. Philbrick's car and Wally's car were needed for the first day of filming. Philbrick's car, Collins' car, and a Dodge Highway Patrol car were needed for the second day of filming.

Locations for episodes 108 and 109:
Poinsetta Park at Fuller and Romaine
Wally's apartment house
1320 North Alta Vista
1321 North Alta Vista
1331 N. Poinsetta, exterior Susan's apartment house
833 N. La Cienega
Mobil Gas Station, 8383 Melrose
King's Row and Melrose
Crescent Heights and Melrose
7120 Pacific View Drive
7400 W. Mulholland Drive

Episode #110 "COUNTERSPY'S WIFE"
Production # 1110 / 110B
Typescript (annotated), by Rik Vollaerts, January 20, 1956
Master mimeo (annotated), January 27, 1956
Revised master mimeo, January 27, 1956
Revised pages (annotated), March 9, 1956
Filmed March 14 and 15, 1956

Cast: Richard Carlson (Herbert A. Philbrick); John Zaremba (Special Agent Jerry Dressler); Virginia Stefan (Eva Philbrick);

John Manfield (Dan Wilson); Dorsey Keaton (Jean Wilson); and Granville Dixon (Comrade Bob Morgan).

PRODUCTION CREDITS

PRODUCTION CHIEF:	JACK HERZBERG
DIRECTOR:	LAMBERT HILLYER
FIRST ASSISTANT DIRECTOR:	DON VERK
SECOND ASSISTANT DIRECTOR:	BRUCE SATERLEE
FIRST CAMERAMAN:	CURT FETTERS
SECOND CAMERAMAN:	BOB JOHANNES
FIRST ASSISTANT CAMERAMAN:	GEO LEPICARD
SOUND MIXER:	JAY ASHWORTH
RECORDER:	ROY CROPPER
BOOM MAN:	BILL FLANNERY
FIRST COMPANY GRIP:	CARL MIKSCH
SECOND COMPANY GRIP:	ROBERT DABKE
PROPERTY MASTER:	VICTOR PETROTTA
ASSISTANT PROPERTY MAN:	WALTER BRODFOOT
SET DECORATOR:	BRUCE "BUD" MACDONALD AND LOU HAFLEY
WARDROBE MAN:	AL BERKE
SCRIPT SUPERVISOR:	JEANNE LIPPMAN
FILM EDITOR:	DUNCAN MANSFIELD, A.C.E
GAFFER:	S.H. BARTON
SET DIRECTOR:	BILL BENTHAM
CONSTRUCTION CHIEF:	DEE BOLIUS
ELECTRICIANS:	MIKE HUDSON, MR. HOUNSHELL AND CHARLES STOCKWELL

PLOT: Dan Wilson is really a counterspy for the F.B.I. and before he can testify against the Party, his wife Jean has been kidnapped in return for his silence. In order to gain info about the whereabouts of Jean Wilson, Philbrick attempts to schmooze with Comrade Bob Morgan, a top-level member of Party Security. Days later, Philbrick gets the promotion and loses no time in peaking into Comrade Morgan's files. After verifying his information, Philbrick informs Special Agent Dressler, who makes plans to save the woman. In the meantime, Comrade Morgan brings both Dan and Jean Wilson to Security Headquarters, and threatens physical harm to Jean since Dan won't confess his involvement with the F.B.I. As they torture Jean, Philbrick wonders just how Eva would cope under similar conditions. Philbrick cleverly gives Dressler and his men a signal to move in, and the F.B.I. rescues the Wilsons, who are reassigned to Washington.

Production Notes: Three electricians, one cableman, one third-grip, one stand-in, and one extra were needed on the first day of filming. One electrician, one motorcycle policeman, four drivers, one stand-in, and two extras were needed on the second day of filming. Philbrick's car, a camera car, Dressler's car, and Morgan's car were needed for the second day of filming. A crab dolly was rented for the first day of filming.
Total Crew Hours: 19

Location Shots:
Fuller across from gate
Poinsetta Park at Fuller and Romaine
Stage #3 at ZIV Studios

Episode #111 "DYNAMITE"
Production # 1111 / 111B
Typescript (annotated) by Lee Berg, January 30, 1956
Master mimeo (annotated), February 6, 1956
Revised pages (annotated), February 17, 1956
Revised master mimeo, February 17, 1956
Filmed February 20—22, 1956, (episodes 111 and 112 were filmed on the same days)

Cast: Richard Carlson (Herbert A. Philbrick); George Becwar (Comrade Oswald); Steve Ritch (Comrade Berrigan); Mercedes Shirley (Louise Crown); Tom Dillon (Jack Porter); George Spaulding (Peters); and Charles Maxwell (Special Agent Joe Carey).

Production Credits

Director:	Henry S. Kesler
Production Chief:	Henry S. Kesler
First Assistant Director:	Mack V. Wright
Second Assistant Director:	Bob Templeton
First Cameraman:	Curt Fetters
Second Cameraman:	Bob Johannes
First Assistant Cameraman:	Jim Bell
Sound Mixer:	Garry Harris
Recorder:	Lloyd Hanks
Boom Man:	Elmer Haglund
First Company Grip:	Carl Miksch
Second Company Grip:	Robert Dabke
Property Master:	Ygnacio Sepulveda
Assistant Property Man:	Walter Brodfoot
Set Decorator:	Bruce "Bud" MacDonald
Wardrobe Man:	Al Berke
Script Supervisor:	Jeanne Lippman
Film Editor:	Jack Woelz
Gaffer:	Al Ronso
Set Labor:	Herb Pritchard
Construction Chief:	Dee Bolius
Electricians:	Mr. Pizante, Mr. Whitman and Charles Stockwell
Drivers:	Ray Stoddard, Mr. Balzerette, Arnold Ballard, J.A. Brown and Ernie Reed

Plot: Comrade Berrigan's ambitions to rise in the Party by framing a cell leader are thwarted courtesy of a report by Philbrick, which does not make Cell Leader Oswald very happy. Angry over the treachery, Berrigan plots with Comrade Rose (who also has ambitions to rise in the Party) a devious attempt to kill Philbrick and Oswald in one swat. Purchasing a couple sticks of dynamite and rigging a timer, a homemade bomb is set to go off ten minutes after a scheduled hearing in a warehouse. After Rose and Berrigan plant the bomb, and check the warehouse to ensure no escape passage, Rose knocks Berrigan out and runs outside to hide. When Philbrick and Oswald arrive and enter the warehouse, Comrade Rose locks them in from the outside and runs away. The men soon discover the treachery when Berrigan comes to, and spend the next few moments finding a means of escape. They succeed and later, Philbrick learns from Special Agent Joe of the F.B.I. that Jack Porter, proprietor of the hardware store where the sticks of dynamite were purchased, was suspicious of Berrigan and sold the Comrade defective caps. The bomb would never have gone off. Comrade Rose was picked up for speeding.

Production Notes: Four electricians, five drivers, two stand-ins, and one extra were needed for the first day of filming. Four electricians, two stand-ins, and one extra were needed for the second day of filming. Four electricians, five drivers and one extra were needed for the third day of filming. A bus, Herb's car, Oswald's car, and Berrigan's car were needed for the first and third days of shooting.

Location Shots:

Interior of hardware store and exterior, 6370 West 3rd Street
Orange Grove, Santa Monica
Service Station
Lumber Yard, Fuller Street
Across from Studio
Electrical Department of ZIV Studios
Interiors on Stage # 7 at ZIV Studios
Willoughby, 920 Kings Rd.
San Vencinte and Santa Monica Blvd.
Limmerman's Warehouse, 8796 Santa Monica Blvd.

Episode #112 "LEGATION"

Production # 1112 / 112B
Typescript (annotated), by Stuart Jerome, February 11, 1956

Master mimeo (annotated), February 15, 1956
Revised master mimeo, February 15, 1956
Filmed February 20—22, 1956, (episodes 111 and 112 were filmed on the same days)

Cast: Richard Carlson (Herbert A Philbrick); John Zaremba (Special Agent Jerry Dressler); Joyce Vanderveen (Maria Eskovar); Lester Sharpe (John Bryson); Tim Sullivan (Gorin); and Bob Harris (Moritz).

Production Credits

Director:	Henry S. Kesler
Production Chief:	Henry S. Kesler
First Assistant Director:	Mack V. Wright
Second Assistant Director:	Bob Templeton
First Cameraman:	Curt Fetters
Second Cameraman:	Bob Johannes
First Assistant Cameraman:	Jim Bell
Sound Mixer:	Garry Harris
Recorder:	Lloyd Hanks
Boom Man:	Elmer Haglund
First Company Grip:	Carl Miksch
Second Company Grip:	Robert Dabke
Property Master:	Ygnacio Sepulveda
Assistant Property Man:	Walter Brodfoot
Set Decorator:	Bruce "Bud" MacDonald
Wardrobe Man:	Al Berke
Script Supervisor:	Jeanne Lippman
Film Editor:	Jack Woelz
Gaffer:	Al Ronso
Set Labor:	Herb Pritchard
Construction Chief:	Dee Bolius
Electricians:	Mr. Pizante, Mr. Whitman and Charles Stockwell
Drivers:	Ray Stoddard, Mr. Balzerette, Arnold Ballard, J.A. Brown and Ernie Reed

Plot: Maria Eskovar, a concert pianist in the U.S., wishes to become a citizen of the United States, having escaped from behind the Iron Curtain. Presently on the top of the Communist's hit list, Maria is kidnapped by a Communist Goon Squad and taken to a secret location. When Philbrick tells Special Agent Dressler of the kidnapping, the F.B.I. starts a manhunt for the girl. Philbrick, meanwhile, learns from an inside source where Maria is being held captive and after sneaking into the warehouse, finds the girl and convinces her that he on her side. When Comrade Bryson arrives on the scene, Philbrick trips the burglar alarm to notify the police. While Bryson and his thugs attempt to take Maria to a freighter bound for her homeland, Special Agent Dressler arrives on the scene and asks Maria, as a political refugee, if she demands police custody. At first she hesitates, but stands up to her captives when she pleads for help and gains the protection she asked for. Bryson and his men leave the country, having failed their mission, knowing just what is in store for them when they arrive.

Production Notes: Four electricians, five drivers, two stand-ins, and one extra were needed for the first day of filming. Four electricians, two stand-ins, and one extra were needed for the second day of filming. Four electricians, five drivers and one extra were needed for the third day of filming. A bus, three cars were needed for the first and third days of shooting.

Location Shots:

Interior of Hardware store & exterior, 6370 West 3rd Street
Orange Grove, Santa Monica
Service Station
Lumber Yard, Fuller Street
Across from Studio
Electrical Department of ZIV Studios
Interiors on Stage # 7 at ZIV Studios
Willoughby, 920 Kings Rd.
San Vencinte and Santa Monica Blvd.
Limmerman's Warehouse, 8796 Santa Monica Blvd.

Episode #113 "DISCREDIT POLICE"

Production # 1113 / 113B
Typescript (annotated), by Robert Wesley (a.k.a. Gene Roddenbery), February 6, 1956
Revised pages (annotated), February 14, 27, 1956
Revised master mimeo, February 27, 1956
Filmed February 29—March 2, 1956. (filmed at same time for episode #114)

Cast: Richard Carlson (Herbert A. Philbrick); John Zaremba (Special Agent Jerry Dressler); Richard Devon (Comrade Will Bancroft); Carl Princi (Comrade Jarvis); Jonathon Haze (Potter); and Gene Marlowe (the uniformed officer).

Production Credits

Production Chief:	Herbert L. Strock
Director:	Herbert L. Strock
First Assistant Director:	Eddie Stein
Second Assistant Director:	Bob Templeton
First Cameraman:	Robert Hoffman
Second Cameraman:	Dick Rawlings (first and second day only)
Second Cameraman:	(third day only)
First Assistant Cameraman:	Jim Bell
Sound Mixer:	Gary Harris
Recorder:	Lloyd Hanks
Boom Man:	Elmer Haglund
First Company Grip:	Mel Bledsoe
Second Company Grip:	Earl Mussey
Third Company Grip:	Sailor Dow (first and second day only)
Third Company Grip:	Carl Miksch (third day only)
Property Master:	Tom Shaw
Assistant Property Man:	John Cengia

Set Decorator:	Clarence Steenson
Wardrobe Man:	Al Berke
Script Supervisor:	Larry Lund
Film Editor:	Jack Woelz
Gaffer:	S.H. Barton
Set Director:	Claude Means
Construction Chief:	Dee Bolius
Electricians:	Mr. Hounshell, Mr. Creiger and Mike Hudson
Drivers:	Mr. Houston, Ted Garber and Ernie Reed

Plot: Comrade Will Bancroft explains the details about the "Police Action Committee." The program involves brutality complaints, minority group persecution, with the Party even making their own incidents. Their job is to destroy civilians' confidence in the police. Philbrick's assignment is to meet the kidnapper of a recent ransom case that involved a murder, and exchange marked money for unmarked money—much in the favor of the Party. Philbrick meets with the gunman/kidnapper and convinces him to exchange the funds for unmarked bills. Comrade Will, happy that things are going according to the plan, then orders Philbrick to sneak into the house of a Police Captain and plant the marked money—framing the local police. Things almost go according to plan, until the kidnapper is shot down by the police, and the money disappeared—switched with newspaper by the F.B.I. Comrade Will, who is accused of stealing the money, is labeled a deviationist and traitor to the Party.

Production Notes: Three electricians, one cableman, one third-grip, three drivers, one stand-in, and one extra were needed on the first day of filming. Three electricians, one cableman, one third-grip, and one stand-in were needed on the second day of filming. Three electricians, one cableman, three drivers, one stand-in, and four extras were needed for the third day of filming. Animals needed were pigeons on the first day and pets in the store on days one and two. Electrical equipment rented was a crab dolly for three days. Philbrick's car, a sound and camera car, a Commie car (black

Plymouth), and an F.B.I. car were needed for the film.
Total crew hours for episodes 113 and 114 was 33 hours.
Make Ready and Shooting: 32 hours
Travel Time: 1 hour

Location Shots:
Outside the ZIV Building
Water Department, 936 North Poinsetta
Exterior Capital House, 857 North Fuller
Stage # 4 at ZIV Studios
Exterior Courthouse, Poinsetta Park at Fuller and Romaine
Park and bench, and street shots in this vicinity

Episode #114 "HEART ATTACK"
Production # 1114 / 114B
Original copyright for production #1114, June 2, 1956.
Original Registration # LP49171
Typescript (annotated), by Jack Rock, February 13, 1956
Revised pages (annotated), February 16, 27, 1956
Revised master mimeo, February 27, 1956
Filmed February 29—March 2, 1956 (filmed at same time for episode #113)

Cast: Richard Carlson (Herbert A. Philbrick); Bruno Vesota (Comrade Gayman); Helene Stanley (Comrade Louise); John Beradino (Special Agent Steve Daniels); Charles Maxwell (Special Agent Joe Carey); Leo Needham (Comrade Paul); Larry Barton (Judge Halsey); and George Cisar (the bailiff).

Production Credits
Production Chief: Herbert L. Strock
Director: Herbert L. Strock
First Assistant Director: Eddie Stein
Second Assistant Director: Bob Templeton
First Cameraman: Robert Hoffman

Second Cameraman:	Dick Rawlings (first and second day only)
Second Cameraman:	(third day only)
First Assistant Cameraman:	Jim Bell
Sound Mixer:	Gary Harris
Recorder:	Lloyd Hanks
Boom Man:	Elmer Haglund
First Company Grip:	Mel Bledsoe
Second Company Grip:	Earl Mussey
Third Company Grip:	Sailor Dow (first and second day only)
Third Company Grip:	Carl Miksch (third day only)
Property Master:	Tom Shaw
Assistant Property Man:	John Cengia
Set Decorator:	Clarence Steenson
Wardrobe Man:	Al Berke
Script Supervisor:	Larry Lund
Film Editor:	Jack Woelz
Gaffer:	S.H. Barton
Set Director:	Claude Means
Construction Chief:	Dee Bolius
Electricians:	Mr. Hounshell, Mr. Creiger and Mike Hudson
Drivers:	Mr. Houston, Ted Garber and Ernie Reed

Plot: Comrade Louise arranges for a Communist meeting in the private chambers of a Superior Judge, where the fate of an entire nation is about to be turned over to Communist rule and top-level plans are revealed. During the meeting, Comrade Gayman, in charge of the executive direction of the revolution, has a heart attack and all of the Comrades escape, except Philbrick, who finds himself trapped in the building when the judge and a bailiff arrive. When the police are phoned, the bailiff is ordered to close all entrances until the detectives arrive. Philbrick is forced to play a game of cat-and-mouse within the courtroom walls in hopes of evading the police. Eventually he is stuck on the roof of the courthouse where Philbrick signals Special Agent Steve Daniels and Special Agent Joe Carey to rescue him in the nick of time.

PRODUCTION NOTES: Three electricians, one cableman, one third-grip, three drivers, one stand-in, and one extra were needed on the first day of filming. Three electricians, one cableman, one third-grip, and one stand-in were needed on the second day of filming. Three electricians, one cableman, three drivers, one stand-in, and four extras were needed for the third day of filming. Animals needed were pigeons on the first day and pets in the store on days one and two. Electrical equipment rented was a crab dolly for three days. Philbrick's car, a sound and camera car, a Commie car, and an F.B.I. car were needed for the film.

TOTAL CREW HOURS FOR EPISODES 113 AND 114 WERE 33 HOURS.
MAKE READY AND SHOOTING: 32 HOURS
TRAVEL TIME: 1 HOUR

LOCATION SHOTS:

WATER DEPARTMENT, 936 NORTH POINSETTA
EXTERIOR CAPITAL HOUSE, 857 NORTH FULLER
STAGE # 4 AT ZIV STUDIOS
EXTERIOR COURTHOUSE, POINSETTA PARK AT FULLER AND ROMAINE
PARK AND BENCH AND STREET SHOTS IN THIS VICINITY

EPISODE #115 "EVA PURGED"

PRODUCTION # 1115 / 115B
ORIGINAL COPYRIGHT FOR PRODUCTION #1115, JUNE 9, 1956.
ORIGINAL REGISTRATION # LP49172
TYPESCRIPT (ANNOTATED), BY LEONARD HEIDERMAN, FEBRUARY 21, 1956
REVISED PAGES (ANNOTATED), MARCH 1, 1956
REVISED MASTER MIMEO, MARCH 1, 1956
FILMED MARCH 7 AND 8, 1956.

CAST: Richard Carlson (Herbert A. Philbrick); John Zaremba (Special Agent Jerry Dressler); Virginia Stefan (Eva Philbrick); Patricia Morrow (Connie Philbrick); Mary Lou Hennessy (Comrade Karen Leeds); and Joe Sargent (Comrade Phil Butler).

PRODUCTION CREDITS

PRODUCTION CHIEF:	JACK HERZBERG
DIRECTOR:	LES GOODWIN
FIRST ASSISTANT DIRECTOR:	DON VERK
FIRST CAMERAMAN:	ROBERT HOFFMAN
SECOND CAMERAMAN:	BOB JOHANNES
FIRST ASSISTANT CAMERAMAN:	BILL RANALDI
SOUND MIXER:	JAY ASHWORTH
RECORDER:	ROY CROPPER
BOOM MAN:	BILL FLANNERY
FIRST COMPANY GRIP:	MEL BLEDSOE
SECOND COMPANY GRIP:	KENNETH DAW
PROPERTY MASTER:	WALTER BRODFOOT
ASSISTANT PROPERTY MAN:	EVERETT RICHARDSON
SET DECORATOR:	BRUCE "BUD" MACDONALD
WARDROBE MAN:	AL BERKE
SCRIPT SUPERVISOR:	LARRY LUND
FILM EDITOR:	JACK WOELZ
GAFFER:	AL RONSO
SET DIRECTOR:	SOL INVERSO
CONSTRUCTION CHIEF:	DEE BOLIUS
ELECTRICIANS:	MIKE HUDSON, CHARLES STOCKWELL AND MR. HANGER
DRIVERS:	J.A. BROWN, JOHN CALZARETTI AND FRANK COURTNEY

PLOT: When Eva is given an assignment from Comrade Karen, and fails to obey those orders on the grounds that family comes first, she is called in by Comrade Phil Butler for suspicion. After considerable questioning, Eva is accused of being more faithful to capitalism, and labeled a "hypocrite." As a result, Herb's loyalties are also put into question. It is also recommended to the Central Committee that Eva be expelled from the Party. Effective immediately, and will be official as soon as the Committee acts. Herb is asked to leave his wife, in fear of her turning against the Party and offering testimony to the authorities. Philbrick, however, talks to Comrade Butler personally and accepts the task Eva would not accept, and together, both Eva and Herb arrange for clothes and passports, making ready to leave in a few days for Europe. The passports and clothes are handed over to Commies leaving abroad, and are picked up at the airport, courtesy of Herb's tip-off to the Feds. Suspicion is removed from Herb and Eva after the Feds are overheard saying how they were trailing the fleeing fugitives for weeks. Eva is reinstated into the Party and Herb's record cleared of suspicion.

PRODUCTION NOTES: One electrician, one motorcycle policeman, four drivers, two stand-ins, and one welfare worker were needed on the first day of filming. Four electricians, one cableman, one third-grip, and two stand-ins were needed on the second day of filming. A 33-passenger bus, Philbrick's car (a Plymouth Sedan), a camera and sound car, and Dressler's car were needed for the first day of filming. A crab dolly was rented for the second day of filming.

TRIVIA, ETC. This episode derives from a section in the Philbrick book that relates to the visit Eva received at home. Alice Mills, a member of the Communist Party Review Commission, pays an impromptu visit on Eva Philbrick, ostensibly just a social call. Eva, also officially a member of the Party, finally convinces Alice that a house and four daughters keep her so busy that she can't possibly attend Party functions. But Alice isn't through. She stays a long time to "chat." In the course of the afternoon Alice expounds the Party line relative to mothers and children. She probes Eva's attitudes on racial discrimination, economic problems, etc. Since there are no boys in the family, there is no question of male chauvinism here, but Alice makes it very clear that girls as well as boys must learn the meaning of the picket line. The Party censorship of children's literature is revealed. Only approved books should be in the house, and these definitely do not include such "bourgeois accretions as Mother Goose . . . Little Black Sambo . . . etc." When Philbrick arrives home, Eva is somewhat incensed at Alice's prying into their home life. Philbrick calls his wife the most reluctant Communist on record.

Location Shots:
346 North Larchmont
418 North Larchmont
361 North June Street
417 North June Street
Corner of June & Oakwood
7200 Block Mulholland Drive
Stage # 3 at ZIV Studios

Episode #116 "STUDENT CONTEST"
Production # 1116 / 116B
Original copyright for production #1116, June 16, 1956.
Original Registration # LP49173
Typescript (annotated), by Ellis Marcus, March 7, 1956
Revised pages (annotated), March 19, 1956
Revised master mimeo, March 19, 1956
Filmed March 21—23, 1956 (episode 116 and 117 were filmed at the same time)

Cast: Richard Carlson (Herbert A. Philbrick); John Zaremba (Special Agent Jerry Dressler); Alan Paige (Comrade Vic); John Bennes (Comrade Karl); Ann Spencer (Comrade Gerta); and Linda Brent (Shari Bruner).

Production Credits

Production Chief:	Jack Herzberg
Director:	Jack Herzberg
First Assistant Director:	Eddie Stein
Second Assistant Director:	Bob Templeton
First Cameraman:	Monk Askins
Second Cameraman:	Dick Rawlings
First Assistant Cameraman:	Jim Bell

SECOND ASSISTANT CAMERAMAN:	CONRAD HALL (FIRST DAY ONLY)
SOUND MIXER:	GARY HARRIS
RECORDER:	LLOYD HANKS
BOOM MAN:	ELMER HAGLUND
FIRST COMPANY GRIP:	CARL MIKSCH
SECOND COMPANY GRIP:	ROBERT DABKE
PROPERTY MASTER:	YGNACIO SEPULVEDA
ASSISTANT PROPERTY MAN:	VICTOR PETROTTA
SET DECORATOR:	BRUCE "BUD" MACDONALD
WARDROBE MAN:	AL BERKE
SCRIPT SUPERVISOR:	LARRY LUND
FILM EDITOR:	DUNCAN MANSFIELD, A.C.E
GAFFER:	AL RONSO
SET DIRECTOR:	SOL INVERSO
CONSTRUCTION CHIEF:	DEE BOLIUS
ELECTRICIANS:	CHARLES STOCKWELL, S.H. BARTON, AND SOMEONE NAMED MCGEE
DRIVERS:	J.A. BROWN, HARRY DALSTROM, TED GARBER, RAY STODDARD AND JACK OSBORN

PLOT: Comrade Vic, assistant to the District Director of the Communist Party, sends Philbrick behind the Iron Curtain to meet Comrade Karl and Comrade Gerta. They operate an essay contest at a local university and they want Philbrick, an American, to help select a group of promising youths—American students from abroad—who can help benefit the Party and be shaped into true Communist loyals. Philbrick's assignment is to help lure the youth of today into a false sense of security. The winners have already been selected and all of them are loyal Communists, and all influential to other youths. While behind the curtain, Philbrick meets up with Shari Bruner, a contact for the F.B.I., explaining how the winners will be sent to Europe on a trip, and who will most likely be given assignments when they leave. Philbrick risks his career and his life to acquire a copy of the list from the file cabinet and make a copy for Shari Bruner. An article appears in a Paris newspaper, reprinting the list of intended winners, and the festival and essay is branded a Communist propaganda plot.

Production Notes: Four electricians, one cableman, one motorcycle policeman, one fireman, five drivers, two stand-ins, and one extra were needed on the first day of filming. Four electricians, one cableman, one third-grip, two stand-ins, and one extra were needed on the second day of filming. One electrician, one motorcycle policeman, five drivers, two stand-ins, and two extras were needed for the third day of filming. A 33-passenger bus, Philbrick's car, an insert car, a standby car, Dressler's car, and Karl's car were needed for the film. A crab dolly was rented for the second day of filming.

Location Shots:

The Furniture yard in the opening scene is a real Furniture yard located at 3477 Cahuenga.
Roads, path & country, roads, bridges, and fence, 3964 Oeste Ave.
Harvard Military Academy
Parisian Florists, 7528 Sunset
Stage #3 at ZIV Studios
Alley #1, Next to house at & 7531 Fountain, Poinettia pk.
Alley # 2, Genessee South of Fountain
Monk Askin's home, 1400 North Genessee
Hawkins Bungalow, Mrs. Block's Home
1309 North Genessee (Alt) 1345 North Genessee

Episode #117 "COMMIE SON"

Production # 1117 / 117B
Original copyright for production #1117, June 23, 1956.
Original Registration # LP49174
Typescript (annotated), by Stuart Jerome, March 6, 1956
Master mimeo, March 6, 1956
Revised pages (annotated), March 19, 1956

Filmed March 21—23, 1956 (episode 116 and 117 were filmed at the same time)

Cast: Richard Carlson (Herbert A. Philbrick); John Zaremba (Special Agent Jerry Dressler); Mary Newton (Mrs. Hawkins); and Robert Roark (Steve Hawkins).

Production Credits

Production Chief:	Jack Herzberg
Director:	Jack Herzberg
First Assistant Director:	Eddie Stein
Second Assistant Director:	Bob Templeton
First Cameraman:	Monk Askins
Second Cameraman:	Dick Rawlings
First Assistant Cameraman:	Jim Bell
Second Assistant Cameraman:	Conrad Hall (first day only)
Sound Mixer:	Gary Harris
Recorder:	Lloyd Hanks
Boom Man:	Elmer Haglund
First Company Grip:	Carl Miksch
Second Company Grip:	Robert Dabke
Property Master:	Ygnacio Sepulveda
Assistant Property Man:	Victor Petrotta
Set Decorator:	Bruce "Bud" MacDonald
Wardrobe Man:	Al Berke
Script Supervisor:	Larry Lund
Film Editor:	Duncan Mansfield, a.c.e
Gaffer:	Al Ronso
Set Director:	Sol Inverso
Construction Chief:	Dee Bolius
Electricians:	Charles Stockwell, S.H. Barton, and someone named McGee
Drivers:	J.A. Brown, Harry Dalstrom, Ted Garber, Ray Stoddard and Jack Osborn

Plot: Mrs. Hawkins turns to Herb Philbrick, the most important man in the neighborhood, for help. She suspects her son Steve of being a Communist, having found material in his room and overhearing conversations between her son and other Commies. She wants to stop her son before he does any harm, but she fights the urge to turn her own son over to the police. Herb begins investigating and soon after, the Commie Goon Squad visits Mrs. Hawkins, turns her house upside down and breaks her arm, warning worse if she spoke to anyone again. Angry at what they did to his mother, Steve loads a second-hand gun. Philbrick drives Steve to Commie headquarters personally, hoping to talk the lad out of a mistake, and tries to use common sense words to convince the youth to turn to the F.B.I., and when that fails, he takes the gun away from the boy. Steve cries, claiming all he wanted to do was to become important. When Steve realizes how much he will succeed if he turns over names to the authorities, he makes a phone call—on Philbrick's dime.

Production Notes: Four electricians, one cableman, one motorcycle policeman, one fireman, five drivers, two stand-ins, and one extra were needed on the first day of filming. Four electricians, one cableman, one third-grip, two stand-ins, and one extra were needed on the second day of filming. One electrician, one motorcycle policeman, five drivers, two stand-ins, and two extras were needed for the third day of filming. A 33-passenger bus, Philbrick's car, an insert car, a standby car, Dressler's car, and Karl's car were needed for the film. A crab dolly was rented for the second day of filming.

Location Shots:
Roads, path & country, roads, bridges, and fence, 3964 Oeste Ave.
Harvard Military Academy
Furniture Yard, 3477 Cahuenga
Parisian Florists, 7528 Sunset
Stage #3 at ZIV Studios
Alley #1, Next to house at & 7531 Fountain, Poinettia pk.

ALLEY # 2, GENESSEE SOUTH OF FOUNTAIN
MONK ASKIN'S HOME, 1400 NORTH GENESSEE
HAWKINS BUNGALOW, MRS. BLOCK'S HOME
1309 NORTH GENESSEE (ALT) 1345 NORTH GENESSEE

I Led Three Lives Proposal: The Unaired Pilot Draft Number One

by Milton Geiger

This teleplay was revised numerous times. The second draft was retitled "I Wore a Red Mask." Neither script made it to the series, and went unproduced. This is the first draft, as it was recently unearthed from a library archive.

"THE RED WEB"

FADE IN

1 EXT.—STREET IN BUSINESS AREA—FULL SHOT—DAY

It is manifestly a big American city but identifiable as no particular one. Keep everything in shot as anonymous as possible.

Herb (OS)

This is a street in an American City.
It happens to be my city but it could
be yours and it probably is, in a pretty
urgent and practical sense . . .

DISSOLVE

2 EXT—ANOTHER STREET, DIFFERENT IN FEELING—DAY

Again a big city street but quite different; perhaps a poor residential section to help symbolize the extremes of the economic and social scale that are touched and that touch upon our theme.

Herb (OS)
It's your city too, and your street too, because you're facing the same problem in them that I faced—for nine corrosive years . . .

DISSOLVE

3 EXT.—LARGE OFFICE BUILDING—MED. LONG SHOT—SAY

It is between rush hour so that there is no unusual traffic into or out of the building that would indicate any particular moment in the day. Neutral in that respect. A typically and purposely undistinguished office building.

Herb (OS)
Weekdays, I faced that problem here, where I also had to meet the problem of bread and shelter and human comforts and decencies. Two problems under one roof—very closely related; but not allied. Get that very straight. They were as opposed as any two ideas you can locate on earth . . .

4 INT. FAÇADE OF OFFICE BUILDING—DAY—PEOPLE

The CAMERA angles on the elevators.

Herb (OS)
An average downtown office building, with the usual complement of law offices, travel bureaus, a barber and a beauty shop, advertising agencies, business services and a miscellany of fly-by-nights. My mask called for a firm face to wear it on . . .

DISSOLVE

5 INT. CORRIDOR OF OFFICE BUILDING—CLOSE SHOT—DOOR

The legend on the frosted glass panel of the door reads:
"DELL, HORNER & KADE, INC. ADVERTISING"

Herb (OS)

I worked there—under two flags, and
for three masters. Dell, Horner & Kade,
Advertising—was just one of my masters . . . .

DISSOLVE

6 INT. OFFICE—CLOSE UP—DAY

We are on a large framed facsimile of the Declaration of Independence. "In Congress, July 4, 1776—"

Herb's Voice

— I have been in conference several times
this past week with Mr. Dell and key
members of our staff . . .

The CAMERA pans slowly and minutely around the office—a bookcase with a large trophy or cup or other fairly substantial award . . . another framed object which on close CAMERA INSPECTION is an ARMY-NAVY "E"—then a TV set next to a large playback turntable—the CAMERA then holds, looking out the window a moment.

HERB PHILBRICK meanwhile has been talking, dictating, OS.

Herb (OS)

We are in utter sympathy with your particular
problem and I think we are prepared to
make our proposals to you within the next ten

> days. At that time we shall present in detail our recommendations to integrate smoothly and completely a campaign of advertising along with merchandising, right up to the point where the consumer enters your retail outlet . . .

HERB enters the shot and stands at the window and looks out as he completes the above. Almost as a matter of habit—unempathitically he leans out the window, both hands braced on the sill and 'cases' the street below.

7. EXT. LONG SHOT—THE STREET—FROM HIS ANGLE

The press of big city traffic in perspective below.

8. EXT—MED. CLOSE SHOT—HERB

In window. CAMERA shoots at him as from within. Office in BG blurred out of detail. HERB seems to think he notices something unusual below and reacts, looking keenly but again not over—emphasis.

9. EXT—MED. LONG SHOT—FROM ABOVE—FAÇADE—MAN.

This is a shooting down shot but from a closer altitude at a MAN standing to one side of the façade, wearing a dark hat; he has a folded paper under his arm. The MAN looks up, NOT at the window (CAMERA) squinting innocently enough at something out of shot.

10. EXT—WINDOW—MED. CLOSE SHOT—HERB

He is satisfied that the MAN is casual. He turns from the window.

11. INT.—OFFICE—MED. MOVING SHOT—HERB; THEN BETTY

The CAMERA trucks back as he advances slowly, dictating, going to his chair and sitting down, putting his feet up on an opened drawer: CAMERA angling around and pulling back to include BETTY.

Herb

Read back the last thing I said, will you?

Betty

Right up to the point where the consumer enters your retail outlets.

Herb

What's the matter with that? I like that.

Betty

I'm delighted.

Herb

Ummh . . . enters your retail outlets. Either I or Mr. Dell himself or both of us will be available for conferences or whatever questions you choose to direct at us, once the presentation is in your hands. I think you may regard this short letter as a report of quite definite progress.

The TELEPHONE rings on his desk and BETTY picks it up.

Betty

Mr. Philbrick's office. Who is calling please?

(To Herb)

Someone who says he's your cousin Jack, now.

Herb

Oh, yes; give it to me.

12. MED. CLOSE UP—HERB

He has the telephone now and settles himself to talk to "Jack"

Herb

Jack, how are you, where've you been keeping yourself? Tonight? Great! What station? I'll pick you up . . . .

13. INT. PHONE PAY STATION—MED. CLOSE SHOT—JACK

JACK is seated in the booth which has a little shelf under the more modern type telephone. There are two more dimes in readiness on the shelf. JACK doesn't look like the kind of friends or relative HERB would have. He is not swarthy or sinister; but he is smoldering and seems constantly out of patience with things, always the appearance of not quite approving; he has a habitual disgusted twitch of the mouth even when there is no occasion for disgust. A temperament habituated to dissent. Withdrawn but has a sort of deadpan, acid humor.

Jack

Seven o'clock; same station as three weeks ago. I've got to hang up now, pretty busy.

HE hangs up bluntly. He picks up another dime, lifts receiver, drops coin and starts dialing again.

14. MED. CLOSE UP—HERB

He still smiles automatically but lifts his eyes quickly to look off at BETTY as he affects to continue speaking into dead phone.

HERB

Wonderful, Jack; how's Aunt Frances—or we can talk family when I pick you up. Right, boy! Right.

HE hangs up.

15. FULL SHOT—HERB AND BETTY

HERB

That's all, Betty; you don't have to get that out now.

(Looks at his watch)

Why don't you start home and avoid the rush?

BETTY

(Stands up)

Kinder words were never spoken, thank you, Herb.

CAMERA pulls back a bit and angles on door as BETTY goes to door.

HERB

Before you go, Betty—will you call my home, I'd like to speak to my wife.

BETTY smiles and goes out. HERB gets up, the CAMERA moving with him to a wardrobe where he takes out his hat; he is in a study as he forms the hat, fixing its dents. Takes out a light raincoat without putting it on and CAMERA trucks him back to his desk. TELEPHONE RINGS. He picks up.

HERB

(Absently)

Yes? Oh hello, dear, how are you? Kind of day did you have?

16. INT. LIVING ROOM—MED. SHOT—EVA

SHE is at the telephone on table at end of sofa.

EVA

Did you know we have a genius in the house? Well, we have a genius in the house. Sandra Ruth came home with an I.Q. test grade that makes me afraid to talk to her. Are you leaving the office now, dear?

17. INT.—OFFICE—MED. CLOSE SHOT—HERB.

HERB

I am but it's the slow train to home sweet home again tonight I'm afraid . . .

18. INT. LIVING ROOM—EVA

EVA

Oh dear, another meeting? All right. Maybe I'll take the children to a movie, they can sleep tomorrow.

19. INT. OFFICE—HERB

HERB

I'll try to cut this one short but I've got to give a short address tonight. Don't wait up for me.

20. INT. LIVING ROOM—EVA

EVA

I'm sorry too. Do you have time to listen to how we've got a genius in the house? It'll give you something to sneer mentally at the others tonight when they're beating you down.

21. INT. OFFICE—HERB

HE looks at his watch, but relaxes then and listens with a grave smile on his face that becomes detached as we hear his voice OS. Sometimes his lips move in pantomime.

HERB

I wanted to hear about Sandra Ruth,
of course. I had a moment, and even if I
didn't have a moment, I did have a family
and an obligation to them and what
interested my wife and children. That
counted too . . . as well as my rendezvous
tonight, received in code from a manufactured
"cousin" named "Jack" coming in on a
dream train where I was to meet him at
a fancied station . . . Code.

22. INT. LIVING ROOM—EVA

She smiles and speaks and is silent by turns in pantomime.

HERB'S VOICE (OS)

It was getting hard to speak to Eva; to try
to seem casual about my after-office-hours
meetings and conferences . . . and still keep
a sense of guilt and subterfuge out of my
voice. I knew she didn't care too much for
some of the company I kept and that I even
had to bring home with me at times . . .

23. INT. PHONE BOOTH—CLOSE SHOT—JACK

He is speaking into a phone in pantomime. Hands up at end.

HERB'S VOICE (OS)

She must have realized that some of them—a
lot of them were communists; or that they

leaned pretty heavily to port if they hadn't already capsized in the Red Sea . . .

JACK hangs up and drops another dime . . .

24. INT.—OFFICE—HERB—ON PHONE

Herb's Voice

I kept talking to Eva, timing myself to arrive at the cell meeting neither too early nor too late. Too eager a beaver was always as suspect among my cell-mates as a reluctant one. Experience had perfected my timing. I know just when to hang up . . .

HERB finishes in a flurry of pantomime smiles and hangs up. He looks drawn by experience and relieved to hang up.

25. INT.—LIVING ROOM—EVA

Eva also smiles extravagantly, hangs up and at once her face darkens with misgivings. She looks OS

26. CLOSE UP—MANTLE CLOCK

It is about ten minutes to six.

27. EXT. MED. SHOT—HERB'S OFFICE BLDG.—FAÇADE—HERB AND CROWD

HERB emerged from the semi-gloom of the foyer into the late afternoon sunlight, carrying his raincoat and pauses to take in his surroundings, looking bland and pleasant.

Herb's Voice

Five minutes to six. I was the last to leave the office and I closed up. I arrived at street

HERB'S VOICE (CONTINUED)
level looking no more relaxed than a busy man should look at the end of a routinely busy day. I took a few seconds for the sort of inventory that had become second nature with me—almost unconsciously checking the street for strange looking loiterers; then I stepped into traffic . . .

He steps down and starts angling through the crowd to be near the curb as he can get without actually bucking counter—moving traffic. This gives a curbside CAMERA the closest possible shot on him that is natural.

28 EXT.—MED. LONG SHOT—SIDEWALK—MOVING SHOT—HERB, CROWD

HERB, DISTINGUISHED BY HIS VERY LIGHT raincoat over his curbside arm moves with pedestrian traffic, the CAMERA moving parallel to him.

HERB'S VOICE
It relieved and relaxed me to move into the crowd; for a while it made me lose my identity and become a part of those people's lives and their candid existences. I was like a card flipped back into the deck for reshuffling, before being dealt into a very different sort of hand. It was a breather. Time to change over—from one master to another—from above board to Underground . . . .

29. MED. SHOT—STORE ENTRANCE—HERB

It is a store where we can reasonably expect to find a pay station telephone. HERB enters the shot, looks down with his usual veiled carelessness and goes inside . . .

30. INT.—STORE—MED. SHOT—PAY TELEPHONE BOOTH

HERB enters the shot and goes into the booth closing the folding doors. As his VOICE comes OVER we see him find a coin, dial.

HERB'S VOICE
It's a funny little thing—but when you
want conversation that's really private—you
go to a public pay station. I had to make a
call that I didn't dare make from my office,
with its frequently crossed wires, and people
walking in unexpectedly.

He finishes dialing and waits, his chin on his chest.

31 INT.—OFFICE—CLOSE UP—TELEPHONE

The telephone jangles a couple of times. A man's hand reaches into the SHOT. The CAMERA follows the phone to his ear, and pulls back at the same time to show BLAKE. HE is capable, almost affable, but with a resistance point of non compromise beneath the easy exterior. Watchful but not piercing; not humorless but not given to fooling.

BLAKE
Hello? Oh, hello!
(listens)
Well good. Uh-huh . . .

The CAMERA angles on the door where a SECRETARY, dressed for the street enters and comes to the desk.

32 INT. OFFICE—MED. SHOT—ANOTHER ANGLE—BLAKE, SECRETARY

The CAMERA shoots past the girl, to Blake behind desk.

BLAKE
Go on, I'm listening.

The GIRL turns her wristwatch toward BLAKE and taps it and waves a small goodbye with her fingers. BLAKE taps the wire basket on his deck and she takes out the outgoing mail.

Blake (Continued)

Anything of particular interest or
that's new, get all the details you can.

The GIRL turns and goes toward open door which is so ajar as to have its edge to the camera and the panel therefore illegible as yet.

33 INT. CORRIDOR—MED. SHOT ON THE DOOR—GIRL, BLAKE

The girl is just coming out of the door, BLAKE at his desk is BG

Blake

Include it all in your report and include
it early . . . Good luck!

The girl closes the door and leaves the shot abruptly.

The CAMERA moves in a short zoom on the panel:
"FEDERAL BUREAU OF INVESTIGATION"

34 INT.—CLOSE SHOT—PHONE BOOTH—HERB

Herb is hanging up. He leaves the booth and stands outside it a moment, mopping perspiration from forehead and lip and chin.

Herb's Voice

In a telephone booth on a warmish day,
anybody can sweat; that's the way I want
to come off, anyhow . . .

HE starts walking out of SHOT.

35 EXT. SIDEWALK—MOVING SHOT—HERB IN CROWD AGAIN

HERB'S VOICE

I wasn't afraid. I don't say I wasn't nervous and maybe even very nervous. But I always tried to make it seem like the humidity or the close quarters or the brisk pace . . .

36. EXT. PARKING LOT—MED. LONG SHOT—HERB

He is entering a parking lot, well stocked with cars but he is the only person on the lot as he slants across toward where his car is parked. Try to shoot down on this from a first or second story window.

HERB'S VOICE

Six-oh-five and I'm pretty much on schedule for this kind of evening of Party business. To an outsider, to the parking lot attendant in his booth, to the cops on the beat, to parking-lot nodding acquaintance, I look the same on evenings like this . . . .

37 EXT. PARKING LOT—MED. SHOT—CAR—HERB

HERB'S car is a conservative sedan, not new, well kept.

HERB enters the shot and gets behind the wheel. Starts car.

HERB'S VOICE

Routine. Inconspicuous. Retiring. That's the ticket. Anything that made me stand apart from the crowd would bring me under closer scrutiny by my tight, strangling little circle . . .

HE PULLS out of the space and the CAMERA pans him around a ninety-degree curve into the out-drive and the street . . .

38 EXT.—CAR—MED. CLOSE SHOT—HERB (PROCESS)

Shooting through windshield at HERB behind the wheel, glassy.

HERB'S VOICE

"If you're exposed publicly as a communist, you may lose your job." They told me that at the F.B.I. and I took 'em on anyhow. "You can't call on us, as the F.B.I to justify your position." That's what they told me. "If you're arrested as a communist—we never heard of you. You're on your own." That's exactly what they told me . . .

DISSOLVE:

39 EXT. STREET—FULL SHOT—DUSK

The CAMERA shoots toward an intersection, free of traffic at the moment. HERB'S car wheels out of the intersection in a right-hand turn, into the SHOT and pulls up at the curb to park, in FG. HERB gets out.

40 EXT. STREET—MED. LONG SHOT—HERB

Shooting from opposite curb. HERB crosses the street toward CAMERA with elaborate nonchalance. CAMERA TURNS with him as he reaches the sidewalk and then truck with him back to the intersection, around the right turn to a place where two or three busses are parked at the curb. THE CAMERA keeps moving parallel to curb and loses HERB behind the last parked bus; when it gets past the first parked bus it does not pick up HERB coming out from behind them. THE CAMERA TILTS UP to a sign:

"BUS TERMINAL "

41 INT. BUS TERMINAL—MED. SHOT–BANK OF TEN AND TWENTY-FIVE-CENT LOCKERS

Herb enters the shot and puts a key into a lock and takes out a battered brief case. Locks locker again.

HERB'S VOICE
If you join the Party for the F.B.I. . . . not
even your wife must know what you're doing.
Nobody will know—

42 CU—BRIEF CASE

It is worn and nondescript and without initials and has a lock.

HERB'S VOICE
Your operation must be thoroughly
secret . . .

HERB starts walking. We see his hand, his shoes perhaps, incidental to the MAIN INTEREST of the BRIEF CASE as CAMERA FOLLOWS in CLOSE MOVING SHOT.

HERB'S VOICE (CONTINUED)
You will send us regular reports—facts
about the Party, its members and their
activity. Facts only. You will of course stay
on your regular job.

CAMERA STOPS and widening its angle, PANS HERB to an exit. HERB going away from CAMERA . . .

43 EXT. STREET—MED. SHOT—BUS STOP—DUSK

It is almost dark. The bus stop and street seem deserted as a BUS veers into shot and stops at the curb to disgorge HERB. He waits as the BUS starts away and out of the shot. He looks hard at his wristwatch to discern the time. Walks.

HERB'S VOICE
I was too early. I didn't want to arrive at

Herb's Voice (Continued)
Sally Throwers apartment before anybody else. Sally was slick and sleek and graceful and beautiful and so was a cobra and I didn't care to be left alone with her. She had too much of a faculty of making you say things you'd prefer to keep to yourself or possibly the F.B.I. Whereas if Jenny Billings got there first, I felt more comfortable . . .

The CAMERA has been moving along with HERB in a slow pace.

Herb's Voice
I slowed up—to give Jenny Billings ample time to get to Sally's before I got there . . .

DISSOLVE:

44 CLOSE UP—FRAMED SAMPLER—

The legend is of course 'GOD BLESS OUR HAPPY HOME"

Herb (OS)
I don't know why people like plumpish Jenny Billings join the Party, but they do. They ought to stay at home and make antimacassars and samplers and raise children. That may be my answer . . .

Jenny (OS)
Yeah. Yeah Honey . . . Dolly—I've got to go out again this evening. I've got a meeting . . .

THE CAMERA TILTS DOWN to a table in a breakfast alcove where comfortable, round-faced homebody JENNY BILLINGS is at the phone, her hat on, wearing a crocheted apron, and standing at the table with her ankles crossed and her elbows on the table—relaxed even as she phones.

JENNY

What do you mean why don't I stay at home once in awhile? Couple times a week I go to a meeting or do work for the club, you scream. How many times . . . huh? How many times—I'M screaming? How many times you call up you're going bowling with the boys and I've got a good dinner on the table?

SHE scrounges around on one elbow to look OS

45 CLOSE SHOT—ELECTRIC CLOCK

It is like a teakettle, on the wall and it says 6:33

JENNY (OS)

I've got dinner for you. I left a note. Yeah.

46. MED. SHOT—JENNY

JENNY

It's in the broiler and the oven's on low; use the pot holder, you don't burn the ever-lovin' hide off you. What? In the pot. Yeah. I won't be home late so don't you. Yeah, Dolly. Yeah, the club . . .

CAMERA MOVES IN for a big CLOSE SHOT showing JENNY'S perfectly open, unfalsifying shape . . .

JENNY

My political discussion group! What else?! Take care, Dolly.

SHE hangs up.

47 FULL SHOT—KITCHEN

THE CAMERA shoots toward the alcove at the far end of the neat, clean kitchen. Jenny puts the telephone on top of a portable radio on the table, comes toward the CAMERA and discovers she still has her crocheted half-apron and goes out through the swinging door . . .

48 EXT. STREET—MED. SHOT ON SMALL HOME—EVENING

It is a nice small old home with a low porch. JENNY comes out bustlingly in a light Spring coat, fumbling busily in a huge carry-all that we will see also contains her needlepoint. She bustles down the walk turns into sidewalk and walks away from the CAMERA busily. KEEP her in sight as long as necessary, walking away . . .

Herb (OS)

This was Comrade Jenny, authority on pie
but enthralled, enchanted by the Red authorities
on pie-in-the-sky. Comrade Jenny, as plain as
pins—and as inscrutable in her way as the
Man in the Kremlin. She always made me
think with her ways and her needlepoint of
Madame DeFarge in A Tale of Two Cities
with her knitting. And her instinct for Death
and killing only awaiting the right time . . .

FADE OUT

49 INT. CLUBROOM—MED. SHOT—FLAG

It is a large banner hanging from a staff over a mantelpiece which is itself magnificent in old oak paneling. It is a large dark flag with a large white "T" sewn into its middle. Arched across the T is the Latin "SEMPER EADEM"

Herb (OS)

The motto was ancient, traditional Tilton
University was a model of solid conservatism.

"Semper Eadem"—Good Queen Bess's own
motto, that meant 'always the same' . . .

50 INT. CLUB ROOM—MED. SHOT—CHAIR—GOMER CLARK

In the large leather chair in front of the unlit fireplace is GOMER CLARK, fifty-five, affluent, content. He is reading a pocket novel and sipping a tall drink.

HERB (OS)

Gomer Clark played halfback for Tilton
when the flying wedge was considered good,
clean fun.

A steward enters the SHOT and takes out a pocket watch and whispers to CLARK who reacts, and nods appreciatively. The steward leaves, CLARK rises, takes a last pull on the drink, dog-ears his paper novel prodigiously and stows it away in an inside breast pocket. While—

HERB (OS)

The solid Tilton Alumni Club of Rock-fast
Old Tilton U! It scared me to think that the
same ten cents worth that called me to my
cell meeting was all it took to reach Gomer
Clark—and for the same purpose . . .

CLARK leaves the shot. The Steward comes in again to remove the ashes from CLARK'S ashtray in a silent butler and to remove his drink.

HERB (OS)

If Clark was going to be there I wanted
him ahead of me too—the chuckley Colonel
Blimpish way he had with Sally Thrower
kept her off my neck and saved me some
pretty bad moments . . . Hurrah for Dear
Old Tilton . . . !

DISSOLVE:

51 EXT. STREET—EVENING—MED. SHOT—HERB

He is walking toward the CAMERA at a leisurely pace, timing his arrival at SALLY'S. A large slick sedan, its lights on approaches from the far BG and slides past HERB into full foreground and stops close to CAMERA. SIDNEY BLALOCK slides across the driver's seat and sticks his head out.

Blalock
(Tentative)
Hey? Philbrick?

HE Backs up exuberantly. Herb in BG stops, puzzled.

52 MED. SHOT—AT CURB—HERB

The car backs into the shot and BLALOCK and HERB almost can rub noses. BLALOCK is fifty-ish, looks affluent and shows the usual exuberance in meeting an acquaintance out of their sphere of contact.

Blalock
(Confirmed)
Philbrick! What's Dell, Horner & Kade Advertising, doing in this neck of the woods, this time of the day? Or the night!

53. CLOSE SHOT—HERB

Mute with consternation.

Blalock
Don't tell me Dell, Horner & Kade Advertising has got you soliciting business door to door!—

54 TWO SHOT—FAVORING BLALOCK

BLALOCK
Pretty small punkin's Philbrick, pret-t-ty petty. Moves me to want to take my business someplace else.

HERB
(Finally can talk)
I . . . we wrote your advertising department a letter today.

BLALOCK
Get it in the mail tomorrow. Where you headed, Herb?

HERB
Just . . . visiting some friends around.

BLALOCK
You're way off your beat.
(Looks down OS)
You are in trouble!

55 CLOSE SHOT—BRIEFCASE—BATTERED!

BLALOCK (OS)
Call that a briefcase? Dell, Horner & Kade, A.D.V.G.? Is that for bringing stuff in to your 'friends' or for bringing the silver out?

56 TWO SHOT—FAVORING HERB

He is badly flustered. But the surface is fairly calm.

HERB
I've got a little work to do when I get home. I didn't want to have to go back to the office for it.

BLALOCK swings open the door.

Blalock
Come on, I'll drop you off.

Herb
Oh, no, I wouldn't hear of it.

Blalock
You're hearing of it now.

Herb
It's only a little way. Just around the corner.

Blalock
Oh, get in; I'M wasting gas idling here.

Herb
I'm in that office all day, believe me I'm glad to walk like this.

Blalock
Maybe I want to talk to you, Philbrick!

Herb
(Feebly)
It's . . . just around the corner.

He hesitates only a moment more and slips in beside BLALOCK, closing the door. The car starts away from the curb.

57. INT. CAR—BLALOCK AND HERB

Blalock
It's a small world—my meeting you like this, way out this end of town.

Herb

As Aristotle said—the improbable is most probable to happen.

Blalock

Well, bully for Aristotle. Tell me when to turn.

Herb

The next corner.

Blalock

Left or right.

(no answer)

Turn left or right at the next corner?

Herb

Oh . . . uh . . . right.

Blalock

You don't visit these friends very often do you?

Herb

Why?

Blalock

If it takes you time to figure out if they live left or right.

(Looks at Herb)

Maybe you don't live right?

Herb

(jokes weakly)

Maybe not.

Blalock

Right?

He changes the position of his hands on the wheel for a right turn.

58. EXT. INTERSECTION—LONG SHOT—NIGHT

The car comes up one angle and wheels right, squealing its tires and continues down the new direction.

59 INT. CAR—TWO SHOT—REVERSE OF FORMER CAR TWO SHOT

Blalock
Say when, Philbrick.

Herb
(Peering)
Slow up about a hundred feet past that
next street light.

BLALOCK doesn't answer, just looking askance a bit at HERB: unempathetic, though. After a moment.

Blalock
Yes, sire. Bully for Aristotle. Now.

Herb
This is good enough.

60. EXT. STREET—NIGHT—CAR, HERB, BLALOCK

The car swings in at low speed and stops at the curb in front of a doorway; car close to CAMERA. HERB gets out.

Herb
Thank you, Mr. Blalock

Blalock
Is this the place or are you just being nice
to me?

Herb

This is it all right.

Blalock

(nods)

It's to let.

HERB turns for the view that BLALOCK has had normally.

61 MED. SHOT—HOUSE FRONT

The windows are vacant and TO LET signs are in all of them.

62 CLOSE SHOT—HERB AND BLALOCK—FAVORING HERB

HE has recovered much of his poise now and takes this new small shock pretty much in stride; but he is not debonair!

Herb

Oh, sure. It's down a couple of doors. I can walk fifty feet can't I, please, Mr. Blalock.

Blalock

Bully for you too, Philbrick.

(Almost saturnine)

Have a nice friendly visit.

BLALOCK reaches across the seat and pulls the door shut. Slips into 'Drive' and slides away.

HERB wipes his upper lip with the back of his hand and over his mouth to wipe his beaded chin. He walks along a moment, CAMERA TRUCKING with him, looking OFF to where car has departed and turns as CAMERA stops and PANS him into a doorway as he pretends to enter.

63. EXT. DOORWAY—HERB

He stands there leaning against the wall, waiting, his eyes closed. He takes a deep breath to steady himself and exhales it. Then he peers out carefully. And steps onto sidewalk again.

64. MED. LONG SHOT—SIDEWALK—HERB

HERB walking away from CAMERA into the night his steps echoing in the deserted neighborhood . . .

DISSOLVE:

65 EXT. STREET—NIGHT—HERB

HERB is approaching the CAMERA in this better neighborhood than in the previous sequence. Unhesitatingly he walks into a pleasant but not rich doorway, without a doorman.

Herb's Voice

(Over preceding)

I was steady again when I arrived in front of Sally Thrower's apartment, a safe five minutes late. It was a place that boasted no doorman and only a self serve elevator . . .

66 INT. VESTIBULE—MED. SHOT—MAIL BOXES AND BELLS—HERB

HERB is standing at the bank of bells; he presses one without scrutinizing the name plate at all. Waits.

Herb

Doormen notice exits and entrances and discuss them with other doormen. Elevator attendants learn your innermost life. There may be a *future* for both professions in the communist scheme for America but there's not much *present.*

There is the SOUND of footsteps ringing loudly on the sidewalk outside. HERB looks OFF quickly. The footsteps come up loudly and take two steps up and JACK of the telephone-booth sequence enters SHOT.

Herb

(Relieved)

Oh . . . hi yuh, Jack.

Jack

(Goes to bell and rings)

What d'ya say?

Herb

I already rang.

Jack

Till that babe makes up her mind to answer the bell!

Herb

Is everyone coming?

Jack

Full house.

Herb

I couldn't make it last week. I had to . . .

Jack

You're here this week aren't you?

Herb

I wanted to explain.

Jack

You'll speak your little piece this week.

HERB
(Lifts briefcase)
Yes, sir!

Jack leans in and pushed the bell again.

JACK
Come on, Flossie move it, move it.

HERB
I'm the one who ought to be biting his nails.

67. TWO SHOT—HERB AND JACK

JACK, being just habitually bilious, looks biliously at HERB but it makes one uncomfortable anyhow.

HERB
What do you do when somebody you know in business finds you on your way to a cell meeting and insists you've got to accept a lift?

THE DOOR BUZZER SNARLS VICIOUSLY OS

JACK
(Sardonically)
Well, how do ye do!

HE makes an elaborately courtly gesture to HERB to precede him. The CAMERA pans them to the glass penciled door that snarls again as HERB opens it and the go in . . .

68 INT. CORRIDOR—HERB AND JACK—ANGLE ON DOOR

HERB and JACK walk down the corridor toward CAMERA and stop at the door. JACK presses the bell and a chime rings inside. The

CAMERA comes in closer as SALLY THROWER opens the door.

Sally

Oh good! Come in!

They step inside.

69 INT. LIVING ROOM—SALLY, HERB, JENNY, JACK

Shooting toward DOOR in FULL SHOT

Sally

Hats, boys. Check your coat sir.

JACK gets out of his light topcoat. HERB reacts.

70 CLOSE UP—HERB

Herb's Voice

Check what coat, sir!? With a jolt I realized I didn't have my raincoat! I'd had it when I left my car. Had I left it in Blalock's car? Was there anything in the pockets to let him know where I was now?

CAMERA PULLS BACK as HERB walks into room, in a kind of stupor.

Herb (Voice)

I didn't think so but I didn't know!

He greets JENNY, sitting on the sofa; she has her big workbag beside her and is needle pointing diligently. JACK waves to her and goes over to an aquarium of goldfish and peers in somberly. SALLY has disappeared with the hats and one coat. HERB sits on the chair across from the sofa.

Herb's Voice

Why wasn't I like Comrade Jack?

71 CLOSE SHOT—JACK—AQUARIUM

HE is looking almost bitterly at the aquarium.

Herb (OS)

Jack didn't leave belongings in oversolicitous people's cars. Why didn't I play airtight ball like him? I looked at the door almost without willing it . . .

72 MED. CLOSE SHOT—DOOR

Herb (OC)

Any second I expected a sturdy pounding or somebody leaning furiously on the chime button and Sally's opening the door for Blalock to come in with my raincoat over his arm. It was all I needed—having a big client meet my friends and spending the next few weeks sidestepping Blalock's sharp eyes and questions . . .

73 PANNING SHOT—AROUND ROOM

The CAMERA slowly pans around the room, counterclockwise starting at the door.

Herb (OS)

I looked slowly around the room trying to see it objectively, as Blalock would see it. It was a good room, I thought—smelling faintly and pleasantly of Sally and not of candle-in-a-bottle conspiracy.

CAMERA stops at a doorway just as SALLY comes in and treats herself to a cigarette from a stand and stands lighting it and relishing it a moment.

Herb (OS)
Sally was presentable in the best finishing school society but with Babbling Blalock she'll take come explanation in terms of my wife . . .

SALLY turns right, from the door and CAMERA in its journey in the same direction pans her sauntering over to JACK; she looks into aquarium with him, talking pleasantly in pantomime.

Herb (OS)
Comrade Jack was another matter. He came closest to the popular conception of the International Communist, closest to type. I watched Sally explaining the fish to him and for the tenth time probably, that one of them was a cannibal and had to be kept apart from the others. Jack was the one who might gobble me up; Jack was a hard one to explain to Blalock.

74 MED. CLOSE SHOT—JENNY

She needle points happily, contentedly.

Herb (OS)
And oddly enough—Jenny was a danger point. Somebody's aunt, sure. But unless I lied flatly to Blalock, what was I doing associating with people's aunts.

75 CLOSE SHOT—HERB

The little creature of drying his lip and chin with the back of his hand or a knuckle.

Herb's Voice
The only one in the cell who fitted me was

Herb's Voice (Continued)
Gomer Clark, the Tilton grad . . . and he wasn't here!

76 FULL SHOT ROOM—FEATURE HERB IN FG

Herb
Where's Gomer, Sally?

SALLY turns from aquarium and comes in; Jack cuts across the BG going to bookshelves as CAMERA tightens up on SALLY, JENNY, HERB, excluding JACK finally from shot.

Sally
We're missing one member for the time being so why don't we just relax till he comes. He'll be here.

SHE sits on sofa next to JENNY, across from HERB.

Sally
How is it coming, Jen?

Jenny
I'm wondering who I'll give this one too. Do you want it, Sally?

Sally
Ask me again when it's finished. So tell me how've you been, Herb?

Herb
Lousy, thank you.

Jenny
It's the business you're in.

HERB
A lot you know about the business I'm in!

JENNY
Your occupational disease is ulcers, isn't it? Your business?

HERB
Not for me.

JENNY
You're young yet.

77. ANOTHER ANGLE—INCLUDING JACK AT BOOKSHELVES

JACK
(Dourly)
I'm young yet and I've got 'em.

HERB
You're the type. Lean, tall, highly strung, brilliant.

SALLY
Flattery will get you nowhere, Herb.

HERB puts down book and goes toward group.

78 GROUP SHOT—HERB, SALLY, JENNY, JACK.

JACK
(To Herb)
You're stupid?

HERB
It figures.

SALLY stands up.

Sally
A fine figure of a hostess I am! What will you cheerful people have to drink? Jacques?

Jack
I'm tall, thin and brilliant. No thanks.

Jenny
I'd love a little lime juice in water and some sugar, Dolly.

SALLY turns to Herb

Herb
Nothing thanks.

Sally
That's easy.

SHE leaves SHOT.

79. CLOSE SHOT—HERB

Herb's Voice
Most of all I kept on wondering about Sally Thrower . . .

80. MEDIUM SHOT—SALLY

She is at a simple bar squeezing a lime into a glass between puffs on a cigarette which she takes up and puts down during the other process. She leaves with the glass to get water.

Herb (OS)
A fine figure of a hostess and no kidding.

Where was the lean, boney ascetic concept of the lady—zealot; where was the dump unkempt haired version of the female communist?

81. CLOSE UP—HERB

HERB'S VOICE

Sally was striking—and a hit with young people in her American Youth for Democracy work—Red front. She headed a national religious group of young people and they liked her too—strictly non communist . . . so far.

82. MED. SHOT—SALLY

The SHOT is on the doorway out of the kitchen. SALLY is coming out with the glass filled with water and ice now. The CAMERA trucks with her and then pans her into a group shot with the rest. Hands drink to JENNY.

HERB'S VOICE

Sally Thrower, unorthodox Red, tall and charming and beautiful and therefore infinitely more dangerous than the other, newspaper cartoon version of the distaff Commie . . .

THERE is the almost shocking chime of the door chime.

83. CLOSE SHOT—HERB

Quick panic leaps into his eye. His head turns sharply, looking OS.

84. MED. SHOT—DOOR

SALLY enters the shot briskly and opens the door. Sure enough . . . there stands BLALOCK with the raincoat over his arm.

Sally

Come in!

BLALOCK comes in, all affability as SALLY closes door. They start toward CAMERA.

85. MED. SHOT—HERB

He follows their approach tautly. The CAMERA pulls back as SALLY and BLALOCK approach, for a group shot (5) HERB'S mouth is dry; BLALOCK holds HERB'S raincoat over his arm still.

Sally

Comrades—this is the new member of our cell. He's here on transfer. Comrade Sidney or just Comrade Sid. That's Jenny . . . Jack . . . Herb.

Blalock

Hello, folks. Sorry I'm late.

HE smiles most affably of all at HERB.

86. THREE SHOT—HERB, BLALOCK, SALLY, FAVORING HERB.

Sally

Give me your coat and let's get started.

After a moment's hesitation that must be an eternity to HERB, BLALOCK affects to remember the coat over his arm and surrenders it to SALLY who leaves the shot.

Blalock

Yes, sir. Small, small world.

87. GROUP SHOT—HERB, JENNY, SID, SALLY, JACK.

HERE WE CONDUCT A CELL MEETING WITH SOME DIRECT DIALOGUE, LARGELY NARRATION FROM HERB GOING INTO DIRECT FOR ESSENTIAL HIGH MOMENTS.

HERB IS GIVING HIS REPORT BASED ON ARTICLE ON COMINFORM BULLETIN DEALING WITH CIVIL DISOBEDIENCE.

SALLY GROWS MORE AND MORE STERN AND DISAPPROVING AND FINALLY LASHES OUT AT HIM IN ALL THE VICIOUSNESS THAT IS INHERENT IN HER DANGEROUS NATURE.

THE UNCOMPROMISING ZEALOT REALLY AROUSED. USE THE LINE ABOUT "WE MUST ARM THE WORKERS FOR THE COMING CIVIL STRIKE."

(WHOLE SCENE FOR PERHAPS 4 PAGES)

31-32-33-34

ASSUME about 15 SHOTS taking us to SHOT 93.

WE WILL DISSOLVE FROM FINAL SHOT IN THIS SEQUENCE SHOWING HERB, scolded and reprimanded by SALLY, putting his lecture notes back into the battered briefcase as SALLY tells them the meeting is over, to leave one by one at five-minute intervals . . . as usual. Blalock goes first taking coat with him, revealing nothing.

DISSOLVE:

93. TWO SHOT—HERB AND SALLY—FAVORING SALLY

They were sitting on the sofa; Herb looks uneasy. SALLY is her former assured, charming, refreshing 'self' as she sits on the sofa, one leg curled under her.

SALLY

You can leave in another minute.
(She looks provocatively at him)
What did you think of our new member?

HERB

You could have knocked me over with a subpoena. Quite a shock.

SALLY

(All smiles)
He's been in the Party for three years. He turned in a very good report on you. Knows your employers at first hand of course. They like you. They've no inkling of your other connections.

94. TWO SHOT—ANOTHER ANGLE—FAVORING HERB

HERB

I'm pretty careful.

She looks at him steadily with a look that may mean much or absolutely nothing. It is bland and relaxed and unwinking and utterly unselfconscious.

SALLY

It's been a good meeting.

SHE stands up. HERB reaches down for his beat-up briefcase and stands also. The CAMERA pans them to the door.

SALLY

Good night, Herb.

HERB

Good night, Sally.

He is about to close the door. She pulls it back and he is drawn into the room.

SALLY
Didn't you have a hat???

Her smile may be friendly and meaningless or it may be an enigma or it may be taunting him about his raincoat. He can't be sure.

But she doesn't need an answer. She smiles at him, closing the door from the corridor and leaves him standing there as she leaves the shot.

The CAMERA moves in for a CLOSE SHOT of HERB looking wrung out and worried and apprehensive.

DISSOLVE:

95. BUS STOP—MED. SHOT—HERB—NIGHT

HERB stands at the bus stop sign looking very solitary, holding his brief case in his hand.

HERB'S VOICE
I was shaken and confused—confused by the shock of learning that Sidney Blalock, of the new breed of benevolent tycoon was a comrade—had been for three years. And had been observing me.

96. CLOSE SHOT—HERB

HERB'S VOICE
He'd given the Party "a good report" on me. No inkling of my other connections. It had sent a shiver along my neck, there in Sally's apartment.

He starts walking, THE CAMERA FOLLOWING HIM as he walks slowly back and forth, CAMERA PULLING BACK A LITTLE FOR FULL SHOT.

Herb's Voice

The malevolence of Sally's attack on me had shaken me. She headed a religious youth group! Didn't she realize that the revolutionary stuff she pleaded so bitterly meant murder in the streets? Ruin, and the final denial of all Christian principles!

A light from an automobile falls on him and sweeps past as BLALOCK'S car whispers to an idle beside HERB.

97 MED. CLOSE SHOT—CAR SEAT—BLALOCK

He leans toward HERB, smiling pleasantly.

Blalock

Taxi, mister?

98. MED. SHOT—HERB AND BLALOCK

Shooting past BLALOCK at HERB on curb. HERB opens the door without a word and gets in. Blalock drives off.

99. INT. CAR—HERB AND BLALOCK

They ride silently a moment. Then BLALOCK looks quizzically at HERB.

Blalock

Talk about the Emperor's new clothes, huh?

(He looks ahead, smiling faintly)

How do I look in Red?

Herb

It was quite a surprise.

Blalock

Umh-hmh. Bully I always say. For Aristotle.

DISSOLVE:

100. EXT INTERSECTION—NIGHT

It is the corner near which Herb's car is parked.

BLALOCK's car appears from the left and makes a left turn and stops in the middle of the street, near Herb's car.

101 MED. SHOT—HERB AND BLALOCK

Herb gets out with his briefcase.

Herb

Thanks!

Blalock reaches into the backseat and hands Herb his raincoat. Herb takes it without a word. BLALOCK waves slightly and pulls away. Herb watches the car diminish, OS. Then, his face stonily noncommittal now, Herb goes to his car, CAMERA trucking with him and gets in. The car starts away as its lights snap on . . .

DISSOLVE:

102 CELLAR STEPS—MED. SHOT—NIGHT

We shoot from the bottom of the stairs, up, in semi gloom.

The SOUND of a typewriter off in basement can be heard.

HERB'S VOICE
It was late when I got home. I didn't want to disturb Eva. It was late anyhow—and my report had to be mailed to the F.B.I. through a drop, early in the morning . . .

A door has opened at top of the stairs out of shot. A bar of light falls into the stairwell and EVA comes down the steps during the above.

HERB'S VOICE
I went down to my hideaway in the basement where I did my extracurricular paper work and closed the door behind me and started on the rather unsettling events of the evening . . .

103 MED. MOVING SHOT—EVA

Shooting from behind now, the CAMERA trucks after EVA as she walks through the basement past the furnace, to the rear.

The SOUND of the typewriter comes up more distinctly; a strange, stealthily sound in the basement.

HERB'S VOICE
It was a little room I'd built behind the furnace and even in daylight it would take close study to reveal that there was a room behind that false wall and carefully masked door . . .

EVA has reached the wall during above, feels along its surface and opens the door. HERB looks up from the B.G

104. REVERSE SHOT—HERB IN FG—EVA IN DOORWAY

HERB
(Smiling)
Oh . . . hello, darling . . .

She comes in, closing the door, into a close TWO SHOT. He gets up and takes her in his arms gently and kisses her.

Herb
I didn't want to wake you. I had some work to do.

SHE searches his face.

Eva
Are you all right, dear?

Herb
Sure I'm all right.

EVA still looks at his face studiedly.

Eva
Was it a hard evening?

Herb
There were some rough spots.

Eva
But it's all right.

Herb
Perfectly.

Eva
All right.

Herb
Socializing with Mr. Sid Blalock, as a matter of fact!

105. TWO SHOT—CLOSE FAVORING EVA

EVA

Don't be up too late, darling.

The CAMERA studies her a moment as she tries to understand more than she does, then she smiles.

106. MED. SHOT—TWO SHOT—HERB AND EVA

She goes to the door and goes out, closing it carefully.

107. MED. CLOSE—HERB

He looks perplexed a moment. Then with a sort of sigh, sits down again. He starts typing strenuously . . .

FADE OUT:

FADE IN:

108 INTERIOR—FULL SHOT—BARBER SHOP MORNING—BARBER: MAN.

We shoot past the barber chair at the window and door at a sunny vista of side street. The barber has a customer in the chair, almost reclining.

A MAILMAN comes in.

MAILMAN

Well! Nice morning!

BARBER

Put it on the counter.

The mailman goes to the counter against the mirror and shuffles out a few letters with a magazine and a paper.

The Barber goes to the nearby sink to wring out a hot towel and ostriches a look at the pile of mail.

BARBER
Bills. Please remit. Go away, Uncle Sam.

The mailman laughs and goes out.

109 MED. CLOSE SHOT—BARBER

He glances through the mail selects one envelope that is fat but ordinary legal stock. He goes to the customer and spreads the steaming towel over his face. CAMERA going with him; then back to the envelope. Without ceremony or secrecy he goes to the telephone.

110 MED. SHOT—BARBER

He drops a dime and dials, looking at the letter noncommittally.

BARBER
Hello? This is Jeff. You got a letter here
for you any time you want to pick it up. Yeah.

He hangs up. The CAMERA trucks with his two or three steps to a small scissors drawer in the back bar where he puts the envelope. Then screwing his pinky in his left ear to scratch it deeply he goes back to his customer . . .

DISSOLVE:

111 EXT. PARK BENCH—MED. SHOT—DAY—MAN ON BENCH

A man is reading a newspaper on the bench. He is hidden behind the paper even when he turns a page though this should be entirely unostentatious.

112 EXT. MED. LONG SHOT—PARK WALK HERB

HERB is walking toward the CAMERA idly, enjoying the air. As he comes full on CAMERA he gets a stone in his shoe and looks for a bench. The CAMERA pulls back and widens to include the bench in BG and Heb starts out of SHOT for it.

113 PARK BENCH—MAN; THEN HERB

Herb sits on the bench and takes off his shoe and emptied it. He does not look up as he talks.

Herb

Did you get the envelope?

Blake

(It is he)

Umh-hmh.

Herb

Pretty shocking, I thought.

HE puts back shoe and starts lacing it.

114 ANOTHER ANGLE—SHOOTING FROM BEHIND, AT THEM

Blake

I don't know.

HERB is startled onto flashing a look at BLAKE.

Blake

We've had our eye on Mister Blalock for two and a half years.

HERB STARES at him.

115 ANOTHER ANGLE—SHOOTING FROM IN FRONT.

BLAKE closes the newspaper, folds it and puts it in his pocket. Without the least recognition of HERB and leaves the shot lazily.

116 CLOSE SHOT—HERB—LOOKING OS

He looks OS in astonishment . . .

117 MED. LONG—BLAKE

The F.B.I. man is sauntering away from the CAMERA; he pauses once to crouch and toss an invisible peanut to an OS squirrel. Then he stands again and continues on his apparently objective-less way.

118 CLOSE SHOT—HERB

A look of pride, relief, admiration all blend in his face. He stands up as CAMERA PULLS BACK for a FULL SHOT.

With a look of renewed confidence and assurance HERB turns, and walks back in the direction from which he came . . .

THE CAMERA HOLDS ON HIM as he walks away in the opposite direction from BLAKE'S. Jauntily.

FADE OUT

Appendix A: The Church Story

UNUSED CHURCH IDEA FOR *I LED THREE LIVES* (PROPOSAL)

BY JACK ROCK

In Philbrick's new territory he meets the Pastor of a small Community Church. In a burst of confidence the Pastor complains of his congregation, ending with the remark that "You'd almost swear the congregation was going Communistic."

Philbrick quietly goes about investigating the situation, and the results prove that communists are infiltrating the churches in an effort to lay the ground work for the eventual abolishment of all religious institutions. The story develops into a complete exposure of what is going on here and behind the iron curtain as far as churches are concerned.

This is not to be a story about religion. It is the story of an outside and abortive attempt to deprive man of his right to worship the God of his choice, and we also could bring out that the Godless state of existence which the communists are fighting for at the moment is very liable to prove their eventual complete downfall.

Could be a powerful story, completely authentic, and of tremendous importance.

RESPONSE FOR CHURCH STORY

Sir Jack:
Re: Church idea for LTL

It may be coincidental, or it may be recognition of the country's need at the moment, but newspapers, television and radio stations are all working for a spiritual wakening on the part of the people and when you read articles like the attached you can understand why.

Destruction of the church—all churches—is part of the communist apparatus and they are working on it right now, infiltrating memberships in an attempt to create discord and division.

Jack Rock

Appendix B: The Case of the Filched Funds

(Unused Plot Outline)

It is about time that we clobbered one of the Comrades' special techniques and biggest assets . . . that of the use of Communist Fronts to fraudulently obtain vast sums of money from large numbers of innocent, well-meaning Americans.

This particular technique is still being used, despite all of the exposes; for example, we will probably never know how many hundreds of thousands of dollars were contributed by well-meaning but unthinking people to an outfit called "The Committee to Secure Justice in the Rosenberg Case." (Later on, a script on this particular campaign.)

Over the course of years, the Communist criminal conspiracy has used hundreds of "Front" organizations as a means to obtain unnumbered hundreds of thousands of dollars. Technically, the Communist Party obtains its funds from four general sources:

> From the Communist Party Membership itself in the form of contributions. Although this is considerable, it probably represents the smallest source of funds for the Communist Party.
>
> From the Soviet Union itself. This Money, although considerable, is practically all limited to espionage and intelligence.
>
> From business operations secretly and subversively controlled and operated by the Comrades. A number of such business operations have existed in the past, and quite a few are still running today. We have already treated one of them on a former script, in "The Case of the Parcels to Poland" . . .

(Parcels to Russia was Licensed to the U.S.S.R.) A number of export-import firms managed to make a considerable profit for the Party; the Comrades also operated some fur and leather firms, a couple of linen and gift stores, book stores, a big insurance-benefit company, and so forth. Money obtained from these sources is channeled directly into the hands of the top Communist Party bosses in the Country.

The fourth and by far the largest source of funds for the Communist criminal conspiracy is obtained through the use of Communist Front organizations. For clarification, obtain and examine the booklet entitled "Guide to Subversive Organizations and Publications." Therewith you will find about 150 pages, each page listing six to seven Communist controlled organizations, some of which have gone out of business, but most of which are still operating today.

TELEVISION SCRIPT OUTLINE #23
"The Case of the Filched Funds"
December 17, 1953

One of the organizations still functioning today, which has had perhaps the greatest success of any Communist Front in obtaining money from non-Communists to be used for Communist purposes, is an organization called "The National Council of American-Soviet Friendship." We will use this organization as an example in this theme outline, although we could use almost any of them.

Philbrick Comments on "CONFUSED COMRADES" . . . sent with memo of December 22, 1953 by Jack Rock.

Pg. 1 . . . Communist Hdqts . . . urgently suggests that if at all possible you slap up big oversized photos or drawings of Joe Stalin and Lenin. I never saw a Party hdqts without 'em . . . and we can give our little viewers a chance to hiss, boot, spit and stamp. Audience participation!

Pg. 4 and 5 . . . Brissen catching h a p at files . . . . Woe is me, I'm afraid not. If this had ever happened, little ol' Herby wouldn't be sitting here now. My wife would have collected on my Accident Insurance for sure.

Pg. 7 . . . bottom page. Just a thought . . . but we've given these art layout boys a lot of plugs already . . . how about us copywriters getting into the game with the *real* ammunition . . . hard selling copy!

Pg. 9 . . . In last few scripts we haven't re-sold the "three lives" to possible new viewers . . . how about in here putting a voice over line . . . for Herb Philbrick, advertising is a good way to make a living . . . . Or to pay for baby's shoes or Eva's hat . . . but for comrades, it's just good cover for a secret member of the communist underground.

Pg. 8 . . . Dressler, half way down . . . instead of saying "clear lobby," he would say "stake out" or "security check" in lobby for Philbrick . . . and still page 8, when Philbrick comes through lobby, he's wondering: "Who's who, Which one could be the comrade . . . *the* comrade . . . with Philbrick's number? And which one is a special agent of the F.B.I.?" It's funny . . . It's not the thing you *know* that jangle your nerves . . . It's the things you don't know . . ." Pass the nerve pills, please.

Pg. 10 . . . Any way we can say, "Laycock is extremely suspicious . . . he's almost convinced himself that I went through the files. Silly thought, wasn't it?

Pg. 12 . . . again, Party hqts, how about some revolutionary posters on the walls? Such as the Picasso peace dove (if you want a real switch, put up the one that goes "boom"! Wonder if anybody would notice).

Pg. 12 . . . Peace, it's wonderful.

Pg. 12 . . . Comrade Herb *of the Educational Commission or of the District Agit-Prop division.*

Pg. 13 . . . Boy! This guy Rock will make quite a comrade! Just a couple of words switched, ". . . rampant in the minds of capitalist imperialists from the beginning of the exploitation of man for profit can be conquered etc etc."

Same pg . . . still good . . . ". . . Are we afraid of Communism." Ridiculous! A few individuals here and there whose ideas and political opinions etc etc . . .

Pg. 14 . . . Dane 2: This would be "a directive from national headquarters."

Brissen: same . . . the new directive

Page 14: Dane: instead of saying "we expect your 100%, Cooper." . . . he says, "Comrade Earl Browder, national whop-la of the Party, has been found guilty of gross deviationism for his failure to agree to the new policy. He will be . . . I mean he *was* expelled . . . yesterday." The comrades simply love this business of giving you the business in a back-handed fashion. By letting you know what happened to the other knuckle-head, no matter how big he was, they let you know just what'll happen to you if you are a knuckle-head too. But since the Party decides who are knuckle-heads and who are not, you are *always* in danger.

Pg 15 top . . . Philbrick's natural reaction would be one of disgust. "Well, I'll be!! The ink isn't even dry on this pamphlet I batted my brains out on, and now they pull a complete flip-flop!!"

I interjected here for what it is worth that possibly the audience will be much happier and pleased to know that Philbrick is just exactly like them . . . no genius . . . and the gimmick can be not that he very craftily spotted this immediately as a Party blunder, but for two reasons: one, he was sore and two he could use a bit of disagreeableness. Only later on does the Party discover its fatal error and then decide that Philbrick was "right" all along. It was one of those things that was about like hitting the jack-pot. Philbrick was just plain damn-fool lucky.

Pg. 16, 17: Good going, "Comrade" Rock!! Not bad for morale: but . . .

Pg. 18 Brissen, end: It is completely against our Party rules of Party discipline and of democracy centralism.

Pg. 19 top Brissen: terrific. Never heard a comrade say it so simply, but that is sure the idea!!

Pg. 19 . . . violence here o.k. Incidentally if you want to know a good comradely of getting a man down on the ground fast so you can kick his kidneys in, just try this: approaching your man from the side, swing your *knee* up and around, catching him with the point of your knee and half way up on the side of his leg between his knee and thigh. Only, be very cautious in practicing it . . . you won't break any bones, but you won't be able to walk for a week. In any case, your victim drops like a stone.

Pg. 23 . . . in connection with the labor violence, this may be too strong medicine for the TV audience, but there is a fact: Since communist activity consist not only in creating labor violence but race hatred, a favorite trick is to get a big bundle of Jewish or Yiddish newspapers . . . appear on the scene with the papers rolled up . . . but with an 18 or 24 inch section of lead pipe inside. When the dust clears, police and witnesses pick up the pipe . . . and the paper . . . and an anti-Semitic hate wave is on.

Pg. 32 . . . For laughs, you might have one of the thugs very proudly wearing an oversize patch on his head. To get your skull cracked for the Party? Ah! A great honor! If the scar doesn't show afterwards, he will be greatly disappointed.

Pg. 34 . . . Good work, Rock.

Pg. 35 . . . middle down . . . instead of hundred percent cooperation . . . . Why not expel another comrade? Beria liquidates Yexhov . . . and then they liquidate Beria. It's all perfectly good Party practice.

Pg. 36 and 37 . . . Maybe this too darned fictional to put into the teleplay . . . but believe it or not, Philbrick, because of this, had this happen:

PARTY BOSS: Comrade, you are now one of the members of the Agit-prop division?

HAP: Yes, comrade.

PARTY BOSS: Since your Marxist theory has been correct from the very beginning, and because of the vital importance of re-educating all of our members in conformance with the new directive, you are promoted to be in complete charge of all leaflet, pamphlet, and propaganda production in District One of the Communist Party, U.S.A."

Memo from H A P

RE: Infra Red by Siodmak and Jerome Fine
dated December 23, 1953

Foist, what happened between the former scripts and this one? Somebody snuck in some firearms and stuff. See preliminary comments to this.

Pg. 1,2,3 . . . all good . . . except Philbrick would *not* try to kid Gilbert. He might say, "you don't mean the Federal Building," to which Gilbert could still reply . . . "Who are you kidding, Herb, you know the F.B.I.'s address like, etc."

The real fact of the matter was, I avoided the Federal Building like the plague . . . never went nearer than a block to it, going out of my way to get around it if necessary.

Incidentally . . . I think we'd better change the name Gilbert. So happens that one of my former comrades named Gilbert was indicted by a Grand Jury for conspiracy and is now free on bail awaiting trial.

Pg. 5: F.B.I. man coming while I am being observed by comrades; good; this indeed happened more than once. However, since such circumstances were anticipated, we had a simple but effective means of "breaking contact" signals. I can't reveal specifically what they were, so use anything you wish. I've often thought that breaking an expensive watch might do it, but maybe that's too corny.

Pg. 7 . . . Turkish baths. Good. One of Boston's fellow travelers was found murdered in a Turkish bath. Never solved.

Pg. 8 & 9 . . . O.K. on the rough stuff, but again . . . the use of fear is a far more effective weapon than physical violence itself . . . . The fear of what *might* happen is sometimes much worse than anything that *will* happen.

Pg. 11 . . . bottom page . . . good . . . fear of the steam room is much more effective than being tossed into the steam room.

Pg. 12 . . . Niet! Niet! No such thing as a NKVD card . . . but never never. This boy could only do so much as possibly reveal himself to be a TASS representative, or Armtorg, or SOVFOTO or something like that . . . This would be a tip-off, but not necessarily proof, that the guy was an MVD agent.

Pg. 14 . . . scene 32 . . . 'tis now we are departing from the straight and narrow. Normally, "Tailing" is given to Party "grubbers" who get all the dirty work . . . But o.k., I'll go along with you . . . Could happen in a most unusual circumstance. But Philbrick wouldn't like it . . . it would not be the Philbrick's or any other pro-group member through such shenanigans.

Pg. 14 . . . scene 34 . . . This is really and truly something which would never happen . . . For about ten thousand reasons! Among them, again, any pro-group member must be preserved *at all cost*, even that of the loss of any evidence concerning comrade Ziroc; Party would not expose H A P to danger of being picked up without a permit to carry; and Philbrick certainly isn't going to let the comrade know that he does carry, or even, or that matter, that he knows how to handle a firearm.

If anything goes wrong, Comrade Ziroc knows full well that the long arm of the Soviet MVD is going to catch up with him, sooner or later, even to the ends of the earth. The eventual fate of Comrade Trotsky, who got "his" thousands of miles from Moscow, is a perennial example held forth by the communist bosses to cowed members.

Pg. 16 . . . scene 40 . . . Voice over . . . Delima here does not indicate that Philbrick must necessarily kill a communist . . . what it really means is that if Ziroc *IS* a traitor to the Party . . . Then he is ON OUR SIDE . . . and Philbrick might very well be signing the death warrant of one of our own men! This is a helluva lot more disastrous than the mere loss of another comrade (good riddance!).

Last voice over, therefore, on page 41, can still be the same . . . But with much more impact. If Ziroc's goose is to be cooked, it may mean the disastrous loss of one of our own counterspies; if, on the other hand, Ziroc comes through with the information, it might mean the end of another counterspy who happens to be Philbrick.

Second part of script: O.K. generally except for the gat-play. Also, I can't seem to figure out precisely why the comrades all trouped over to the Federal Building only to duck out of there and pick up the film in a movie house . . . but maybe the audience won't know why either so I guess it is all right. Use of the movie house for the switch is very good and strictly in accordance with good communist practice.

Pg. 3-86 . . . why not have the F.B.I. say, "Ever hear what happens if radium comes near undeveloped film??"

OVERALL: Terrific; idea, tension, etc. Only bad thing is gun gizmo.

Appendix C: Story Material for Script Writers

Below are reprints of material gleamed from the book from the producers, material to be handed to the writers for possible inclusion and background for their film scripts. None of which made it into film scripts for the series.

Danger of discovery by boss

1948—Mundt-Nixon bill in Congress. Mass hysteria and red-baiting becomes the order of the day and Philbrick's job as a counterspy is made all the tougher. In topical discussions with business acquaintances, he opposes outlawing the Communist Party, just as J. Edgar Hoover did, because such action would drive the Party underground and make it more dangerous.

At home, Eva feeds Philbrick's alarm. Will someone expose them? Will the office remember that he was the treasurer of the A.Y.D., chairman of the Cambridge Youth Council, etc.? Suppose a busybody, fired by the sound and fury in Congress, should start a broad smear campaign against the Philbricks. Eva and the children would suffer worst of all.

Philbrick makes detailed plans to move Eva and the children to another part of the country under a different name if the Mundt [or Mundy?]-Nixon bill should land him in jail or expose him. Strain builds from day to day until July 20th, with the Grand Jury indictment descends on the Twelve.

Danger of discovery by Party

Philbrick attends the convention at which the C.P.A. (Communist Party Activities) is dissolved and the Party is reconstituted in repudiation of Browder. As he watches the swing to the left get out offhand, he is reminded of a cell meeting on Beacon Hill more than a year before, when he tried "rocking the boat" a little, as an experiment. Then he had rebelled against Browder's new Party line of cooperation with the capitalist, and supported his arguments with quotations from Marx and Lenin. His comrades turned on him with such force that he was afraid he had been too rash, but he managed to bring the discussion around to a peaceful conclusion by agreeing to go along with them for the sake of the Party.

Now Don Tormey, a two-fisted labor leader, veers off on an extreme left-wing slant, calling for an end to the no-strike pledge, and immediate conversion of the imperialist war into a civil war and revolution. Philbrick sends his name to the speaker's stand, but is not called on. The National Committee is alarmed at the turn of events, fears a split in the Party, calls a night meeting, to which Philbrick is not invited. At the next day's session, the dispute continues, as each section of the Party platform is discussed, and when the votes are taken there are many abstentions—an unheard of thing in the Communist Party where there must be unanimity. When Alice Gordon rises to the defense of the National Committee's position, she mentions that some in the Party were always doubtful of Browderism and cites Philbrick as an example. He flushes. Did she have to point him out? But his fellow comrades look on him with more respect.

At the next high-level meeting at Boston Party headquarters, he asks Anne Burlak what their topic will be, and she flashes back, "Party discipline." He wonders whether she refers to him or to Tormey.

Before the August convention, Tormey is reprimanded and blacklisted. Philbrick's Party stock, and consequent value to the F.B.I., rises. Now Philbrick has to do something about that nervous flush—his worst security flaw . . .

A hint of this outline was featured in episode #26 "Confused Comrades."

Another danger of discovery by Party

Philbrick is ordered by the F.B.I. never to be seen publicly talking with anyone from the Bureau office. He therefore avoids curbstone conversations with any acquaintances—comrades must not get suspicious.

He returns to his office after a two-week vacation to find a coded message—call the F.B.I. office. He calls and leans that a personal contact has been set up: he will be picked up by a car on a certain corner, at a certain time. Must be something unusual.

He arrives at the corner a few minutes ahead of time. As he approaches the intersection, Comrade Roy falls into step with him. Is it a coincidence? Philbrick has met Roy only once or twice—doesn't know his mission. He takes in the intersection at a glance, spots the F.B.I. car, returns Roy's greeting without breaking stride, and Roy accompanies him across the street. Stopping at a cigar stand, Philbrick waves to the agent in the car, "I'm being picked up by a friend. Sorry to duck off, Roy, but I have a business appointment uptown." Then, quickly banking on the agent's discretion, he adds, "Could I give you a lift?" "No, thanks," says Roy. "Just going up the block a step." Philbrick gets into the car. As the agent pulls away from the curb, Philbrick directs him quickly out of the Scollay Square area, sits back silent until Comrade Roy is well out of sight.

ANOTHER DANGER OF DISCOVERY BY PARTY

At the 26th anniversary of the meeting of the Communist Party in Boston, a young man with spectacles attaches himself to the Philbricks, trying to engage Herb in conversation. He talks about himself and his work in the Party, and seems to be deliberately setting up opportunities for a government agent to go after info. Philbrick recognizes something like crude spying, and doesn't fall into the trap. Instead he makes an excuse to leave the meeting early, and warns the bespectacled youth not to talk so much—it isn't wise!

A few days later, Louis Budenz publicly bolts the Party and rejoins the Catholic Church. At a secret meeting held to discuss the Budenz affair, a stranger known only as Comrade Sam addresses the group. Certain phrases in his speech, delivered at high tension in a small room lit by one bare bulb, to a silent audience of about twenty, strike fear into Philbrick—until he realizes that his twenty comrades around him are as much afraid as he is, with less cause.

Comrade Sam: ". . . Budenz was incorrectly promoted without sufficient testing . . . We are not only surrounded by the class enemy. The enemy's agents are at work within our ranks too. We will find them out."

Another danger of discovery by Party

On the way to a cell meeting, Philbrick pulls his car over to the curb to relax for a minute from the constant strain of living a triple life. Then he scans the textbook for the evening's discussion, which he is to lead, and "shifts his brain into Marxist high gear."

At the cell meeting, he finds an old friend from his A.Y.D. days, a beautiful and brilliant young girl, who presides over the meeting. A minor shock—although by now Philbrick may expect to find almost anyone at a cell meeting. New security regulations are brought in person by Pete the courier—a young military man with a crew cut and a belted trench coat. All phones are considered to be tapped. Never mention a member of another cell at your cell meeting. Don't meet in your homes—stick to public places like restaurants. The attorney general may be planning some raids soon.

Then follows the discussion period. Philbrick sells the literature and expounds on certain sections of it, then proceeds to the questions period. But his handling of the discussion is too tame for the girl. She attacks him, breaks into an eloquent revolutionary tirade. Outside the Party she campaigns for Henry Wallace, but here she frankly denounces him as a social reformer and an idle dreamer. She rages against all liberals. Demands that civil disobedience be regarded as only the prelude to armed revolt—arm the workers for the revolt NOW.

Philbrick leaves the meeting squelched, troubled, and downright scared. He gets home, and unable to sleep he goes into his secret room to type his report to the F.B.I. He knows that this female firebrand, this charming revolutionary, is going to be the chairman of the pro-cell now, and he sees the direction in which the Party is taking him. He may not be able to keep up the appearances much longer . . .

Exploitation of Negroes

Philbrick is invited to help organize the Cambridge Committee for Equal Opportunities—a Communist front, purportedly devoted to Negro Welfare. He visits homes in the Negro section, which is as squalid as most Negro sections in the North, and he sees a fertile field for C.P. recruitment and development.

The Party stages rallies. They remind the Negro people vividly of every injustice and every discrimination practiced against them. They rub salt in the wounds. The Party organizes a picket line. Some scattered incidents, but nothing sufficiently explosive. (A comrade comments to Philbrick that once one of these people gets cracked over the head by a nightstick we don't have to convince him of police brutality.)

The Party circulated a petition for a mixed battalion of Negroes and whites in the army to put an end to segregation under arms. Philbrick comments that it would be a wonderful thing to set up such a battalion. A comrade enlightens him: "Don't kid yourself. We don't expect these petitions to bring any results. But they give us a wedge—a hearing among these people so that we can accomplish our educational work among them."

Educational work—propaganda—involves selling literature. When Philbrick sees these poor people dig down for money for the Party coffers, he combats the communist campaign whenever he can.

Appendix D: Photography Movies of Scollay Square

This word-for-word story suggestion became episode #3, "Dope Photographic."

The office force knows that Philbrick is devoted to his photographic hobby. When the suggestion of setting up a motion picture camera in the office window overlooking Scollay Square to film the odd and amusing characters and incidents of Boston's honkytonk center, they are all for it. Actually, Philbrick is acting under F.B.I. orders. The Bureau is on the lookout for 200 tons of dope from China, which the Communist Party offered to the British in Hong Kong, but was turned down. The Bureau has word that servicemen in the Scollay Square area have been getting hold of this stuff. The American C.P. must be in back of it, and Philbrick's office is right there, so his job is to keep shooting pictures of the square until the missing links in the underground dope chain can be identified.

The camera is set up, and for several days the staff has a grand time with it. But so far, nothing of much use to the Bureau . . .

Then a reporter pops up, and wants to do a story on Philbrick and his movies of Scollay Square. Philbrick doesn't know this guy—is he a reporter or not? And even if he is, Philbrick can't tell him anything or the whole plan would be ruined. A quick call to the Bureau. Keep the reporter waiting until the Bureau checks on him and calls back. He's a reporter all right, but don't breathe a word to him. Philbrick has a rough time getting rid of the reporter, but finally succeeds . . .

For the next couple of weeks, the movie project continues. The staff has adopted one of the Square's characters as their favorite—

Ragpicker Joe. They grab every opportunity to film him. When the F.B.I. "screens the rushes" they sometimes get actually tired of watching the old scavenger pick up butts and old papers off the street, and empty the corner ashcan gradually into his shopping bag—until they notice something: Joe makes a habit of smoothing out every piece of paper, every rag, carefully before putting it away. But, in emptying the ashcan (to do which he almost has to stand on his head) he takes one bundle of newspapers and drops it directly into the bag without refolding it. The agents investigate and their suspicions are confirmed: the ashcan is the drop, and Ragpicker Joe is the missing link in the drop chain.

Philbrick suddenly tires of the movies of Scollay Square.

APPENDIX E: THE FORMATION OF THE CAMBRIDGE YOUTH COUNCIL: THE ORIGIN

BY HERBERT A. PHILBRICK

The following is a scenario taken from the book, written on March 25, 1953, specifically for the scriptwriters to adapt into a teleplay, which became production #1020.

The news events of 1940 were stressful for the entire world. On June 9, 1940, Norway had surrendered. Russia seized Lithuania, Latvia and Estonia in the same month. By July 12th, Britain and Russia had signed a twenty-year mutual aid pact. At the same time—even after the fall of France—saw a continuation of the peace movement in this country. Congress argued over and barely passed the first peace-time conscription act. Everyone in the country was caught up in the debate as the war came nearer. A Gallup poll taken at this time showed that more than 90% of the people of the country, when asked the question, "Shall the Yanks go overseas?," answered, "No!"

Thus the time was ripe for organizing the Cambridge Youth Council, a supposedly pacifist organization. But the organization of the Youth Council confronted Philbrick with problems he had never before faced. It was one thing to mobilize his close friends in Baptist church groups for a particular task, but it was quite another thing to start from scratch on a community level in a large city, among people whom he knew only slightly or not at all.

I would have been lost, if it had not been that at each turn I found the way paved ahead. Mrs. Mills was good enough to facilitate the first part of the job by giving me the names of youth leaders in Cambridge who could help me the most, and then at each step along the path there appeared a helping hand to take me along to the next step. One person gave me the name of another to see, and that one in turn made other names available to me. Looking back on it of course, the skids were well greased and I was sucked into this movement by a very simple expedient that I didn't know about at the time. What was happening behind the scenes, was that one comrade, without my knowledge would telephone ahead to the next individual, alerting him for my visit, and preparing the way for a proper reception.

One of these people was Toni Grosse. It so happened that this was not her real name, but Philbrick didn't know that at the time.

The office of the Harvard Student Union, at the time, was 40 Boyleston Street in Cambridge. No. 1 Boyleston Street was right on the corner of Harvard Square, right across the street from the Harvard University buildings. No. 40 was in the same block—a garage building—one of these double-deck ramps, of concrete structure . . . a small spa on the corner, and a doorway between the spa and the ramp into the garage, leading upstairs to the second story. On the second floor there was a long, concrete hallway and the office of the Cambridge Youth Council was way down the hallway at the farthest and on the right-hand side.

In the office directly next to the Harvard Student Union was one of those telephone jukebox arrangements. Jukeboxes were located in the various establishments around Cambridge, wired into the office. When you put your nickel into the jukebox, a voice would come out of the machine, saying, 'What number do you wish to have played?' or something to that effect, and you would request your number. In this office, there were three or four telephone operators, who sat at the switchboards, and then overhead they had all the records lined up in stacks, and they would reach up and select the record that has been requested and place it on a turntable at their side and the record would be played over the jukebox. This was a very popular gag at the time, but unfortunately, it didn't pay off and most of those places have since gone out of business. I know the one in Cambridge did, at least.

Well, the door to the Harvard Student Union had a large frosted glass on which the words Harvard Student Union had been lettering. You opened the door, walked in—and here was a very snappy looking blonde—a big, blonde attractive gal, very fair but with a deep tan, her long blonde hair was worn free. She was a picture of splendid health, clean living, an extrovert, an outdoors girl, such as one might expect to encounter on a summers excursion through the youth hostels, which were then popular with college groups. Incidentally, I forgot to mention that that concrete hallway was a very noisy one, and as you walked down through it, you got a big echo from your footsteps.

Toni received me most cordially. The office of the Harvard Student Union appeared to be very much like the office of the Massachusetts Youth Council. It too, had a mimeograph machine, a telephone, several desks and a great deal of literature, much of it very similar to the peace literature that I had seen at the Massachusetts Youth Council office. Toni indicated that she was highly receptive to the idea of a Cambridge Youth Council. She said it was exactly what college and other community youth organizations needed to orient their thinking and action on the current problems of war, jobs, racial discrimination, military service, on-the-job-training and other pertinent issues. And she promised me the full support of her organization, showing me that when the council was called into session delegates from the Student Union would attend. Her group, she said, represented not only Harvard Students, but also students from the womens' college in the Boston area as well—Radcliffe and Simmons among them. Some of the things we discussed in the nature of organizing, were first of all, how to get material mailed out to prospective members. My own four-room apartment by now was getting crowded out with nursery equipment, and so it wasn't easy to operate there, although I had my own mimeograph and typewriter and other advertising production equipment. Toni offered me the complete services of her office. She said she would be glad to have me come in and use the typewriter and mimeograph machine, and then suggested that we would want to have a mailing address. I acknowledged that that was true, and she offered to let us have the mailing address into which they were going to move, right around the corner from Boyleston Street in Harvard Square at 1384 Massachusetts Avenue. Not only that, but she would be glad to answer any telephone messages that would come in. Since I was working full time in my advertising sales job, I would have little time, if any, to spend during the day, and with telephone messages coming into this office with Toni to take the messages, I could pick them up after work.

This looked like a very good arrangement to me. Of course, what I did not know was that Toni Grosse was a highly trusted, although secret member of the Communist Party. What this meant therefore, was that every single move that was made, either by myself or by other comrades, and especially by important non-Communists—every move we made was picked up and charted for the intelligence of the Communist Party. What it meant was that they were two jumps ahead of me all the time. They not only knew what was going on, but had ample time after picking up these messages to put their own heads together and to discuss these various things and to figure out just how to handle me and each matter as it came up. A Communist Party member leaves nothing to chance; he plans every detail of such an important project very carefully.

But of all of this, I knew absolutely nothing. And so Toni Grosse gave me additional names of Youth leaders in the Cambridge area, men and young women, on whom she was certain I could rely. Very soon after these meetings began I became aware of the presence of Arthur Solomon, his brother, Sidney Solomon, Stanley Beecher, and a gal by the name of Alice Solomont. Alice Solomont was a very splendid girl, a Negro, and one of the finest people I have ever had the opportunity to know. She was a youth leader and an employee in the YWCA, and she still is in the YWCA today, working for them at their national headquarters in New York City.

Arthur and Sidney Solomon lived in Cambridge, at 118 Trowbridge Street. (It is interesting to note that at a later date the Communist Party gave me a "Party name"— and that name was Arthur Trowbridge.) Their father was a tailor, with his own shop in Cambridge, who had been a member of the Communist Party for many years. Arthur and Sidney Solomon were like Mutt and Jeff. Arthur was small, quick, nervous, very alert and very sharp. His brother, by comparison, seemed almost twice as tall. He was slow-moving, dull-witted Stanley Beecher, was a bruiser—a burley boy. In addition to the contacts established through Mrs. Mills and her colleagues, I personally enrolled many of my friends as staunch supporters of the Cambridge Youth Council.

One of them was Gordon Case, a schoolmate and a Methodist

youth leader, whose deep loyalty, I discovered later, made it impossible for him to disown me completely. As with others, I contacted Gordon Case, told him about the wonderful new youth organization we were founding, and prevailed upon him to join.

At this period of time, I met Nat Mills, husband of Alice Mills. He called me at my office one day and suggested a luncheon meeting at a restaurant in Harvard Square. I found Nat to be tall and thin, dressed very conservatively, almost to the point of severity. He had a self-conscious formality, but he talked easily and a soft drawl, disclosing a well-educated mind. He had, in fact, studied at Amherst University, and in addition, had put in some time studying for the ministry. So far as I know, he was never ordained as a minister. He had dark, straight, unruly hair, which kept falling over his forehead and I recall his habit of pushing the hair back up again with his left hand.

It was Nat Mills who told me how to get the thing really started. The first thing to do, he told me, was to organize a provisional forming committee. He said it should include a dozen members as a good workable number, and a representative one, too. Then he said, "You must have sponsors, and I think I can suggest some names for the sponsoring committee." "What is their job?" I asked. "Well, first of all, they will lend their personal support, and perhaps the support of organizations which they represent. But, they will also serve as a sort of point of reference to others in the community who do not know you or the younger members of your forming committee. We give the organization adult stability, which is essential, especially if you have to raise funds, and you probably will to carry on your work. They also can give direction to your politics. We always try to get well-known sponsors at every level of our organizational work, local, state and national." He showed me a list of names of American Youth Congress sponsors. I recall the name of Mrs. Franklin D. Roosevelt, the wife of the President, John L. Lewis, and many others.

On the local level, Nat Mills showed me the names of several prominent individuals; a prominent doctor, Dr. Albert Dieffenbach; Professor Kirtley A. Mather, a prominent professor at Harvard University; the Rev. F. Hastings Smythe, from the Oratory of St. Micheal, Society of the Catholic Commonwealth; and Professor

Birk J. Struik, a world-famous mathematician at the Massachusetts Institute of Technology.

I swallowed this stuff hook, line and sinker, proposed some additional names of adult sponsors on his own. These included some of his personal friends who were equally unaware as to what was going on or that the Communist Party had any interest in this movement at all. Looking back on it now, the whole thing looks pretty stupid; but at that time I knew nothing about Communism—so far as I knew I had never met a Communist in my whole life—and so the idea simply never occurred to me.

But as Nat Mills explained the way in which to set up a sponsoring committee, and initiating committee, I began to see the light. Together we went over the names of youth leaders in the community to serve on the forming committee and of others to be invited as sponsors. I suggested a few, and Nat readily accepted them. He also filled in his own suggestions. From that point, with frequent assistance from Mr. Mills, we moved rapidly toward the organization of the forming committee.

There followed a series of committee meeting at Toni Grosse's office, in which I was elected as Provisional Chairman. It is usually the case in an undertaking of this kind that out of any assembled group a hard nucleus ultimately develops. It did not therefore seem at all odd to me that that happened in this case. During this series of preliminary meetings, there emerged the influence of Arthur and Sidney Solomon and Stanley Beecher. Between these three there was nothing that I couldn't get done and some things I didn't think of doing. I came to regard them as the "Three Musketeers," not for any sense of chivalry, but because of their underlying unanimity and the manner in which their personalities played against each other toward a common objective. And so they motivated the show almost from the very beginning. The drive to get the Council set up by Autumn carried out by three to whom the council idea was an afterthought. But at this point I was still going under the assumption that they had come into the Cambridge Youth Council by invitation; that they didn't start it.

In any event, the Solomons and Beecher got things done. If a letter had to be turned out in mass quantities, one of them had an immediate answer. In a day or two they would come back with mimeographed copies produced by "friends"; that was very helpful for the sake of our nearly empty treasury, became as a rule there was no charge for the work, except sometimes for the cost of the paper. But my uneasiness grew into an uncomfortable awareness that a chairman was scarcely necessary for the functioning of the Cambridge Youth Council.

By early fall, we sent to more than one hundred Cambridge organizations our first call for a meeting of the full Council. A long, three-page letter was drawn up by my three sides for my signature. It contained a platform of issues that we considered within our province. The paramount issue of course, was the war; we pointed out that the vote for President Roosevelt in the last election just completed was a vote for his peace promises; and we raised the possibility that the President was leading the country down the road to war instead. The letter discussed the military conscription law, recommenced action on a community level to provide services to drafted men, send out parties for conscripts, correspondence with many camps to keep them in touch with affairs and attitudes at home and support the legislation that would help them.

There were one or two points in the circular with which I disagreed, and I remember voicing exceptions. One, as I recall it, was the recommendation that the conscripts be given more frequent furloughs. I felt if men were going to war they needed not furloughs, but all the training they could get. However, the objections all seemed to be minor points, and the letter was already mimeographed anyway, and so it seemed best to let it go as it was.

In a subsequent circular two weeks later, we fixed the date for the first full council meeting as December 6, 1940. We had received a good response from our initial call; we had an impressive list of local sponsors, all of them well-known in Boston's circles. The principal speaker of the evening was to be Nat Mills, head of the Massachusetts Youth Council. The agenda worked out with the assistance of the Solomons and Beecher centered upon the issue of job-training for industry, an issue selected for the reason that was to become part of a familiar pattern—because it would be expected to stir up interest and provoke a lively discussion, and yet develop no strong disagreement.

Representatives of more than 30 youth organizations attended the opening session, and from the standpoint of numbers we considered it a marked success. Almost all of the local church groups were represented, the YMCA, the YWCA—we held our meeting in the YMCA building in Central Square, Cambridge.

This was an old building, probably an old wooden schoolhouse that had been converted for YMCA purposes. It was a clapboard job, painted in a dark grey and located in the business and shopping center in town, in a very convenient location near the subway, streetcars and other transportation.

Arthur Solomon stood up and gave the progress on the job-training programs in Cambridge and guided the discussion. Nat Mills was unable to appear to make a keynote address, but Mrs. Mills came in his place. She spoke smoothly, with confidence, and with what I considered to be an amazing amount of ability. She discussed conscription, racial discrimination in both military and community life and other pertinent topics.

Thanks to the machinery worked out in advance the electricians were quickly dispensed with. Somebody proposed my name as chairman, the nomination was accepted by the assemblage and I was named the permanent chairman of the Cambridge Youth Council. Arthur Solomon was made Secretary Treasurer.

I did not know it then, but all of this had obviously been well worked out behind the scenes and without my knowledge in advance. Because the hard work of the "Musketeers" brought its rewards, too. All three of them were elected to serve with me. We set meetings for the full Council to be held once a month, first Friday of each month, while the cabinet was to convene every other Sunday morning at my apartment.

We quickly jumped into all kinds of youth activities and also into immediate trouble. Our first sign of strain came on the questions of job-training, in which Arthur Solomon was particularly interested. From time to time during our organizational phase, letters and circulars on a wide variety of subjects had got up over my name and given to me for my approval and after that sent out to the individuals and groups. But now, I discovered one day, that more than a thousand leaflets of flyers, sponsored by the Cambridge Youth Council and bearing my name as chairman, had been distributed all over the city of Cambridge, without anyone having consulted me in advance. (Philbrick retained a copy of this leaflet for his files for many years after.)

Well, I was shocked that the leaflet had been circulated over my purported signature without my knowledge. It represented to me a lack of scruples on the part of those involved and a brazen seizing of the authority supposedly vested in a chairman by a membership to whom I was responsible for all of my actions.

At the same time, I recognized some of the merits of the programs and my own experience certainly justified support for part-time work for young people. I could not but appreciate the zeal and initiative of the cabinet members, and furthermore, the campaign brought results. The School Committee voted to establish a National Youth Administration Work Experience Center in Cambridge to co-ordinate the search for jobs. It was the Youth's Council first big victory, and so I was placed in the position of not being able to object too strenuously as to the tactics involved in winning this victory.

But, this is one of the first incidents that begun to disturb me in the Cambridge Youth Council. I determined to be more careful, because many of my good friends, sincere respected citizens of Cambridge had thrown their support behind me in the Youth Council. My first responsibility was to them. As chairman of the Council I realized that I must see that the control of the policies and the actions remained where it belonged—and it belonged in the hands of the membership itself. Actually of course, this turned out to be impossible. What happened was this: The Constitution and the by-laws of the council (I discovered upon close examination) stated that in between full meetings of the Council, the cabinet would have the power to make action and make decisions in the name of the Youth Council. It was all very constitutional and legal. Furthermore, it now developed that the top council of the Cambridge Youth Council had been "stacked." As we begun to clash on more and more issues, Alice Solomont and I were always outvoted, three to two. Well, things went from bad to worse and I became more and more uneasy as time went on. Something was wrong. But, I just couldn't put my finger on it. As a matter of fact, this realization came rather slowly and painfully, but probably for the purposes of the TV series we had better do the same things as we did in the book, and that is to take one dramatic incident at which time the light can come on, not only for Philbrick, but for the audience as well.

Again, for that purpose, we can use almost any issue of that day. The one we used in the book was that of military aid to Britain. When these issues came up before the Council, the Solomons and Beecher, all made their position plain. They were always in agreement and quite frequently. They were directly opposed to the views of Alice Solomont and myself, but to the views of the membership.

On the issues of military aid to Britain, the majority of our young people seemed to feel that we should provide help to the Allies, so long as it did not involve the United States in the war itself.

Of course, the Communist Party position at that time, during the Hitler-Stalin pact, was that the United States do nothing in opposition to the ally of Stalin, and of Hitler. So when the issue came up before the cabinet, another battle developed. Alice Solomont was unable to attend this particular session, but I took a firm stand. "Look," I said, "I appreciate how you feel, and you are of course, entitled to your own opinions, but on this same subject there was a meeting of the Council only ten days ago, and although we didn't take a vote on it, the opinion of the majority was that we should provide all help short of war."

Now I faced a three man team: #1—Stan Beecher, the bruiser. No tact. He spoke in a sneering sort of voice, and said, "You're crazy." Well, I got up on my feet to face him down, and said, "As chairman of the Council I can see no choice but—"

At that point, Beecher leaned forward and said, "Agh—sit down." And punctuated the order with a light, firm push against my chest, which caught me off balance and I flopped back into my chair. "Look," he said, before I could recover myself, "the national Board of the American Youth Congress already decided to go ahead. We've got no choice but to send them our hundred percent approval."

"You're confusing the issue," I retorted. "We're not formally affiliated with the Youth Congress."

"We send delegates to it, don't we?"

"Sure, we voted to send delegates to it, but I don't see that ties us to what they do. Besides, this isn't democratic. Our members vote one way, we vote another. How can we function as a legitimate youth organization in that way?"

Now, Arthur Solomon is the diplomatic type. "Naturally, we believe in democratic action." Arthur's eyes darted rapidly from one to the other of us, in his usual fashion he spoke nervously, but his intention was to conciliate. And I didn't want things to get out of hand. Perhaps Arthur could smooth over the argument.

"In most instances of course, we would act in full accord with the vote of the members. I think we can now. A lot of the delegates were absent from the last meeting, you know. Furthermore, they didn't have the time to give full study to the problem. I'm certain that if they had every opportunity to get all of the facts and to analyze them they would have voted the same way as we are now."

Sidney Solomon is always smiling. And he smiles now. "Of course," he echoed his brother, "we have to take action now. We can't wait. The congress wants our report. We know the facts. At the Council meeting all of the facts weren't in and the members weren't fully educated. Don't you see?" And he kept on smiling.

Well, I didn't see. But by this time I wasn't thinking of the issue at hand. Because no amount of quibbling could possibly change my opinion on my stand. But I was also stunned at the realization of how ridiculous my own position was to concern myself with the hairs that these were trying to split. Their minds were made up as much as mine was, and we were on opposite sides of the fence. The problem could never be resolved in meeting with them. But the thing that shocked me most was their attitude toward what they were calling democratic procedure.

"Now," Sidney continued, still smiling, "after all, the National Board is sitting right there in Washington. They studied the situation at first hand and they know what is going on much better than we do. Are we in a better position to make a good decision than they are, right on the spot? Besides, here's another thing. The Massachusetts Youth Council, our own parent organization, has already approved this thing. How can we step out of line? We're just being left way behind in the present trends, Herb, that's all."

Well, this line of reasoning flashed on the light in a corner of my brain. What was it called—this method of thinking? The Communists had a word for it—"Democratic Centralism."

The top policy makers established the line on a particular issue and passed it down through channels to the rank and file. When they are through with it, they rubber-stamped it and passed it back. The policy makers then called it "the will of the people." Democratic centralism, Communist democracy!

My mind was suddenly clear. Very clear. The answer to all of my doubts and questions became apparent. I had walked into a cleverly laid trap. One of the founders, organizers, and the first chairman of the Cambridge Youth Council—in fact, the Council itself—was nothing but a front for the plans and programs of a few behind-the-scenes operators. The Cambridge Youth Council, an organization involving about 35 youth organizations and three to four hundred young people, was being effectively validated and controlled by three individuals.

"Besides," Stan Beecher was saying, "we're being democratic. We're the Board. You're outvoted three to one. What else are you going to do to be democratic?" There was a very plain implication in his tone of voice. I could resign. The three didn't need a chairman anyways.

I left the meeting in black despair. Even if Alice Solomont had been there, I would have been outvoted three to two. The cards were stacked against us. There might have been an easy way out, but if there was I didn't see it at the time. I simply knew that I had to do something. It was fortunate that I didn't act on impulse. First, I turned the problem over and over in my mind. I kept it to myself. In a way, I was too abashed to talk about it to anyone. I didn't even mention it to Eva, my wife. She was very busy now with the new baby, and besides she didn't care very much for some of the people who came around to the house these days.

I knew that many of my friends who had supported and come into the Council at my urging would be terribly shocked if they knew how effectively the Chairman was being controlled. Should I go directly to them? To do so would certainly wreck the Youth Council and destroy all of my work thus far. Should I bring the whole thing out in the open, and make public charges that these people were Communists? I didn't relish a public scene—and besides, I had no proof that these individuals were in fact Communists; although I was completely sure of it in my mind. If I made public charges, I would have been kicked out of the organization, called a Fascist or a Redbaiter, and that would have been the end of Philbrick. Who would listen back in 1940?

I could resign. Beecher made that very clear to me at the meeting. But to resign would solve nothing. Beecher and the Solomons would carry on in the Council anyways, with probably the unknowing help of another front.

I wrestled with the problem day and night, went back over every phrase of the development of the youth council, reviewed my association with these three, who now proved to be my antagonists.

Now I could see that things had been a little too pat, policies too tailor-made, but how did the Solomons and Beecher manage to get so much done? Who did this work for them, and why? Why was it that they were so anxious to take on the heavy jobs? I covered every link in the chain that led me to them in the first place—Nat Mills, Toni Grosse, my first encounter with Mrs. Mills.

Then I began to study the literature that we had published . . . the letters and the circulars. I compared them with circulars from other sources, dumped in the lap by the Solomons, Toni, and the others. Now it began to take shape. Now I had a few booklets and leaflets, but still no proof that these people were Communists. They had never spoken of Communism or of the Communist Party to me. Marxism? Yes, perhaps they mentioned it here and there, but many of our delegates studied Marxism as an academic pursuit. Besides, Marxism was no crime, and even the Communists were a legally constituted group.

I wondered about taking the problem to Nat Mills. As head of the Massachusetts Youth Council he should certainly be concerned, but then, as I thought of the links in the chain, I decided against it. I realized I had little real knowledge of what part he played in this picture. As this went on, the situation grew steadily worse. I saw that I was losing control of the Council completely. I couldn't bring my weight to bear effectively against the opposition in the cabinet. Furthermore, the atmosphere changed from mere difference of opinion to outright fraud. Actions were taken in the name of the

Council and it was my name which did not represent the true sentiments of the membership.

The original platform of the "peace" organization was arbitrarily expanded far beyond its original concept. We became engaged in a "fight against discrimination in the Air Forces." This in turn, was enlarged into a campaign against poll taxes, for Negro housing, and in behalf of many other special issues, which regardless of their merits, had nothing to do with keeping the United States out of war.

The Council became a propaganda sounding board to arouse resentment and ill-feeling. While its spokesmen, the "Three Musketeers," fought for non-intervention in Europe, they were very curiously "interventionist" in what they called China. In their statements declaring that Latin American countries should be "free from American expansionist, colonial policies." Apparently there was no end to the issues which could be dragged into the Council program without consulting either the members or the chairman. I only knew that I was in a bad spot and that it was getting worse every day. I was unable to sleep. It occurred to me that I might go to the Boston police, but I was afraid that they might dismiss me as a crackpot and probably would have. After all, no laws were being broken. Trying to sleep one night, reviewing these things in my mind, I tossed and sweated, sweated without letup. How had I ever gotten into this thing in the first place? Eva slept quietly beside me, and I wanted to awaken her and blurt out the whole story, get it off my chest. I needed to talk to somebody. I was angry—angry with others, as well as myself. I felt tricked, frustrated, and outwitted. Precisely how or when this thing had happened I could not determine. It was no longer possible for me to evade the truth of the situation.

The Youth Council, basically a decent idea with great possibilities for good, had gone completely out of control. It was out of my hands and in the power of others who were distorting it to their own views. The Cambridge Youth Council had been subverted. And me? I had gone briskly along and had been made a fool of. Something had to be done in order to win back my friends and my self respect.

The room was hot despite the cold winter night. I tossed off my blanket, turned over, tried to sleep. Suddenly, I sat upright.

I turned on a dim bedside lamp, and grabbed the telephone book. I looked under the Initial "F." Nothing there. Perhaps it was under Federal. I turned the pages. Nothing there. Then I switched to the back of the book, looked under the columns listed "United States Government" in big, heavy type. Finally found "Justice Department" and then "Federal Bureau of Investigation," 10 Post Office Square, Liberty—1155.

Eva stirred in her sleep. "Is anything wrong?," she asked sleepily. "No," I glanced again at the address. 10 Post Office Square—and closed the book and placed it back on the bedside stand. "No, there's nothing wrong," I said to her, and then continued to myself, "I hope."

Well, we're at the end of this cylinder.

Just when you will want to cut off this particular episode—whether at the telephone episode in the middle of the night or the next morning when I go down to the F.B.I., I don't know. But on the next cylinder I will relate some of the circumstances surrounding my visit to the Bureau the next morning.

Appendix F:
Theory and Tactics of the Bolshevik Party on the Question of War, Peace, and Revolution
by Herbert A. Philbrick

This was one of a handful of brief summaries and essays for the script writers to outline in the television scripts.

This was one of the most astounding lessons I learned in the Communist Party. Put together right by that, I mean so that the TV audience will hang onto their seats while we reveal it on the screen, can render one of the most vital and valuable public services yet presented by TV or by the sponsor. It goes to the very core of the communist conspiracy, making you realize that the Party member is not just another guy but a very special character who is not good for our side.

This lesson comes right out of the "Bible" of the Communist Party, "History of the C.P.S.U. (B)," written by Joe Stalin in person (or so the comrades claim). The "History" book is actually the alleged history of the successful revolutionary overthrow of the Russian Tsarist government. Since it was successful there, the comrades maintain that the same means will be successful everyplace else. Hence we were taught that it should be considered as a "Guide to Action."

Background—lead to cell meeting.

Philbrick, as related in the book, was called to a luncheon meeting with Toni Grosse, a blonde amazon whose bent was toward youth hostels, outdoor life in the socialist sense.

Toni selected a restaurant which significantly had mirrors on the wall by the table. From this vantage point she could keep an eye on the room and on Philbrick at the same time. Self service trays. When a man came by the table and lingered a moment, looking for a spot, she stopped talking.

Philbrick rings the F.B.I.—announcing that the luncheon meeting is to be held. Up to this point she has been to him only a student worker pretty close to the communist movement—but so far as Philbrick was concerned, not a communist. So who is she? What does she want? Is she going to expose Philbrick as a communist? Exposure to Philbrick by an anti-communist would be as disastrous as the Party learning his connection with the F.B.I. An ordinary lunch with an ordinary gal thus becomes critical.

Follow the book on Toni Grosse to the meeting of the Youth Communist League at the Philbrick flat.

This was a motley assemblage of young people—some college kids from Harvard and M.I.T.; an Italian labor union lad from the Central Labor Committee in Cambridge; a couple of Negro community clubs; etc.

It was obvious from the meeting that many of the members already knew the lesson and were prepared to give the "correct" answers to questions by the cell educational leader.

Here is the gist of the material:

It is "wrong" to be a pacifist. It is not scientifically correct. It is bad for a good American to be against every type of war. For example: should an American have been against the Revolutionary War? No—of course not—because that was a war for freedom from Imperialism. Is it correct to be against the Civil War? No, because although there were many wrong aspects to the Civil War—many Northern capitalists participating in it simply as a matter of economics, unable to compete with cheap slave labor in the South—it was a "beneficial" war. Should good Americans have been against the World War (now World War I)? Yes—because this was the only war of interest between great world economic interests, a war for control of world markets.

What is the communist position, therefore? There are two kinds of wars:

a.) Just wars—wars that are not wars of conquest but wars of liberation.

b.) Unjust wars—wars of conquest carried out by capitalists and imperialists to enslave colonial peoples, to control colonial and dependent countries.

Wars of the first kind the communists will support. But wars of the second kind the communist will oppose.

Capitalism creates warfare and sponsors it. Wars are caused by capitalist competition for world markets. A communist must therefore not simply be "against war" but he must fight to eradicate the cause of war, capitalist imperialism, which is run by the 100 (or 50–400, the number makes no difference) biggest capitalists who according to the comrades own and control all U.S.

Hence the Bolsheviks are not mere pacifists who sign for peace and confine themselves to the propaganda for peace, as the Quakers, Social Democrats, and do-gooder Americans.

The communist advocate revolutionary struggle for peace, to the point of overthrowing the decadent, imperialist bourgeoisie.

Any war by the Soviet Union would, of course, be a Just war—a war to free the people from capitalist slavery. (That's us, in case there is any question). Any war by the United States would be a capitalist war, an unjust war. Whose side are we on? Are we on the side of the workers, or are we on the side of the working class?

> We read from the good book (page 167)—Lenins position in 1916; "The Bolsheviks maintain that the lesser evil for the people would be the military defeat of the tsarist government in the imperialist war, for this would facilitate the victory of the people over tsardom and the success of the struggle of the working class for emancipation from capitalist slavery and imperialist wars. Lenin held that *the policy of working for the defeat of one's own imperialist government* must be pursued not only by the Russian revolutionaries, but by the revolutionary parties of the working class in all the belligerent countries." End quote.

The communist therefore, in the event of a war between the U.S. and the U.S.S.R., must not take the incorrect position of pacifist. The communist does not avoid the struggle, he participates in the struggle—on the right side, on the winning side. The communist links the cause of peace with the cause of the victory of the proletarian revolution, holding that the surest way to ending the war and securing a just peace is to overthrow the rule of the imperialist bourgeoisie.

It means that we must convert the imperialist war into a civil war; it means that you do not fight on the side of the capitalists, but that you advance the policy of the defeat of one's own government in the imperialist war.

Hence you are not passive, you are active; this means working against compulsory military training, against the draft, against the war financing, against financial support of the capitalist governments elsewhere, form illegal (underground) revolutionary organizations in the armed forces, all sorts of propaganda against war, setting up "Peace" fronts, involving as many hundreds or thousands of other people . . . and, if and when the actual outbreak of war between the two systems, turning these actions into an uprising against one's own imperialist government.

Under the almost hypnotic influence of the instructor, all of this stuff almost made sense—and did if you accepted the premise that capitalism is bad and socialism is good. And it was obvious that this cell already accepted these "facts" as obvious axioms.

This is also an important indication of the communist considerations of "right" and "wrong." There was nothing at all wrong about teaching and advocating seditious and treasonable activities against one's own country. Any such suggestion was viewed—and is viewed—with scorn. This, too, is accurately reflected and indicated in the History of the C.P.S.U., page 170.

Seems that in 1914 in Russia, the comrades were pursuing this same line; to wit;

> "In November 1914 a conference of the Bolshevik group in the State Duma was convened to discuss policy towards the war. On the third day of the conference all present were arrested. The tsarist government charged them with 'high treason' (quote marks theirs). The picture of the activities of the Duma members unfolded in court did credit to our Party. The Bolshevik deputies conducted themselves manfully."

At yesterday's conference we spoke of the "weeding out" process, the fact that many young people dropped out. This particular meeting might be a good time to illustrate that and to wind up the half hour. These people usually just dropped out, would have nothing more to do with us. We might use this meeting for one of them to quit right before us, leave the meeting.

The position of the Party cell leader: Let him go; we not only don't need him, we don't want him. "The Party consists of only the most class conscious sections of the working class. These individualistic intellectuals fear discipline and organization, and they will indeed remain outside of the ranks of the Party. But that is all to the good, for the Party is spared that influx of unstable elements."

But what did that lad think of Philbrick as he left the meeting. Philbrick stayed in . . . who was wondering by this time if he was not somewhat nuts . . . it would be an excellent idea if he got out too. But at the same time he realized that this new knowledge meant that the Party was a great deal more dangerous then he had originally thought. This group is tied to others. There are Party bosses, more important, directing this thing. Who are they? It was now more important than ever to continue.

Appendix G: Standard Outlines for a Party Meeting

by Herbert A. Philbrick

This was one of a handful of brief summaries and essays for the script writers to outline in the television scripts.

Cells before 1948 numbered 10 to 15 people; after 1948 they were limited, for security reasons, to 5 people.

Officers of the cell: Chairman (who is also representative to next highest echelon); Treasurer; Educational Director; and Literature Director. Sometimes last two combined. Sometimes Chairman would also be Educational Director, with another comrade Literature Director.

Cell meetings in three parts:

1. **Business.** New members, collection of dues, collection of special fees, fund raising, subscription to communist publication; turning in of money obtained from "front" operations; announcement of next meeting, time, place and date; and the sale of literature.

2. **Agitation & Propaganda.** Current activities of cell and members—report of progress, any special problems, assignment of projects for next two weeks. Most projects are fairly long range, with a comrade assigned to a front, where he carries on without much trouble.

3. **Education.** Usually the longest session, unless Educational Session of the Zdanov Report.

Meeting at Martha Fletcher's apartment . . .

During the business meeting, the housewife—Treasurer—takes a very tiny piece of paper, about 1/3 of one 3x5 card, from her pocketbook. There are some meaningless notations and numbers on the card, designed to give no clue to a Party spy, wrecker, of member of J. Edgar Hoover's secret police. In fact, the notions are so meaningless that even Peg cannot remember what they meant at the meeting two weeks ago. Somebody jibes her while she figures out that—oh, yes—only one-half of somebody's dues were paid, and now that it is a new month. That means one month's dues plus ? month's dues or $25.00 plus $12.50 equals $37.50.

Somebody else had contributed—as a prominent "non-communist" liberal—with a public flourish to the Women's International League for Peace and Freedom. The cell had decided last week to put that comrades' monthly dues in as part of the contribution which was rather heavy—$250.00—for two months.

While the money banter is going on, Philbrick picks up the bag he has obtained from the subway locker, opens it, and begins to spread the contents on the desk. Some special problem in the "Agit-Prop" session. The "Educational" session was also, to Philbrick, the most dull and boring, although the comrades lapped the stuff up. We have recently been avid supporters of Eisenhower or Stevenson who would cling to every last word of their candidate with worshipful attention and complete acceptance. Multiply this by two for the comrades listening to the words of Stalin, Lenin, Zdanov, Jacques Duclos, etc. Especially Stalin. At big communist convention before going underground they had a song "Stalin is our Leader, we shall not (something or other)." If the television audience says is disgust, "Well for God's sake!," you will be right—because that is the way I felt and I was used to it. Slightly sickening, but also amazing that these otherwise intelligent people should be so.

The Educational section led by one of the members of the cell, rotated, with sometimes a visiting specialist coming in.

MATERIAL STUDIED: Marxist classics, using "Little Lenin Library" books, and taking from ? to 1 Chapter per meeting . . . in the pro-group cell, the latest directives in "For a Lasting Peace, For a People's Democracy," or in magazine "Political Affairs," or from some current American Communist Party publication on a special subject, such as a "draft resolution" from the National Committee of the Communist Party.

DISCUSSION: The comrades are permitted to "discuss" the subjects but only within a very narrow framework of Party discipline. You may indulge in criticism—so long as it is "self-criticism" and no criticism of the Party or its leaders. Most discussion took a peculiar form which consisted of one member saying something (in accordance with Party policy) and then the next one saying the same thing over again but with a word selection designed to get even closer to the Party line. A refining process, all in the opposing points of view.

In case of any slight difference of opinion, the whole cell would stop right where it was until the erring member was "straightened out" in his thinking. And if any real difference persisted, the chairman always had the last word. Everything done within the framework of "Democratic Centralism," which works as follows:

DEMOCRATIC CENTRALISM. Party rules adopted at the Sixth Congress, Petograd, July & August 1917. . . and reaffirmed at the 19th Party Congress held last October and November, 1952 . . .

(1) All directing bodies of the Party, from top to bottom, shall be elected.
(2) Party bodies shall give periodical accounts of their activities to their respective Party organizations.
(3) There shall be strict Party discipline and the subordination of the minority to the majority.
(4) All decisions of higher bodies shall be absolutely binding on lower bodies and on all Party members.

Point No. 4 cancels out the majority rule business of point 3, but leaves in the "discipline." If a majority of a "lower body" should vote "wrong" they can always be overruled by the Party bosses.

THESE INCLUDE: Political Affairs; Masses and Mainstream; Science and Society, a Marxist Quarterly; current Communist Party tracts and pamphlets running from a penny to five or ten cents each . . .

and in this instance, copies of the newspaper, "For a Lasting Peace, For a Peoples Democracy!"

Problem is how to get the one with the Czdanov article. This weekly paper, printed in Bucharest (during the Tito time, in Belgrade), is printed in many languages and mailed to all countries of the world by Air every week. Camera might pick up the block in the paper which tells the language it is printed in, while narration explains that this is the main guide to action for communist parties everywhere. What the F.A.L.P. says this week, the *Daily Worker* will set next week, in terminology to fit the United States.

This paper is referred to by the comrades as the *Cominform Bulletin*. It costs ten cents.

Another interesting book is a pocket-size paper bound job called *State and Revolution*, by V. I. Lenin.

The treasurer having collected the dues, opens for Philbrick who gives a little sales pitch on the literature. He says that the new issue of *Masses and Mainstream* and *Political Affairs* are out . . . that since the *Comminform Bulletin* articles constitute the basis for tonight's discussion, everyone should have one; and that next session the cell was to start on a study series of Lenin's *State and Revolution* . . . those who did not already have a copy should get one, or maybe they'd like to have a nice fresh copy to start off with.

The comrades are still milling about a bit from dues proceedings, and pick up their literature, leaving money on the desk or making change.

Agi-Prop is dispensed with Martha Fletcher's "Any problems?" Nobody responds. Finally somebody says, "No problems," so Martha announces the discussion tonight will concern the most important directives for Party policy of the day—the Czdanov report. "It will be our guide for action for the next period of struggle."

Comrade Herb sits on an uncomfortable wooden bench that has a thin upholstered cover. He has the paper spread across his lap, with penciled notations opposite certain marked sections and circled areas in the article.

This stuff was extremely dull, in spite of whatever manufactured enthusiasm I could master. Furthermore, the comrades, who love to chew on this stuff like a cow on a cud, would, I knew, expect me to hold forth for a good 45 minutes or an hour. It was bad enough dishing out stuff, but it was made worse by the way the comrades ate it up.

According to my best recollection, this is approximately the way it went; the great second war brought on many terrific changes in the world situation, and especially in the world balance of power. Russia has emerged the greatest country in the world, despite terrible losses and destruction. The imperialist countries have suffered great losses, however, and imperialism has been weakened. Only in the United States has capitalism gained in the course of the war. The United States is unquestionable the greatest central power of world capitalism, and as such it will seek to capture the world market formerly held by Great Britain, France, the Netherlands, etc. That means that the United States itself entering into a period of unbridled, unrestrained Imperialism.

We, as communists, know that Imperialism is the highest stage—and the final stage—of capitalism.

This highest stage of capitalism is marked by utmost reaction, with all the forces of reaction rallying behind the banner of fascism and reaction against the working class people's. The colonial countries of the world face enslavement by Imperialist United States, who will seek to exploit them.

But many of the world have been lost to the capitalist bosses. World markets—necessary for the increasing needs of capitalist expansion—have shrunken. And many countries formerly ready to serve as tools and lackeys of capitalist United States have now become People's Democracies.

Hence capitalism is caught in a trap. It needs an increasing world market, but it is faced with a restricted world market. The contradictions of capitalism lead to crisis; and crisis to depression and unemployment.

The world had therefore been divided into two camps. In one camp, the U.S.S.R.—the great victorious socialist sixth of the world, together with the people's democracies and the downtrodden of the colonial countries; and their allies in the working class everywhere . . . (what the heck was this bunch of pro-group members doing in the "working class," I used to ask myself) . . . And on the other side, in the other camp, capitalist, imperialist, reactionary government of the United States . . .

As this discussion went on, the Soviet Union emerged through the "logic" of the talk as the inevitable victor, and the United States as the inevitable looser. Everybody felt pretty much hopped up because they were on the winning side.

It was when I finished the thing off that I slipped, with a weak ending that didn't match the expectations of the comrades. I said something about the Communist Party here having therefore to prepare itself to face increased reaction, greater attacks on the people's movements by the government, speed up and pay outs in industry, the "class struggle" going up another notch. We communists must brace ourselves to meet the blows.

But the balloon was blown up and something was going to explode. It did, in the person of Martha Fletcher, the charming, popular, classical featured gal of such standing with young people. Although I was usually prepared for anything, I was shocked by the sudden and violent transformation. From civilization to savagery in 30 seconds. Her first few words were in slashing rebuke to me . . . In the face of this great world transformation, what was my position? Fiddlefaddle. (etc., from the book itself . . .)

Then she went on somewhat as follows: Matters have changed radically in this new period. The new world crisis is one of open class collisions, of revolutionary action by the proletariat, or proletarian, revolution, we comrades are faced with a new task . . . we must reorganize all Party work on new, revolutionary lines. We must educate the workers in the spirit of revolutionary struggle for power. We must work closely with the workers of the world. We must establish a firm alliance with the liberation movement in the colonies. We cannot hope to win through senseless adherence to parlimentarism . . . that would mean inevitable defeat. That is the stupid way of the Progressive Party, the social democrats and the liberals.

We face the necessity to build a new Party. A militant (Fletcher's voice reached a pitch and fervor at this point which exceeded anything I ever heard at a Revivalist meeting) . . . a revolutionary Party, one bold enough to lead the proletarians in the struggle for power. Without such action it is useless to even think of overthrowing imperialism and achieving the dictatorship of the proletariat. "We must arm the workers for the struggle, and we must arm them now!!"

By this time I was sweating. But everybody happily had forgotten me in their attention to Fletcher and they all acclaimed her correct analysis. The discussion broke up with the usual banalities.

Later that evening, in my attack hideout, I reconstructed the evening for the F.B.I. and especially the outburst by Fletcher. I had the odd feeling that I had experienced a vivid nightmare, shook my head in wonderment despite the unqualified terminology used.

P.S. I forgot to include in Fletcher's remarks some caustic comment about capitalism . . . people were facing a period of untold unemployment and misery.

Appendix H: Standard Communist Party Cell Procedure

by Herbert A. Philbrick

This was one of a handful of brief summaries and essays for the script writers to outline in the television scripts.

Today the Party is mostly underground, and operates according to underground strategy and tactics. Before 1948 (Philbrick was in from 1940 to 1949) the Party operated on two levels, mostly aboveground and only the Pro group underground.

However, even in the "aboveground" level the Party was always very security conscious. Here are some of the rules and regulations;

Regular Party cell meetings (before 1948): 10 to 15 people. First names or nicknames only, or just plain "comrade." Notices of meetings sent by mail, in plain envelopes, first class, and some telephoning done on a cautious basis. Comrades could talk about other communists not present or in other work and cells. We worked directly for the District Headquarters of the Communist Party and discussion quite often would pertain to instructions and orders from Party bosses. Dues ten cents to two dollars per month on income scale. Many members publicly known as Communists.

Pro-Group—deeply underground. This group acknowledges that it operates as the "illegal" arm of the Communist Party. None of the members are known publicly to be communists. Most of them are not known to other communists as communists. Limited to "white collar" above the clerical level; housewives barred unless they could offer culture or money; no laborers.

- First names, nicknames, or Party aliases. Philbrick's Party alias was Arthur Trowbridge.
- Whereas in regular Party cells you knew who your bosses at state

headquarters were, in the pro-group cell you do not know who your boss is, due to the cell organizational structure and breakdown.

- Limited to only five people. You can have no Communist Party business with any comrade outside of your own cell unless on special instructions. Sometimes you would be ordered to work with another person on the "outside" on a special project.
- If you do have some Party business with somebody outside of the cell, the communication must go through your Chairman. He or she takes it to the next level. From there it is handed to the Chairman of the cell of which your "contact" is a member. That means:
   (1) Government agents detect no communication between the two, and yet they are able to work together.
   (2) The eye of Stalin is always on you; you do nothing which is not known in detail by your Chairman. That prevents any shenanigans or counter-plots between members.
- Dues. Pro-group members pay "sustaining fees" to the Party, according to income and the pressure put by Party for money. From five to ten dollars per month up to $100.00 per month in the Boston cell, probably higher in Hollywood. A guy like Frederick Vanderbilt Field could quite conceivably be paying $1,000 to $5,000 per month.
- No written communications or phone calls relative to Party meetings. All phones are considered to be tapped. No Party cards are carried by any pro-group member (they were used in the ranks and file Party). Time and place of next meeting fixed at meeting. Attendance at regular cell meetings is mandatory, unless for a very good reason and it must be a Party reason, not a personal one.
- If contact is broken for any reason, a written notice might say: Herb: a group of friends are dropping in next Wednesday at 8 p.m. Hope you can come. Or, a phone call to the office would make an appointment for lunch, and at luncheon meeting the message would be delivered by word of mouth.
- Everything you did for the Party was done in the good assumption that government agents (fascist secret police, agents of the capitalist) were about. You took security measures not for your own security, but for the security of the Party and your comrades. Hence, when going to Party meetings you were always cautious

that you were not observed or trailed. You did this so that you would not lead the G-Men to your meeting place and to your other conspirators.

- You never called state headquarters, district headquarters, even from a pay station. You never met publicly with a known communist or with a Party boss.
- All of these rules and regulations for underground operation offer limited possibilities for story treatment, all within the limits of factual, documentary content.

It is here you see the wisdom and the reason for the F.B.I. admonition to Philbrick—which is nothing more than standard for any counter-espionage operation; if anything happens, we never heard you.

That meant that Philbrick could not afford to behave any differently from the rest. In fact, he had to be even more cautious, and could afford even less to be careless. This was a guarantee that Philbrick would in every action and word coincide with those of his cell members. This meant, in practical effect, that there was nothing at all different about Philbrick, so far as the Party security agents were concerned. It worked for nine years. But that doesn't mean that Philbrick didn't worry about it *not* working.

IMPORTANT: So far as the cell members were concerned, however, there was little to indicate a "conspiratorial nature." These people were—and are—"pros." Professional communists, professional revolutionists. It's a business and they went about it in a business like manner.

Cell meetings were much in the nature of business meetings. The discussion of problems was in a matter of fact nature, much the same as at a story conference.

In fact, their actions and attitude belied the words they were using. Whereas with the usual cops and robbers story we could use "out of the corner of the mouth" technique, here we may have to use "voice over" to call to the attention of the viewer that what this distinguished business man is talking about is treason and conspiracy.

Pro-Group—Top Party bosses; main business, the tactics and strategy of the Communist Party in the U.S.; what its line shall be, how to accomplish certain ends, timing, people to use, what aspects of America to attack, what groups to infiltrate and which ones to leave along; how to go about the business of weakening the United States, destroying the confidence of the people in their government and in capitalism, how to help the Soviet Union.

In Boston, Mass.; between 70 to 80 members. Across the country, probably close to 2,000. Doctors, lawyers, teachers, professors, business men, government workers, authors, publishers, etc. The Soviet Union has been working now for 20 years, patiently building this group. Of 20,000 students at a given college, the Party is happy to get exactly one pro-group member in a year. It takes only one Alger Hiss to do the kind of a job the Party wants.

Appendix I: *I Led Three Lives* Summary

by Herbert A. Philbrick

This was one of a handful of brief summaries and essays for the script writers to outline for a television scripts.

It was a day in late Spring. Boston, 1940. We see a young salesman going down through a typical business section of a city. These are not stores—they are business offices—banks—something like Wall Street. The young salesman (Philbrick) is seen walking down the street, shifting his heavy briefcase of advertising samples from one hand to the other, and then coming to an address—7 Water Street. There is a Western Union telegraph window next to the entrance. He appraises his reflection in the Western Union window. He sees the reflection of Herb Philbrick, in the 25th year of the life of a very average Bostonian, an American wage earner pursuing his living.

His appearance is very normal—he has no particular distinguishing marks to set him apart in a crowd—he is neither tall nor short, but of medium build. This complete normality was to prove, in fact, one of my most valuable assets. Together with an extrovert's geniality, it turned out to be my best disguise. But he has one stock in trade—and that is the pipe, which may well become a permanent prop in the series. He wears a light overcoat and a hat.

It may be that we could use a newsstand at this point to pin down the time and date. The spring of 1940, is a year and a half before Pearl Harbor. The greatest Second World War is rapidly embroiling the whole world. We might take a newspaper dated April 9, 1940—the Nazis invade Norway and Denmark; Copenhagen occupied—or on May 10, Nazis invade Netherlands, Belgium and Luxembourg. On the same day—May 10—Chamberlain resigns and Churchill takes over as Prime Minister. These headlines might very well serve to dramatize the particular day when I walked into the office of the Massachusetts Youth Council, 7 Water Street, Boston.

The entrance is a normal business entrance. The building is made of smooth, grey granite rock, and a short hallway leads into an elevator. The elevator has gold, metal filigreed network, so that you can see the elevator through the grillwork coming down on the inside—in other words, it is not enclosed. I pushed the button, the elevator comes down, I went in, go up to the 5th floor, walk down the hallway and call on a company called The Massachusetts Housing Association. This is one of my regular customers, with whom I do business regularly.

Conversation with the customer might establish the advertising business I am in. In this case, I have called to discuss with him a mailing of 5,000 direct mail advertising pieces, and the agency is going to write the copy for the letter, multigraph the letter, put the man's signature at the bottom of the letter, address the envelopes and mail them out. One of the things I have to do on this call is to obtain a signature of the man, which will be duplicated mechanically by a machine.

Fill in material concerning Philbrick will be found on Page 7 to 11 of the original manuscript, concerning Philbrick's background.

Leaving the office of my regular customer, I walked down the hallway of the business firm back toward the elevator, except along the way I examined some of the doorways and the names of the companies inside on these doorways to determine if there might not be another prospective customer. This is what is called "cold canvassing" in the sales field. A few doors down I did find a door and on the door in black letters on the frosted glass is printed "Massachusetts Youth Council." I turn, knock, and then open the door myself into a small room. This room has a single window, with three plain business tables, one of these one-drawer affairs, in the room, two desks set facing the wall next to the window, one facing the right wall and one facing the left wall, both of these have typewriters on them; just to the left of the door as you come into the room there is a mimeograph machine, an old beat up job, a great big thing, but very old; and under and on the tables are stacks of pamphlets and booklets. Under the tables are boxes of envelopes—500 to a box. There is one occupant in the room.

I reach into my upper left hand pocket where I keep my business cards. As I hand over the business card I say, "I'm Herbert Philbrick, and I represent the Holmes Direct Mail Service in Cambridge."

The occupant is a young. mid-twenty girl. Her face is medium-complexioned; she has dark eyes and heavy black eyebrows, although she wears no makeup. Her hair is straight, no jewelry, and arranged in the fashion of a neat, well-disciplined person, but one who had little use for fussy, feminine adornment. Maybe a school teacher. She wears cotton stockings. Then a little gold social badge of protest against Japan, then popular in many circles. Her dress is plain, and her shoes I notice, are comfortable but flat-heeled and very plain.

I glanced around the room again and found the place crowded with desks and tables and all heaped with campaign literature. There were posters on the wall which give an indication of the nature of the organization. For example, one of the posters says, "Don't Be an Unknown Soldier,"—there was a picture of a young child, about four-five years old and it was captioned "To Be Killed in Action." And on the table there were pamphlets, one of the pamphlets labeled, "The Yanks Are Not Coming," another one called, "The Case of Non-Intervention."

I have to apologize a bit because although I sold direct mail advertising, it looked as though they don't have to be sold. They obviously use a great deal of it. I also remarked that the material interested me. "I'm interested in world peace too." "If there was only some way we could avoid becoming embroiled again in one of Europe's eternal squabbles. If there was only some way we could establish world peace without having to send our own soldiers overseas." I indicate that I don't know if that can be done, or if it is possible, but I felt that that was certainly much to be preferred. Mrs. Alice Mills is the name of this girl. She explains to me that they are the Massachusetts Youth Council. "We function as a clearing house for all sorts of organizations." "There are many organizations throughout the country interested in peace—the Women's International League for Peace and Freedom, The Carnegie Endowment for International Peace, The World Peaceways, so on. Peace is one thing we are interested in too, now especially, but we have a broader organization and a broader function. Peace isn't the only thing we are interested in. The groups, and all progressive movements for youth have our support."

Well, "progressive" was a new word to me. It didn't mean anything to me, especially at that time. "Such as?," I said.

Alice Mills answers, "Oh, such as Jobs for Young People, training opportunities, government job counseling. We organize discussions and activities to help out the young people. We believe that the young people should get together and we should discuss these things ourselves, rather than waiting for adults to solve all these problems for us."

Mrs. Mills then asked where I lived. I told her that my wife and I just recently moved to Cambridge, Massachusetts.

"Cambridge," she said, with a detached air as if a thought had crossed her mind. I half sat against a table, and Mrs. Mills took a chair. "We have youth groups all over the state working on joint projects through this organization," she explained. "The YMCA, the YWCA, church affiliates." She paused, waiting for me to say something, but I was still listening.

"As a matter of fact," she gave a toss of her head as though a fresh idea was to be tried, "we know of some people in Cambridge where you live, who have already expressed interest in the possibilities of the Youth Council there. I could put you in touch with them, provided of course you are interested." I assured her I was. We talked for another half hour, during which the Cambridge Youth Council, springing from behind the alert, dark eyes of Mrs. Mills, grew in my vision to a splendid accomplishment.

She gave me ideas, names. And then she referred me to a Toni Grosse at Harvard University, and head of the Harvard Student Union. Toni, she explained, was a very aggressive person and just the one to help me. And then Mrs. Mills explained that her husband, Nat Mills, was the head of the Massachusetts Youth Council, and if I truly wanted to carry on, he would call upon me to give me any assistance he could.

I was very grateful to Mrs. Mills for her interest and enthusiasm, and for her helpful suggestions I left her my business telephone number at the advertising agency I worked for.

When I walked out of Mrs. Mills office' that day, stacks of Youth Council literature mingled with the direct mail samples in my briefcase. I felt very enthusiastic about the future of a Cambridge Youth Council.

It occurs to me that the writer might possibly want to the Philbrick apartment rather than picking him up on the street.

If so, there is a description of the house on Banks Street, Cambridge, Massachusetts. The apartment that my wife and I were living in at the time was a four-family duplex house, two stories high. It was very plain, clapboard construction, flat roof, and very square. A wooden fence went around the house.

Note: It is important that the house be shown on a corner location, with the Philbrick apartment on the corner, because of incidents to take place later in the story.

The apartment was a four-room, cold-water flat. It consisted of four rooms; a long hall from the doorway going down the middle of the house, with doors leading off the hallway to (1. a living room, wherein we had a player piano and simple furnishings; 2. a bedroom, also very simply furnished; 3. at the rear of the house were the back windows overlooking the back stairs and with a clear view down the side street, leading to the Charles River, a kitchen. This kitchen had a plain kitchen table and chairs, a sink, and a most important prop for later developments in the story—a coal-wood burning iron stove, a good sized one. This was used for heating the apartment. During the colder winter months, we also set up a small, pot-bellied stove in the front living room, also a wood burning job. Leading off from the kitchen, on the outside of the house, were a window looking out onto the side street, a small study about eight feet square. The small study had a desk, typewriter, mimeograph machine, a bookcase with reference books on advertising, sales promotion, salesmanship, etc.

The Philbricks at this time had no children, but were expecting one soon. We entertained simply, mostly inviting in our church friends from our old town of Somerville, Massachusetts, most of whom we were to lose as friends when I became closely involved with the Communists and the Communist front organizations.

However at this time we would have them in at the house and had a rollicking good time around the player piano. I had discovered that you could get modern versions of piano recordings on piano rolls. The one piece that used to give us the most rollicking effect was a Fats Waller piano roll recording of "Ol' Man Mose Is Dead." Another recording was that of "Dance Macabre." As a matter of fact, this piece might have had some significance, since it represents the allegorical dance of death in which a skeleton Death leads people to the grave. Another prop which we shall need will be a telephone book, and a lamp on a bedside table in the bedroom.

We had a small backyard, fenced in with the same fence which went around to the front of the house and along the side street. This fence also ran across the back of the lot of the land. This backyard consisted only of a grassed in plot, part of which we dug up for the planting of a very small garden, planting bush beans and a very few tomato plants. The side street led down to Memorial Drive, a couple of hundred feet away, on the other side of which was the Charles River.

Hence, although at the front of the house we had a rather bleak situation; a plain, crowded, city street with concrete sidewalk and no trees—in the back of the house we had green grass, open stretches of land, and the Charles River and the parkway that ran on either side of it.

Technical Problem: I have been wondering how to work in the F.B.I. and the Communist Party, according to our formula of hitting this thing fast.

I have no doubt but that your skilled script writers will be much better at this than myself, but here are a couple of suggestions.

In the beginning, you see, Philbrick was not in touch with the F.B.I., nor did he know that he was running into Communism. So perhaps we can build up the suspense by establishing this happy family unit, and then bringing in the villain, the threat to the happy family, threatening its security and causing suspense.

Although later on in the story, we have Philbrick himself in plenty of trouble and doing lots of worrying, at this stage we will possibly have to let the audience do all the worrying while Philbrick nonchalantly walks in where angels fear to tread. In other words, the audience is let in on the dangerous situation, and can see it coming, although Philbrick doesn't. The old melodrama where the audience hisses to alert the hero.

And on the "public service" level, this particular dramatization can serve to show how easy it is for people to be victimized by the communist conspiracy—something which has happened to thousands of Americans over the past few years, and in fact, is still happening today.

There are two things we can legitimately do at this point. First, after Philbrick walks out of the Massachusetts Youth Council office, we can have Mrs. Mills get in touch with Toni Grosse—as she obviously did. This could probably best be done through a telephone conversation; the trouble is that technically to be correct, Mrs. Mills would not divulge confidential information over a telephone, since every communist always assumes that a telephone is tapped by spies.

What she would do would be to telephone Toni Grosse, and tell her that she has a new prospect coming over, who may be of a help in setting up the Cambridge Youth Council. She would arrange to get together with Toni Grosse to discuss it with her. Upon meeting her, probably in a restaurant, in a railroad station waiting room, or possibly in an automobile, she would then describe to Toni Grosse the character of Philbrick entirely. She would relate to Toni every detail about Philbrick- his background, his interests, his likes and dislikes, his vulnerable points which may be appealing to in order to win his friendship and confidence.

Among these things would be: the fact that Philbrick comes from an old New England family; he has many valuable contacts in the Christian youth field; he has been active in youth organizations for a long time; where he lives, where he works, and even the suggestion that since he is in the advertising field he may have a little more money to contribute to the organization than the average college student or neighborhood youth.

The next element we can legitimately introduce is also the fact that the F.B.I. is on the job also. They too, have observed that Philbrick has visited the office of the Massachusetts Youth Council, and has stayed in the office for a fairly long time in conference with Alice Mills. For example, as Philbrick leaves the office building, he might even then be under observation by an F.B.I. agent. The agent would observe him very carefully and with some curiosity. This is somebody new, and the agent would be thoughtfully appraising the appearance, the physical characteristics, etc., of this new individual. From there, we might move right into the F.B.I. office, where the agent is reporting to his superior. Here again, Philbrick's history is recorded. The superior would want to know if he had any previous contact with the Communist Party or Communist Party members. The agent—"No, he is as clean as a whistle. Came from a good family background, has an excellent reputation in his church and in his business, and has a long record of legitimate youth activity and work." The agent would report how to his superiors that new incidents surrounding the Massachusetts Youth Council and now the Cambridge situation, has all the earmarks of a new front coming up. The superior would advise the agent to keep on top of it.

Of all of this, Philbrick has not the slightest knowledge. He is very blindly becoming enmeshed in something a million times bigger than he possibly could imagine. Incidentally, we can use the same office in the same building for later events.

In one of the subsequent programs, we will show the name of the Cambridge Youth Council being rubbed off the front door of the office and the name of another communist front organization being put up. This, in fact, has happened many times in actual practice. The comrades have used one office for a series of three or four different and new communist fronts, as one became obsolete and another one was established.

Additional Material on the Friends and Surroundings of the Philbrick Apartment: Among the friends of Philbrick at the apartment was one Gordon Case. Gordon Case is a young, Methodist youth leader, who, as the Cambridge Youth Council is formed, Philbrick invites to participate. Another friend is Charles Rice. Charlie was a young electronics expert, who plays the trumpet; at the "jam sessions" he frequently brings his trumpet over to accompany the piano. Another is Arnold Craden; Arnold also plays the trumpet; both of these young men are married and their wives come along with them. Another is Bill Tessen, who is a trombonist (and still is today, as a matter of fact). Still another is Ernest Seely, then studying to enter the ministry. Ernie Seeley, along with Gordon Case, also deserted Philbrick as he became enmeshed in the communist activities.

Appendix J: Plot and Story Outlines

PLOT PROPOSAL #1
"I LED THREE LIVES"—STORY OUTLINE by Stuart Jerome

1. Philbrick is summoned from work by his Party chairman, Comrade Neely, who orders Herb to join him tomorrow for a trip to Lynbrook, a city some 300 miles away, where they will attend an important meeting.

2. As Herb returns to his office, Mr. Snyder, his boss, gives him a friendly caution about cutting down his outside activities before they interfere with his work.

3. At home that night, Herb discusses his dilemma with Eva. He's afraid his job might be in jeopardy if he continues devoting so much time to the Commies; on the other hand, he's helping the F.B.I. Eva agrees that he should attend this meeting; she'll call the office in the morning and say he's sick.

4. Next day, Herb picks up Neely and they drive to Lynbrook. At the meeting, Herb learns their host, Comrade Wilson, wants to furnish guns to select groups against the day when open revolt will be declared. They start discussing it.

5. Back at the Philbrick house, Eva is surprised by a visit from Snyder, who has a favor to ask of Herb. The firm is trying to land a new account, and he would like Herb to work up a short prospectus. Eva says Herb's asleep. Snyder agrees to wait and see

him tomorrow.

6. In Lynbrook, the comrades decide to adjourn until morning. Herb phones Eva, says he can't get away until tomorrow. She tells him about Snyder. Herb is left in a pickle: If he stays, Snyder's going to find out he'd lying, and he might lose his job. If he leaves now, he'll not only have to forego information for the F.B.I. concerning where the guns are coming from, how many, and who's to get them, but he'll also risk Party disfavor.

Act Break

7. At the meeting the next morning, Herb gets all the information he needs. He phones Eva, tells her to notify Snyder he can visit him tonight. But as Herb leaves with Neely, the latter says he has some stops to make to visit Party members; this might delay getting home until tomorrow. Herb objects but Neely insists he follow orders.

8. They work their way home, making one stop after another. It's getting late as Neely makes another visit. Herb, left alone in the car, suddenly drives off. (Voice Over) Herb says to himself that he'll have to take his chances about getting in bad with the Party.

9. Arriving home, Herb barely has time to make some notes on the prospectus and slip into his "sick bed" when Snyder arrives. He compliments Herb's ideas and leaves. Then Neely phones; he's furious with Herb, orders him to an emergency meeting to discuss his actions.

10. At Neely's, Herb is faced by a tribunal of three Party bigwigs. They have voted to expel him from the Party. Angrily insisting on a hearing, Herb says he acted as he did for the Party's welfare; his actions helped his firm land an account that does secret work for the government. Now he'll be in a position to give the Party information they could never receive otherwise. They forgive him his actions, even compliment him.

11. Herb leaves the meeting, thoroughly exhausted. (Voice Over) He says now he's got to prepare his report for the F.B.I. He's very thankful about everything. By some miracle, all three of his lives are still functioning.

PLOT PROPOSAL #2

STORY OUTLINE—Author unknown, possibly Stuart Jerome.

Here's an opportunity to get Herb on a flight, show a major Party meeting in action, as well as develop real conflict in his life as a citizen, both at home and at the office.

Herb gets a call from a comrade that the C.P.A. (Communist Party Activities) is having a major session in New York and Herb is to be the representative of his district. Not wanting the trip or the responsibility of inventing explanations he balks, but not too much since he realizes there may be some interesting tidbits that will come out of this session.

At home we have a scene with Eva where Philbrick tells her he's going out of town for the office for three days. He has to leave early in the morning—please don't get up. He'll call a cab and get to the airport.

Next morning he does just that but with a stopover to call Bill at the office to tell them he's not well and better stay in bed. Don't worry—probably just a little virus. A question of a couple of days. They hang up. We see Herb at the airport, boarding and winging his way, via United (stock footage) to New York (also stock footage).

Back at the office, we see jovial Bill worried and gracious, busy taking up collections for large basket of fruit and flowers for Herb, and Bill feels something like "wouldn't it be wonderful if a couple of us from the office would take the gift over, to make Herb understand they think he's a grand boy and that he's simply been working too hard?"

ACT BREAK

We see Herb at the communist meeting which by this time has broken up into small bands of revolutionists rather then a big group. The Party line, or some such thing has been recapped and now the states or districts are in groups to discuss their individual problems with guidance from the Central Committee.

While back home we see Bill and Berdoni, driving up in a convertible to Herb's house. The back seat practically filled with junk. They approach the door and this can be played straight, not drawn out. There's enough natural tenseness without trying to create some. Eva answers and after they say they'd like to see the patient there is a pregnant pause—Eva finally says she sent him away so he could get a little (peace) and quiet away from the kids. Good old Eva.

Back in N.Y., the meeting breaks up and Herb returns home. Here we can play a slight conflict between the two which ends up in embrace and a display of confidence to each other. The "I know what I'm doing" type of thing—something we haven't touched too much on.

PLOT PROPOSAL #3

Three ideas for I LED 3 LIVES Series by Arthur Fitz-Richard
Dated: November 14, 1953

PLOT # 1. Story suggested by second paragraph, page 161 of the Philbrick book, telling of an uneventful vacation taken by him and his wife. We make it a bit more eventful.

Before Philbrick and his wife park their kids with their sister and take off on a long anticipated bicycle tour in the mountains, he learns the F.B.I. is hunting for two badly wanted Communist saboteurs named Zorek and Clark. Philbrick has heard nothing of them, but as he and Eva approach the mountains, he narrowly avoids running into a woman driving a grocery-laden station wagon, whom he has seen once and knows as Selma, a Party courier, and discovers she is bound for a mountain resort. Without telling Eva why, he detours from their itinerary to the resort, and finds that Selma has male guests at her cabin who are staying awfully close.

He doesn't know whether Selma will recognize him, and he does not take the chance, but Eva now tumbles to what is up and insists on helping. She hates Communists like poison, and Selma has never met her nor is she apt to in the future. A "war of nerves" ensues as Eva makes herself nosey and neighborly with Selma, renting the cabin next door while Philbrick camps in the woods. Philbrick is nervous as a cat, using Eva as a decoy, but he at last gets some camera shots of the two men staying at Selma's and whizzes to the city to his F.B.I. contact. His hunch was right. The men are identified as Zorek and Clark.

Eva's nosiness gets her in trouble. While Selma and Philbrick are both in the city (Selma getting orders for the saboteurs), Zorek and Clark catch Eva eavesdropping as they prepare incendiary materials for a fire job on a defense plant. She pretends complete ignorance of what they are doing, playing dumb as she has with Selma, but they insist on her keeping them company for a tense interval nevertheless, and she knows well enough she is a prisoner. By luck Philbrick returns before Selma, contrives to get Eva safely away from the cabin. They leave on their bikes as fast as possible. When Selma delivers the saboteurs to the "job," they are caught with the goods and they never do know whether it was the fool woman in the mountains who blew the whistle on them.

PLOT # 2. Story suggested by fourth and fifth paragraphs on page 237 of the Philbrick book, concerning Susan, the girl trapped in the Party by fear of blackmail.

Philbrick is ordered by his cell leader to hold himself in readiness for a courier mission, and he accidentally finds out he is to carry a packet of infinite importance to be given him by Wanda, a member of the cell. Wanda is held in the Party by fear she will lose her job and then be unable to support her small daughter Enid. Reporting this to his F.B.I. contact, it turns out Wanda is suspected of stealing secrets from the electronics firm for which she works. She is permitted to photograph drawings and specifications for a new radar tube (these being phonies) and to deliver then to Philbrick. Then she is arrested and grilled. As for Philbrick, his trip to another city to meet the unknown Red spy to whom he delivers Wanda's little packet of film enables the F.B.I. to hook up yet another link in the communications chain of the espionage ring.

Returned home, Philbrick is really sorry to Wanda, who refuses to tell of past thefts or talk at all for fear of Party reprisals on Enid. The child left with neighbors when Wanda was arrested, has disappeared. Though advised by the F.B.I. to keep out of the case and let them find Enid, Philbrick is a parent himself. Knowing the hell Wanda is going through, he gets a line on the youngster at considerable risk and rescues her from the Party members holding her. The F.B.I. men, glad enough to show Enid to Wanda and get a confession, cooperate with Philbrick in whisking the child to a safe home where she will be taken care of until Wanda is out of prison. Of course, at the above turn of events, Philbrick's cell has been hastily disbanded, and when it is reorganized, the cell leader congratulates him on his own "narrow escape."

PLOT # 3. Story suggestion by situation of break-up of Wakefield cell by Gus Johnson's wife, page 88 in the Philbrick book, third and fourth paragraphs.

Joe Evans, a hairy ape type of Communist, member of a cell to which Philbrick once belonged, comes to him and confesses that his virago wife Ruby is threatening to go to the police and expose the cell unless Evans gets out of the Party with her. He loves the Party; it is his life. But he loves Ruby too in his roughneck way and he doesn't want to see her harmed by Communist vengeance. Evans feels relieved when he has told Philbrick, a minor Party functionary, simultaneously begging for time to straight Ruby out.

It puts Philbrick in a hell of a spot—it could be a test, a trap. He talks to Ruby himself, gets nowhere. She went into the Party to please Joe, thinking it might bring them closer together, and now all the human quality has been crowded out of their relationship. She is through, so is Joe, and she dares the Party to do anything about it. Playing his role, Philbrick has to make some dire threats and Evans doesn't like that. The guy fails to realize he too is a danger to the Party—and in danger from his fellow conspirators.

Philbrick reports the situation to the F.B.I., saying that the cell is about to blow up. He is asked to stop Ruby Evans if possible—the F.B.I. has another operative in the cell (they can't tell Philbrick who it is) getting a line on the Communist situation in the labor union to which certain members belong, and they don't want him picked up. Also, Philbrick will have to pass the Evans trouble along to the Party protest himself. He does, is ordered to read both Joe and Ruby out of membership, but fast. At a special cell meeting the Evanses' cards are taken up, in a scene reminiscent of stripping a soldier of insignia in drumming him out of the army, and Joe Evans is utterly stunned. He hates Philbrick.

Meanwhile, someone from Party headquarters has gone through the Evans house and taken every single scrap of literature, lists, etc. which might be used as evidence. But this individual goes too far: he sets some sort of "booby trap" to liquidate the Evanses (poisoned food, a gas leak, a small cyanide bomb, incendiary device?) . . . Philbrick finds out about it, however, and saves them. Ruby, ignorant that she is alive only because of Philbrick, damns him for an s.o.b., but Joe Evans has an inkling of the truth. A cured Communist, he takes Ruby and leaves town, though not before he has gone to the police himself, exposing the cell and the situation in the union—being very careful to leave Philbrick's name out of it. You see, he knows how Philbrick feels about the Party, having been in the same toils himself. And while he thinks Philbrick is crazy to give such unreasoning loyalty to an outfit like Murder, Inc., he is grateful to Philbrick after all.

PLOT PROPOSAL #4
"THE OLD MAN" by Arthur Fitz-Richard
Dated December 23, 1953, this plot proposal did become episode #30 in the production.

Fred Holman, a few years ago an important Communist leader and now supposedly dead—his demise and funeral having been faked by the Party when he became the key figure in a government investigation—is actually living in our city as a humble shoe repairman under an assumed name. He is a sort of fugitive, ironically, from the Party itself. Only his daughter Sarah, a union activist, knows of Holman's whereabouts and she, worshiping her father as a hero, has kept his secrets from the local Party heads. District boss Krug, however, suspects something is wrong and assigns Philbrick to spy on Sarah. Detecting Philbrick and guessing his function, Sarah winds up by dumping the whole problem in his lap. She is worried sick, torn between loyalties, for since his "death" Holman has become a deviationist (which is why he vanished from the Party view six months back), and not only this, he is writing his memoirs.

Such a document could be highly dangerous to the Party, and Sarah, realizing the jig is up from Philbrick's spying, welcomes a chance to confess to Krug. He gives her hell for not reporting Holman long since, orders her to cajole her father's private papers out of him. Philbrick is made responsible for seeing to it that Sarah succeeds—and then he discovers there is a plan afoot to liquidate Holman when his papers are safely in Party hands. The F.B.I. is also interested in Holman and his papers, but there isn't much that can be done to help Philbrick at this point without giving him away as a counterspy. However, Holman's little shop is staked out by Special Agents and he is guarded against any murder attempt.

The blow-off comes when Philbrick finds and steals the hidden memoirs. Holman accuses Sarah of taking them. There is quite a scene between father and daughter—and then both are faced with death as the Party hatchet man closes in. (The method liquidation planned to be worked out.) But the double murder doesn't come off, for Sarah and Holman overcome the killer and escape, they realize that blood is thicker then Communist H2O at showdown. There is no need for the F.B.I. to interfere in this swift climax, and Philbrick is able to do his duty by both his country and Krug when he delivers the memoirs to be photographed by the F.B.I. and then, the originals to Party members.

PLOT PROPOSAL #5

TO JON EPSTEIN
JANUARY 15, 1954
DICTATED JANUARY 14, 1954

DEAR JONNY,

I happened to think about an idea for an LTL script that I believe could be a good one and well off the path of anything that we've done.

This could be the story about a comrade who simply belongs to the Communist Party. He is not a criminal—at least, not yet. He has not broken any laws; he has simply been a member of the Communist Party for years.

Over the years he has been a loyal, conscientious worker. He has risen in the Party, has held various jobs, and over a period of time, of course, has accumulated a wide assortment of information, knowledge, contacts, etc. within the Party.

Somewhere along the line this fellow begins to see the light of day. He would like very much to get out of the Party. However, he knows that he has risen to a point where simply a resignation could not be the answer to his problem. There is only one thing holding him in the Party and that is fear and perhaps a lack of the final inertia to make the decision and reach the breaking point. To Philbrick he appears as a rather unenthused Communist. The man seems nervous, reluctant, worried, pre-occupied, and based on the things that happened in perhaps a cell meeting, an assignment, and a task with Philbrick, Herb recognizes that perhaps here is a high-ranking Communist who perhaps is about to crack. Philbrick realizes that if his observations are correct, if the man would crack, and if a wedge could be driven into that crack, this could be a tremendously valuable person to the F.B.I. Here is a man who if he wished to do so could give the F.B.I. probably far more information than Philbrick ever could, and yet in no way jeopardize or cause the discontinuance of Philbrick's efforts as a counterspy.

On the other side of the fence, because the facts are true, Philbrick would not be the only one who might begin to notice this. The cell leader of other Party members might be aware of the same factors. Now with the help of the F.B.I., and taking some deadly chances, Philbrick enters into what might be a tug-of-war with the comrades, with the shaky comrade as the rope itself. The story can play to a climax where the efforts of Philbrick and the F.B.I. are finally successful to the point where the man appears before some properly constituted body, states that he has been a communist for many years, has committed no crimes, and before it is too late wants to re-instate himself as a good citizen of the United States. He feels it is his duty to tell any interested Party everything he knows about communist activities, secret communist members, etc. In other words, an entire history since he has joined the Party.

Properly spiced I think this might be a great story. If you agree, let's give this to a writer and do for a step-outline. Obviously I haven't created the story, but only the situation. If you prefer, you might drop a line to Philbrick asking for help, as I rather imagine this might be a situation with which Philbrick is familiar, and might even come up with an actual parallel.

Maurice Unger

MORE PLOT OUTLINES, "I LED 3 LIVES" STORY IDEAS

Dated May 18, 1954 by Stuart Jerome

1. A high-ranking American communist has been on trial and has just been found guilty. While this is going on, strange things happen to Philbrick. He is given access by his cell leader to certain supposedly-important papers, and is allowed other opportunities to tell the F.B.I. about communist secrets. Fearing some plot to test his loyalty, Herb keeps all of his information to himself. Then he is summoned to a meeting of high-ranking Party officials who tell him they have been testing his loyalty for an all-important job, concerning their member who has been on trail. This man has just been released from jail on bond pending his sentencing, and the Party orders Philbrick to contact him and follow pre-arranged plans to smuggle this man out of the country. Knowing that his own life, and possibly the lives of his family are at stake, Herb makes no attempt to contact the F.B.I. He follows through on the plan to smuggle out his important Commie, but once again the resourceful F.B.I. comes through in the nick of time.

2. A member of Herb's cell, a man named Gordan, persuades Herb to accompany him on a fishing trip. But too late does Herb learn that Gordan's real plan is to shoot a Congressman, the head of a local Commie-investigation committee, who is also vacationing in the same area. Herb is in a terrible spot—he's somehow got to prevent this assassination, and at the same time do it in such a

manner that the would-be victim and his friends aren't aware of it. If Herb is captured along with Gordan, he's bound to be exposed as a Commie. At the last minute, as Gordan has the congressman in the sights of his high-powered rifle, Herbs knock the gun out of his hands. Gordan turns on him like a maniac, and tries to shoot him. He and Herb have a helluva battle. Herb knocks him out just as other members of the Party come along. They learned of Gordan's plan and were trying to prevent him from carrying it out; knowing what would happen to the Party if he succeeded. Herb becomes a hero in their eyes for his service to the Party. (This storyline would completely eliminate his usual visits and/or phone calls to the F.B.I.)

3. The F.B.I. asks Herb to learn all he can about a mysterious new cell member, a woman named Andrea Lane. Herb plays up to her, involving him in complications with his family, his father and his boss. But his work pays off as he learns that Andrea is a foreigner who has been sent here on an important secret mission. She is about to leave the country when she recommends that Herb be allowed to leave with her. What can Herb do but follow orders? (Any idea of censorable romance can be eliminated by Andrea having a husband; she's interested in Herb only for his great mind.) Herb leaves with Andrea for the airport, on his way out of the country, but the F.B.I. arrests Andrea for illegal entry and Herb gets away.

SELECTED BIBLIOGRAPHY

Miami Harold Fun in Florida Magazine, December 7, 1958

Journal of Criminal Law, Criminology, and Police Science, Vol. 44, No. 4 (Nov.–Dec. 1953), pp. 499-500

TV Guide article, December 4, 1953

Variety Magazine, December 1977

Eduard Bernstein, (1895). *Kommunistische und demokratisch-sozialistische Strömungen während der englischen Revolution*, J.H.W. Dietz, Stuttgart.

Karl Marx, (1845). *The German Ideology*, Marx-Engels Institute, Moscow.

H. Gordon Skilling (April 1966). "Interest Groups and Communist Politics." *World Politics* 18 (3): 435-451.

Arch Getty (1985). *Origins of the Great Purges: The Soviet Communist Party Reconsidered: 1933-1938*, Cambridge University Press.

INDEX

Herbert A. Philbrick is not listed in the index since the entire book is devoted to him and his name appears (real life and the fictional portrayal) throughout the entire book.

Episode Titles

ABOUT THE AUTHOR

Martin Grams Jr. is the author and co-author of more than a dozen books on radio and television including:

Suspense: Twenty Years of Thrills and Chills (1998, Morris Publishing)
The History of the Cavalcade of America (1999, Morris Publishing)
The CBS Radio Mystery Theater: An Episode Guide and Handbook (1999, McFarland Publishing)
Radio Drama: An American Chronicle (1999)
The Have Gun—Will Travel Companion (2000, OTR Publishing)
The Alfred Hitchcock Presents Companion (2001, OTR Publishing)
The Sound of Detection: Ellery Queen's Adventures in Radio (2002, OTR Publishing)
Invitation to Learning (2002, OTR Publishing)
Inner Sanctum Mysteries: Behind the Creaking Door (2002, OTR Publishing)
The I Love a Mystery Companion (2003, OTR Publishing)
Information Please (2003, BearManor Media)
Gang Busters: The Crime Fighters of American Broadcasting (2004, OTR Publishing)
The Railroad Hour (2006, BearManor Media)
The Radio Adventures of Sam Spade (2007, OTR Publishing)

He has also written magazine articles for *FilmFax, Scarlet Street, Old Time Radio Digest* and SPERDVAC's *Radiogram*. He contributed chapters, essays, short stories, and appendices for various books including *Vincent Price: Midnight Marquee Actor*

Series (1998), *The Alfred Hitchcock Story* (1999) and all three volumes of *It's That Time Again* (2002, 2004 and 2005) from BearManor Media.

Martin is the recipient of the 1999 Ray Stanich Award, the 2005 Parley E. Baer Award and the 2005 Stone/Waterman Award. He is presently involved with the annual Mid-Atlantic Nostalgia Convention held annually every September in Maryland. Martin lives in Delta, Pennsylvania with his wife and their three cats.

Silent Stars Speak!

New CD

Thrill to actual voices of the world's greatest stars on *Silent Movie Stars Speak*, a compilation of rare recordings of 21 of the greatest stars of the silent film era. You'll hear these fascinating, lost interviews:

- Blanche Sweet recalling working on Biograph films with D. W. Griffith
- Lillian Gish reminiscing about her first film with her sister, Dorothy Gish.
- Harold Lloyd remembering how he progressed from his early beginnings.
- Stan Laurel thinking back to boyhood tours and working with Oliver Hardy.
- Buster Keaton revealing how he became "the great stoneface" in films.
- John and Lionel Barrymore telling how they rose from obscurity to fame.
- Bronco Billy's thrilling recount of making *The Great Train Robbery.*

You will also witness first-hand performances given on wax cylinder records, 78 rpm records, film, or on live radio broadcasts Ramon Novarro, Mary Pickford, Jackie Coogan, Charlie Chaplin, Laurette Taylor, Sarah Bernhardt, Douglas Fairbanks, Gloria Swanson, John Gilbert, and Greta Garbo. In the finale, William S. Hart is heard in the heartrending speech he gave in a Prologue for the 1930s re-release of his film, *Tumbleweeds.*

Each recording has been digitally re-mastered to improve clarity. They vary in quality, and on some tracks there is slight surface noise that cannot be removed without damaging the recording, but on each, the voices of the great stars come through loudly and clearly.

New CD in factory shrink-wrap. $12.95 + postage
Postage $4.95 on Priority Mail inside the USA only.
$12.00 Global Priority mail outside the USA.
$10.00 Air Mail for Italy only.

BearManor Media · PO Box 71426 · Albany, GA 31708
e-mail: books@benohmart.com
Telephone: 229.436.4265 · Toll Free: 1.800.566.1251 · Fax: 814.690.1559
Or online at: www.bearmanormedia.com

Here's a small sampling of a few more books published by BearManor Media.

Simply go online for details about these and other terrific titles.

www.BearManorMedia.com

CPSIA information can be obtained at www.ICGtesting.com
Printed in the USA
BVOW011709071112

304911BV00007B/121/A